RACE AND ETHNIC RELATIONS IN CANADA

EDITED BY

PETER S. LI

Toronto
OXFORD UNIVERSITY PRESS

For Terence

Oxford University Press, 70 Wynford Drive, Don Mills, Ontario M3C 1J9

Toronto Oxford New York
Delhi Bombay Calcutta Madras Karachi Kuala Lumpur
Singapore Hong Kong Tokyo Nairobi Dar es Salaam
Cape Town Melbourne Auckland Madrid

and associated companies in
Berlin Ibadan

Canadian Cataloguing in Publication Data

Main entry under title:

Race and ethnic relations in Canada

Includes bibliographical references.
ISBN 0-19-540721-0

1. Canada—Ethnic relations. 2. Canada—Race relations. 3. Canada—Politics and government.
I. Li. Peter S.

FC104.R32 1990 305′.8′00971 C90-093225-2
F1035.AIR32 1990

OXFORD is a trademark of Oxford University Press

Design by Marie Bartholomew

4 5 6—96 95

Printed in Canada

CONTRIBUTORS

RODNEY A. CLIFTON, Professor in the Educational Administration and Foundations Department at the University of Manitoba and a Fellow of St John's College, specializes in the sociology of education.

WILFRID B. DENIS is Associate Professor of Sociology at St Thomas More College, University of Saskatchewan. His research focuses on francophones and minority relations, and the sociology of agriculture.

JOHN DE VRIES is chairman of the Department of Sociology and Anthropology at Carleton University, where he teaches statistics, research methods, and demography.

JEAN LEONARD ELLIOTT is Associate Professor of Sociology and Social Anthropology at Dalhousie University. She is the editor of *Two Nations, Many Cultures: Ethnic Groups in Canada*.

AUGIE FLERAS is Assistant Professor in the Department of Sociology, University of Waterloo. He has published widely in the field of ethnic studies both in New Zealand and in Canada.

JAMES S. FRIDERES, Professor of Sociology at the University of Calgary, is Associate Dean of Research for the Faculty of Social Sciences. His research centres on ethnic relations, with a specific focus on Native people in Canada.

NEIL GUPPY is Associate Professor of Anthropology and Sociology at the University of British Columbia. He is co-editor of *Social Inequality in Canada* and *Uncommon Property: The B.C. Fishing Industry*.

WARREN E. KALBACH, Professor of Sociology and director of the population research unit at Erindale College, University of Toronto, is engaged in research on the costs of maintaining culturally distinctive minority groups in a bicultural and bilingual society.

EVELYN KALLEN, Professor of Social Science and Anthropology at York University, has written numerous publications on ethnic relations and human rights. In 1989-90 she is honorary Chair of Human Rights at the Human Rights Centre, University of Ottawa.

HUGH LAUTARD, Professor of Sociology at the University of New Brunswick, has written numerous articles on ethnic relations in Canada, as well as two research reports for the Department of Indian and Northern Affairs.

LANCE W. ROBERTS is Associate Professor of Sociology and Fellow of St John's College, University of Manitoba. He has written several articles with Professor Clifton; he also has a chapter forthcoming in the *Handbook of Clinical Sociology*.

VIC SATZEWICH, Assistant Professor of Sociology at the University of Saskatchewan, specializes in the sociology of migration and racism. His book *Racism and the Incorporation of Foreign Labour: Farm Labour Migration to Canada Since 1945* is forthcoming.

DAIVA STASIULIS, Associate Professor of Sociology at Carleton University, has published several articles on racism, state policies, and ethnic relations in Canada and is currently working on a book on anti-racist politics.

K. VICTOR UJIMOTO is Professor of Sociology at the University of Guelph and Research Associate at the Gerontology Research Centre. He has written extensively on Japanese Canadians, multiculturalism, and the health and aging of ethnic minorities.

CONTENTS

PREFACE

Intended for students and researchers interested in the sociology of race and ethnicity, this reader carries a simple message: it is impossible to understand race and ethnic relations in Canada without finding out how state policies influence these relationships and how academics theorize about them.

The book is organized in three parts. The introductory section provides a theoretical exposition and a demographic overview. In the first chapter, a theoretical discussion of the concepts of race and ethnicity, I argue that race and ethnic relations are often not the products of a natural evolutionary process. Kalbach's demographic overview identifies the population trends of racial and ethnic groups in Canada from 1871 to the present.

Each of the five chapters in the second section, 'Race, Ethnicity, and the State', addresses a major policy issue that has produced profound effects on race and ethnic relations in Canada. These policy issues pertain to immigration, human rights, native people, multiculturalism, and language rights. The chapter by Elliott and Fleras discusses the evolution of Canadian immigration policy, and how it has affected the racial and ethnic composition of Canada. Kallen's chapter on ethnicity and human rights shows how statutory and constitutional law strengthens the protection of all minorities. The chapter by Frideres deals with four government policies towards Canada's Native people that affect them severely in the areas of self-government, land claims, education, and economic development. Roberts and Clifton present a theoretical typology of multiculturalism and discuss its policy implications. Denis's chapter, the last one in this section, examines the detrimental effects that language and education policies have had on minority languages.

Under the heading 'Perspectives on Race and Ethnicity' there are also five chapters, each dealing with a major theoretical perspective. John Porter's 'vertical mosaic' thesis, which laid the foundation for many subsequent studies in Canada, is re-examined by Lautard and Guppy using updated census figures. Ujimoto's chapter provides a comprehensive summary of the major theories of ethnic identity and race studies. The chapter 'Language and Ethnicity', by de Vries, argues that language is an important component of ethnicity, and that language shift reflects the weakening of ethnicity. Satzewich offers a critique of the sociology of race relations from the standpoint of political economy. The last chapter, by Stasiulis, is an ambitious attempt to theorize the connections among the concepts of race, gender, ethnicity and class.

Comprehensive in its coverage of the major policy and theoretical issues of race and ethnicity, this book is intended to allow readers to grasp the essential elements of race and ethnic relations in Canada in the most succinct way possible. All the contributors are authorities in their respective fields who have researched and written extensively on their subject matter. As the editor, I am pleased and honoured to have their contributions.

It has been my pleasure to work with Oxford University Press. Dr Richard Teleky, the managing editor, coming from an academic background himself, has shown tremendous understanding and sympathy for academics who are struggling to meet publishing deadlines; I appreciate in particular the encouraging support Richard has given this project since its inception. I would also like to thank Sally Livingston, who copy-edited the manuscript with care.

Finally, it has been a great challenge for me, in trying to answer the curiosity of my six-year-old son, Terence, to come up with a simple explanation of what 'white people' and 'non-white people' mean. To him, it is strange that I should use colour to describe people, especially when he is convinced that the people I call 'white' are not really that colour. His innocence convinces me ever more that the concept of race is not a logical genotype or phenotype, but a product of the social categorization that children unfortunately have to learn. It may be wishful thinking that some day adults will be able to sustain the simple and innocent approach towards people that they too had as children.

PETER S. LI

PART ONE

INTRODUCTION

ONE

RACE AND ETHNICITY

PETER S. LI

Despite the popular notion that Canada is a multi-ethnic and multicultural society, several common assumptions about race and ethnicity prevail. These assumptions colour the way many people look at Canadian society, especially those contentious and antagonistic aspects that involve racial and ethnic groups.

It is widely assumed that biological and cultural features provide scientific grounds for classifying people into what are commonly known as racial and ethnic groups. Superficial physical traits are regarded as logical grounds for classifying people into racial groups; skin colour in particular is generally held to be the most salient characteristic in differentiating between 'white' and 'coloured' people. The combination of physical and cultural traits provides an ever-widening basis for discriminating between ethnic groups. Throughout the history of Canada, physical and cultural characteristics, whether real or presumed, have been used to justify segregating and discriminating against groups such as Chinese, Jews, Ukrainians, and Indians.

In a more extreme view, those biological and genetic features that are believed to have produced racial and ethnic groups are also held to determine people's mental, social, and cultural capacities. Accordingly, racial and ethnic groups are seen as forming a hierarchy, based on alleged abilities and potentials, in which some groups are supposedly superior to others. This inherent ranking of racial and ethnic groups along a scale of superiority and inferiority is the essence of racism.

And there are other misconceptions. For example, it is generally assumed that ethnic groups are the same as cultural groups, and differences in people's achievements, values, and behaviours are often automatically attributed to culture as a cause. Culture is seen as a primordial feature that mechanically exerts its influence on people's lives. This line of reasoning puts disadvantaged groups in an even more disadvantaged position, since their culture becomes the source of their misfortunes. Thus the economic problems of Native people are often seen as caused by their own inaptitudes and cultural inadequacies. Not only is equating ethnicity with culture incorrect, but it also leads to blaming the victims for their own woes by attributing their problems, which in many instances are caused by societal forces, to their supposed cultural deficiencies.

This mechanical view of culture and ethnicity also distorts the way ethnic relations are interpreted. Since culture is believed to be the primary mover of human behaviour, ethnic adaptation and survival become a question of the capacity of a cultural group to maintain its own identity and resist the evolutionary process of assimilation. This interpretation of ethnic relations has become such a powerful intellectual force in the post-war era that every aspect of human life concerned with ethnicity is evaluated within the framework of assimilation. Ethnic groups are seen as extensions of Old World cultures transplanted to the New World; the Old World culture provides immigrant groups with the internal logic and communal base on which to reconstruct their lives. Strangely, in this New World, it is always internal culture and never external force that determines ethnic survival. If external force is considered, it is only in so far as it facilitates or impedes ethnic groups' assimilation.

UNDERSTANDING RACE AND ETHNICITY

Sociologists have taken many positions regarding the question of racial and ethnic origin. These positions represent theoretical orientations that stress different aspects of intergroup relations, and the particular choice is more than a preference of style. The ways in which ethnicity and race are defined have a definite bearing on the types of questions raised and the kinds of answers that emerge.

The term 'ethnic' derives from the Greek *ethnos*, referring to heathen nations or peoples not converted to Christianity. In its contemporary usage, 'ethnic' refers to people of a common heritage. Sociologists, following this contemporary meaning, use the term to refer to a group of people who presumably share a common experience and origin.

Many sociologists have unquestioningly adopted the concept of ethnic identity as a basis for defining ethnicity and, at times, race. Accordingly, ethnicity is ascribed, or given at birth. The important aspect of an ethnic group is that its members share a sense of peoplehood or identity based on descent, language, religion, tradition, and other common experiences (Weber, 1968: 385-98). According to this view, ethnic identity provides a basis for members of an ethnic group to develop closures (ibid.: 388), or boundaries, within which ethnic institutions, neighbourhoods, beliefs, and cultures are developed and maintained. To the extent that an ethnic identity is accepted by outsiders, it becomes a convenient way for members of the group to distinguish themselves and for others to distinguish them. In the case of a racial group, there is the added feature of its members' having observable physical traits, the most commonly recognized of which is skin colour.

The study of ethnicity as a matter of identity is favoured by many sociologists. In a review of major sociological journals in the United States and Canada between 1945 and 1971, Isajiw (1974) identifies over seventy elements used in defining ethnicity, of which the most often mentioned are ancestry, culture, religion, race, and language. Regarding the formation of an ethnic community, Driedger (1978: 9-22) has suggested that there are six components of identification: ecological territory, ethnic culture, ethnic institutions, historical symbols, ideology, and charismatic leadership. When ethnicity is seen in terms of identity, in the sense that it is a question of self-definition and definition by others (Aboud, 1981; Akoodie, 1984; Haas and Shaffir, 1978), it is logical to inquire what factors help to maintain such an identity and what forces compel it to change. This is essentially the question raised by sociologists when they study assimilation and pluralism—a question of how ethnic identity is either weakened or reinforced.

Another approach is to examine race and ethnicity as consequences of unequal relationships, produced and maintained by differential power between a dominant and a subordinate group. According to this view, racial and ethnic groups are constructed on the basis of social relationships, not on genetic differences or primordial features. Here the focus is on the institutional framework within which groups are defined as racial or ethnic and how social interactions are organized accordingly (Bolaria and Li, 1988). Physical and cultural traits are the basis for defining social groups only in so far as they are socially recognized as important. In other words, race and ethnicity take on social meaning and importance when physical and cultural traits are paired with social attributes, such as intellectual, moral, or behavioural characteristics. Whether such associations are alleged or real is often irrelevant. What is important is that the dominant group has the power to define socially what constitutes a subordinate group, using physical and social features (ibid.).

The process of defining ethnic and racial groups is much more apparent when such definitions are legally sanctioned, and when the consequences of labelling are reinforced by law. For example, Blacks in South Africa are not defined by whether people subjectively consider or identify themselves as Blacks; rather, they are officially and legally classified as such. In Canada, status Indians are legally defined in the Indian Act, and they have certain entitlements and restrictions that do not apply to non-status Indians and Métis. The differences between status and non-status Indians, therefore, are based on legal and bureaucratic considerations and have little to do with people's cultural attributes.

Throughout the history of Canada, there have been numerous occasions when the federal government has passed laws concerning various racial and ethnic groups, sometimes in the name of protecting thom, and at times to restrain them. These laws not only provide a legal and therefore a formal basis for identifying groups as ethnic or racial, but also define the institutional framework within which subsequent race and ethnic relations are to take shape. For example, besides the Indian Act of 1876 and the many treaties signed with the Indians, both provincial and federal governments have passed numerous laws restricting the rights of Chinese in Canada (Li, 1988a). These statutes inevitably provided a legal meaning and interpretation to the groups targeted; they also produced social consequences that affected how these groups would relate to the dominant group in society. In recent decades, the Official Languages Act of 1969, the Canada Act of 1982 (which contains the Charter of Rights and Freedoms), and the Multiculturalism Act of 1988 are examples of how the government attempts to legislate race and ethnic relations, and in doing so, redefine race and ethnicity.

The concept of 'race' is particularly controversial since it is often incorrectly linked to genetic factors; indeed, the United Nations Educational, Scientific and Cultural Organization (UNESCO), through a number of scientific conferences, has issued several definitive statements regarding these misconceptions. The only difference between population groups that can be attributed to biological heredity alone is found in blood groups; but populations sharing the same blood group do not coincide with racial groups as they are commonly understood. The concept of race is not a useful scientific one by way of classifying people into population groups. Consequently, it is incorrect to attribute cultural characteristics to genetic inheritance (Bolaria and Li, 1988). On the grounds of overwhelming findings, Rex has concluded that the term 'race' is a social construct, and that rather than looking at the biological basis of race, it is more meaningful to inquire 'how it is that men come to be classified as racially different' (1983: 5).

Some sociologists (e.g. van den Berghe, 1984: 216-18) use the term 'social races' rather than 'races' to emphasize that they are not genotypes—that is, biological subspecies based on a common genetic constitution. Although superficial physical differences, especially skin colour, play an important part in the social classification of people into racial categories, phenotypes—types determined by common visible characteristics, as distinguished from hereditary traits—are often illogically constructed, and do not correspond to genetic typologies. For this reason, some sociologists (Banton, 1977; Miles, 1982; Bolaria and Li, 1988) advocate the term 'racialization' to draw attention to the social process whereby groups are singled out for unequal treatments on the basis of real or imagined phenotypical characteristics. Miles has further challenged the use of the term 'race' by social scientists on the grounds that in using it they treat what is basically an abstraction as though it were real. He argues (1982: 34-5) that if racial groups do not have the same job opportunities, it is not 'race' *per se* that operates as an active agent affecting job choice; rather, it is the decision of an employer who refuses to hire someone. When social scientists speak of race as a cause of job opportunities, they are confusing race as an abstraction with inequality as a reality. In this way race is reified, or treated as though it were a concrete form when in fact it is not.

In the social construction of race and ethnicity it would appear that different types of traits are used. As Wilson (1973: 6) points out, ethnic groups are distinguished by socially selected cultural traits, and racial groups are determined by socially selected physical traits. The exploitation of racial minorities is predicated on racist ideologies that endorse an inherent racial order. Superficial physical differences provide convenient grounds for justifying the mistreatment of subordinate groups (Bolaria and Li, 1988). A good example is the policy of apartheid, which is based on race and not ethnicity; likewise, the immigration policies of many capitalist countries are governed by racial rather than ethnic considerations (Grove, 1974: 320-1). However, Miles (1982) argues that it is difficult to make the distinction between racial and ethnic groups using phenotypical traits for the former and cultural criteria for the latter, since both sets of characteristics are used jointly in social categorization. Perhaps the clearest explanation of the difference between race and ethnicity is given by

Banton (1979), who argues that ethnicity reflects the positive tendencies of identification and inclusion, while race reflects the negative tendencies of dissociation and exclusion.

THE LIMITATIONS OF CULTURAL EXPLANATIONS

It is common in studies of race and ethnic relations to rely heavily on culture to explain human behaviours, since ethnic groups are often seen as primarily cultural entities. While no one would disagree that culture exists, the controversy has to do with the unrefined use of the all-embracing concept of 'culture' to account for all aspects of behaviours that are related to race and ethnicity.

Although there are many ways of defining it, few would disagree that culture represents a way of life that a group of people develops in order to adapt to a set of external and pre-existing conditions. In addition to language, religion, and social institutions such as the family, culture consists of values and orientations that are learned through socialization.

Proponents of cultural theories argue that culture provides the key to understanding why people of various ethnic and racial origins behave differently and, in particular, why they perform unequally in the labour markets of advanced capitalist countries. Different ethnic or cultural groups are believed to have different sets of values, shaped partly by past experiences and partly by present conditions. These cultural values are seen as affecting individuals' psychological composition, thus producing ethnic differences in cognitive perception, mental aptitude, and logical reasoning.

Although the specific cultural trait identified as salient may vary from one study to another, the reasoning remains similar. Because of alleged cultural and sometimes genetic characteristics, different ethnic groups are believed to place unequal emphasis on cognitive and mental development in the process of socialization. Consequently, certain ethnic groups are more capable of promoting among their members those psychological aptitudes and value orientations that are conducive to high achievement (Li, 1988b).

There is an abundance of social-psychological literature that purports to show how ethnic differences in values and intelligence levels affect subsequent educational and occupational performance. For example, Rosen (1956, 1959) argues that differential ethnic mobility in North America may be explained by ethnic variations on what he calls an 'achievement syndrome'. In an empirical study of six ethnic groups, he shows that Greeks, Jews, and white Protestants are likely to rank higher in achievement motivation, achievement values, and educational aspirations than Italians, French Canadians, and Blacks.

These differences, according to Rosen, explain their different mobility rates.

In his study of Canadian Indians and Orientals, Vernon (1984) reports that these groups show profound differences on intelligence tests. He attributes the remarkable abilities and achievements of Orientals in North America to the traditional values preserved in the family; in contrast, Native culture has been violently disrupted by white settlers.

The theme of cultural deprivation and low economic achievement is echoed in many sociological writings. Perhaps the clearest statement in this respect comes from Wagley and Harris (1959), who argue that the adaptive capacity of a minority group determines its socio-economic status, and that such a capacity is dependent upon the group's cultural preparedness. Hence the Jews and French Canadians are economically more successful than Natives and Blacks because of the high adaptability of the former groups.

While at one end of the cultural spectrum there are those whose handicapped culture deprives them of the capacity to achieve, then, at the other end there are those ethnic families that encourage their members to develop an identity conducive to economic achievement. Thus traditional Jewish scholarship, preserved in the religious heritage, gives rise to modern Jewish professionalism in North America (Herberg, 1960; Wagley and Harris, 1959). The Jewish family in Canada is a continuation of the *Shtetl* of Europe, providing the context in which the achievement orientation of the next generation is nourished (Kallen, 1976). Similarly, the recent occupational mobility of Orientals in America is explained in terms of their cultural and institutional heritage (Hsu, 1972; Light, 1972).

Critics of cultural theories argue that there are far too many assumptions made about culture, and that the linkage between culture and ethnicity is tenuous at best (Li, 1988b). First, since culture is largely people's responses to external conditions, it is not static. But supporters of cultural theories often treat culture as primordial and eternal. Ethnic groups are believed to have transplanted a monolithic culture from their country of origin. Over time, as these ethnic groups interact with the dominant group in the host country, their identity with their ethnic culture is believed to weaken. Second, people of the same ethnicity do not necessarily share a common culture. Indeed, whatever cultural homogeneity may have existed among different peoples of the world, the expansion of capitalism since the sixteenth century has radically transformed the population and culture of many parts of the world (Wallerstein, 1979). Today there is no simple correspondence between people, culture, and nation. The European conquest of colonized territories historically and the international migration of peoples in contemporary times have meant that people with an apparent common origin may not even share the same experience, let alone a uniform culture (Li, 1988b). It is therefore incorrect to assume that people having the same ethnic label would necessarily have a common culture.

Aside from the fundamental flaw of equating ethnicity with culture, there are other drawbacks to using culture as an explanation of ethnic variations in behaviours and economic performance. There is little doubt that many ethnic groups show differences in intelligence tests and cognitive scales. But it is not clear whether these differences are a consequence of differential learning opportunities or of an ethnic culture (Samuda, 1984). After all, IQ tests measure developed abilities and past learning rather than innate capacities or general adaptation to life (McClelland, 1973). It has also been noted that many standardized aptitude tests are in fact culture-bound and class-based, so that minority children from lower-class backgrounds are in double jeopardy. Samuda (1984) also warns of the potential problem in using psychological tests as a basis for excluding minority children in favour of those of high ability, usually from the dominant group. In this sense, subsequent educational disparity may be further polarized, not so much because of alleged cultural differences, but because of how test results are used by educators and policy-makers (Cicourel and Kitsuse, 1963; Mercer, 1971).

Even if the results of many standardized tests between ethnic groups were accepted as *prima facie* evidence, it is debatable whether these ethnic differences originate from culture, and whether test results in the early years imply unequal capacities that cause subsequent occupational achievement. Furthermore, when IQ and other psychological scores are included in status-attainment models, their effect tends to weaken appreciably at successive stages of the occupational career, especially after adjusting for variations in social origin and educational level (Featherman, 1971; Jencks et al., 1972).

Perhaps the strongest objection to cultural explanations lies in the way ‘culture’ is used. Conceptually, almost every aspect of human life can be included under the rubric of culture: hence it can explain no aspect of human life. Cultural variations are assumed when comparisons are made between ethnic groups, and the presumed difference is often affirmed by IQ and other psychological test results that mostly measure past learning experiences. Whether the correlation between ethnic origin and standardized test scores implies a relationship between culture and socio-economic performance is highly questionable. Among the strongest critics of the misuse of the culture concept is Valentine (1968) who points out a potential tautology in using culture as both a description and an explanation. He argues that there is an important distinction between those material conditions that exist prior to, and therefore apart from, culture, and culture itself. Consequently, disadvantaged racial and ethnic groups cannot be held responsible for those material conditions that are external to them—conditions to which they have little choice but to learn to adapt. In this sense, lack of opportunity and the structural constraints of ethnic ghettos are *causes* of cultural deprivation, but cannot be *consequences* of culture. There is also strong historical evidence to indicate that the plight of many racial and ethnic groups is the result of structured inequality and racial oppression, and that their subsequent cultural destruction can be directly linked to colonial domination (Frideres, 1983; Milner and Milner, 1973; Bolaria and Li, 1988). In other words, if cultural deprivation and economic failings tend to coexist, it is because they originate from the same cause.

In recent years the transplanted cultural thesis, widely used to explain immigrant lives, has been under attack. There are many versions of this thesis, but the basic argument is that immigrants to North America bring with them an Old World culture that largely influences their adjustment, achievement, and community development in the New World. In their excellent account of emerging ethnicity in America, Yancey, Ericksen, and Juliani (1976) argue that the development of ethnicity is more closely related to structural conditions in the cities to which ethnic groups immigrate and the economic opportunities available to them there than to the primordial culture. Ethnicity—and, for that matter, culture—is not fixed, but constantly changing under different external conditions. They conclude (1976: 400) as follows:

> The assumption of a common heritage as the essential aspect of ethnicity is erroneous. Ethnicity may have relatively little to do with Europe, Asia or Africa, but much to do with the exigencies of survival and the structure of opportunity in this country.

ACADEMIC THEORIES AND STATE POLICIES

While it is becoming increasingly uncertain what role culture plays in shaping race and ethnicity, two social forces previously ignored are continuously changing the way ethnic and racial groups relate to each other. The first of these forces arises from academic theorizing about race and ethnic groups, which influences the way the government and the public react to existing racial tensions and ethnic conflicts. The second has to do with actions and policies of the state that have the effect of influencing the composition of race and ethnic groups, and reshaping the contours of intergroup relationships.

Sociologists affect the way people view race and ethnic relations in several ways. Miles (1982: 33-6) has probably presented the harshest critique of how the sociology of race relations has reified the phenomenological appearance of race into an empirical reality. According to Miles, this is what academics do when they present to their survey respondents contextual questions that reinforce the existence of racial groupings and racial problems, and when they communicate their research findings in such a way as to confirm that racial and ethnic categories are natural biological groupings. Sociologists also influence others when their dominant theories are popularized as expert explanations of what the state of affairs is, thus converting abstract academic ideas into concrete popular beliefs.

In the area of race and ethnic studies, no perspective has had such a profound influence as the theory of assimilation—despite its numerous shortcomings. Among the many versions of assimilation theory are the melting-pot thesis, the Anglo-conformity perspective, and the theory of pluralism (Gordon, 1964). The terms 'assimilation' and its variant 'melting-pot' are difficult to define, and their meanings are largely assumed. 'Assimilation' and 'Anglo-conformity' imply that there are standards of behaviour and values that ethnic groups can acquire and thereby become similar to the dominant group; yet such standards are often impossible to define. In the absence of objective criteria, any sign that suggests an ethnic group is adhering to presumed non-English behaviours or culture is taken to reflect incomplete assimilation, no matter how irrelevant these behaviours may be to living in North America. Conceptually, moreover, it is impossible for ethnic minorities, particularly racial groups, to assimilate. Empirically, from the vantage point of assimilation theory, it is irrelevant to try to find out whether members of the dominant group are indeed as assimilated as they are assumed to be, since assimilation, being undefined, is not a problem for them. Where the theoretical options for studying assimilation are exhausted, sociologists turn to the study of pluralism, the opposite of assimilation. Underlying the notion of pluralism is the belief that some ethnic groups will not assimilate; the focus of research is to find out how different they are. Pluralism—or, in its Canadian version, multiculturalism—is widely seen by academics and policy-makers as a liberal policy enabling racial and ethnic groups to preserve their own heritage and distinctiveness. In fact, pluralist theory and multicultural policy have been elevated to such a level that they are almost considered a liberating force of ethnic culture.

Yet for many racial and ethnic minorities, the idealism of the multicultural society is hard to reconcile with the reality of inequality. On the one hand, multiculturalism encourages cultural uniqueness;

yet on the other, it is precisely those minorities' alleged distinctiveness that puts them in a disadvantaged position in the labour market. But this is not a contradiction for academics who follow the pluralist model religiously, since the problem of race and ethnic inequality falls outside the intellectual domain of assimilation and pluralism. If Canadians have been too complacent about multiculturalism but indifferent about race and ethnic inequality, they have been influenced, at least in part, by the intellectual favouritism that many academics have shown to assimilation and pluralism as the most important tools in unravelling the meaning of race and ethnicity.

If academic theories can change the way people think about race and ethnicity, then state policies certainly carry the weight to shape race and ethnic relations. Historically, there have been numerous instances in which the Canadian state has defined, in precise legal terms, what groups were to be racialized, and how they were to be incorporated into Canadian society (Bolaria and Li, 1988). For example, the Indian Act of 1876 consolidated and revised all previous legislation dealing with Indians, and provided the legal and bureaucratic foundation for the way Indians were to be treated in Canada. The statute defined virtually every aspect of life affecting Indians, and institutionalized many restrictions on them. Despite many revisions, the original Indian Act has basically been maintained to the present day. Because of its pervasive and destructive impact on the Indians, Frideres (1983: 33) has described it as 'the most vicious mechanism of social control that exists in Canada today'. Thus the state policy towards the Indians, more than anything else, stands out as the most salient factor in explaining the relationship between Native and white Canadians.

The case of the Chinese in Canada is another example of how state policies marginalized a minority group and legalized its unequal treatment. Between 1875 and 1924, numerous bills were passed at both provincial and federal levels to restrict the rights of Chinese Canadians. These statutes severely affected their opportunities in the labour market, retarded the development of the Chinese community, and influenced the way other Canadians viewed and treated the Chinese (Li, 1988a). This is a clear example of racialization by state policies, through which phenotypical features become racial characteristics and take on social significance.

The Canadian state has also played a key role, through its immigration policy, in determining the volume and nature of immigrants recruited from different source countries. Historically, Canada has followed a policy of recruiting immigrants from the United Kingdom, Northern Europe, and the United States, while restricting those from Asia and other Third World countries (Li and Bolaria, 1979). The policy of favouring Europeans was maintained until the changes in immigration policy in 1962 and later in 1967 (Hawkins, 1988). For many minority groups the Canadian immigration policy is probably the single most important factor in determining the size and composition of their ethnic communities. Moreover, the differential treatment of racial and ethnic groups in the history of Canadian immigration also means that the entrance status of various groups into Canadian society is not the same ('entrance status' refers to the social status of immigrant groups as compared to that of the charter groups [Porter, 1965]). Thus the unequal social status and position of race and ethnic groups in Canada are further reinforced.

In recent decades the Canadian state has made more radical policy changes that are reshaping ethnic and race relations. In the area of English and French relations, perhaps the greatest effects have been brought about by the Official Languages Act of 1969. Among its many consequences are mandatory language requirements for many jobs in the civil service, the expansion of opportunities for bilingual francophones, and changes in the French language programs in the school system both inside and outside Quebec. The same language act also prompted renewed antagonism towards francophones and the French language, especially in English Canada. Relations between English and French Canada are further strained as a result of the repatriation of the constitution in 1982 without Quebec's consent. Although the Canada Act of 1982 put in place the Charter of Rights and Freedoms, the Quebec question and the Aboriginal-rights question are by no means resolved. This is evident in the subsequent dispute over the Meech Lake Accord, which has continued into late 1989 with several provinces in English Canada objecting to the special status Quebec would have if the accord were approved.

While attempting to mediate between English and French Canada over the past two decades, the Canadian state has also made policy changes that affect other ethnic groups. In 1971 Canada adopted a multicultural policy with the stated purpose of preserving the language and heritage of all ethnic groups, and removing social obstacles towards equality. The multicultural policy was put into law in the Canadian Multiculturalism Act of 1988. Although the ethnic revival of the 1970s in the form of folk festivities and heritage-language classes was spontaneous to the extent that ethnic groups responded to opportunities of financial support for ethnic activities, it was largely engineered by the state's various multicultural programs. Critics have argued that if the multicultural policy fails to combat racism and discrimination, it succeeds in managing race and ethnic relations within a state apparatus (Bolaria and Li, 1988). The state, through its funding of multicultural activities, exercises fiscal control over ethnic associations. This means that the nature, duration, and amounts of grants that ethnic associations receive must fall in line with the officially defined priorities of multicultural programs. Ethnic associations that do not follow the official priorities run the risk of losing the financial support necessary for their existence, while those that depend on government funding face the threat of losing organizational autonomy (Stasiulis, 1980).

There is no doubt that the power and resource base of racial and ethnic groups has been constantly restructured by state policies. In this sense it is fair to say that race and ethnic relations do not naturally fall into place as a result of cultural evolution; on the contrary, they are often the result of actions and policies on the part of the state that reflect competing interests in society.

REFERENCES

Aboud, Frances E.
1981 'Ethnic Self-identity'. Pp. 37-56 in R.C. Gardner and R. Kalin, eds, *A Canadian Social Psychology of Ethnic Relations*. Toronto: Methuen.

Akoodie, Mohammed Ally
1984 'Identity and Self-concept in Immigrant Children'. Pp. 253-65 in R.J. Samuda, J.W. Berry, and M. Laferriere, eds, *Multiculturalism in Canada*. Boston: Allyn and Bacon.

Banton, Michael
1977 *The Idea of Race*. London: Tavistock.
1979 'Analytical and Folk Concepts of Race and Ethnicity'. *Ethnic and Racial Studies* 2: 127-38.

Bolaria, B. Singh, and Peter S. Li
1988 *Racial Oppression in Canada*. 2nd ed. Toronto: Garamond.

Cicourel, Allen V., and John I. Kitsuse
1963 *The Educational Decision-Makers*. Indianapolis: Bobbs-Merrill.

Driedger, Leo, ed.
1978 *The Canadian Ethnic Mosaic: A Quest for Identity*. Toronto: McClelland and Stewart.

Featherman, David L.
1971 'The Socioeconomic Achievement of White Religio-ethnic Subgroups: Social and Psychological Explanations'. *American Sociological Review* 36: 207-22.

Frideres, James S.
1983 *Native People in Canada*. Scarborough, Ont.: Prentice-Hall.

Gordon, Milton M.
1964 *Assimilation in American Life*. New York: Oxford University Press.

Grove, J.
1974 'Differential Political and Economic Patterns of Ethnic and Race Relations: A Cross-national Analysis'. *Race* 15: 303-29.

Haas, Jack and William Shaffir
1978 *Shaping Identity in Canadian Society*. Scarborough, Ont.: Prentice-Hall.
Hawkins, Freda
1988 *Canada and Immigration*. 2nd ed. Kingston and Montreal: McGill-Queen's University Press.
Herberg, Will
1960 *Protestant, Catholic, Jew*. New York: Doubleday.
Hsu, Francis I.K.
1972 *Challenge of the American Dream: The Chinese in the United States*. San Francisco: Wadsworth.
Isajiw, W.
1974 'Definitions of Ethnicity'. *Ethnicity* 1: 111-24.
Jencks, Christopher S., et al.
1972 *Inequality*. New York: Harper and Row.
Kallen, Evelyn
1976 'Family Life Styles and Jewish Culture'. Pp. 145-61 in K. Ishwaran, ed., *The Canadian Family*. Toronto: Holt, Rinehart and Winston.
Li, Peter S.
1988a *The Chinese in Canada*. Toronto: Oxford University Press.
1988b *Ethnic Inequality in a Class Society*. Toronto: Wall and Thompson.
Li, Peter S., and B. Singh Bolaria
1979 'Canadian Immigration Policy and Assimilation Theories'. Pp. 411-22 in J.A. Fry, ed., *Economy, Class and Social Reality*. Toronto: Butterworths.
Light, Ivan H.
1972 *Ethnic Enterprise in America*. Berkeley: University of California Press.
McClelland, D.C.
1973 'Testing for Competence rather than Intelligence'. *American Psychologist* 28: 1-14.
Mercer, J.
1971 'Institutionalized Anglocentrism: Labelling Mental Retardates in the Public Schools.' Pp. 311-38 in P. Orleans and W. Russell, eds, *Race, Change and Urban Society*. Los Angeles: Sage.
Miles, Robert
1982 *Racism and Migrant Labour*. London: Routledge and Kegan Paul.
Milner, Sheilagh Hodgins, and Henry Milner
1973 *The Decolonization of Quebec*. Toronto: McClelland and Stewart.
Porter, John
1965 *The Vertical Mosaic*. Toronto: University of Toronto Press.
Rex, John
1983 *Race Relations in Sociological Theory*. 2nd ed. London: Routledge and Kegan Paul.
Rosen, Bernard C.
1956 'The Achievement Syndrome: A Psychocultural Dimension of Social Stratification'. *American Sociological Review* 21: 203-11.

1959 'Race, Ethnicity, and the Achievement Syndrome'. *American Sociological Review* 24: 47-60.
Samuda, Ronald J.
1984 'Assessing the Abilities of Minority Students within a Multiethnic Milieu'. Pp. 353-67 in R.J. Samuda, J.W. Berry, and M. Laferriere, eds, *Multiculturalism in Canada*. Boston: Allyn and Bacon.
Stasiulis, Daiva K.
1980 'The Political Structuring of Ethnic Community Action: A Reformulation'. *Canadian Ethnic Studies*. 12: 19-44.
Valentine, Charles A.
1968 *Culture and Poverty*. Chicago: University of Chicago Press.
van den Berghe, Pierre L.
1984 'Race: Perspective Two'. Pp. 216-18 in E.E. Cashmore, ed., *Dictionary of Race and Ethnic Relations*. London: Routledge and Kegan Paul.
Vernon, Philip E.
1984 'Abilities and Achievements of Ethnic Groups in Canada with Special Reference to Canadian Natives and Orientals'. Pp. 382-95 in R.J. Samuda, J.W. Berry, and M. Laferriere, eds, *Multiculturalism in Canada*. Boston: Allyn and Bacon.
Wagley, Charles, and Marvin Harris
1959 *Minorities in the New World*. New York: Columbia University Press.
Wallerstein, Immanuel
1979 *The Capitalist World-Economy*. London: Cambridge University Press.
Weber, Max
1968 *Economy and Society*. Vol. 1. New York: Bedminster.
Wilson, William J.
1973 *Power, Racism, and Privilege*. New York: Free Press.
Yancey, William L., E.P. Ericksen, and R.N. Juliani
1976 'Emergent Ethnicity: A Review and Reformulation'. *American Sociological Review* 41: 391-403.

TWO

A DEMOGRAPHIC OVERVIEW OF RACIAL AND ETHNIC GROUPS IN CANADA[1]

WARREN E. KALBACH

The exploration and settlement of the North American continent was a direct consequence of the agricultural, commercial, and industrial revolutions in Europe. Expanding populations intensified the competition for new territories and access to the riches of the New World. It was the dominant economic and political powers of the seventeenth and eighteenth centuries that put in place the foundations of the social order that has evolved in North America. In that part of the New World that was destined to become Canada, it was the French who gained the initial foothold and established their political, economic, and social institutions. After almost a century of French rule, the British won control in 1763, but even though the French succumbed to the political and economic dominance of the British, their cultural influence has persisted for more than two hundred years.

Through most of its history, Canada has been perceived to be predominantly British in its orientation, even though its two founding groups have provided it with a somewhat unique bilingual and bicultural character. At the time of Confederation, 60 per cent of the population was of British origin and 30 per cent French. Now, with generally declining fertility and continuing immigration from different source countries, Canada has become more ethnically and culturally diverse. Yet as recently as 1981 the British and French still comprised almost 70 per cent of the nation's total, with 40 and 27 per cent respectively.

The move towards an official multiculturalism policy would appear to have been instigated by French Canada's efforts to secure a bilingual and bicultural policy that would entrench and protect their language and cultural rights. Clearly, there has been increasing concern that the historical position of the French in Canada, vis-à-vis the British, is in jeopardy. The bicultural and bilingual character of Canada had been maintained over the years through the continuing high fertility of the French Canadian population and the continuing immigration of individuals of British origins from the United Kingdom and elsewhere (Kalbach and McVey, 1979). But the changing character of immigration to Canada through the twentieth century and the dramatic acceleration of the decline in fertility following the Second World War have the potential to significantly alter the basic nature of Canadian society and the relationships between the two 'founding' cultural groups and the other diverse ethnic and racial groups that have established themselves in Canada over the past twenty to thirty years.

As in the past, the relationships between these various ethnic and racial groups will be influenced not only by unique historical factors, but also by the degree of similarity between the arriving immigrants and those groups already established in Canada with respect to their culture and language, demographic factors, and various social and economic characteristics. This chapter briefly discusses some of the problems of identifying populations in terms of their ethnic and racial characteristics and examines some of the changes that are occurring in Canada's ethnic and racial composition and distribution.

IDENTIFICATION OF POPULATIONS BY ETHNIC AND RACIAL ORIGINS[2]

The validity and reliability of ethnic/racial population data are highly dependent upon the government's recognition of the importance of data collection and its commitment to the development of systematic and comprehensive national censuses and vital statistics registration systems. Fortunately for Canada, as for most of the developed countries, the government has carried out systematic and comprehensive censuses throughout its history. And, perhaps because of the country's basic bicultural nature, and its persistent concerns about the kinds of immigrants it receives, the major national censuses have always included questions on ethnic and racial origins, country of birth, religion, mother tongue, and period of immigration. The realization that questions on ethnic or racial ancestry tend to have an above-average potential for response error (Boxhill, 1986) has resulted in periodic attempts to improve the wording of the questions as well as the instructions to enumerators and respondents. Such definitional improvements between 1871 and 1971 probably have not seriously affected either the comparability of the data or their general usefulness for historical analyses for this period of Canada's history. However, continuing efforts to improve the quality of ethnic-origin data collected in the 1981 and 1986 censuses produced significant changes in definitions and data-management procedures. As a result, the 1981 and 1986 ethnic-origin data, as obtained from the respondent or produced in census tabulations, are directly comparable neither to each other nor to data collected in earlier censuses (Statistics Canada, 1987).

In 1981 the census allowed respondents to use either the paternal or the maternal line of descent to describe their ethnic origin, and to report more than one origin if they wished. In 1986 the 1981 census question on ethnic origins—'To which ethnic or cultural group did you or your ancestors belong on first coming to this continent?'—was shortened to make it more appropriate for the aboriginal population, by dropping the last phrase 'on first coming to this continent'. In addition, greater provision was made for possible multiple responses, in anticipation of the results of revised instructions requesting respondents to mark or specify as many groups as apply. In 1986 two more 'write-in' spaces were provided than in the previous census. These changes were thought to contribute significantly to an increase in 'multiple responses' reported in the 1986 census (Statistics Canada: 1989a). While the validity of the ethnic-origin data collected in the 1981 and 1986 censuses may have been greatly improved, the cost of these changes to the researcher has been considerable in terms of the loss in comparability of historical data. Extending analyses of ethnic compositional trends beyond 1971, for anything other than the broadest groupings of ethnic-origin categories, is no longer possible.

Whether one is doing research using census ethnic-origin data or reading about the research of others, it is important to remember the difference between census data that reflects 'origins' and 'ancestry' and data that might indicate current membership in, or identity with, some ethnic community. The census data presented and discussed here are 'origin' or 'ancestry' data, and can be used only indirectly, or in conjunction with other ethnic characteristics, to infer the strength of ethnic identity or the extent of current 'ethnic connectedness' to some ethnic community. It is important not to confuse the meanings or the use of the two concepts 'ethnic origin' and 'ethnic identity', while trying to understand the relationships between them.

Because of difficulties in conceptualizing and defining ethnicity and race, and in establishing a set of unambiguous subcategories that are valid, reliable, and reasonably accurate, accumulating a useful historical series is problematic at best. Canada's censuses have consistently collected data on ethnic/racial origins of the population, emphasizing 'ancestry' rather than the individual's current degree of identification with particular ethnic/racial groups. It is quite possible that in the future, it may be necessary to add a question to the census in order to determine the nature of respondents' current 'ethnic identities' as well as their 'origins', if a better understanding of the nature of Canadian society is to be achieved.[3]

POPULATION GROWTH

The demographics of the early settlement and rapid growth of the populations of New France and British North America have been discussed in considerable detail elsewhere (Beaujot and McQuillan, 1982; Kalbach and McVey, 1979). About the time of Confederation, Canada's population had reached 3.7 million. Somewhat more than 80 per cent of the population was concentrated in Quebec and Ontario, and those of British and French origins comprised 61 and 31 per cent of the total respectively. The French were still dependent on natural increase to maintain their position in Canada in relation to the British, while the latter relied, as they have continued to do, on immigration to maintain their numerical dominance. Since then, both populations have gone through a demographic transition from high to relatively low levels of vital rates as the overall annual growth rate declined from a high of 2.9 per cent during the early 1900s to a much lower rate, approaching one per cent, in recent decades (Kalbach, 1987).

Canada's population, 1871-1986

In the period between Confederation in 1867 and 1986, Canada's population increased from 3.7 million to 25 million. The average annual rate of growth varied considerably, ranging from a high of close to 3 per cent during the 1901-11 decade of the great European migration to North America, to a low of 1.0 per cent during the decade of low immigration in the economically depressed 1930s, and recovering to 2.8 per cent by the middle of the post-war economic expansion and 'baby-boom' years (Kalbach and McVey, 1979).

The volume of immigration varied considerably over this period. It was greatest in the first three decades of the 1900s, when approximately 4.6 million immigrants arrived (mostly from European countries). After the virtual cessation of immigration during the economic depression and the Second World War, immigration surged again with Canada's unprecedented post-war economic expansion and the 'baby boom' of the 1950s. Over 1.5 million immigrants arrived in

Canada during this decade. All together, 4.4 million immigrants were landed between 1951 and 1981 (Employment and Immigration, 1988).

These totals provide some indication of immigration's impact on Canada's population. However, they can be misleading, since the population base increased significantly between the early 1900s and the post-war period, and emigration was not taken into account. For these reasons, the impact of immigration on Canada's population can be better appreciated by examining changes in the size of the foreign-born population in relation to the total population growth as shown in Figure 2.1.

Figure 2.1 Canada and the Foreign-Born Population, 1871-1986

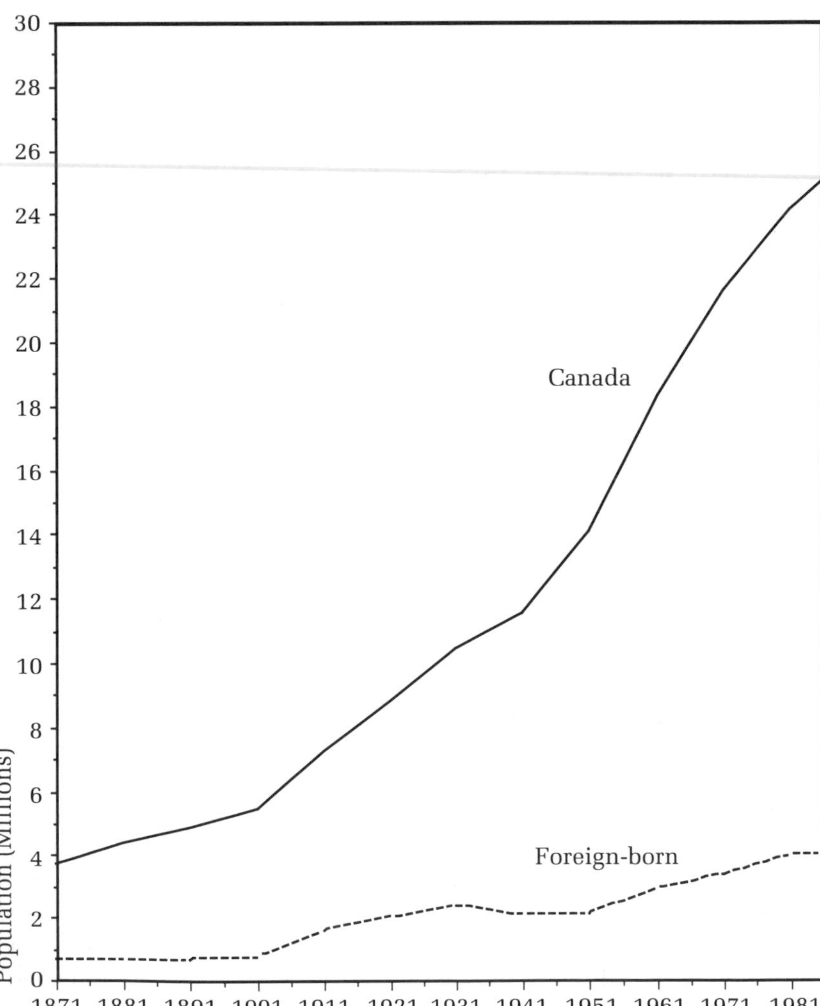

SOURCE: See Table 2.1. Population Research Lab., Erindale College, University of Toronto.

Examination of the data in Table 2.1 shows that the surge of immigration in the early 1900s not only resulted in significant increases in the number of foreign-born residents in Canada between 1901 and 1931, but boosted their proportion of the total population from 13 per cent in 1901 to 22 per cent in 1911 and slightly over 22 per cent for both 1921 and 1931. The increase in post-war immigration did not begin to reverse either the relative or the absolute decline in the foreign-born during the depression and war years until the 'baby-boom' decade. At that time the numbers, as well as their proportions, began to increase again. From a low of 14.7 per cent in 1951, the proportion of foreign-born had increased to 15.7 per cent at the time of the census in 1986. Note that with the exception of the 1930s, the foreign-born population has increased in numbers every decade since 1871, but that its rate of growth has not always kept pace with that of the native-born.

Ethnic and racial composition, 1871-1971

The full impact of continuing immigration on Canadian society depends not only on the relative size of the immigrant streams, but on their ethnic and racial composition as well. Clearly, a continuation of immigration from the same major source countries that contributed during Canada's early history would have minimal effect on the es-

Table 2.1
Population Increase, Immigration, and the Foreign-born Population: Canada, 1871-81 to 1981-86

Decade	Total population[a] ('000)	Percentage increase (%)	Number of immigrants ('000)	Total foreign-born ('000)	Percentage foreign-born (%)
1871-1881	3,689	17.2	353	625	16.9
1881-1891	4,325	11.8	903	603	13.9
1891-1901	4,833	11.1	326	644	13.3
1901-1911	5,371	34.2	1,759	700	13.0
1911-1921	7,207	21.9	1,612	1,587	22.0
1921-1931	8,788	18.1	1,203	1,956	22.3
1931-1941	10,377	10.9	150	2,308	22.2
1941-1951	11,507	21.7	548	2,010	17.5
1951-1961	14,009	30.2	1,543	2,060	14.7
1961-1971	18,238	18.3	1,429	2,844	15.6
1971-1981	21,569	12.9	1,447	3,296	15.3
1981-1986	24,343	2.8[b]	511[b]	3,867	16.1
1986-	25,022	—	—	3,937	15.7

SOURCE: *Censuses of Canada*, 1871 to 1986; Employment and Immigration Canada, *Immigration Statistics*, 1986 (Ottawa: Minister of Supply and Services Canada, 1988).

[a]Population at the beginning of the decade.
[b]For the five-year period 1981-85.

tablished social, economic, and political institutional structures. Conversely, a major shift in the principal source countries and in the ethnic/racial origins of immigrants would seem to have considerable potential for affecting change. But the nature of these changes and their implications for the future of Canadian society are difficult to determine. Uncertainties about the cultural, socio-economic, and political consequences of changes in the ethnic/racial origins of the population are giving the government some cause for concern and a reason for adopting a more cautious approach to its annual review of immigration and the setting of immigration levels (Employment and Immigration Canada, 1988a).

It is evident from the data on the ethnic/racial origins of Canada's population from 1871 to 1971, presented in Table 2.2, that the combined population of British and French origins retained its majority position, even though each of the 'founding' groups experienced relative declines. This is especially significant in view of the fact that these declines occurred during the period of Canadian history when immigration was controlled by policies that encouraged immigration from most European countries while discriminating against those source countries whose cultures and life-styles, etc., were noticeably different from those found in Canada. The changing pattern in ethnic composition during the period when immigration selection policies discriminated primarily on the basis of ethnic and racial origins is quite clear in Figure 2.2. It is apparent that most discriminatory policies had little overall effect in stemming the decline in the proportion of British since the 1930s. On the other hand, they may have pre-

Table 2.2
Ethnic Composition of Canada's Population, Selected Ethnic Origins: 1871 to 1971

Ethnic-Origin Group	1871	1881	1901	1921	1941	1961	1971
British Isles	60.5	59.0	57.0	55.4	49.7	43.8	44.6
French	31.1	30.0	30.7	27.9	30.3	30.4	28.7
Other European	6.9	6.9	8.5	14.2	17.8	22.6	23.0
Asiatic	—	0.1	0.5	0.8	0.6	0.7	1.3
Other[a]	1.5	4.0	3.3	1.7	1.6	2.5	2.4
Total:							
Percentage	100.0	100.0	100.0	100.0	100.0	100.0	100.0
Number ('000)	3,486	4,325	5,371	8,788	11,507	18,238	21,568

SOURCE: *Censuses of Canada;* D. Kubat and D. Thornton, *A Statistical Profile of Canadian Society* (Toronto: McGraw-Hill Ryerson), 1974.

[a]Includes Native people, Blacks and other non-European.

Figure 2.2 Ethnic Composition of Canada's Population, 1871-1961

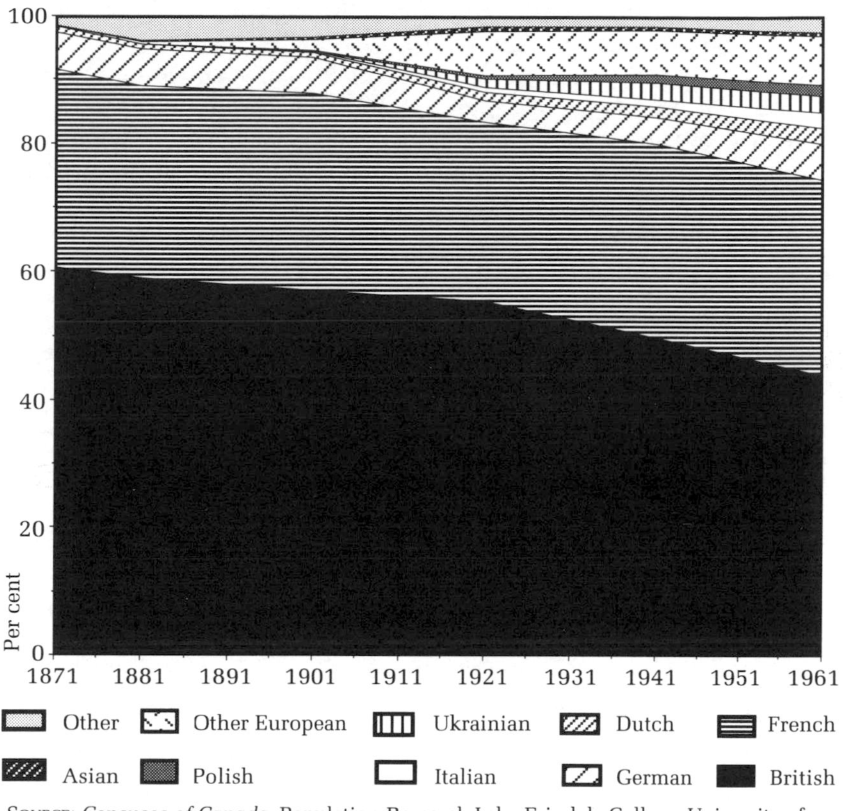

SOURCE: *Censuses of Canada*. Population Research Lab., Erindale College, University of Toronto.

vented an even larger and more rapid decline than would have occurred otherwise.

During the post-war period of massive reconstruction in Europe and Asia, major political realignments and new regional conflicts, large-scale population displacements and growing numbers of refugees made it increasingly apparent that Canada's traditional selective immigration policies, based on ethnic/racial and cultural suitability criteria, were too outmoded and morally indefensible for Canada to retain. As a consequence, the government eliminated any suggestion of 'preferred ethnic/racial origins' from its selection process and introduced a more universal set of criteria based on occupational skills, education, work experience, and other factors thought appropriate to expedite the social and economic integration of immigrants into Canadian society (Manpower and Immigration, 1974, vol. 2).

The major effect of liberalizing Canada's immigration policy and implementing a more objective selection process, free of ethnic and racial biases, was a significant shift in the rank order of the leading source countries of immigrants. Note in Table 2.3 that throughout the post-war period Britain and the United States continued to rank high in the list of leading sources. However, the dominance of European countries in 1951, 1960, and 1968 has given way to non-European source countries. Since 1984 Poland has been the only European country besides Britain to remain among the top ten sources. Hong Kong ranked fifth in 1968 and has remained in the top five for each of the subsequent years for which data are shown. South, East, and Southeast Asian countries have been increasing their numbers in the list of leading sources, as have the countries in the Caribbean and Central and South America. There seems to be little doubt

Table 2.3
The Leading Source Countries[a] of Immigration to Canada, Selected Years: 1951 to 1986

1951	1960	1968
Britain	Italy	Britain
Germany	Britain	United States
Italy	United States	Italy
Netherlands	Germany	Germany
Poland	Netherlands	Hong Kong
France	Portugal	France
United States	Greece	Austria
Belgium	France	Greece
Yugoslavia	Poland	Portugal
Denmark	Austria	Yugoslavia
1976	**1984**	**1986**
Britain	Vietnam	United States
United States	Hong Kong	India
Hong Kong	United States	Vietnam
Jamaica	India	Hong Kong
Lebanon	Britain	Poland
India	Poland	Britain
Philippines	Philippines	Jamaica
Portugal	El Salvador	Philippines
Italy	Jamaica	Guyana
Guyana	China	El Salvador

SOURCE: Department of Manpower and Immigration, *The Immigration Program*, vol. 2, *A Report of the Canadian Immigration and Population Study* (Ottawa: Information Canada, 1974), Table 3.3, p. 84; *1976 Immigration Statistics*, Table 3; Employment and Immigration Canada, *Annual Report to Parliament on Future Immigration Levels*, 1985 (Ottawa: Minister of Supply and Services Canada, 1985), Statistical Appendix; *1986 Immigration Statistics* (Ottawa: Minister of Supply and Services Canada, 1988), p. 13.

[a]Country of last permanent residence

that Canada has become a prime destination for potential immigrants from the world's developing countries. This dramatic shift during the last twenty-five years can be seen in Figure 2.3.

Ethnic and racial origins in the 1980s[4]

With the acceptance of multiple ethnic origins in response to the 1981 census question of ethnic origins, and the greater encouragement given to elicit and record multiple responses to the 1986 census question, it is much more difficult to make precise estimates of changes in specific ethnic-origin populations after the 1971 census. Yet rough estimates of broad changes in ethnic composition between 1971 and 1981 are still possible. Data in Table 2.2 showed that the combined categories of British and French represented 73 per cent of the total population in 1971. For 1981, data in Table 2.4 show that the combined British and French origins could still account for 73 per cent, but only if those who reported multiple origins involving only the

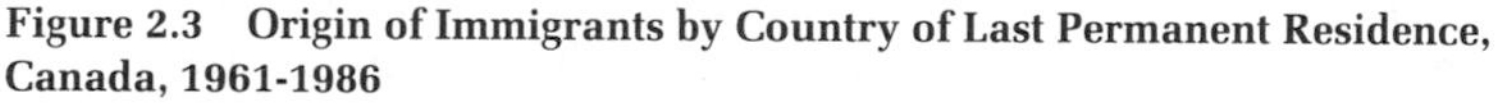

Figure 2.3 Origin of Immigrants by Country of Last Permanent Residence, Canada, 1961-1986

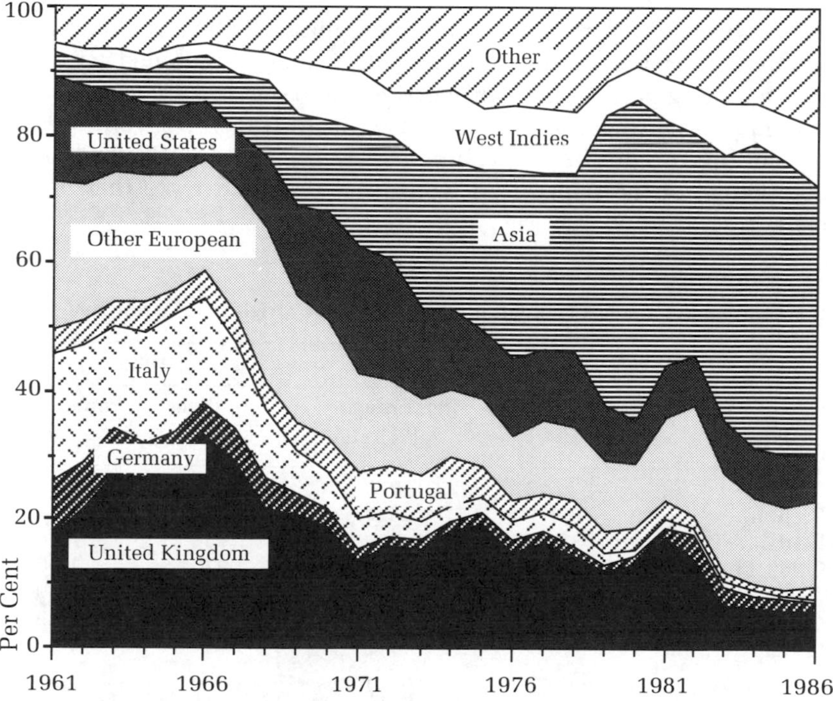

SOURCE: Immigration Statistics, Annual Reports, Employment and Immigration Canada, 1961-1986. Note: 'Other' includes Africa, Australia, Central and South America, and Oceania. Population Research Lab., Erindale College, University of Toronto.

British and French were also included. There appears to be little evidence of any significant change vis-à-vis these combined 'founding' groups during the 1970s. The picture for the European origins is somewhat different. Even if the 'multiple-origin' Europeans were combined with the single origins, the Europeans would still show a decline from 23 to 20 per cent. The relatively small numbers of Asians and other non-Europeans, on the other hand, showed significant gains from 1.3 and 2.4 per cent respectively in 1971 to 3.1 in 1981. The 1986 census revealed further declines in the proportions of single British, French, and other European origins, and a continuation of the post-war trend of increasing numbers and proportions for Asian origins, whose numbers grew by approximately 228,000 during the five-year intercensal period. The most notable change in the 1986 results was the increase in the proportion reporting multiple origins other than combined British and French. The increase from one to 23 per cent probably accounts for most of the decline between 1981 and 1986 reflected in the data for the British, French, and other Europeans shown in Table 2.4. Nevertheless, the single British and French origins, combined with just the British-French multiples, still comprise 54 per cent, or a majority of Canada's population. If all of the multiple-origin responses involving either British or French are removed from the 'other multiple' category and combined with the two founding groups, their proportion increases to 75 per cent. The non-European single origins increased from 6 to 7 per cent, and if the multiple origins involving only non-Europeans are included, their component of the population would not be much more than 8 per cent.

Table 2.4
Composition of Canada's Population, Selected Ethnic Origins: 1981 and 1986

	1981		1986	
Origins	Number ('000)	Percentage (%)	Number ('000)	Percentage (%)
British	9,674	40.2	6,333	25.3
French	6,439	26.8	6,099[a]	24.4
British & French	1,522	6.3	1,139	4.6
Other European	4,627	19.2	3,913	15.6
Asian	753	3.1	981	3.9
Other Single	707	3.1	715	2.9
Other Multiple	317	1.3	5,847	23.3
Total	24,084	100.0	25,022	100.0

SOURCE: *1981* and *1986 Censuses of Canada.*

[a]Includes 6,000 French-only multiple origins.

Multiple origins

Whatever the difficulties that have been caused for historical analyses through the encouragement of multiple-ethnic responses, they will probably be more than compensated for by what more accurate data on ethnic mixing will reveal about the nature of Canadian society. The proportions of ethnically endogamous and exogamous marriages have been used as indicators of acculturation and assimilation (Kalbach and Richard, 1989) and can provide clues as to the degree to which the minority ethnic groups are being integrated and assimilated into Canadian society.

Consideration of population size alone might suggest that the concept of multiculturalism would have rather limited relevance beyond the British and French groups in Canada today. However, data on the types of ethnic mixing and differences in relative sizes of mixed-ancestry populations can now be used to assess the relative validity of the various assimilation and cultural-pluralism models for Canada's ethnic/racial populations. It is interesting to note, in Table 2.5, that of northern, western, and eastern European origins, the British have the highest proportions reporting multiple origins. However, this is what might be expected, given the historical cultural dominance of the British in Canada, and the major role played by their European-origin populations during the early settlement of the country. Neither is it surprising that the Asian populations, which have been an increasingly dominant component of post-war immigration, showed the lowest proportions of multiple origins. In general, the Asians are culturally very different from the Europeans and have had relatively little time to become acculturated and integrated into Canadian society. The intermediate levels of mixed origins reported by the other non-European-origin populations reflect a variety of cultural and historical circumstances that have facilitated their acculturation and integration into Canadian society.

POPULATION DISTRIBUTION

The impact that specific ethnocultural populations may have on the host society depends not only on their size but also on their geographical distributions and degree of regional and local concentration. French Canadians, for example, would not likely have the cultural and political influence they enjoy today had they been fewer in numbers and not so heavily concentrated in Quebec. In 1981, slightly more than three-quarters of the French-origin population lived in Quebec, where they comprised 80 per cent of the population (Kalbach, 1987). Table 2.6 presents data on the ethnic composition of the

Table 2.5
Single and Multiple Origin Responses for Selected Ethnic Origin Groups: Canada, 1986

Ethnic-origin group	Single-origin responses ('000)	Multiple-origin responses ('000)	Multiple responses as percentage of total response
British origins	6,333	6,039	48.8
French origins	6,093	2,030	25.0
British & French	—	1,702	—
Other European			
Northern European	212	479	69.3
Western European	1,321	2,014	60.4
Southern European	1,242	463	27.2
Eastern European	888	998	52.9
Asian origins			
Arab	72	31	30.1
West Asian	41	10	19.6
South Asian	267	47	15.0
East & S.E. Asian	601	88	12.8
Other non-European origins			
Aboriginal	373	338	47.5
Blacks	175	85	32.7
Caribbean	48	33	40.7
Latin, Central, & S. American	32	18	36.0
Pacific Islanders	7	4	36.4

SOURCE: *1986 Census of Canada*, Cat. 93-154, Table 1.

population by province for 1901 and for 1986 based on the most recent definition of ethnic origin. These data show that the population claiming only French origin still comprised 78 per cent of Quebec's population in 1986, while outside the province the British still outnumber those of French origin. However, only in the Atlantic provinces have the British approximated or exceeded the degree of concentration exhibited by the French in Quebec. The most significant change in the character of the population since 1901 that can be detected with these data is the decline in the proportions of British and French in Canada and the increasing proportion of other origins. According to the 1981 data (Statistics Canada, 1984), the combined British and French populations experienced a decline of 17 per cent, while the remaining combined origins increased by 118 per cent. A more accurate and up-to-date comparison of changes up to 1986, based on the new 1986 question and coding procedures, shows a similar but smaller decline of 14 per cent in the proportion of the

Table 2.6 Percentage Composition of the Population by Ethnic Origins for Provinces of Residence: Canada, 1901 and 1986

	Ethnic-Origin Group	Total Canada	New-found-land	Prince Edward Island	Nova Scotia	New Bruns-wick	Quebec	Ontario	Mani-toba	Saskat-chewan	Alberta	British Columbia	Yukon	North-west Terri-tories
1901	British	57.0	—	85.1	78.1	71.7	17.6	79.3	64.4	43.9	47.8	59.6	39.2	0.5
	French	30.7	—	13.4	9.8	24.2	80.2	7.3	6.3	2.9	6.2	2.6	6.5	0.2
	Other	12.3	—	1.5	12.1	4.1	2.2	13.4	29.3	53.2	46.0	37.8	54.3	99.3
	Total	100.0	—	100.0	100.0	100.0	100.0	100.0	100.0	100.0	100.0	100.0	100.0	100.0
1986	British	25.3	79.8	47.4	48.4	35.8	5.0	32.4	21.4	22.3	25.3	30.6	23.1	13.5
	French	24.4	2.0	8.9	6.1	33.1	77.7	5.9	5.3	3.4	3.3	2.4	3.3	2.9
	Multiple Br. & Fr.	4.6	4.3	12.1	9.3	10.0	2.7	5.7	3.3	2.8	3.8	3.7	5.0	2.8
	Other European	15.6	0.5	2.0	5.0	1.7	6.9	20.3	27.8	27.0	22.1	17.4	11.5	5.4
	Northern European	0.8	—	0.1	0.2	0.2	—	0.6	1.5	2.6	2.1	2.1	2.0	0.7
	Western European	5.3	0.4	1.5	3.6	1.0	0.7	5.4	12.5	14.6	10.5	7.8	5.6	2.7
	Eastern European	3.5	—	0.2	0.5	0.2	0.8	3.9	10.6	9.1	7.1	3.8	2.9	1.3
	Southern European	5.0	0.2	0.1	0.5	0.2	4.1	9.0	2.0	0.5	2.0	3.1	0.9	0.8
	Other European	1.0	—	—	0.2	0.1	1.3	1.4	1.3	0.1	0.3	0.5	0.1	—
	Asian	3.9	0.4	0.5	0.8	0.4	1.7	5.0	3.6	1.6	5.1	8.2	1.0	1.3
	Arab & Western	0.5	—	0.3	0.3	0.1	0.6	0.6	0.1	0.1	0.5	0.2	0.1	—
	South Asian	1.1	0.2	0.2	0.2	0.1	0.3	1.5	0.7	0.3	1.3	2.4	0.2	0.1
	East & S.E. Asian	2.4	0.2	0.1	0.2	0.2	0.9	2.9	2.8	1.1	3.4	5.5	0.8	1.1
	Other non-European	2.9	0.7	0.4	1.7	0.8	1.8	2.5	6.7	6.4	3.5	3.1	16.1	53.7
	Aboriginals	1.5	0.7	0.3	0.7	0.6	0.8	0.6	5.2	5.6	2.2	2.1	14.0	52.2
	Blacks[a]	0.7	—	0.1	0.9	0.1	0.6	1.2	0.4	0.1	0.3	0.2	—	0.2
	Caribbean	0.2	—	—	—	—	0.2	0.3	0.1	—	0.1	—	—	—
	Other	0.5	—	—	0.1	0.1	0.2	0.4	1.0	0.7	0.9	0.8	2.1	1.3
	Other multiple	23.4	12.4	28.6	28.7	18.2	4.2	28.2	31.7	36.5	36.8	34.5	39.9	20.3
	Br., Fr. & Other	20.9	12.2	28.4	27.6	17.9	3.7	25.8	26.0	30.1	31.5	30.8	35.8	17.2
	Other multiple	2.5	0.2	—	1.1	0.3	0.5	2.4	5.7	6.4	5.3	3.7	4.1	3.5
	Total per cent	100.0	100.0	100.0	100.0	100.0	100.0	100.0	100.0	100.0	100.0	100.0	100.0	100.0
	N ('000)	25,022	564	125	864	702	6,454	9,001	1,049	997	2,340	2,850	23	52

SOURCE: *1961 Census of Canada*, Bull. 7:1-6 (Ottawa: Queen's Printer, 1966), Tables 1,2,3; *1986 Census of Canada*, Cat. No. 93-109 (Ottawa: Minister of Supply and Services, 1989), Table 1.

[a]Includes Canadian Blacks, African Blacks, and other Blacks.
— Less than 0.5 per cent.
Percentages based on data rounded to the nearest 1000s and may not add to 100.0 per cent because of rounding.

population with either some single or multiple British and French origin, and a somewhat smaller, but still impressive, increase of 102 per cent for the remaining combined origins.

Definitional changes for the 1986 census are responsible for the reduction in the proportion reporting single British origins, with the possible exception of Newfoundland, which continues to have one of the most culturally homogeneous populations of any province in Canada. In 1981 the British origins were numerically dominant in Ontario and the western provinces. In 1986, the much lower proportions of British origins (excluding multiple responses) were still larger than the proportions for other European origins, except in the two prairie provinces of Saskatchewan and Manitoba. Populations in these two provinces, like the others in the west, had higher proportions reporting multiple origins other than those involving just British and French. The settlement of the west by a variety of European-origin groups during the early years of the twentieth century produced the most ethnically diverse provincial populations in the country. Historically, Manitoba and Saskatchewan have been the most ethnically diverse, in contrast to Newfoundland, PEI, and Quebec, which have been the most homogeneous. Clearly the settlement pattern of the west has been more conducive to mixing the various European groups through intermarriage than has been the case elsewhere.

The single Asian and other non-European origins accounted for only 3.9 and 2.9 per cent of the country's 1986 population respectively. While they are clearly under-represented in the eastern provinces, the Asians are still to be found in above-average numbers in Ontario, Alberta, and British Columbia. The other non-Europeans, except single-origin Blacks and Caribbeans, are relatively overconcentrated in all of the Canadian west and in the north. This is due mainly to the above-average proportions of those with aboriginal origins in Manitoba (5 per cent), Saskatchewan (6 per cent), the Yukon (14 per cent), and the Northwest Territories (52 per cent).

To the extent that ethnic mixing is affected by the size and distribution of the various ethnic-origin populations, by their cultural characteristics, and by the historical circumstances surrounding their immigration to Canada, the data in Table 2.6 provide some interesting answers to the question as to where the conditions for ethnic intermarriage have been greatest. As might be expected, the proportions of provincial populations reporting multiple British and French origins were smallest in Newfoundland and Quebec, and largest in the remaining Atlantic provinces. For mixed ancestry involving either British or French and some other ethnic origin, the largest proportions are to be found in PEI, Nova Scotia, Ontario, and the remaining western provinces and northern Territories. Clearly, the demographic and cultural constraints on ethnic intermarriage are still strongest in Quebec and Newfoundland and weakest in the west and north. To the extent that Canada's immigrant population continues to become accultured and assimilated into Canadian society, the greatest change can be expected in the regions west of Quebec.

Urbanization of ethnic populations

The present distribution of Canada's population reflects not only the original settlement patterns but the effects of urbanization as well. The forces that have led to an urbanization level of 77 per cent for Canada as a whole (Population Reference Bureau, 1989) have not affected all its regions, or their ethnic populations, in the same way. More of the early immigrants were drawn to the rural areas, while those coming later, when Canada had become more industrialized, were more likely to settle in the towns and cities. Thus we find more Native people, French Canadians, Ukrainians, Germans, and Scandinavians still entrenched in the rural areas; the British origins more evenly distributed between rural and urban areas; and the more recent immigrant groups increasingly concentrated in the urban centres, especially in the larger Canadian cities. All groups have been affected in one way or another by urbanization, but have varied considerably with respect to their individual contribution to the rural-urban shift in population. At one extreme are the ethno-religious groups, like the Hutterites, who have always lived in rural colonies; and the native Indians, who have been kept on their reserves in rural areas. At the other extreme are groups that have almost always been urban dwellers. As early as Confederation, two-thirds of those of Jewish origins lived in urban areas, and almost all (99 per cent) were urban dwellers in 1981. Of the two founding groups, the French origins have generally remained more rural than the British, but the two groups have been converging slowly over the years as the country's population has become increasingly concentrated in urban areas. By 1971, both the British and the French had the same proportions living in urban areas (76 per cent).

As late as the immediate post-war period, government officials still thought that more farmers and agricultural workers were needed in Canada, even as more and more Canadians left rural areas for the cities and increasing number of immigrants headed for Canada's largest urban centres. Attempts to correct regional imbalances in population and economic development by recruiting agricultural workers abroad, as well as by offering inducements to immigrants to settle in less populated areas, have not proved very effective in the past (Manpower and Immigration, 1974). Immigrants continue to be drawn to those areas where economic opportunities are believed to be greatest.

Since 1981 Ontario has continued to be the intended destination for almost half of the immigrants being landed in Canada (Employment and Immigration Canada, 1988b). Both non-European and some of the more recent European immigrants have been settling almost exclusively in urban areas. Of the Asian groups shown in Table 2.7, only the Japanese had less than 96 per cent living in urban areas (as recently as 1981). For some of the more recent European origins—the Greeks, Portuguese, and Spanish—the proportions of urban dwellers were all 96 per cent or more. The Chinese, Greek, and Jewish populations have been almost totally urbanized. Data on populations of mixed origins (not included in Table 2.7) also showed above-average proportions with urban residence, varying between 77 and 88 per cent (Statistics Canada, 1984).

A further distinction in the propensities for urban settlement can be made from the data presented in Table 2.7. There seems to be a significant variation in ethnic preferences for residence in the larger metropolitan places. The two founding groups, as well as the more established populations of German and Ukrainian origins, exhibit the lowest propensities for settlement in the largest urban centres,

Table 2.7
Percentage of Selected Ethnic-Origin Populations Residing in Urban, Rural, and Census Metropolitan Areas: Canada, 1981

	Urban				Rural	Census Metropolitan
Ethnic origin	Total	500,000 and over	100,000-499,999	1,000-99,999	Total	Total
			(%)			
German	68.3	30.1	13.8	24.4	31.7	48.4
French	73.3	40.9	6.9	25.5	26.7	60.6
British	74.5	34.9	12.5	27.1	25.5	53.0
Ukrainian	76.1	44.3	11.9	19.9	23.9	59.6
Italian	94.9	74.4	10.9	9.6	5.1	88.0
Spanish	96.0	82.9	5.6	7.5	3.9	88.0
Portuguese	96.6	75.6	10.2	10.8	3.4	87.0
Greek	97.9	84.4	7.4	6.1	2.1	93.2
Jewish	98.5	92.1	3.6	2.8	1.5	96.2
Japanese	91.6	73.7	3.3	14.6	8.3	77.6
Indo-Pakistani	95.8	75.4	6.9	13.5	4.2	84.0
Indo-Chinese	96.0	64.5	10.5	21.0	4.0	74.0
West Asian	96.0	77.4	12.2	6.4	4.0	90.0
Chinese	98.0	82.2	7.0	8.8	2.0	90.4

SOURCE: Statistics Canada, *1981 Census*, Cat. 92-911, 1984, Table 2; and special tabulations.

whether the latter are defined as urban places with populations of 500,000 or more, or as all the census metropolitan areas. With the one exception of the Indo-Chinese, the same groups exhibit the highest propensities for residence in urban places of under 100,000, and also tend to have higher propensities for settlement in the intermediate-size places of 100,000 to 500,000 population. The picture is quite different for those of Jewish origins, the more recent southern Europeans, and those of Asian origins, who have shown a marked preference for residence in the largest urban centres in Canada. Changes in the ethnic composition of the immigrant streams following the Second World War, and their increasing concentration in Canada's metropolitan areas, are changing the ethnic diversity of Canada's population both nationally and regionally, and especially in the major metropolitan areas.

Ethnic diversity and residential segregation

There is no reason to believe that the forces underlying the settlement of the prairies and the emergence and persistence of the ethnic communities there would not have relevance for understanding the emergence and persistence of ethnic neighbourhoods in the cities. The persistence of ethnic identity and loyalty, the natural desire to continue to use the ethnic language in the home, the need for specialized ethnic-related institutional services, and variations in the socio-economic status of arriving immigrant groups, all would appear to contribute to ethnic concentrations and the emergence of ethnic communities and neighbourhoods in the larger cities (Driedger and Church, 1974; Driedger, 1979).

Recent research has acknowledged the importance of such factors as period of immigration, timing of arrival in relation to other groups, and size of the host community in explaining variations in the degree of observed residential segregation. The size of a group in relation to the dominant group has also been shown to be a factor in accounting for the presence of ethnic institutions and the visibility and persistence of ethnic communities (Balakrishnan, 1976). Much of the controversy in residential-segregation research has revolved around the question of the relative importance of economic and cultural factors as explanatory variables (Darroch and Marston, 1969), and the extent to which ethnic communities tend to be transitory, as suggested by Burgess (1925) in his early theory of urban growth, or more or less a permanent feature of immigrant-based societies such as Canada.

Research in Canada has shown that the various ethnic-origin populations in the larger cities vary considerably in their propensities for residential segregation. Studies have found some evidence to suggest that the degree of ethnic segregation had declined somewhat between 1951 and 1961 (Balakrishnan, 1976), but there is little evidence that the trend continued after 1961 (Balakrishnan, 1982).

Recent studies have found hierarchical patterns of ethnic segregation, similar to those revealed in Table 2.8, for a selected number of census metropolitan areas in 1981. Inter-city comparisons reveal lower levels of ethnic segregation in the west than in the east. Average indexes for Montreal and Quebec City of 57.3 and 52.9 respectively are significantly higher than those for Edmonton and Vancouver, at 36.5 and 36.2. There are also variations in the rank ordering of particular groups within the larger urban metropolitan areas that may reflect differences in the dominant cultural setting of each city, as well as differences in the size of cities, the degree of ethnic and religious diversity, and the timing and order of arrival of the various immigrant groups in Canada.

Historically, the population of Jewish origins has continued to be one of the most highly residentially segregated groups in Canada's largest metropolitan areas. In contrast, the largest, and culturally dominant, population of British origins has been the most widely dispersed of any group relative to the other populations. The northern, western, central, and eastern Europeans show somewhat greater tendencies for segregation from the rest of the population than is the case for those of British origins. In contrast, some of the more recent southern European immigrants, who have not been in Canada as long, exhibit rather high propensities for segregation, as do many of the Asian and other non-European origins. In some metropolitan areas, the Portuguese and the Pacific Islanders have exhibited the same high degree of residential segregation that has characterized the Jewish population. In this case, the high levels of segregation are probably the result of significantly different combinations of social, cultural, and economic factors.

The economic theory underlying the assimilation model of immigration suggests that ethnic residential segregation in an industrial society characterized by high population and social mobility is only a transitory stage that will ultimately disappear. Rising educational levels, along with the acquisition of greater technical skills and experience for the immigrants or their children, are expected to facilitate their acculturation and integration into the broader community. An analysis of the 1971 census data, based on ethnic origin, generation, and educational-attainment data for immigrant populations, has provided limited support for an assimilation model, but only for some ethnic-origin groups (Richmond and Kalbach, 1980). For the Toronto metropolitan area in 1971, the assimilation pattern of diminishing residential segregation through successive generations appeared to be

Table 2.8 Indices of Dissimilarity and Ethnic Diversity for Selected Census Metropolitan Areas: 1981

	Census Metropolitan Area (CMA)									
Ethnic-origin group	Vancouver	Edmonton	Regina	Winnipeg	Toronto	Hamilton	Montreal	Quebec	St John's	Group Average[c]
	Indices of Dissimilarity[a]									
British	17.4	12.3	11.7	20.8	26.3	15.1	45.8	21.1	18.0	16.2
German	15.9	14.9	12.8	20.0	19.4	17.1	40.7	39.3	30.1	20.0
French	21.1	15.4	10.9	39.0	19.8	18.4	47.8	23.2	17.7	21.4
Ukrainian	15.8	20.2	11.6	27.9	34.4	22.4	47.9	—	—	23.8
Polish	20.9	19.8	14.3	27.9	38.8	27.8	44.2	—	—	25.8
Dutch	25.1	21.8	17.8	24.9	32.5	34.0	57.1	—	—	27.2
Scandinavian	16.3	13.6	13.1	18.3	33.8	31.7	67.5	—	—	27.9
Hungarian	24.7	28.4	23.8	33.6	30.9	23.8	53.8	—	—	31.1
Italian	44.8	41.0	31.1	33.8	50.5	37.3	56.5	38.9	—	36.6
Czech & Slovak	34.6	34.4	29.5	31.9	38.1	32.4	64.0	—	—	37.1
Balkans	34.7	37.8	43.6	47.4	32.4	44.8	56.7	—	—	40.0
Native peoples	39.5	37.2	37.6	49.2	44.7	51.6	45.4	61.0	—	42.9
Baltic	46.4	50.1	—	51.8	39.9	43.1	64.2	—	—	46.6
Russian	28.7	35.4	25.4	34.8	54.1	65.6	69.3	—	—	47.2
Finnish	32.6	40.7	—	53.9	43.2	61.8	—	—	—	47.5
Chinese	50.9	36.2	37.4	45.2	45.2	50.8	60.5	72.7	61.0	49.1
Indo-Pakistani	38.9	48.1	44.0	51.6	40.9	49.3	61.4	—	46.4	49.2
Latin American	46.7	42.3	59.0	40.7	38.6	52.5	48.6	66.8	—	49.9
Asian Arab	62.3	47.3	—	60.7	46.9	65.3	52.5	61.7	—	53.0
Greek	48.2	51.2	67.1	53.6	46.1	45.7	65.6	—	—	53.0
Spanish	43.6	44.9	58.6	56.8	48.5	72.6	48.0	68.4	—	59.0
Jewish	55.9	65.5	59.1	72.5	74.1	67.9	83.1	—	—	61.0
Pacific Islands	44.6	54.2	64.2	61.2	48.7	67.1	78.2	—	—	61.9
Portuguese	58.9	63.3	—	68.2	63.2	64.0	60.0	76.1	—	62.8
CMA Average[d]	36.2	36.5	33.6	42.7	41.3	44.3	57.3	52.9	34.6	
Indices of Ethnic Diversity[b]	.765	.846	.851	.865	.782	.695	.564	.116	.134	

SOURCE: L.S. Bourne et al., *Canada's Ethnic Mosaic: Characteristics and Patterns of Ethnic Origin Groups in Urban Areas* (Toronto: University of Toronto Press, 1986).

[a]The Index of Dissimilarity measures the unevenness in the spatial distribution of each ethnic origin group as compared to the distribution of the balance of the CMA population. The maximum value of 100 represents complete segregation, while the minimum value of 0 indicates that the two populations being compared have identical distributions.

[b]The Index of Diversity measures the extent to which the population of a CMA is ethnically mixed. The Index varies between zero (ethnically homogeneous population) and one (maximum heterogeneity).

[c]Arithmetic mean of indices for each group across CMAs.

[d]Arithmetic mean of indices for all groups within CMA.

— index not calculated since ethnic group represents less than 0.05% of CMA population.

valid only for the British-origin groups and the French, as well as for a few of the older northern and western European immigrant groups. For most of the smaller and more recently arrived ethnic groups, higher levels of segregation persisted, and for some they even increased in subsequent generations. For Montreal, the level of ethnic segregation has tended to be higher, but the direction of intergenerational change just the reverse for those of French origin. In this case the Canada-born population of French origin has been much more segregated than the foreign-born. The dominant presence of the French culture and language obviously must be taken into account in developing any valid explanation for the patterns of ethnic residential segregation observed in Montreal.

Patterns of intergenerational change in ethnic residential segregation have been found to vary considerably among the ethnic populations of Canada's larger urban communities. They are affected by both cultural and socio-economic status factors. These ethnic differences in patterns of residential segregation change but do not disappear when the effects of socio-economic status differences are held constant (Kalbach, 1981). It is becoming increasingly clear that in Canada, at least, the socio-economic-status factor is not sufficient in itself to explain ethnic differences in residential segregation. Its importance varies for different groups, as does the cultural factor. Other factors, such as the relative size of the various ethnic populations in relation to the dominant economic, political, and cultural group; differences in their generational structures; and social and economic characteristics must be taken into account to improve our understanding of ethnic relations in Canada's changing ethnic mosaic.

VARIATIONS IN SOCIO-DEMOGRAPHIC CHARACTERISTICS

The increasing concentration of immigrant populations in the largest cities and the persistence of ethnic residential segregation are consequences of the urbanization process affecting Canadian- and foreign-born populations alike. The ability of various ethnic and racial immigrant groups to become successfully integrated and acculturated depends to a great extent on their specific socio-demographic profiles at the time of their arrival in Canada and their ability to gain access to the relevant opportunity structures. To date, the latter has required cultural origins and demographic profiles not too unlike those of the Canadian-born, or possession of characteristics in demand that are in short supply among the Canadian-born population.

The demographic characteristics of immigrant groups, as of other groups, change over time as their populations age, acquire more education, and improve their language and occupational skills. In contrast to the others, however, the demographic profiles of immigrant groups can change dramatically as the characteristics of arriving immigrants change. But, regardless of the change that occurs, the immigrants' characteristics at the time of arrival in Canada are particularly important in determining their initial social and economic standing in the community.

During the early decades of the twentieth century, prior to the Second World War, most of the so-called 'new' immigrants from eastern and southern Europe had relatively low levels of education, too few job skills, and little if any facility in either of the official languages. They were, however, in the prime working ages, and generally from cultural backgrounds not too dissimilar to the European and Christian roots of the two charter groups. Achievement of upward status mobility for the immigrants and their children has generally followed their gradual acculturation and assimilation as they acquired more education and occupational skills and greater facility with the official languages. Generally, those from the most visibly different cultural origins have had the greatest difficulty in acquiring the skills and work experience necessary to improve their level of social and economic status. As recently as the 1961 census of Canada, 59 per cent of the pre-war immigrant population had only elementary schooling or none at all. Apart from the British, only those of French and Netherlands origins had lower than average proportions with so little schooling, while the remaining European and non-European groups exceeded the average (Kalbach, 1970). The Ukrainians, for example, with 88 per cent, exhibited the lowest educational attainment levels, followed closely by the Italian, Polish and Asian groups with 82, 81, and 80 per cent respectively. Clearly, education was not so important a requisite for social and economic integration during the settlement of the west as it has been during Canada's period of industrialization and economic growth.

The post-war period of economic growth increased the demand for immigrants of a different kind than those required for the settlement of the west and the early stages of industrialization. With the elimination of ethnic and racial origins as the major criteria for selecting immigrants in the 1960s, immigration policy has become more selective with respect to those characteristics thought to be most highly associated with socio-economic success in a highly urbanized and industrialized population: that is, professional and technical occupational skills, and high educational attainment (Manpower and Immigration, 1974). The immigrants now being selected are those who have already been partially acculturated to Western industrial society. While this may facilitate rapid and successful economic integration, it does not necessarily insure the minimal degree of acculturation that is often required to promote greater social integration and moderation of historical ethnic and racial prejudices. Even though the current selection criteria for independent immigrants headed for the labour force are designed to improve the socio-economic/demographic profiles of immigrant populations settling in Canada, the majority of recent immigrants have been admitted under provisions of the family reunification and refugee policies (Employment and Immigration, 1988a). Not being subject to selection criteria, the admission of refugees and family members might tend to increase cultural diversity, reinforce existing cultural distinctiveness, and possibly reduce the rate of social and economic integration. Nevertheless, as has been pointed out by others (Anderson and Frideres, 1981), however favourable or unfavourable a group's demographic profile may be at the time of arrival, it does change over time and will continue to do so as the source countries for Canada's immigration continue to urbanize and industrialize.

For some non-European groups, current immigration selection policies do appear to be producing demographic profiles with higher potential for social and economic status achievement than those for such recent European immigrants as the Portuguese and Greeks. Note in Figure 2.4 that the 1961-81 immigrant cohorts of Greek and Portuguese origins, 15 years of age and over, had the lowest proportions with some university education or degree. They also had the lowest

Figure 2.4 Socio-economic Characteristics for Selected Ethnic Origin Groups of the 1961-1981 Cohort, Canada, 1981

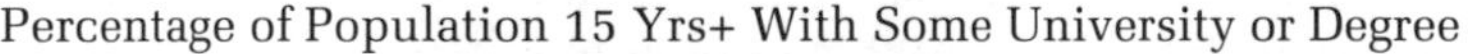

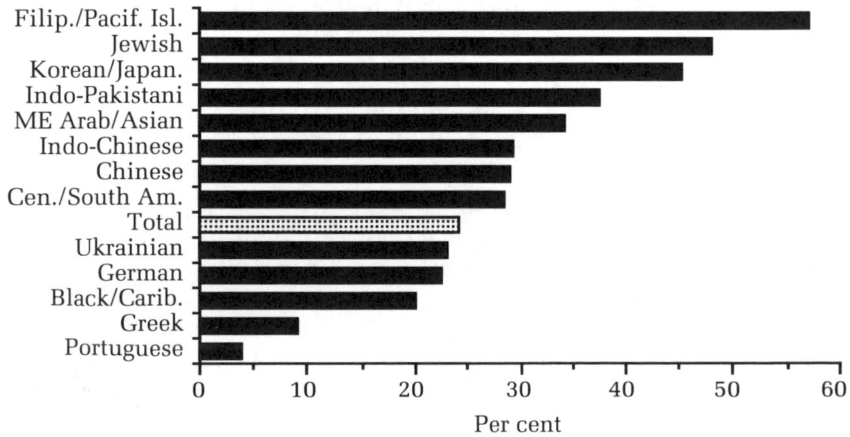

Percentage of Male Labour Force in Managerial, Administrative, Professional and Related Occupations

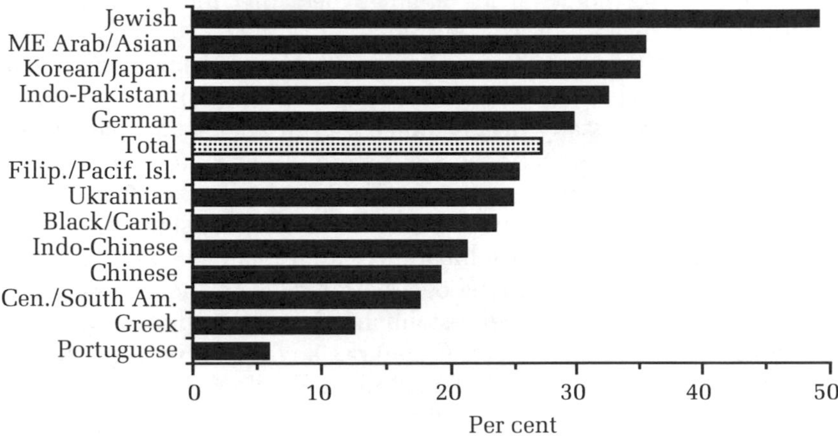

Percentage of Individuals 15 Yrs+ in Census Families Reporting Total Family Incomes of $50,000+

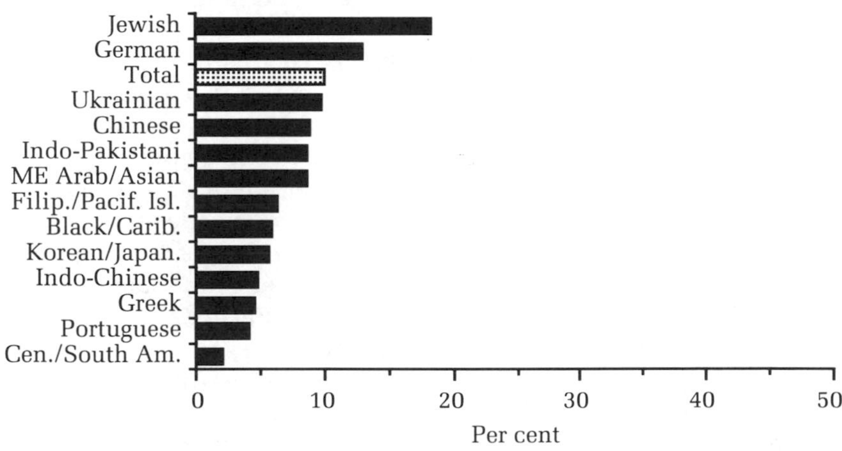

SOURCE: Statistics Canada, *1981 Census of Canada*. Special Tabulations. Charts prepared by the Population Research Lab., Erindale College, University of Toronto.

proportions of their male labour force in high-status managerial, administrative, professional, and related occupations. In contrast, seven of the eight non-European groups shown had above-average proportions with some university or degree, and three had above-average proportions in high-status occupations.

Just how the processes of urbanization, industrialization, and centralization/decentralization will affect inter-group relations in general is difficult to predict. But one might expect that increasing the diversity and concentration of ethnic groups in a few major urban centres would contribute to an increased potential for ethnic- and racial-group conflict, especially if some groups continue to be either socially or economically disadvantaged, even after being selectively screened for high educational attainment levels and occupational skills. It has already been shown in Figure 2.4 that the 1961-81 immigrant cohort of Indo-Pakistani origins ranked considerably above average with respect both to educational attainment levels and to their proportion in the higher-status occupations. Given the general positive correlation that has been established between education, occupational status, and income for Canada as a whole, it is surprising to see in Figure 2.4 that the Indo-Pakistanis fall below the average with respect to their percentage of individuals (15 years and over) in census families reported total family income of $50,000 and over. Note that this is also the case for all of the other non-European immigrants who had above-average proportions with some university or degree, as well as those who had above-average proportions in the higher-status occupations.

For many of the non-European 1961-81 cohorts of immigrants, it seems that their high educational and occupational status gained them admission to Canada but failed to produce economic rewards commensurate with their qualifications. Part of this apparent status inconsistency might be explained in terms of the relative recency of their immigration to Canada and their lack of experience. But this would not explain why the non-Europeans would experience a greater disadvantage than the European-origin groups in the same 1961-81 cohort. The education and occupation credentials of the non-Europeans would appear to have been discounted to a greater degree than has been the case for recent European immigrants. Any explanation that does not take into account the possible existence of ethnic and racial prejudice is avoiding the issue. The evidence, although somewhat indirect, should alert those interested in promoting equity in employment and wages to a potential source of ethnic- and race-relations problems.

The data in Figure 2.4 may also raise questions as to why some European ethnic groups, with such low educational, professional, and technical qualifications, should have been admitted in significant numbers under an immigration policy designed to admit only the most educated and skilled workers required by the labour force. Neither Greece nor Portugal could be considered seriously as a source of political refugees, which would have permitted special exemptions from the admission requirements for independent immigrants destined for the labour force. Immigrants of both Greek and Portuguese origins appear to have been admitted on the basis of levels of education and occupational skills that would not have qualified most non-European groups for admission to Canada. With respect to the Portuguese immigrants during this period, the only apparent positive characteristics would seem to be a generally younger population, higher fertility, a plentiful supply of unskilled workers, and a generally greater similarity of cultural background to the dominant Anglo-Saxon culture of Canada than is the case for non-Europeans.

The two population pyramids—i.e., distributions of age and sex groups—shown in Figure 2.5, for the Chinese and Portuguese populations in Canada at the time of the 1981 census, provide further evidence of how differential application of selection criteria might affect the demographic character of immigrant ethnic groups in this country. For example, the population pyramid for the Chinese clearly has disproportionately greater numbers of males and females in the younger labour-force age groups. However, while the Portuguese also appear to be a generally younger population, they show no evidence of the specific age-sex selectivity that is characteristic of those of Chinese origins. Obviously, it cannot be said for certain that the differences in the population characteristics of the Chinese and Portuguese immigrant cohorts that arrived between 1961 and 1981 are the result of discriminatory application of the selection criteria. But, whatever the reasons, it seems clear that the immigration process has been less selective of the Portuguese with respect to age, education, and occupational characteristics than it has been with respect to the Chinese. While all references to ethnic/racial origins, or religion as selection criteria have been removed from statements of immigration policy and regulations since the 1960s, subtle differences in the operation of the selection process and the application of objective selection criteria with respect to non-Europeans vis-à-vis Europeans may continue to affect the demographic profiles of Canada's immigrant ethnic and racial groups. Inter-group differences in demographic profiles that appear to reflect ethnic and racial differentials, whether in the opportunity to apply for immigration or in the application of objective selection criteria for determining eligibility, are not apt to pass unnoticed.

Canada's largest urban centres are continuing to become more ethnically and racially diverse, with clusters of the more visibly different minority groups living in relatively close proximity to each other. It is not clear how these emerging conditions will affect present patterns of ethnic residential segregation, ethnic-group cohesion, or the distribution of economic rewards or opportunities for socio-economic

Figure 2.5

Age-Sex Distribution, Chinese Population, Canada, 1981

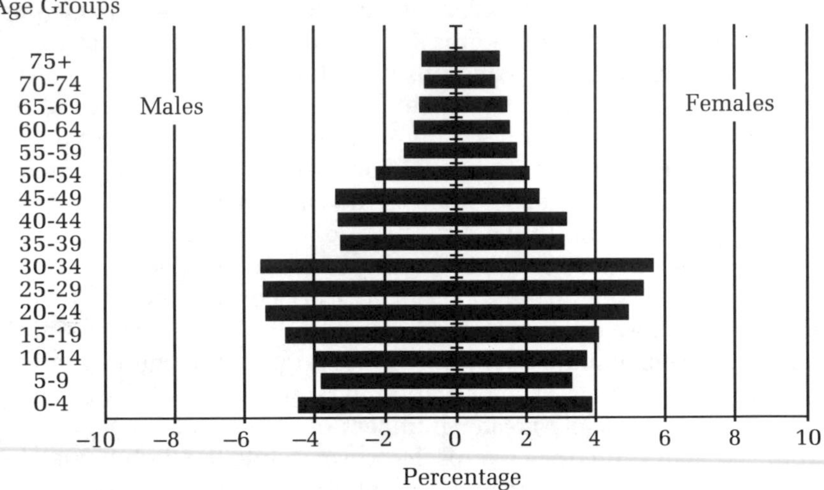

Age-Sex Distribution, Portuguese Population, Canada, 1981

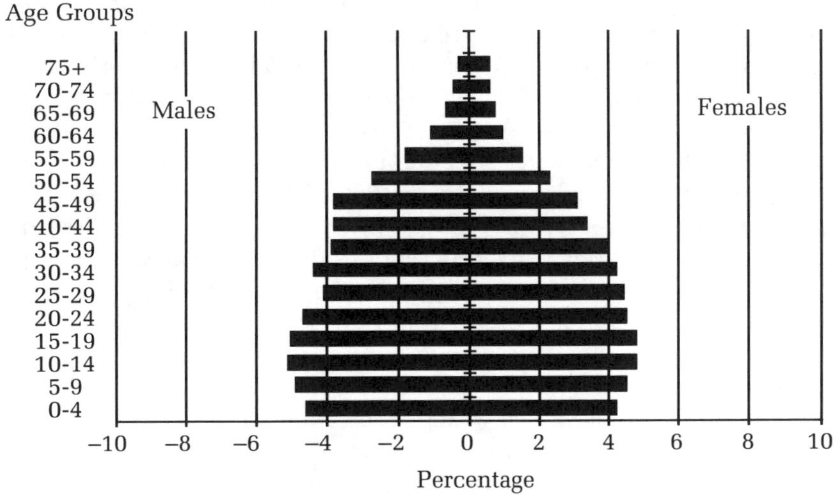

SOURCE: Statistics Canada, *1981 Census of Canada*. Special Tabulations. Charts prepared by the Population Research Lab., Erindale College, University of Toronto.

status mobility. With ethnic diversity and socio-economic inequality, however, the demographic potential for inter-group conflict would appear to be great.

NOTES

[1]Data presented in this paper for which specific references are not provided have been taken from Canada census publications and special tabulations produced by Statistics Canada, to whom a continuing indebtedness is acknowledged.

[2]For an excellent review of the development and use of the census question on ethnic origin, see J.M. Kralt's article 'Ethnic Origin in the Canadian Census, 1871-1981' in W.R. Petryshyn, ed., *Changing Realities: Social Trends Among Ukrainian Canadians* (Edmonton: Canadian Institute of Ukrainian Studies, 1980), pp. 18-49.

[3]Another important question for the understanding of cultural and language maintenance is the 'birthplace of parents' question necessary for identifying the second-generation children of the foreign-born in Canada. Included in both the 1931 and 1971 censuses, it was dropped after the 1971 census without explanation or comment.

[4]Prior to the 1981 census, only the respondent's paternal ancestry was to be reported and multiple origins were not recorded. In 1981 the restriction to paternal ancestry was removed and multiple origins were allowed by providing one write-in option in addition to the mark boxes. The 1986 census questionnaire made provision for writing in up to three ethnic origins not included in the mark boxes, and respondents were instructed to 'Mark or specify as many as applicable'. Prior to 1986, respondents were asked 'To what ethnic or cultural group did you or your ancestors belong *on first coming to this continent*'. The latter phrase was dropped from the 1981 census questionnaire to make the question more appropriate for North American Indians, Métis, or Inuit (Statistics Canada, 1986 Census, *Census Dictionary*, Catalogue 99-101E, 1987). As the order in which the ethnic origin groups are presented is known to affect the respondents choice, the question as it appeared in the 1986 census schedule is shown below:

To which ethnic or cultural group(s) do you or did your ancestors belong?

Mark or specify as many as applicable

☐ French ☐ Italian ☐ Polish
☐ English ☐ Ukrainian ☐ Black
☐ Irish ☐ Dutch (Netherlands) ☐ Inuit
☐ Scottish ☐ Chinese ☐ North American Indian
☐ German ☐ Jewish ☐ Métis

Other ethnic or cultural group(s). For example, Portuguese, Greek, Indian (India), Pakistani, Filipino, Japanese, Vietnamese.
(specify below)

			________________
			Other (specify)
			________________
			Other (specify)
			________________
			Other (specify)

REFERENCES

Anderson, A.B., and J.S. Frideres

1981 *Ethnicity in Canada: Theoretical Perspectives*. Toronto: Butterworths.

Balakrishnan, T.R.

1976 'Ethnic Residential Segregation in the Metropolitan Areas of Canada'. *Canadian Journal of Sociology* 1 (4): 481-97.

1982 'Changing Patterns in Ethnic Residential Segregation in the Metropolitan Areas of Canada'. *The Canadian Review of Sociology and Anthropology* 19 (1): 92-110.

Beaujot, R., and K. McQuillan

1982 *Growth and Dualism: The Demographic Development of Canadian Society*. Toronto: Gage.

Boxhill, Walton

1986 *A User's Guide to 1981 Census Data on Ethnic Origins*. Catalogue 99-949, Occasional. Statistics Canada. Ottawa: Minister of Supply and Services.

Burgess, E.W.

1925 'The Growth of the City: An Introduction to a Research Project'. In R.E. Park, E.W. Burgess, and R.E. McKenzie, eds, *The City*. Chicago: University of Chicago Press.

Darroch, A.G., and W.G. Marston

1969 'Ethnic Differentiation: Ecological Aspects of a Multidimensional Approach'. *International Migration Review* 4 (Fall): 71-95.

Driedger, Leo

1979 'Maintenance of Urban Ethnic Boundaries: The French in St Boniface'. *Sociological Quarterly* 20 (Winter): 89-108.

Driedger, Leo, and G. Church

1974 'Residential Segregation and Institutional Completeness: A Comparison of Ethnic Minorities'. *Canadian Review of Sociology and Anthropology* 11 (1): 30-52.

Employment and Immigration Canada

1988a *Future Immigration Levels: 1988 Consultation Issues*. Ottawa.

1988b *Immigration Statistics, 1986*. Ottawa: Ministry of Supply and Services.

Kalbach, W.E.

1970 *The Impact of Immigration on Canada's Population*. 1961 Census

Monograph, Dominion Bureau of Statistics. Ottawa: Queen's Printer.

1981 'Ethnic Residential Segregation and Its Significance for the Individual in an Urban Setting'. Ethnic Pluralism Paper No. 4. University of Toronto: Centre for Urban and Community Studies.

1987 'Growth and Distribution of Canada's Ethnic Populations, 1871-1981'. In Leo Driedger, *Ethnic Canada: Identities and Inequalities*. Toronto: Copp Clark Pitman.

Kalbach, W.E., and W. McVey

1979 *The Demographic Bases of Canadian Society*. 2nd ed. Toronto: McGraw-Hill Ryerson.

Kalbach, W.E., and M.A. Richard

1989 'Ethnic Intermarriage and the Changing Canadian Family'. In Legare et al., eds, *The Family in Crisis: A Population Crisis?* Ottawa: Royal Society of Canada.

Manpower and Immigration

1974 *The Immigration Program*. Vol. 2. A report of the Canadian immigration and population study (Green Paper). Ottawa: Information Canada.

Population Reference Bureau

1989 *1989 World Population Data Sheet*. Washington, DC: Population Reference Bureau.

Richmond, A.H., and W.E. Kalbach

1980 *Factors in the Adjustment of Immigrants and Their Descendants*. 1971 census monograph. Ottawa: Ministry of Supply and Services.

Statistics Canada

1984 1981 Census of Canada. Cat. 92-911. *Ethnic Origins*. Ottawa: Ministry of Supply and Services.

1985 *1986 Census of Population Question*. Ottawa: Statistics Canada.

1987 1986 Census of Canada, Cat. 99-101E. *Census Dictionary*. Ottawa: Ministry of Supply and Services.

1989a 1986 Census of Canada, Cat. 93-154. *Profile of Ethnic Groups*. Ottawa: Ministry of Supply and Services.

1989b 1986 Census of Canada, Cat. 93-109. *Ethnicity, Immigration and Citizenship*. Ottawa: Ministry of Supply and Services.

1989c 1986 Census of Canada, Cat. 93-155. *Profile of the Immigrant Population*. Ottawa: Ministry of Supply and Services.

PART TWO

RACE, ETHNICITY, AND THE STATE

THREE

IMMIGRATION AND THE CANADIAN ETHNIC MOSAIC

JEAN LEONARD ELLIOTT
AND AUGIE FLERAS

INTRODUCTION

Canada became one of the first official multicultural nations with the passage of the 1988 Multiculturalism Act. As a 'nation of immigrants', we are encouraged to celebrate our differences and take pride in the fact that we have all contributed to Canada's cultural diversity. The journey towards this end, however, has not been without obstacles. Canada's immigration policies and multicultural initiatives leading up to the 1988 Act have been met with claims that call into question the balance between collective and individual rights. While Canada as a whole has benefitted from immigration, the gains have not been equally realized by all regions and ethnic groups. And, of course, the impact on the First Nations has been devastating.

It is simplistic and misleading, in the most fundamental sense, to view Canada as a 'nation of immigrants'. Freda Hawkins (1972: 34) was referring to immigration when she wrote: 'this is not the central fact of Canadian history. The fact is the existence of the two founding races [*sic*] and the relations between them.' In addition to charter-group relations, the First Nations also should be included. With this revision, the 'central fact' of Canadian history becomes the relations between the charter groups, the aboriginal peoples, and the subsequent newcomers.

Immigration is pivotal in understanding the relations between the three main sectors of Canadian society: charter groups, native peoples, and newcomers. In the post-Confederation era, immigration as a nation-building strategy was received ambivalently. French Canada has been acutely aware that growth of the non-francophone sector of the population represents a threat to the survival of the French language. The First Nations have been powerless to object in a systematic fashion. Tragically, cultural genocide continues unabated in spite of their opposition to the invasion and alienation of their lands.[1]

In addition to general opposition to immigration from charter groups, aboriginal peoples, and interest groups such as religious bodies and organized labour, there has been specific opposition from federal and provincial governments to particular categories of immigrants and certain source countries. Our policies have incorporated our prejudices.

The first immigrant group to be regulated were the Chinese, when in 1886 the first of a series of head taxes was put into place, eventually leading to a ban on Chinese immigrants in 1923 (Li, 1988). It is curious to note that in the decade of the 1980s, the Chinese ethnic groups have tended to contribute the lion's share of immigrants to Canada; moreover, immigration from Asia has surpassed immigration from Europe (Table 3.1). This dramatic turnaround in policy from exclusion to acceptance has occurred over approximately sixty years and is indicative of the vast social change that Canada and the world community alike have witnessed. Given the high and low points in the history of policy governing Chinese immigration to Canada, it is perhaps the most vivid illustration of the progress Canada has made towards the goal of immigrant acceptance and cultural promotion as

Table 3.1
Selected Major Source Countries of Immigrants[a] (1980-1986)

Country (rank order, 1986)	1986	1984	1982	1980	1980-1986 (all years)
China[b]	9,144	11,202	11,347	13,426	80,556
West Indies[c]	8,948	5,696	8,717	7,515	53,171
India	7,481	6,082	8,858	9,531	53,694
Vietnam	6,201	10,185	5,945	24,593	70,731
US	6,094	5,727	7,841	8,098	49,166
Poland	5,283	4,640	9,259	4,222	38,313
Great Britain	4,612	4,657	14,525	16,445	68,094
Philippines	4,203	3,858	5,295	6,147	33,261
France[d]	1,124	970	1,821	1,461	9,288

SOURCE: *Immigration Statistics*, Employment and Immigration Canada, 1980-86.

[a]The immigrant is recorded by country of birth.
[b]Includes the People's Republic of China, Hong Kong, and Taiwan.
[c]Includes total Caribbean area.
[d]Included for comparative purposes only.

exemplified by the Multiculturalism Act of 1988 (see Appendix). Thus the challenge presented by immigration is not primarily one of citizen education; it is the challenge of balancing the Canadian equation: charter groups, aboriginal peoples, and newcomers. While we have not yet struck a satisfactory new balance, legislation like the Multiculturalism Act is a move in that direction.

Although immigration has been a response to national needs, the arrival of vast floods of humanity—3 million between 1896 and 1914, for example—has evoked concern, in some quarters, as to immigration's potential threat to the social fabric. It can be argued that multiculturalism has evolved in an attempt to allay these fears and address the increasing heterogeneity and assertiveness of Canada's ethnic and immigrant populations. To what extent, then, is calling our nation 'multicultural' a present-day exercise in myth-making? What functions does multiculturalism—as myth or reality—serve? How has immigration contributed to the institutionalization of multiculturalism? And, in turn, how is multiculturalism affecting our current immigration policy? These are the main concerns that this chapter will explore, beginning with a brief overview of immigration policy.

THE EVOLUTION OF IMMIGRATION POLICY

While Canada's immigration policy has been influenced by domestic factors—economic, demographic, social, and political—some issues have been more in the forefront than others in certain eras. Likewise, 'push' and 'pull' factors influence international migration and operate in both the sending and the receiving society. The following summary of immigration history and policy is offered with an eye towards highlighting major developments from the perspective of cultural pluralism, social conflict, and the mosaic that has resulted.

1. *Immigrant promotion: the 1896 Immigration Act*

Four events that occurred within the last two decades of the nineteenth century were to set in motion population dynamics that would irrevocably change Canada from a land inhabited by French/English settlers and aboriginal peoples to a cosmopolitan society representative of the world's cultures. While there had been ethnic diversity from the days of early settlement, there was no coherent policy in place actively promoting immigration until the first Immigration Act of 1896.

The first event of profound significance to immigrant recruitment was the completion of the Canadian Pacific Railroad (CPR) in 1885.

A main purpose of the railroad was to 'open' the west to settlement. While Chinese labourers had been used extensively in the construction of the CPR, the coolies were never considered to be other than transient cheap labour. Also, the Chinese labourers were not acceptable as agriculturalists, and the latter were sought to break, till, and sow the soil. CPR agents and steamship companies took an active role in promoting immigration.

Second, the last battle of the so-called Métis rebellion also took place in 1885. Canadian troops were quickly transported to the west on the railroad; the CPR presented the government with a bill of $852,231.32 for its services. Wade (1968: 412) ironically observed that without 'the railroad's transportation skill, the expedition might have come to grief. The cost in national unity proved to be incalculable.' The provisions of the Manitoba Act of 1870, guaranteeing the Métis title to their land and French language rights, were violated.

The Manitoba lawyer Clifford Sifton's appointment as Minister of the Interior in 1896 by Prime Minister Laurier was the third factor of note. Working hand in glove with business interests, he authored the first Immigration Act, which put an end to the free-entry period; at the same time, it aggressively pursued farmers wherever they could be found. For example, by 1899 seven thousand Doukhobors—a rural, religious sect from Russia—had been resettled by Sifton on land occupied until recently by the Métis (Woodcock and Avakumovic, 1977: 148).

Fourth, French Canadian emigration to the United States in the last decades of the nineteenth century occurred at a sufficiently high level for Joy (1972) to refer to the episode as 'the fatal hemorrhage'. By going south to jobs in the US textile industry rather than west to homestead the prairies, they ensured the death of George Etienne-Cartier's dream of a Quebec in the west. The US census of 1900 indicated that one-third of all French Canadians in North America resided south of the Canadian border. Once again the CPR was implicated. 'It was more expensive for an inhabitant of Rivière-du-Loup to go to Alberta than for a Jew from Galicia or a peasant from the Danube'; this charge was made by the French Canadian nationalist Henri Bourassa in attacking Sifton's policy of immigrant subsidization (Peterson, 1955: 122).

With the defeat of the Métis and the demographic swamping of the French Canadians, one might have predicted the immediate triumph of English Canadian culture in the west. While Anglo-ascendancy did occur eventually, the west enjoyed a brief period of multiculturalism from 1890 to 1917 (Jaenen, 1981: 187). During this era, Manitoba had a public school system that permitted instruction in English and another language. The Icelanders who settled on the prairies in 1875 preferred to assimilate to English, but the Mennonites, for example, opted for German-English schools, as did the Ruthenians. French was deemed an immigrant language that could be taught as long as English was taught as well.

This period of relative tolerance existed until the beginning of the First World War. With the outbreak of war, German and Ukrainian, for example, were considered enemy languages and no longer permitted. However, this brief period of cultural pluralism may have set the stage for the experiment with multiculturalism that was to come three-quarters of a century later. As Jaenen (1981: 201) has observed, 'The Canadian West's French roots made the Prairies more receptive to polyglot and multicultural development . . . Today only a lack of historical perspective could obscure the fact that multiculturalism has arisen out of dualism.'

2. 'Preferred nations' and 'prohibited classes' (1914-1966)

In the years leading up to the outbreak of the First World War in 1914, there was a noticeable shift in recruitment policy, which turned its attention from agriculturalists to unskilled labourers. This change in policy was accompanied by a change in ethnic composition. In 1907, for example, 20 per cent of the immigrants were from central and southern Europe; by 1913 the figure had reached 48 per cent (Avery, 1979: 37).

The shift in ethnic mix coincided with a significant increase in numbers. In 1913, over 400,000 newcomers were recorded, the largest arrival in any given year. The task of accommodating them was hindered by the fact that Canadians from British Isles and Northern European backgrounds tended to regard the immigrants from Central and Southern Europe as 'culturally inferior', valuable only for their brute strength and manual labour. These ethnocentric beliefs, fashionable at the time, combined with a fear that the Russian Revolution of 1917 might be exported, led to a series of measures directed at limiting immigration to 'preferred countries'. This illiberal era in immigration policy was to last for approximately fifty years.

Following the end of the First World War, and in the midst of an economic recession, the government in 1919 passed an order-in-council under the Immigration Act of 1910 that was to set the tone of immigration until the 1960s. A class of immigrants was created that was

> deemed undesirable because of climatic, industrial, social, educational, labour or other conditions or requirements of Canada, or because their customs, habits, modes of life and method of holding property were

> deemed to result in a probable inability to become readily assimilated. Selection would also be carried out on the basis of whether applicants belonged to "preferred" or "non-preferred" countries. (Malarek, 1987: 11)

Between the Immigration Act of 1910 and the Immigration Act of 1952, the list of preferred countries underwent adjustments, but the basic discriminatory logic remained unchanged. By the time of the 1952 Immigration Act, the Governor-in-Council could 'prohibit [certain candidates] by reason of: nationality, citizenship, ethnic group, occupation, class or geographic area of origin' (Hawkins, 1972: 102). While Canada did provide a haven for refugees and post-war immigrants in numbers up to what Prime Minister Mackenzie King termed our 'absorptive capacity', there were numerous atrocities in this period before and following both World Wars. A sampling is provided:

(a) In 1914, 400 would-be immigrants from India landed in Vancouver aboard a Japanese freighter, the *Komagatu Maru*. Although they were citizens of the British Empire, they were denied entry and forced to turn back (Samuel, 1980).

(b) At the time of the First World War in Canada, 8,000 Ukrainians, many of them Canadian citizens, were rounded up as 'enemy aliens' and interned without due process (Malarek, 1987: 11).

(c) In 1939, a passenger ship, the *St Louis*, with 900 Jewish refugees from Nazi Germany on board was refused landing in Halifax and returned to France. It is believed that many of the refugees were killed by the Nazis (Abella and Troper, 1982).

(d) With the outbreak of the Second World War, several hundred German and Italian Canadian residents and citizens and 22,000 Canadians of Japanese descent were interned in prison camps in Canada. After the bombing of Pearl Harbour, Hawaii, by the Japanese in 1941, all Japanese residents, including citizens were removed from the coast of British Columbia. No person was ever charged with an act of disloyalty (Malarek, 1987: 13). The families of the Japanese were not offered an 'apology' by the Canadian government until 1988.

The post-1945 period in Canada was characterized by rapid industrial growth and expansion. Immigrants tended to settle in southern Ontario's 'golden horseshoe'; the rural-to-urban migration was in full swing. By the start of the 1960s, it was recognized that the Immigration Act of 1952 was antiquated and did not reflect the vision that Canada had of its future or address its immediate need for human resources. In 1966 the Department of Manpower (*sic*) and Immigration was established (Hawkins, 1972: 192). From this point forth, there would be an attempt to dismantle the ethnocentric and racist immigration legislation and replace it with universalistic and humanitarian guidelines that would also supply Canada with human resources and cultural enrichment.

3. Universalistic criteria (1967-present)

The mid-1960s was a time of serious soul-searching in Canada. Quebec had undergone the 'quiet revolution' and had emerged wanting to take a firmer hand in the recruitment of immigrants. Immigration was a matter of joint jurisdiction under the BNA Act; but prior to the new nationalism of the quiet revolution, the Quebec government of Duplessis had tended to be hostile or indifferent to immigrants fearing cultural dilution (Hawkins, 1972: 225-6). With a falling birth rate and a desire for economic development, Quebec had no alternative other than immigrant recruitment. By the mid-1970s, language legislation, namely Bills 22 and 101, was in place that prohibited immigrant children from attending English-language schools (Veltman, 1988: 50).

In 1967 the 'points system' was introduced; immigrants were to be selected on the basis of points that they earned in nine areas such as education, occupation, and language. Country of origin, ethnic, and racial criteria were eliminated. The Immigration Regulations of 1967 established three classes of immigrants: family, independent (selected worker), and refugee (Keely and Ewell, 1981). The effect this system had on stimulating immigration from the Third World can be seen in Table 3.2.

Table 3.2
Selected Major Source Countries of Post-war Immigrants[a]

Country (rank order, 1979)	1979	1976	1973	1970	1946-1969
Great Britain	11,806	19,257	23,533	23,688	836,349
China[b]	9,858	13,301	15,997	5,647	64,139
West Indies[c]	6,535	15,066	19,809	13,286	62,767
India	5,486	8,562	11,672	7,089	36,406
Portugal	3,742	6,194	14,417	8,594	75,330
Italy	2,134	4,008	6,176	8,659	455,424
France	1,547	2,415	2,411	2,958	72,984
Greece	1,187	2,429	5,800	6,440	97,626
Total	50,116	85,510	121,206	97,220	1,930,146

SOURCE: *Immigration Statistics,* Employment and Immigration Canada, 1973-1979.

[a]The immigrant is recorded by country of birth.
[b]Includes the People's Republic of China, Hong Kong, and Taiwan.
[c]Includes total Caribbean area.

The 1976 Immigration Act and subsequent regulations retained the 1967 classification schema with some modifications. For example, the family class has been expanded in keeping with the principle of family reunification, and the independent worker category has been expanded to include two types of business immigrants: investors and entrepreneurs. These changes are consistent with the demographic and economic objectives of the current policy (Passaris, 1984).

The refugee class consists of convention refugees as defined by the United Nations, and designated classes—persons deemed to be refugees by Canada under the terms of Bill C-55 and C-84 (Employment and Immigration, 1988). In 1987 Canada received the United Nations Nansen medal for its refugee efforts—the first time the honour has been bestowed upon an entire nation. So as not to end on a self-congratulatory note, however, Malarek (1987: 198) calls our attention to the fact that our lack of response to the plight of the Afghan refugees, for example, is every bit as callous and unforgiving as our behaviour in the era before the points system.

FORMATION OF THE MOSAIC

Before tracing the development of multiculturalism as a response to immigration, it is wise to detail the ethnic mix in the mosaic, paying attention to the composition of first-generation immigrants and the relative size of immigration flows.

1. *Ethnic-minority composition*

Of Canada's total population in 1986 (25,022,005),[2] nearly 9.5 million (9,377,015), or 37.5 per cent, report having some non-British or non-French ethnic origins.[3] More than 6 million are recorded as being of neither British nor French extraction. By way of contrast, those with British ancestry (33.6 per cent), with French only (24.4 per cent), and with both British and French (4.6 per cent) have declined in relative numbers. The ethnic background of 28 per cent of Canadians included more than one ethnic origin (Statistics Canada, 1989a).

Of those reporting non-British and non-French ethnic origins, Germans (nearly 1 million) and Italians (.75 million) are the most populous. They are followed by Ukrainians (475,000), Aboriginal peoples (375,000), Chinese and Dutch (350,000), Jewish and South Asians (250,000), Black/Caribbean and Polish (225,000), and Portuguese (200,000; totals are approximate). But while 'invisible minorities' ('white, Europeans') remain numerically predominant, 'visible minorities' ('non-whites, non-Europeans'), at 6.3 per cent of Canada's total population, are an increasingly conspicuous feature. If present immigration trends continue, moreover, visible minorities are destined to reach 9.6 per cent of Canada's population by 2001 (Samuel, 1988). Arguably, then, the ethnic component (those with some non-British and non-French origins, or no such background whatsoever) has evolved to the point where it must be taken seriously as an emergent force in Canadian society.

Regional and municipal variations in ethnic composition are noticeable. Ontario, with 4 million members of ethnic minorities, is home for the largest number of people with non-British, non-French origins. It is followed by British Columbia and Alberta with just over 1.5 million each, and Quebec with just under 1 million. The remaining prairie provinces each contain about .5 million non-British and non-French people. The Atlantic provinces have relatively small totals. None of this imbalance should obscure the impact that a proportionately small number of immigrants can have on provinces with low population totals (Tepper, 1988).

Ethnic minorities continue to reside in large urban concentrations. Both in absolute numbers and in percentage terms, Montreal, Toronto, and Vancouver are more diverse than their respective provinces or the national average (Tepper, 1988). Just under 1.5 million of those who reported ethnic origins other than French or English live in Toronto. Another half million are found in each of Vancouver and Montreal. These three metropolitan regions are also important centres for visible minorities, with Toronto's total standing at 14 per cent of its entire population.

2. *First-generation (foreign-born) immigrants*

With respect to immigrants per se, nearly 4 million members of ethnic minorities were born outside Canada. The proportion of immigrants to the total population (16 per cent) has remained about the same since 1951 (Statistics Canada, 1989b). Ontario ranked first among the provinces, claiming 53 per cent of this total, followed by British Columbia, Quebec, and Alberta with significantly lesser amounts. Nearly 23 per cent of the population in Ontario and British Columbia is composed of first-generation immigrants. Of all immigrants in Ontario, about 53 per cent (or 1.2 million) reside in Toronto. Similarly, Montreal has over half a million immigrants, while Vancouver possesses just over a third of a million. With nearly two-thirds of all immigrants between 1976 and 1986 inside the three metropolitan centres, Canada can best be described as a homogeneous society but with urban pockets of cultural and racial diversity (see Shifrin, 1989).

Also evident are the changes in the composition of new Canadian immigrants. Between 1945 and 1971, when 4.4 million individuals disembarked, the vast majority of immigrants arrived from Europe.

From 1971 onwards, however, the sources of immigration have shifted to incorporate non-conventional countries of origin. Since 1981, for example, 43 per cent of those entering Canada originated in Asia, whereas only 29 per cent arrived from European countries. Other sources included South and Central America (10 per cent), the United States (7 per cent), the Caribbean (6 per cent), and Africa and Oceania (5 per cent). Combined, nearly two-thirds of Canada's immigration totals are now derived from countries that boast large concentrations of visible-minority populations.

As implied earlier, the influx of visible minorities is especially apparent in the major urban centres, accounting for 8.2 per cent of the population in Toronto, Montreal, and Vancouver. To be sure, because of earlier immigration flows, Europeans still comprise 62 per cent of persons born outside Canada, compared with Asians at 18 per cent. Nevertheless, this flow of immigration from the Third World has the potential to alter the direction of Canadian nation-building as the proportion of ethnic minorities with no French or British extraction increases.

3. *Past and present immigration flows*

Only 8 per cent of Canada's population was not British or French at the time of Confederation, in 1867 (Palmer, 1975). Between 1896 and 1914, the balance began to shift when up to 3 million immigrants—many of them from Central and Eastern Europe—arrived to settle the west. Immigration increased substantially prior to and just after the First World War, reaching a peak of over 400,000 in 1913. Another wave of Eastern European immigrants during the 1920s brought the non-British, non-French proportion up to 18 per cent. The post-Second-World-War period resulted in yet another influx of refugees and immigrants from the war-torn European theatre. Similar increases occurred during the 'baby boom' era, reaching 282,000 in 1957 and 218,000 as recently as 1974.

The number of immigrants allowed into Canada between 1977 and 1986 has fluctuated from 84,000 to 143,000 (Figure 3.1). In 1987 and 1988, a total of 135,000 immigrants were accepted (eventually 150,000 arrived in 1988). Of these, 50,000 were set aside for family reunification, 40,000 for the selected-worker category, 20,000 refugees (of which 13,000 were government-sponsored), and 4,000 entrepreneur class (Toronto *Globe and Mail,* 30 October 1987). For 1989, the government set a goal of between 150,000 and 160,000 immigrants (*Globe and Mail,* 24 December 1988). Projected totals for 1990 are estimated at around 175,000, and current government estimates indicate a gradual relaxation of quotas to a ceiling of about 200,000.

These projections are regarded as barely adequate because of declining birth rates and out-migration.

Various reasons have been put forward to justify increased immigration flows. With its aging population pyramid and declining totals (due to birth rates below replacement levels), Canada is dependent on immigrants to ensure a steady population growth (Tepper, 1988). As producers and consumers, immigrants are regarded as important for stimulating ('kick-starting') economic growth. They not only ease labour shortages caused by capitalist expansion, but also take jobs that many Canadians are unwilling to do. With the relatively young age of most immigrants, they are likely to underwrite the future costs of servicing an increasingly aging and shrinking population. Finally, the energy and commitment of immigrants in setting down roots in Canada is rarely disputed.

Yet acceptance of unlimited numbers of Third World immigrants is not widely endorsed by the public. Criticisms range from those who regard immigrants as unfair economic competition to those who resent the 'problems' (divided loyalties, drugs, gangs, etc.) associated with visible minorities. Foremost is the fear of undermining the WASP-ish character of Canadian society through unrestricted entry. This transcript of a pre-recorded telephone message taken from the Aryan Nations headquarters in Alberta (1987) is reflective of an admittedly fringe element:

Figure 3.1 Immigration by Calendar Year, 1972-1986

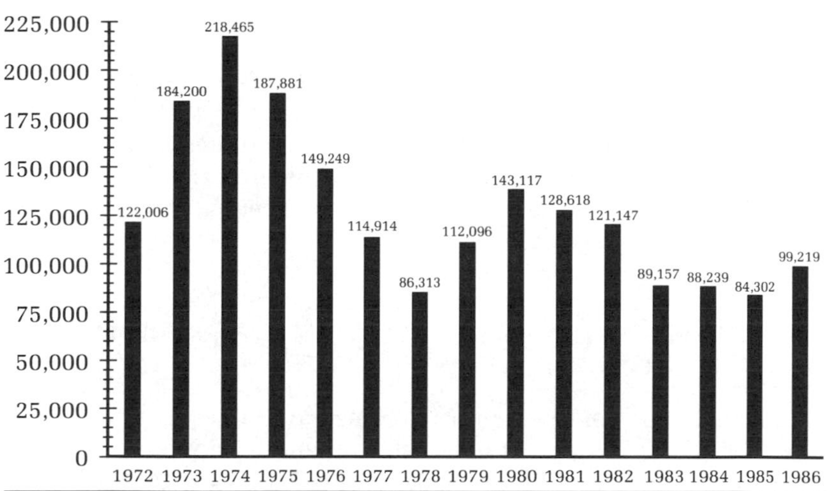

SOURCE: *Immigration Statistics*, 1986, Employment and Immigration Canada (Ottawa: Minister of Supply and Services, 1988).

> Canada's current open door immigration policy spells national suicide. Hello, you contacted the Church of Jesus Christ Aryan Nations. Facts are facts, there has never been a single successful multi-racial society. But no matter what hard evidence appears in history's back drop, our gutless bleeding heart politicians are oblivious to Canada's future, when it comes to the recent flood of Third World immigrants. One wonders when considering our unemployment and debt-ridden economy, how we are able to accept these so-called helpless refugees. Without having to speak on their free-welfare handouts, 5-star hotel stays, and round air-trips, accommodations anywhere in Canada being generously supplied by you the taxpayer . . . Did you know that numerically whites will be a racial minority by the year 2020? Now do you see why we believe the way we do? We in Aryan Nations worry about the future and preservation of the white race and we desperately need your spiritual and financial support.

Interestingly, a massive three-year study commissioned by the federal government to study Canada's changing demographic makeup has reached a similar—albeit more muted—conclusion (*Toronto Star*, 4 April 1989). Unless a preference is shown for English- and French-speaking immigrants who are willing to adapt to Canadian society, the preliminary report concludes, the potential for ethnic and racial strife in the twenty-first century will escalate.

Multiculturalism in Canada must be analysed within this context of increased immigration and ethnic diversity. Put simply, the influx of culturally diverse immigrants has elicited debate over questions pertaining to Canadian unity and identity. This is especially true following the displacement of conventional immigration sources by those from non-French- and non-English-speaking Third World nations. For this reason alone, the government has had to look to multiculturalism as an instrument for solving the 'immigrant' problem. In this sense, immigration can be viewed as the 'driving force' (Tepper, 1988) behind Canadian pluralism and its multicultural response. At the same time, multiculturalism has taken on a significance of its own in redefining the rules that govern the agenda underlying government-ethnic relations.

CANADIAN MULTICULTURALISM: FROM POLICY TO LAW

Canada is but one of several liberal-democratic states that have taken advantage of the immigration influx for the promotion of national identity and nation-building (Hudson, 1987). Multiculturalism since 1971 has served not only as a guideline for government policy at both the federal and provincial levels, but also as a framework for national discourse on the reconstruction of Canadian society. Originating in response to the growing immigrant presence and the political dilemmas it poses (Palmer, 1975; Burnet and Palmer, 1988), multiculturalism has been perpetuated for a variety of social and political objectives, among them the following: (a) to encourage peaceful race relations and intercultural exchanges; (b) to eliminate discrimination and promote national unity; (c) to reduce the social and economic disadvantages of ethnic minorities; (d) to assist ethnic groups in the preservation of their identities; (e) to educate the public regarding the merits of cultural pluralism. But in reaction to growing assertiveness among the three major ethnic forces (aboriginal, charter, landed-immigrant), Canadian multiculturalism has experienced a shift in content, objectives, and scope. Early policy initiatives (from 1971 to 1981) have given way to an entrenchment of multiculturalism as a fundamental characteristic at constitutional and statutory levels (from 1981 to 1988). These changes in the agenda underlying government-ethnic relations have redirected Canadian nation-building in a direction scarcely conceivable even a generation ago.

1. *Defining Canadian multiculturalism*

Despite its importance as a concept, multiculturalism continues to elude any simple and straightforward definition. Part of the problem derives from the different senses (or 'levels') implied within multiculturalism—namely, as demographic reality, ideology, government policy, or social movement (Kallen, 1982).[4] For our purposes we can define multiculturalism as a political doctrine that officially promotes cultural differences as an intrinsic component of the social, political, and moral order. Defined in this manner, multiculturalism involves the establishment of a novel working relationship between the government and ethnic immigrants (Hawkins, 1982).

Several assumptions underlie multicultural initiatives: these include a belief that ethnic cultures constitute living and lived-in realities that impart meaning and security to adherents during periods of rapid social change. Emphasis, however, is directed at promoting expressive concerns ('identities', 'roots', and 'belonging'), rather than instrumental goals or collective rights. Individuals are allowed the right to voluntarily affiliate with the cultural tradition of their choice without fear of discrimination or exclusion. Instead of being dismissed as incompatible with national goals, cultural differences are endorsed as integral components of a national 'mosaic', a reflection of the Canadian ideal, and a source of enrichment and strength. Ethnocultural affiliation does not imply an element of mental inferiority, stubbornness, or lack of patriotism. Instead, for as long as this diversity remains within a common set of overarching values, laws, and institutions, ethnic differences can be forged into a workable national framework ('unity within diversity'). In addition, a commitment to multiculturalism reflects the premise that those secure in their cultural background will concede a similar right to others (Berry et al., 1977). By capitalizing on this somewhat contentious proposal, the government is departing from conventional strategies of nation-building, which focused on obliterating differences in pursuit of unity.

2. *Early policy initiatives (1971-1981)*

Multiculturalism is the most explicit response of the federal government to the enhanced status of ethnic minorities—especially those from Third World countries (Tepper, 1988). Prior to the 1960s, however, policy debates over cultural pluralism were rarely pursued in any systematic fashion. Successive Canadian governments overlooked the value of ethnic heterogeneity, concentrating instead on assimilating the minority element into the mainstream. But with the publication of the report of the Royal Commission on Bilingualism and Biculturalism in 1969, a shift in priorities occurred. In an attempt to (a) identify a uniquely Canadian identity (Weinfeld, 1985), (b) defuse the threat of American-style race riots, (c) shore up political strength in Ontario, and (d) neutralize prairie-province grievances (Burnet and Palmer, 1988), a policy of multiculturalism within a bilingual framework was inaugurated when Prime Minister Pierre Trudeau rose in Parliament and announced on 8 October 1971:

> There cannot be one cultural policy for Canadians of British or French origins, another for the originals, and yet a third for all others. For although there are two official languages, there is no official culture. Nor does any cultural group take precedence over another . . . We are free to be ourselves. But this cannot be left to chance . . . It is the policy of this government to eliminate any such danger and to safeguard this freedom.

In rejecting the notion of a single culture as commensurate with national identity and prosperity, the all-party agreement sought to take 'into account the contribution made by the other ethnic groups to the cultural enrichment of Canada'. Federal assistance was promised (a) to assist minorities in maintaining their cultural identity; (b) to foster full and equal involvement in Canada's social and economic institutions; and (c) to encourage harmonious links through elimination of racism and discrimination at all levels of society.

In an attempt to put these principles into practice, specific initiatives for language and culture maintenance received funding (nearly $200 million since 1971). A multicultural directorate within the Department of the Secretary of State was instituted in 1972 for the promotion of social, cultural, and racial harmony (Special Committee on Visible Minorities, 1984). Later developments included the creation of a Ministry of Multiculturalism to monitor government departments. The Canadian Consultative Council on Multiculturalism was set up in 1973, then restructured and renamed the Canadian Ethnocultural Council in 1983 in hopes of improving its advisory, research, and monitoring capacities. Five Canadian provinces eventually endorsed multiculturalism as official government policy (Saskatchewan became the first government anywhere to pass a multiculturalism act in 1975) with a variety of programs in cultural awareness and anti-racism. Finally, provincial and federal efforts to improve the access to and responsiveness of services to ethnic minorities have resulted in a restructuring of various social institutions such as education (Samuda et al., 1984) and the police (Fleras and Desroches, 1989).

3. Recent multicultural initiatives (1981-1988)

Recent multicultural developments have assumed an even higher profile in redefining government-ethnic relations. On 3 August 1988, Canada provided a legislative base for multicultural initiatives (Secretary of State, 1987). Directed towards the 'preservation and enhancement of Canadian multiculturalism', the Multiculturalism Act sought to promote cultures, reduce discrimination, and accelerate institutional change to reflect Canada's multicultural character. It also focused on the right of individuals to identify with the cultural heritage of their choice, yet retain access to equal involvement in Canadian life (see Gans, 1979). In other words, the Act put into a statutory framework what had existed as *de facto* government policy since 1971 (see Appendix).

Equally noteworthy was the Bill's intent to expand government spending in support of ethnic activities and research. Funds totalling $192 million for five years were set aside to (a) promote harmonious race relations, (b) enhance cross-cultural understanding, (c) preserve heritage languages and cultures, (d) ensure full and equal participation of ethnic minorities, and (e) foster cross-government commitment for all federal institutions. Admittedly, the Act's failure to heed a number of the recommendations proposed by the Joint House of Commons Committee on Multiculturalism has drawn criticism (Standing Committee, 1987). However, by rationalizing government objectives and by laying down a comprehensive basis for legislative activity in this area, multiculturalism now provides a formal point of departure for revising government-ethnic relations.

The new Multiculturalism Act is consistent with the Canadian Charter of Human Rights and Freedoms that came into effect in April 1985 (see Beckton, 1987). Like its predecessors—namely, the Canadian Bill of Rights in 1960 and the Canadian Human Rights Act of 1977—the Charter sought to impose safeguards for the protection of individual rights (Secretary of State, 1987). But the Charter's equality provisions did not preclude the possibility of balancing individual and multicultural rights. According to Section 27 of the Canadian Charter, 'The Charter shall be interpreted in a manner consistent with the preservation and enhancement of the multicultural heritage of Canadians.' The constitutional implications cannot be overlooked. With its emergence as a tool of interpretation at the highest levels of national decision-making, multiculturalism reaffirms a fundamental human right in Canadian society—that is, the right to be different ('culture') as well as the right to remain the same ('equality'). Moreover, by shifting its jurisdiction from elected officials to the court system, multiculturalism has ensured for itself the legal and moral authority to co-exist 'in harmony with' (and equal to) the principle of biligualism in Canada.

Other changes on the multicultural front are evident. As an ongoing activity, the focus of multiculturalism has shifted from culture and community affairs to race relations and institutional adjustments to cope with diversity (Tepper, 1988). A federal department of multiculturalism and citizenship has been proposed to monitor institutional compliance with the principles of multiculturalism. Further adjustments towards the elimination of racism and the accommodation of cultural diversity within the institutional framework are anticipated as the scope of multiculturalism expands through employment-equity initiatives for visible minorities.

MULTICULTURALISM AS RESOURCE: THE POLITICS OF ENTITLEMENT

In spite of criticism over its meaning, scope, and impact,[5] multiculturalism has been widely extolled as contributing towards a positive reconstruction of Canadian society (see Berry et al., 1977).[6] Politicians and bureaucrats have routinely looked at multiculturalism as a resource with economic or political potential, to be exploited at national or international levels for practical gain. Similarly, ethnic minorities have taken advantage of multiculturalism as leverage for solving problems concerning 'culture' and/or 'equality'. This section will focus on the politics of multiculturalism by examining its role as a renewable resource of value for competing interests.

1. Political perspectives: 'multiculturalism means business'

Politicians are attuned to the political value of multiculturalism—if only to avert a potential crisis in government-ethnic relations. Confronted with the growing heterogeneity of Canada's population, all political parties have made a concerted drive to capture the ethnic vote through promises of increased representation, funding, and affirmative action at federal levels (*Globe and Mail*, 31 May 1988). In addition there has been a growing realization of multiculturalism's potent economic value. Increasingly, authorities have embraced the principle of ethnic involvement in commercial activities, especially when promoting Canadian exports (ibid., 7 March 1986). Prime Minister Brian Mulroney outlined this challenge in a speech at the 'Multiculturalism Means Business' conference in 1986 at Toronto when he stated:

> We, as a nation, need to grasp the opportunity afforded to us by our multicultural identity, to cement our prosperity with trade and investment links the world over and with a renewed entrepreneurial spirit at home . . . In a competitive world, we all know that technology, productivity, quality, marketing, and price determine export success. But our multicultural nature gives us an edge in selling to that world . . . Canadians who have cultural links to other parts of the globe, who have business contacts elsewhere are of the utmost importance to our trade and investment strategy (Secretary of State, 1987).

The message is clear: in contrast with the past, when cultural differences were routinely dismissed as impediments to progress, the promotion of diversity through multiculturalism has now evolved into a 'resource' with marketable value (Moodley, 1983). This emphasis on the economic dimension is consistent with the notion of multiculturalism as a renewable resource with the potential to harness lucrative trade contracts and export markets through international linkages and mutually profitable points of contact.

2. Immigrant and ethnic perspectives: multiculturalism as resource

Multiculturalism in Canada is directed primarily at the 'ethnic' sector. This sector includes those landed immigrants (both visible or invisible) or descendants of immigrants who claim neither charter-group status nor aboriginal ancestry. Canada's ethnic minorities vary in terms of what they expect of multiculturalism. On the surface, invisible ('European') minorities appear more interested in expressive concerns (cultural promotion and language maintenance), as noted by Burnet and Palmer (1988: 226). Government funding in these areas is positively received in part because of the political legitimacy conferred by federal support of ethnic activities.

In contrast, visible minorities and recent Third World arrivals are inclined to see multiculturalism as a resource for the attainment of practical goals (Burnet, 1981). Their needs are basic: they want to become established, to expand economic opportunities for themselves and their children, to eliminate discrimination and exploitation, and to retain access to their cultural heritage without loss of citizenship rights. Multiculturalism is employed as a tool for opening up economic channels through eradication of barriers in the areas of employment, education, housing, and criminal justice (Special Committee on Visible Minorities, 1984). Recourse to multiculturalism has been instrumental in securing redress from the government for past indiscretions. In the case of Japanese Canadians, compensation for their relocation and dispossession during the Second World War is symbolic of the revised moral order that ethnic minorities can exploit. Also important is the role of multiculturalism in serving as a buffer between minority members and the Canadian public, many of whom are thought to entertain racist attitudes towards visible minorities (Henry and Tator, 1985). In taking advantage of the growing unacceptability of racial discrimination, visible minorities are increasingly reliant on multicultural appeals as a resource to combat racism (Fleras and Desroches, 1988; Burnet and Palmer, 1988).

For landed immigrants, the resource value of multiculturalism is evident in other ways. The combination of geographical dispersal, cultural heterogeneity, and a vulnerable status with negligible negotiatory powers has left them relatively powerless in influencing central policy structures. But in threatening to embarrass the Canadian government by holding it accountable for failure to uphold multicultural principles (see Dyck, 1985), an otherwise 'powerless' sector now possesses the leverage to prod and provoke central policy structures. References to the moral authority underlying multiculturalism are thus calculated to arouse political and public sympathy over the perceived mistreatment of ethnocultural minorities. In short, multiculturalism provides symbolic support, sets the tone for what is acceptable ('behaviour cues'), establishes a legal basis for action, and sends out signals regarding notion of justice and equality (Tepper, 1988). By legitimizing the presence of visible minorities, multiculturalism has furthered Canada's experience with nation-building from a mosaic of cultures and races.

3. *Multiculturalism: the politics of power*

The politicization of multiculturalism has reflected and reinforced the growing assertiveness of visible (and invisible) minorities. The politics of multiculturalism are increasingly less concerned with the promotion of pizza, polka, and perogy festivals. Debate instead is focused on the issue of power- and resource-sharing within the context of a revised set of relationships between the government and immigrant/ethnic minorities. With the formal legitimation of multiculturalism in Canadian society, a new set of rules involving government-ethnic relations has appeared. These revisions imply the creation of a new moral authority in which ethnic minorities are seen as legitimate contenders in the competition for power and resources.

Nowhere is this more evident than in institutional responses to enhanced levels of ethnicity (Tepper, 1988). Federal and provincial institutions have been created to mediate and manage the process of cultural and racial accommodation. Existing institutions have undergone internal reform ('mainstreaming') as part of an overall process to 'multiculturalize' federal agencies, to facilitate immigrant adaptation and integration, and to meet the absorptive capacity of the 'new pluralism'. Institutional 'preparedness' has revolved primarily around the principles of *access* ('openness to visible minorities'), *representation* ('reflect the population mix'), and *equity* ('equality of opportunity and removal of systemic bias'). The extent to which multicultural initiatives can keep pace with changing patterns of immigration and the needs of visible minorities for promotion of their special needs remains to be seen.

APPENDIX: THE MULTICULTURALISM POLICY OF CANADA

WHEREAS the Constitution of Canada provides that every individual is equal before and under the law and has the right to the equal protection and benefit of the law without discrimination and that everyone has the freedom of conscience, religion, thought, belief, opinion, expression, peaceful assembly and association and guarantees those rights and freedoms equally to male and female persons;

AND WHEREAS the Constitution of Canada recognizes the importance of preserving and enhancing the multicultural heritage of Canadians;

AND WHEREAS the Constitution of Canada recognized the rights of the aboriginal peoples of Canada;

AND WHEREAS the Constitution of Canada and the Official Languages Act provide that English and French are the official languages of Canada and neither abrogates or derogates from any rights or privileges acquired or enjoyed with respect to any other language;

AND WHEREAS the Citizenship Act provides that all Canadians, whether by birth or by choice, enjoy equal status, are entitled to the same rights, powers and privileges and are subject to the same obligations, duties and liabilities;

AND WHEREAS the Canadian Human Rights Act provides that every individual should have an equal opportunity with other individuals to make the life that the individual is able and wishes to have, consistent with the duties and obligations of that individual as a member of society, and, in order to secure that opportunity, establishes the Canadian Human Rights Commission to redress any proscribed discrimination, including discrimination on the basis of race, national or ethnic origin or colour;

AND WHEREAS Canada is a party to the International Convention on the Elimination of All Forms of Racial Discrimination, which Convention recognizes that all human beings are equal before the law and are entitled to equal protection of the law against any discrimination and against any incitement to discrimination, and to the International Covenant on Civil and Political Rights, which Covenant provides that persons belonging to ethnic, religious or linguistic minorities shall not be denied the right to enjoy their own culture, to profess and practise their own religion or to use their own language;

AND WHEREAS the Government of Canada recognizes the diversity of Canadians as regards race, national or ethnic origin, colour and religion as a fundamental characteristic of Canadian society and is committed to a policy of multiculturalism designed to preserve and enhance the multicultural heritage of Canadians while working to achieve the equality of all Canadians in the economic, social, cultural and political life of Canada;

(1) It is hereby declared to be the policy of the Government of Canada to:
(a) recognize and promote the understanding that multiculturalism reflects the cultural and racial diversity of Canadian society and acknowledges the freedom of all members of Canadian society to preserve, enhance and share their cultural heritage;

(b) recognize and promote the understanding that multiculturalism is a fundamental characteristic of the Canadian heritage and identity and that it provides an invaluable resource in the shaping of Canada's future;

(c) promote the full and equitable participation of individuals and communities of all origins in the continuing evolution and shaping of all aspects of Canadian society and assist them in the elimination of any barrier to such participation;

(d) recognize the existence of communities whose members share a common origin and their historic contribution to Canadian society, and enhance their development;

(e) ensure that all individuals receive equal treatment and equal protection under the law, while respecting and valuing their diversity;

(f) encourage and assist the social, cultural, economic and political institutions of Canada to be both respectful and inclusive of Canada's multicultural character;

(g) promote the understanding and creativity that arise from the interaction between individuals and communities of different origins;

(h) foster the recognition and appreciation of the diverse cultures of Canadian society and promote the reflection and the evolving expressions of those cultures;

(i) preserve and enhance the use of languages other than English and French, while strengthening the status and use of the official languages of Canada; and

(j) advance multiculturalism throughout Canada in harmony with the national commitment to the official languages of Canada.

(2) It is further declared to be the policy of the Government of Canada that all federal institutions shall:

(a) ensure that Canadians of all origins have an equal opportunity to obtain employment and advancement in those institutions;

(b) promote policies, programs and practices that enhance the ability of individuals and communities of all origins to contribute to the continuing evolution of Canada;

(c) promote policies, programs and practices that enhance the understanding of and respect for the diversity of the members of Canadian society;

(d) collect statistical data in order to enable the development of policies, programs and practices that are sensitive and responsive to the multicultural reality of Canada;

(e) make use, as appropriate, of the language skills and cultural understanding of individuals of all origins; and

(f) generally, carry on their activities in a manner that is sensitive and responsive to the multicultural reality of Canada.

Excerpts from the Canadian Multiculturalism Act, July 1988

NOTES

[1]A recent example of aboriginal opposition to European influence concerns the struggle of the Innu in Labrador to prevent NATO from using their land for low-flying training flights that imperil the caribou—the main component of their traditional way of life. See, for example, 'NATO centre would be "push over the cliff" for Innu, court told' (*Globe and Mail*, 7 April 1989: A9).

[2]Unless otherwise stated, much of the statistical information in this section is derived from the 1986 census data as prepared by the Policy and Research Division, Multiculturalism, Secretary of State, in a draft paper entitled 'Multiculturalism in Canada'.

[3]Sociologically speaking, all persons in Canada can be regarded as 'ethnics' since each of us has the potential to affiliate with a particular cultural tra-

dition. In terms of public policy, however, the government restricts the label to immigrants or descendants of immigrants with some non-British and non-French origins. Aboriginal peoples are not regarded as ethnic minorities since their legal status is based on a different set of principles and priorities.

[4]Multiculturalism can be discussed from different points of departure, including (a) reality, (b) ideal, (c) policy, and (d) social movement (see Kallen, 1982; also Fleras, 1984; Fleras and Desroches, 1986). As *reality*, multiculturalism makes an empirical statement about 'what is'. The existence of aboriginal, charter, and landed-immigrant groups as the three major forces in Canada attests to the inescapable fact that Canadian society is multicultural in composition (Elliot, 1981). Multiculturalism as an *ideology* refers to a normative statement of 'what ought to be'. It prescribes a preferred course of thought or action, consistent with the principles of cultural pluralism and modelled after the virtues of freedom, tolerance, and respect for individual differences. In terms of *policy* multiculturalism consists of government initiatives to transform multicultural ideals into practice at the level of programs and funding. The essential policy problem for liberal-democratic states is the reconciliation of national unity out of emergent diversity. Lastly, as *social movement* multiculturalism refers to the activities of ethnic and immigrant groups in their attempts to redefine their relational status in society along multicultural lines.

[5]Despite moves to make multiculturalism a cornerstone of Canadian society, many observers of Canada's political scene have chastized the government's initiatives in this area (Peter, 1978; Kallen, 1982; Burnet, 1984; also Bullivant, 1981). Critics have taken political officials to task for employing the term indiscriminately, with little regard for its use outside of conflict resolution. Some have accused authorities of using multiculturalism as an expedient device for defusing ('depoliticizing') minority assertiveness over political and economic issues. As an exercise in state control and assimilation through 'divide and rule', multiculturalism is viewed as co-opting ethnic minorities into certain occupational structures and residential arrangements, thereby preserving the prevailing distribution of power and wealth (Porter, 1965; Anderson and Frideres, 1981; Moodley, 1983). Others have argued that government policy is willing to lavish funds on folk festivals and ethnic performing arts, but is reluctant to support minority demands for collective rights or socio-economic enhancement (Kallen, 1987). In all fairness to the central policy structures, however, it comes as no surprise that Canada's multicultural policies have encountered resistance when confronted by diverse claims for balancing state, ethnic, group, and individual rights.

[6]Although Canadians as a whole are supportive of multiculturalism (in principle if not always in practice), public endorsement is not unanimous. Although residents of Ontario and western Canada appear receptive, French Canadians (Bourassa, 1975; Ryan, 1975) and Native Indians (Sanders, 1987) have demonstrated less enthusiasm. Both sectors have rejected multicultur-

alism as diminishing their collective rights as 'distinct' populations with special rights.

REFERENCES

Abella, Irving, and Harold Troper
1982 *None is Too Many*. Toronto: Lester and Orpen Dennys.

Anderson, Alan, and James Frideres
1981 *Ethnicity in Canada: Theoretical Perspectives*. Toronto: Butterworths.

Avery, Donald
1979 *Dangerous Foreigners*. Toronto: McClelland and Stewart

Beckton, Clare F.
1987 'Section 27 and Section 15 of the Charter.' Pp. 1-14 in Canadian Human Rights Foundation, ed., *Multiculturalism and the Charter: A Legal Perspective*. Toronto: Carswell.

Berry, John W., Rudolph Kalin, and Donald M. Taylor
1977 *Multiculturalism and Ethnic Attitudes in Canada*. Ottawa: Minister of Supply and Services.

Bourassa, Robert
1975 'Objections to Multiculturalism'. Letter to Le Devoir, 17 Nov. 1971. Reprinted in Palmer (1975).

Bullivant, Brian
1981 'Multiculturalism: Pluralist Orthodoxy or Ethnic Hegemony'. *Canadian Ethnic Studies* 13 (2): 1-22.

Burnet, Jean
1981 'The Social and Historical Context of Ethnic Relations'. Pp. 17-36 in Robert C. Gardiner and Rudolph Kalin, eds, *A Canadian Social Psychology of Ethnic Relations*. Agincourt, Ont.: Methuen.
1984 'Myths and Multiculturalism'. Pp. 18-29 in Ronald J. Samuda, John W. Berry, and Michael Laferriere, eds, *Multiculturalism in Canada*. Toronto: Allyn and Bacon Inc.

Burnet, Jean, and Howard Palmer
1988 'Coming Canadians.' *An Introduction to the History of Canada's People*. Toronto: McClelland and Stewart in conjunction with the Multicultural Directorate within the Secretary of State.

Dyck, Noel
1985 'Aboriginal People and Nation-States: An Introduction to Analytical Issues.' Pp. 155-71 in Jens Brosted, ed., *Native Power: The Quest for Autonomy and Nationhood of Indigenous Peoples*. Oslo: Universitetforlaget AS.

Elliott, Jean Leonard, ed.
1981 *Two Nations, Many Cultures: Ethnic Groups in Canada*. Scarborough, Ont.: Prentice-Hall.

Employment and Immigration Canada
1988 *Annual Report 1987-1988*. Ottawa: Minister of Supply and Services.

Fleras, Augie

1984 'Monoculturalism, Multiculturalism, and Biculturalism: The Politics of Maori Policy in New Zealand.' *Plural Societies* 15: 52-75.

Fleras, Augie, and Frederick J. Desroches

1986 'Multiculturalism: Policy and Ideology in the Canadian Context.' Pp. 17-24 in Brian K. Cryderman and Chris N. O'Toole, eds, *Police, Race, and Ethnicity. A Guide for Law Enforcement Officers*. Toronto: Butterworths.

1988 *Peel Regional Police Force Reports on Race Related Incidents: A Five Year Analysis (1983-1987)*. Unpublished report for the Peel Regional Police Force.

1989 'Towards a Multicultural Policing in Canada'. *Canadian Police College Journal* 13(3): 154-64.

Gans, Herbert J.

1979 'Symbolic Ethnicity: The Future of Ethnic Groups and Culture in America'. *Ethnic and Racial Studies* 2: 1-20.

Hawkins, Freda

1972 *Canadian Immigration: Public Policy and Public Concern*. Montreal: McGill-Queen's University Press.

1975 'Recent Immigration Policy'. Pp 71-5 in Howard Palmer, ed., *Immigration and the Rise of Multiculturalism*. Toronto: Copp Clark.

1982 'Multiculturalism in Two Countries: The Canadian and Australian Experience'. *Journal of Canadian Studies* 17: 64-80.

Henry, Frances, and Carol Tator

1985 'Racism in Canada: Social Myths and Strategies for Change.' Pp. 321-35 in Rita M. Bienvenue and Jay E. Goldstein, eds, *Ethnicity and Ethnic Relations in Canada* 2nd ed. Toronto: Butterworths.

Hudson, Michael R.

1987 'Multiculturalism, Government Policy and Constitutional Enshrinement—A Comparative Study'. Pp. 59-122 in Canadian Human Rights Foundation, ed., *Multiculturalism and the Charter: A Legal Perspective*. Toronto: Carswell.

Jaenen, Cornelius J.

1981 'French Roots in the Prairies'. In J.L. Elliott, ed., *Two Nations*. Scarborough, Ont.: Prentice-Hall.

Joy, Richard

1972 *Languages in Conflict* (esp. Chap. 11). Toronto: McClelland and Stewart.

Kallen, Evelyn

1982 'Multiculturalism: Ideology, Policy, and Reality'. *Journal of Canadian Studies* 17: 51-63.

1987 'Multiculturalism, Minorities, and Motherhood: A Social Scientific Critique of Section 27'. Pp. 123-38 in Canadian Human Rights Foundation, ed., *Multiculturalism and the Charter: A Legal Perspective*. Toronto: Carswell.

Keely, Charles B., and P.J. Ewell

1981 'International Migration: Canada and the US'. In M.M. Kritz et al., eds, *Global Trends in Migration: Theory and Research on Interna-*

tional Population Movements. New York: Center for Migration Studies.

Li, Peter S.
1988 *The Chinese in Canada*. Toronto: Oxford University Press.

Malarek, Victor
1987 *Haven's Gate*. Toronto: Macmillan.

Moodley, Kogila
1983 'Canadian Multiculturalism as Ideology'. *Ethnic and Race Studies* 6 (3): 320-32.

Palmer, Howard, ed.
1975 *Immigration and the Rise of Multiculturalism*. Toronto: Copp Clark.

Passaris, C.
1984 'The Economic Determinants of Canada's Multicultural Immigration'. *International Migration* 22 (2): 90-100.

Peter, K.
1978 'Multi-cultural Politics, Money, and the Conduct of Canadian Ethnic Studies'. *Canadian Ethnic Studies Association Bulletin* 5: 2-3.

Peterson, William
1955 *Planned Migration*. Berkeley: University of California Press.

Porter, John
1965 *The Vertical Mosaic*. Toronto: University of Toronto Press.

Richmond, Anthony H.
1988 *Immigration and Ethnic Conflict*. Basingstoke, Eng.: Macmillan.

Ryan, Claude
1975 'Biculturalism or Multiculturalism?' Speech (1972). Reprinted in Palmer (1975).

Samuda, Ronald J., Berry, John W., and Michel Laferrière, eds
1984 *Multiculturalism in Canada: Social and Educational Perspectives*. Toronto: Allyn and Bacon.

Samuel, John T.
1988 'Immigration and Visible Minorities in the Year 2001: A Projection'. Ottawa: Centre for Immigration and Ethnocultural Studies.

Samuel, Raj
1980 'Some Aspects of East Indian Struggle in Canada 1905-1947'. In K. Victor Ujimoto and G. Hirabayashi, eds, *Visible Minorities and Multiculturalism: Asians in Canada*. Toronto: Butterworths.

Sanders, Douglas
1987 'Article 27 and the Aboriginal Peoples of Canada.' Pp. 155-66 in Canadian Human Rights Foundation, ed., *Multiculturalism and the Charter: A Legal Perspective*. Toronto: Carswell.

Secretary of State
1987 *Multiculturalism . . . Being Canadian*. Ottawa: Minister of Supply and Services.
1988 *Multiculturalism in Canada*. Draft prepared by the Policy Analysis and Research Division. Ottawa.

Shifrin, Leonard
1989 'Immigrants could halt declining population'. *Toronto Star*, 23 Jan.: A13.

Special Committee on Visible Minorities in Canadian Society
1984 *Equality Now*. Bob Daudlin, MP, Chairperson. Ottawa: Queen's Printer.
Standing Committee on Multiculturalism
1987 *Multiculturalism: Building the Canadian Mosaic*. Gus Mitges, MP, Chairperson. Ottawa: Queen's Printer.
Statistics Canada
1989a *Dimension*. Profile of Ethnic Groups. Ottawa: Minister of Supply and Services.
1989b *Dimension*. Profile of Immigrant Population. Ottawa: Minister of Supply and Services.
Tepper, Elliot L.
1988 *Changing Canada: The Institutional Response to Polyethnicity*. The Review of Demography and Its Implications for Economic and Social Policy. Ottawa: Carleton University.
Veltman, Calvin
1988 'Impact of International Migration on the Linguistic Balance in Montreal'. *The Review of Demography and Its Implications for Economic and Social Policy: Update Number 5*. Ottawa: Health and Welfare, Winter.
Wade, Mason
1968 *The French Canadians*. Vol. 1 (esp. Chap. 8). Toronto: Macmillan.
Weinfeld, Morton
1985 'Myth and Reality in the Canadian Mosaic: "Affective Ethnicity"'. Pp. 65-86 in Rita M. Bienvenue and Jay E. Goldstein, eds, *Ethnicity and Ethnic Relations in Canada*. Toronto: Butterworths.
Woodcock, George and Ivan Avakumovic
1977 *The Doukhobors*. Toronto: McClelland and Stewart.

FOUR

ETHNICITY AND HUMAN RIGHTS IN CANADA: CONSTITUTIONALIZING A HIERARCHY OF MINORITY RIGHTS

EVELYN KALLEN

INTRODUCTION

Throughout both of the 1980s' constitutional debates, the 1980-82 debate giving rise to the Charter of Rights and Freedoms, and the ongoing debate on the Meech Lake Accord (1987), amendments designed to further entrench the special and dominant status of Canada's two founding peoples—the English/Protestant and French/Catholic 'charter groups'—have assumed top priority. Accordingly, the collective (linguistic, religious, and broader cultural) rights of this country's majority ethnic groups have consistently taken preference over the corresponding rights of Canada's ethnic minorities.[1] In parallel vein, throughout both debates, the minority rights of subordinate, non-ethnic populations in Canada have been accorded lower priority than the rights of ethnic collectivities.

From a human-rights perspective, this paper will analyse the provisions for minority rights in the Charter and in the Accord. This analysis will reveal that both constitutional amendments entrench a hierarchy of ethnic and non-ethnic minority rights in Canada. Further, it will show that the provisions of the Accord can be seen to seriously undermine constitutional protections for minority rights guaranteed in the Charter.

THE HUMAN-RIGHTS APPROACH

Both individual and collective human rights derive from the fundamental nature of humankind as a species. Individual human rights represent the principle of biological unity, the oneness of all human beings as members of humankind. Collective human rights represent the principle of cultural diversity, the distinctiveness of the diverse ethnocultures developed by different ethnic groups within the human species. Together, individual and collective human rights represent the twin global principles of human unity and cultural diversity.

As specified in the International Bill of Human Rights (IBHR) and related covenants, protections for individual and collective human rights essentially represent international *moral guidelines*, the global standards to which the laws of ratifying states should conform. What this means is that human-rights principles are *prior to law*: laws themselves may violate or endorse them.

When laws *endorse* human-rights principles, then human rights become *legal* rights that can be claimed by individuals or groups who can provide evidence to show that their human rights have been violated. In other words, a legal framework of human-rights protection allows those whose rights have been violated to bring forward claims for legal redress and recompense.

Individual human rights are rooted in the premise that all human beings are full and equal persons. As such, all have a fundamental right to life and to freedom, equality, and dignity in all life pursuits. Freedom to decide, equality/equivalence of opportunity, and dignity of person can be conceptualized as 'natural rights' that accrue to every human being simply by virtue of belonging to the human species. Insofar as human rights are natural rights, they do not have to be earned; they can be claimed equally by all human beings regardless of differences among individuals in their particular abilities, skills, resources, or other personal attributes, and regardless of differences in group status or class membership. Individual human rights can be said to be inalienable, but in their exercise they are not absolute. For the exercise of each person's individual human rights is conditional upon non-violation of the rights of others. Human rights thus entail social responsibilities: each human being must respect the human rights of others.

The basic principle behind *collective human rights* is the right of ethnic communities *as collectivities* to legitimately and freely express their cultural distinctiveness. The distinctive elements of ethnocultures may be expressed in language, religion, politico-economic design, territorial links, or any combination of these and/or other defining group attributes. Regardless of the specific cultural attributes emphasized at any given time, insofar as a people's ethnoculture is in itself consistent with human-rights principles, every ethnic group has the collective right to develop, express and transmit through time its distinctive design for living (Kallen, 1982a: 14-17).

The one component of ethnicity that differentiates the kinds of collective claims that may be put forward by particular ethnic groups is that of territoriality. Internationally, a 'people' whose territorial/ ethnocultural boundaries potentially or actually coincide with the geo-political boundaries of a state unit can be conceptualized as a 'nation'. As applied to ethnic groups within the boundaries of a given state unit, this interpretation is more problematic. Nevertheless, there is growing support among legal scholars not only for the view that all ethnic communities can claim collective cultural rights, but also for the argument that all ethnic communities that can demonstrate a continuing, integral association between the people, its ancestral territory, and its distinctive ethnoculture within the boundaries of a given state unit can claim collective national rights (nationhood claims).

MINORITY RIGHTS IN CANADA: INDIVIDUAL, CATEGORICAL, AND COLLECTIVE CLAIMS[2]

The importance of human-rights instruments, at both the international and national levels, is that they provide standards upon which minorities can base claims alleging human-rights violations. In Canada the legal framework of human-rights protections is based on a three-tiered system of standards governing human relations within the state. International human-rights instruments (the International Bill of Human Rights and related covenants) apply to relations between states and provide the global standards to which all state legislation should conform. Constitutional rules, under the Charter of Rights and Freedoms and related sections of the Canadian constitution, apply to relations between governments within the state and provide the national standard to which all statutory laws (federal and provincial human-rights legislation, as well as other laws) should conform. Statutory human-rights legislation applies to relations between individuals and organizations within the state and should conform to the guarantees for human rights in the Charter and related constitutional provisions.

Under statutory human-rights legislation at the provincial and federal levels, all Canadians, as individual persons, can put forward claims for redress against perceived violations of their individual human rights by other individuals or by organizations. Additionally, under the constitutional provisions of the Charter, individuals can put forward claims that challenge governments when their laws, policies, or practices do not conform with the guarantees for human rights in the Charter. Under the equality-rights provisions of the Charter, section 15(2) permits members of disadvantaged minorities to put forward claims, individually or collectively, for redress against the adverse impact of systemic discrimination upon the minority as a whole. Parallel legislation has been enacted by federal and provincial governments, allowing these kinds of claims to be put forward under statutory human-rights laws.

In order to distinguish between *individual-rights claims*, put forward under statutory law and/or under the Charter, and claims for redress against the adverse impact of systemic discrimination similarly put forward, I will refer to the latter as *categorical-rights claims*.

In addition to individual- and categorical-rights claims, members of ethnic minorities who perceive that their collective cultural rights have been violated can make *collective-rights claims*. Ethnic minorities who perceive that their collective right to freely express their distinctive religion, language, or other ethnocultural attributes has been denied or diminished can bring forward claims under the combined provisions of s.15 (equality rights) and s.27 (multicultural rights) of the Charter. These collective-rights claims essentially represent claims for ethnocultural equality.

COLLECTIVE ETHNIC CLAIMS: CULTURAL VS. NATIONAL RIGHTS

For purposes of analysis, I propose a three-fold division among Canadian ethnic groups, on the basis of the differential nature of their collective claims: founding (English/French), multicultural (immigrant), and aboriginal (Indian, Inuit, and Métis) peoples. While all ethnic groups are able to put forward cultural-rights claims, not all ethnic groups can legitimately make national-rights claims. Insofar as immigrant/multicultural ethnic groups cannot provide evidence for ancestral/territorial links to a particular geographical area within Canada, they cannot—justifiably—make nationhood claims. Alternatively, the collective nationhood claims put forward by founding/charter and some aboriginal peoples derive their legitimacy from a demonstrable link between ethnicity and territoriality. The constitutionally recognized and historically grounded link between Franco-Québécois and Quebec—their ancestral homeland—underscores their claims to nationhood. Aboriginal peoples' nationhood claims rest on the demonstrable link between particular aboriginal peoples, their traditional aboriginal territories, and their living, *land-based* ethnocultures.

RESOLUTION OF MINORITY CLAIMS

The foregoing typology of minority-rights claims, as well as its potential value to minority claimants, can be illustrated through an examination of legal cases that have been brought forward by minority claimants under the provisions of human-rights legislation in Canada.

1. *Individual-rights claims*

My first example deals with a claim of racial discrimination made against a Victoria restaurant and the Victoria police by a Black citizen of Canada. The complainant, born in St Vincent, holds master's degrees from two Canadian universities and works as a health coordinator in British Columbia (*Canadian Human Rights Advocate* [*CHRA*], Sept. 1988). While visiting Victoria, the complainant, a registered guest at a motor inn, went into the restaurant at the inn and sat down at the only available table. All other tables were occupied by non-Black patrons. He placed his order with a waiter, but within five minutes was informed by a waitress that he would have to move so that she could seat two other persons at his table. He refused to move because he could see no other table available and because he had not, as yet, received his order. The police were called. Victoria police questioned him about his citizenship, threatened him with deportation, searched and handcuffed him, and then hauled him off and locked him in jail for eight hours. The complainant brought his case to the BC Human Rights Council, which found that the only reasonable inference that could be drawn was that the complainant was the subject of racial discrimination. The complainant was awarded $2,000 for humiliation, embarrassment, and damage to self-respect in the settlement of his claim against both the restaurant and the police.

This case, and others like it, reveal that under human-rights legislation the employer is held responsible for the discriminatory acts of employees. Thus what may appear to be an act of individual discrimination is treated as an act of institutional discrimination; hence the onus is on those who control organizations to ensure that they respect the human rights of all persons associated with them.

A second and somewhat parallel case involves a claim alleging institutional discrimination on the part of the RCMP (*CHRA* Jan. 1987). A Chinese-Canadian, born in Halifax, filed a complaint of racial discrimination under the (federal) Canadian Human Rights Act, because an RCMP officer, who had stopped him for a driving offence, asked him whether he was a Canadian citizen and then whether he was born in Canada. An internal RCMP investigation following the lodging of the complaint revealed that the RCMP officer in question customarily interrogated members of visible ethnic minorities in the same way when he stopped them for speeding. The Commission found that this officer's action was not an isolated case, but represented accepted RCMP practice. The Commission concluded that the RCMP discriminated against suspects on the basis of racial origin and that such discrimination was unjustifiable. The Commission ordered the RCMP to cease the practice in question and to issue a directive to this effect to all members of the Force. The Commission also recommended that the RCMP provide educational instruction to members of the Force on the right to equal treatment of citizens from visible minorities. The RCMP was ordered to pay the complainant $250 for hurt and affront to dignity.

A third example illustrates the way in which human-rights cases are resolved when an apparent conflict of rights is involved. The Supreme Court of Canada has ruled (in the Bindher case) that on a construction site a member of the Sikh faith may not insist that he be allowed to wear his turban (a required religious observance) in preference to a safety helmet ('hard hat') (*Affirmation* [newsletter of the Ontario Human Rights Commission], Sept. 1986). The original case was brought forward under federal jurisdiction by a CN employee. The position of the Supreme Court was that considerations of public safety take precedence over religious freedom. This position is consistent with the general human-rights principle (derived from the American Bill of Rights) that where there is evidence of 'a clear and present danger', individual rights may be abrogated in the interests of the 'greater good'.

On the other hand, when such overriding considerations are not at issue, under human-rights legislation, religious freedom must not be denied. Accordingly, the Metro Toronto Police have amended some of their regulations so as to permit a police officer of the Sikh faith to wear a turban on duty, instead of the customary officer's cap. The turban has been specially designed to accord in colour with the customary police cap and also features the officer's badge. In addition, the clean-shaven rule of the police has been amended to permit a Sikh to wear the beard required by his religion.

What these contrasting examples illustrate further is the difference, under human-rights legislation, between a *bona fide* job requirement, which cannot be held to be discriminatory (the hard hat, in the first case) and a non-essential or non-job-related requirement, which can be held to be discriminatory (the customary police cap and the clean-shaven requirement, in the second case).

2. *Categorical-rights claims*

Categorical-rights claims may seek redress against the collectively disadvantaging effects of past discrimination through programs of affirmative action (allowed under section 15(2) of the Charter and parallel statutory provisions). This kind of claim has been suggested in the recommendations for mandatory programs of affirmative action for visible minorities put forward in two 1984 federal-government reports: the Daudlin (*Equality Now*) report and in the Abella (*Equality in Employment*) report. Both reports identified a variety of systemic discriminatory practices in the workplace, including word-of-mouth recruiting, 'Canadian experience' criteria, culturally-biased interviews and tests, limited exposure to new job openings, and many other practices that block hiring and promotion opportunities for visible minorities. Both reports strongly recommended that programs of affirmative action for visible minorities be made mandatory, because the voluntary approach to affirmative action has not led to widespread adoption of programs for visible minorities. The *Equality Now* report pointed out that a number of Canadian organizations have voluntarily adopted affirmative-action programs to increase employment opportunities for aboriginal peoples (1984: 34). Even in the case of aboriginal minorities, however, for whom affirmative-action incentives have been in place for almost two decades, the voluntary approach has produced meagre results in terms of redressing long-term categorical disadvantage.

3. *Collective-rights claims*

While collective cultural claims have been far less common than individual- and categorical-rights claims, two important cases have rested at least in part on collective claims. The first was the Sandra Lovelace case, brought forward by an Indian woman who had lost her legal Indian status and her right to reside on her reserve (in New Brunswick) because she married a non-Indian (Kallen, 1982a). After divorcing her husband, she wished to return to her reserve, with her children, to be with her family and ethnic community. She was not allowed to do so because, under the provisions of the Indian Act, when an Indian woman married out, she and her descendants automatically lost their legal Indian status. Lovelace argued that the relevant provisions of the Indian Act discriminated against women because, when an Indian man married out, his wife and descendants automatically gained legal Indian status. Thus the Act endorsed and enforced a sexist double standard. Lovelace took her claim to the New Brunswick Human Rights Commission, and eventually to the Supreme Court of Canada, but was unsuccessful. Having exhausted all legal avenues in Canada, she took her claim to the United Nations Human Rights Committee and won her case. The interesting aspect of the UNHRC decision was that it did not rest on sexism, but on cultural discrimination. The committee argued that by denying Lovelace (and, by implication, all Indian women who married out) access to her reserve, she and her children were being denied their right to practice their distinctive ethnoculture. This, they argued, was in conflict with article 27 of the International Covenant on Civil and Political Rights, which protects minority cultural rights. (This article states that no member of a minority community should be denied the right to practice his/her distinctive religion, language or [broader] culture together with other members of the community.) This was a landmark case, for it succeeded where all previous cases had failed in persuading the federal government to amend the relevant provisions of the Indian Act (1985).

The second case, again, is a landmark with regard to minority cultural-rights claims. On 24 April 1985 the Supreme Court of Canada unanimously struck down the federal Lord's Day Act on the grounds that it conflicted with the guarantee of freedom of religion under s.2a of the Charter. This was the first Supreme Court decision interpreting the right to freedom of religion in the Charter, and the Supreme Court interpretation represented a sharp break with pre-Charter decisions, which had interpreted that freedom very narrowly (*CHRA*, May 1985). What is most interesting about the interpretation is that it took into account equality rights, even though s.15 of the Charter was not yet in effect, as well as s.27 of the Charter, the multicultural provision. In this way the Court broadened its interpretation of freedom of religion from the customary interpretation as an individual right (freedom of choice) to one reflecting the principle of ethnocultural equality, which includes collective (religious) rights: i.e., the right of minorities to express their difference from the dominant religious culture.

In connection with this particular case, it is important to point out that it may not necessarily be precedent-setting for parallel provincial legislation, insofar as the Supreme Court has indicated that statutes requiring businesses to remain closed on Sunday may be valid if it can be demonstrated that they are designed to ensure workers a day off (a common pause day) rather than to enforce religious beliefs. In September 1984 the Ontario Court of Appeal, in considering the Ontario Retail Business Holiday Act—which requires many businesses to remain closed on Sunday—found that the purpose of this law was not to protect the Christian Sabbath, but to ensure a day off. For that reason the Court held that the law was not invalidated by the Charter for most purposes. However, the Court recognized that the unintended effect of the law was to discriminate against religious minorities whose Sabbath day of rest fell on another day of the week. Therefore the Court held that those who closed on another day because of religious beliefs were exempted from the law and could remain open on Sunday (*CHRA*, May 1985). The act is still in effect, but the Ontario government has amended it so as to shift the onus of decision-making on the question of Sunday closing to the municipalities (*Toronto Star*, 8 Feb. 1989).

4. *Nationhood claims*

A full discussion of these claims would necessitate another paper, but it is important to note that they have been brought forward, for example, by the (original, 1976) Dene Nation, by the Inuit of Nunavut, and by the Franco-Québécois. To date, in no case has the desired goal of nationhood (including self-government) been achieved.

In the following pages I will analyse, from a human-rights perspective, constitutional protection for minority rights in Canada. My analysis of the provisions of the Charter and the Accord will reveal that, contrary to international guidelines, an entrenched hierarchy of minority rights can be discerned. Further, it will demonstrate that the provisions of the Accord can be seen to undermine constitutional protection for minority rights secured under the Charter.

MINORITY RIGHTS AND THE CONSTITUTION: EQUALITY OR DIFFERENTIAL TREATMENT?

Insofar as constitutional provisions are in accordance with fundamental human-rights principles, they should afford equal/equivalent protection not only for the individual rights of all persons but also for the collective rights of all ethnic groups within the state. Yet Canada, from Confederation, has been constitutionally predicated on the inegalitarian notion of special group status. Under the Confederation pact and the subsequent Constitution Act of 1867, Canada's 'founding peoples'—the English/Protestant and French/Catholic ethnic groups—acquired a special and superordinate status as the majority or dominant ethnic collectivities, each with a claim for nationhood within clearly delineated territorial boundaries (Upper Canada/Ontario; Lower Canada/Quebec). Moreover, under the terms of s.93 and s.133 of the 1867 Constitution, the collective, religious/educational and language rights of the two 'charter groups' were protected even outside their respective territorial jurisdictions, in localities where their members constituted *numerical* minorities.

By way of contrast, under the terms of s.94(24) of the 1867 Constitution, aboriginal nations—lumped together under the racist rubric of 'Indians'—became Canada's first ethnic minorities. The provisions of s.94(24) gave the Parliament of Canada constitutional jurisdiction to enact laws concerning Indians and lands reserved for Indians. Under ensuing legislation, notably the various Indian Acts, aboriginal nations that were once proud and independent, living and governing themselves within the territorial bounds of their indigenous homelands, acquired a special and inferior status as virtual wards of the state.

Later immigrant ethnic groups, *without* constitutional provisions for *special* status—superior or inferior—have come to constitute a third (multicultural) category of ethnic groups, whose collective claims rest on a goal of *equal* ethnic status and *equal* ethnocultural rights (Kallen, 1982b).

For the purposes of this paper, the significance of constitutionally rooted status differences among founding, aboriginal, and multicultural ethnic groups is that they afford differential bases for collective claims: claims based on special (founding or aboriginal) status and claims based on equal (multicultural) status. Moreover, a direct consequence of this tripartite division is that minority-rights claims put forward by representatives of each of the three categories are in competition, if not in direct conflict with each other.

The crucial questions, at this point are: To what extent have each of the three sets of claims been recognized during the two constitutional debates of the 1980s, and to what degree have the collective rights of minority claimants been specified and protected through ensuing (1982 and 1987) amendments?

The analysis to follow may serve to shed light not only on the ethnic priorities underscoring the amending process but also on the concomitant version of Canadian 'unity in diversity'—on both ethnic and non-ethnic grounds—entrenched through constitutional amendments.

PHASE ONE: THE CHARTER OF RIGHTS AND FREEDOMS (1980-82)

Throughout the 1980-82 constitutional debate legal scholars who voiced support for constitutional entrenchment of a Charter of Rights and Freedoms argued that an entrenched Charter would override existing legislation and would thus render all discriminatory laws throughout the country inoperative (Kallen, 1982a, Chap. 9). Moreover, it was argued, an entrenched Charter would serve to eliminate existing disparities in the provisions of federal and provincial human-rights legislation as it would provide the standard to which all legislation should conform (ibid.).

It follows from this line of argument that a constitutionally entrenched Charter should provide all Canadian minorities with an equal/equivalent basis for claiming redress against perceived human-rights violations. But is this in fact the case? Is the Charter truly an egalitarian human-rights instrument, or is it informed by established ethnic and non-ethnic group priorities that serve to render some categories of Canadians *more equal* than others?

In order to answer this question at least three variables relating to the nature of the provisions of the Charter must first be taken into account.[3]

1. *Negative vs. positive protections.* Negative protections guarantee only non-interference by the state in the exercise of human rights by individuals or groups. Positive protections, on the other hand, obligate the state to take appropriate measures, including the provision of resources out of public funds, in order to guarantee the full exercise of rights.

2. *Specified vs. unspecified protections.* Unspecified protections apply generally; they do not specify particular target populations. Specified protections, on the other hand, apply specifically to particular, enumerated target populations.

3. *Undefined vs. defined rights.* Undefined rights are not spelled out with regard to meaning and content. Accordingly, the nature of the state obligations and of the protections to be afforded are neither clarified nor elaborated. Defined rights, on the other hand, are spelled out with regard to meaning and content, and the protections to be afforded by the state are delineated.

When the foregoing variables are taken into account in assessing the provisions of the Charter, it becomes evident that the Charter is not a truly egalitarian human-rights instrument. Rather, together with related (1982) constitutional provisions, it can be seen to perpetuate and further legitimate long-institutionalized status inequalities between and among different ethnic and non-ethnic populations in Canada.

ETHNIC INEQUALITIES

The special and superordinate status of Canada's two founding peoples is reconfirmed and bolstered through Charter provisions protecting their collective rights. Under Charter s.16-21 and s.23, *positive, specified* protections are afforded for *clearly defined* English and French language and educational rights. Under Charter s.29, the constitutionally entrenched, *positive, specified* protections for the *clearly defined* religious denominational education rights of Protestant and Catholic religious collectivities throughout Canada are reconfirmed.

Conversely, there are no parallel protections for the collective linguistic and religious rights of multicultural or aboriginal minorities. Charter s.27 mentions the 'multicultural heritage' of Canadians, but the vagueness of this provision leaves its interpretation entirely in the hands of the courts. Certainly s.27 affords no *positive* protections for minority rights, as this provision neither *specifies* nor *defines* the nature of the rights alluded to. Similarly, Charter s.22 provides only a vague, *negative* protection for non-official language minorities by allowing their linguistic rights but neither *specifying* nor *defining* them.

Constitutional amendments (s.35 and Charter s.25) represent a positive move to improve the constitutionally entrenched special and inferior status of Canada's aboriginal peoples by recognizing their collective aboriginal rights. Yet these provisions afford only *negative* protections for the aboriginal and treaty rights of Indian, Inuit, and Métis minorities. The nature and content of collective aboriginal rights is not elaborated, and, after four constitutional conferences convened for the singular purpose of defining aboriginal rights, these remain *undefined*.

The unwavering priority given the collective rights of Canada's founding peoples over the parallel rights of multicultural and aboriginal minorities was evident throughout the amending process. In the original (1980) version of the Charter, there was no mention of the notion of 'multicultural heritage'. In response to unflagging lobbying by representatives of ethnic minorities, s.27 eventually was added (in the view of many scholars, as a tokenism—a 'motherhood' statement) (Kallen, 1987).

Amendments pertaining to aboriginal peoples' rights proved to be highly vulnerable to the ongoing moves of the intergovernmental political chess game; sections were inserted, deleted, and altered before the (undefined) rights of aboriginal peoples were finally recognized in s.25 of the Charter and s.35 of the Constitutional Act (Kallen, 1982a).

Like aboriginal people's rights, women's rights proved to be negotiable pawns in the constitutional chess game: s.28 of the Charter, guaranteeing the equality of men and women, was added, deleted, and finally reinstated (in response to intensive lobbying by women's rights groups) in the final stage of the negotiations. The end result was the enactment of a Charter that both reflects and entrenches the ethnic and non-ethnic priorities informing the entire debate.

My earlier analysis of the Charter revealed an apparent hierarchy of ethnic groups constitutionalized through its provisions. The following pages will reveal a parallel hierarchy of non-ethnic groups. Moreover, when we compare the Charter's protections for the human rights of ethnic and non-ethnic minorities, we find that the latter clearly are the more 'fragile freedoms' (Berger, 1981).

EQUALITY RIGHTS: CONSTITUTIONALIZING ETHNIC AND NON-ETHNIC INEQUALITIES

Section 15(1) and (2) of the Charter, under 'Equality Rights', provides the key constitutional basis for individual and categorical rights claims for equal status and equal/equivalent treatment. While there is general agreement among scholars that the non-discriminatory grounds of s.15 are 'open'—i.e., claims can be put forward by minorities not enumerated in its provisions—enumerated minorities are afforded *specified* protection for their human rights, while non-enumerated minorities have only *unspecified* protection. Enumerated minorities, specified on the grounds of race, national or ethnic origin, colour, religion, sex, age, or mental or physical disability, thereby have a firmer basis for claims than have non-specified minorities. Even among the different enumerated minorities, a covert status hierarchy can be found. Ethnic (aboriginal and multicultural) minorities and women have specified human-rights protections under other Charter provisions (s.25, s.27, and s.28, respectively), whereas other enumerated minorities do not. In light of the fact that the provisions of s.15 of the Charter are subject to the possibility of provincial government override under s.33, while s.25, s.27, and s.28 are not vulnerable in this respect, it becomes apparent that aboriginal and multicultural minorities and women enjoy greater Charter protections than do other minorities enumerated under s.15.

The foregoing analysis suggests that the provisions of s.15 of the Charter can be seen to underscore a status hierarchy in which enumerated minorities with other constitutional protections (namely, aboriginal and multicultural minorities and women) rank highest; other enumerated minorities (namely, those specified on the basis of race, age, or physical or mental disability) rank second; and non-enumerated minorities (namely, unspecified populations whose minority status is based upon sexual orientation, political belief, criminal record, or other grounds) rank lowest. Given this interpretation, I would tend to agree with Judge Walter Tarnopolsky (1982: Chap. 1) who suggests that it would not be surprising if some version of the American approach to equality rights were to be adopted by the courts in their assessment of equality-rights claims. The American model involves three levels of judicial scrutiny: strict, intermediate, and minimal. This model could be applied to claims put forward by non-enumerated minorities, enumerated minorities without other constitutional protections, and enumerated minorities with other protections, respectively. Should this happen, the discriminatory implications for minorities of the inegalitarian nature of the Charter's provisions could be profound. For it would follow that the lower status of the minority, the greater would be the burden of proof upon the victim of discrimination (ibid.).

Tarnopolsky's suggestion is supported to some extent by judicial interpretation made in connection with the recent ruling of the Supreme Court of Canada in the Andrews and Kinersly case. In releasing its first judgement under s.15 of the Charter, the court ruled that a British Columbia statute (the Barristers and Solicitors Act) stipulating that only Canadian citizens could practise law in that province violated s.15 on the basis of citizenship (*Toronto Star*, 3 Feb. 1989). Citizenship is not enumerated in the non-discriminatory grounds of s.15, but the court ruled that it is akin to the kinds of characteristics listed. Legal observers had been looking to the court for guidance on whether the prohibited grounds of discrimination extended beyond those enumerated in s.15. Judge McIntyre said that, for now, non-enumerated grounds will be judged on a *case-by-case* basis. What this suggests is that claims brought forward on non-enumerated grounds will be more strictly scrutinized than claims brought forward on enumerated grounds. Accordingly, s.15 of the Charter will continue to afford clearer protection for the rights of enumerated that of non-enumerated minorities.

Notwithstanding this observation, it is important to point out the potentially immense gain for Canada's minorities of this first Charter decision under equality rights. In reaching the decision, the court unanimously endorsed the guideposts for claimants challenging allegedly discriminatory statutes under s.15 of the Charter, which were set out by Judge McIntyre. He contended that discrimination is based on the personal characteristics of the individual or group, and that it has the effect of imposing categorical disadvantages not imposed upon others, thereby resulting in the restriction or denial of opportunities available to others.

Representatives of various minorities—including racial minorities, disabled minorities, and women—view this decision as a victory, saying that it will make the fight for equality easier because the Supreme Court rejected the 'similarly situated' test that has been widely used by lower courts in equality-rights cases throughout Canada (*Toronto Star*, 3 Feb. 1989). Under the 'similarly situated' test, a minority complainant has been faced with the difficult task of proving that s/he is similarly situated to a member of a social category with greater advantages. Minority representatives have criticized the 'similarly situated' test because it has given rise to decisions based on minority stereotypes. Judge McIntyre has commented further that the test is seriously deficient, for if adopted literally it could be used to justify Hitler's Nuremburg laws, under which similar treatment [genocide] was contemplated for all Jews.

For Canada's minorities, the decision of the Supreme Court to reject the similarly-situated test in favour of a non-discriminatory test was significant because it made clear that one purpose of s.15 of the Charter is to ensure that people are not treated on the basis of stereotypes.

PHASE TWO: THE MEECH LAKE ACCORD

Will the Accord undermine constitutional protection for minority rights guaranteed under the charter?

In the analysis to follow, I will demonstrate that the 1987 Accord serves to increase constitutionally established status inequalities between and among ethnic and non-ethnic minorities in Canada. Moreover, I will show how the provisions of the Accord can be seen to undermine protection for minority rights secured under the provisions of the Charter.

The precedence accorded Canada's two founding majorities over all of the country's minorities became evident in the earliest stage of the debate, when the First Ministers agreed in April 1987 to recognize Quebec as a 'distinct society', ostensibly for the purpose of bringing Quebec into the Constitution—i.e., to remedy the fact that the patriated 1982 Constitution came into effect without the approval of then Quebec Premier René Lévesque and his provincial government (*Toronto Star*, 21 Aug. 1987). The move provoked immediate concern among aboriginal and multicultural minorities, and their representatives urged the First Ministers to ensure that a 'distinct society' amendment would not erode or diminish their constitutionally recognized collective rights. In response, the First Ministers added a clause to this effect (s.16). Women's groups and other minority organizations soon followed suit, seeking similar protections for their Charter rights in an amended Accord (ibid.). The concern voiced by minority spokespersons was that legal precedent has supported the view that the rest of the Constitution, and, presumably, the Accord, supersedes the Charter (ibid., 22 Aug. 1987).

On 3 June 1987 the Accord, the *Constitutional Amendment, 1987*, was placed before Parliament and the provincial legislatures for adoption (Government of Canada, August, 1987: 1). In the months to follow, Canada's minorities, despite their disparate constitutional concerns, were virtually unanimous in their expressed opposition to the Accord's provisions, especially with regard to s.2(1)a, recognizing the existence of French-speaking Canadians and English-speaking Canadians as a 'fundamental characteristic' of Canada, and s.2(1)b, recognizing that Quebec constitutes a 'distinct society' within Canada.

Spokespersons for Franco-Ontarians expressed the fear that the 'distinct society' provision would relegate the role of Ontario (and, similarly, the other provinces) to French-language preservation without the necessary distinctive cultural context currently provided in French-language schools where history and other subjects are taught from a Franco-Ontarian perspective. Notwithstanding s.2(4) of the Accord, Franco-Ontarians fear that their distinctive cultural heritage within Canada will be lost. Representatives have expressed dissatisfaction with the limitations of the negative protections afford under s.2(4) and have pressed for positive guarantees for their collective rights (*Toronto Star*, 7 July 1987).

Anglo-Quebecers have voiced similar concerns regarding the erosion of their constitutionally recognized rights under the Charter by the provisions of the Accord. Alliance Quebec, a group representing Anglo-Quebecers, has called on Ottawa to amend the Accord so as to make it clear that nothing in the 'distinct society' clause could override constitutional guarantees for their rights under the Charter (ibid., 19 Aug. 1987).

Representatives of multicultural minorities have been even more vehement than spokespersons for 'official-language' minorities in declaring their opposition to the provisions of s.2(1). Some have argued that this section of the Accord sanctions the ensconced superordinate ethnic status of the French and English minorities, thereby relegating non-English and non-French minorities to the status of second-class citizens within Canada. The Canadian Ethnocultural Council, a coalition of more than thirty national ethnic organizations, has contended that s.2(1) of the Accord clearly gives priority to English/French bilingualism over multiculturalism (ibid., 7 July 1987). Multicultural spokespersons have asserted with one voice that the Constitution should be amended so as to include a reference to multiculturalism in its opening clause (ibid., 11 July 1987).

Equally adamant in their rejection of the provisions of s.2(1) of the Accord, representatives of aboriginal organizations have contended that the recognition of Quebec as a 'distinct society' without parallel recognition of aboriginal nations as 'distinct societies' seriously undermines constitutional protections for aboriginal peoples' rights. In this connection, a representative of the Inuit Committee on National Issues asked the Joint Committee for some commitment in the Accord that would obligate Ottawa to address the still outstanding issue of aboriginal self-government (ibid., 17 Aug. 1987). Aboriginal leaders also have expressed concern that the provisions of s.41 of the Accord, requiring amendment by unanimous consent of the provinces, will make it more difficult for the Northwest Territories and the Yukon Territory—jurisdictions representing substantial numbers of aboriginal Canadians—to gain provincial status. Echoing this view strongly, the Justice Minister of the Northwest Territories charged that the Accord treats the two northern territories as 'colonies of Canada' and further reinforces their subordinate status by enhancing the powers of the provinces at their expense (ibid., 19 Aug. 1987). Needless to say, these ardently voiced concerns imply aboriginal minorities' underlying renunciation of the long-institutionalized paternalistic mode of relations between Canadian governments and aboriginal peoples.

Among Canada's non-ethnic minorities, women's groups have been most resolute in articulating their strong opposition to the provisions of the Accord that they view as favouring the collective rights of ethnic groups (majorities and minorities) over the individual and categorical rights of women and other non-ethnic minorities. Women's representatives have objected to s.16 on the grounds that it singles out multicultural and aboriginal groups as minorities whose constitutionally recognized rights are not affected by the Accord amendments, implying (by omission) that the rights of other minorities not mentioned would therefore have less recognition and protection (ibid., 22 Aug. 1987). Similar objections have been raised against s.2(1), which, according to women's lobby groups, could weaken women's equality rights by directing the courts to give priority to policies designed to promote French/English bilingualism (ibid., 27 Aug. 1987). Accordingly, women's organizations have pressed for an amendment to the Accord giving specified protections for women's rights so as to ensure that the courts would give more weight to Charter provisions guaranteeing sexual equality (s.15 and s.28) than to s.1 of the Accord (ibid., 21 Aug. 1987; 27 Aug. 1987).

While these views are strongly supported by women's groups outside Quebec, within that province the 'distinct society' provision has been strongly endorsed by the Fédération des femmes du Québec[4]. Spokespersons for the Quebec Council on the Status of Women also have expressed the view that the 'distinct society' clause will not affect women's equality rights under the Charter (ibid., 1 Sept. 1987).

Briefs to the Joint Commission from a number of national organizations representing other non-ethnic minorities have echoed the concern expressed by many women's groups that the Accord undermines equality rights. There appears to be strong support for the recommendation that a provision be added to the Accord to ensure that the Constitution of Canada will be interpreted in a manner consistent with the Charter (*CHRA*, Sept. 1987).

Towards the end of August 1987 an *ad hoc* coalition of community organizations representing ethnic and racial minorities, women, disabled minorities, unions, and human-rights groups sent an open letter to Canada's premiers calling on them to delay ratification of the Accord in order to allow for public analysis and debate (ibid.). The coalition argued that once again, in 1987 as in 1981, the Canadian Constitution was being amended with virtually no direct participation or input from Canada's minorities. The letter pointed out that the Joint Committee on the Constitutional Amendment had allowed less than two months for briefs from the public, and argued that this highly restrictive time frame had prevented many minority organizations from properly informing and consulting with their membership.

What this implies is that particular minority concerns have been unequally voiced and represented in the constitutional debate over the provisions of the Accord. Moreover, it is apparent that the most vulnerable and least powerful minorities are those least likely to have had their concerns articulated. One is led to ask how the equality-rights amendment demanded by women's groups would protect the more vulnerable rights of disabled women, aboriginal women, black women, Chinese lesbians, and other members of multiple minorities.

The Meech Lake Accord: entrenching a pecking order of minority rights[5]

When the provisions of the Accord are analyzed using the same three variables employed in the earlier analysis of the Charter (negative vs. positive protections, specified vs. unspecified protections, and defined vs. undefined rights), my thesis that the Accord serves not only to reinforce the existing minority pecking order but also to undermine Charter-endorsed minority rights can be seen to have strong support.

As in earlier constitutional provisions, top priority is accorded the collective rights of Canada's two founding majorities, whose superordinate status is reconfirmed through the *positive, specified* protections of s.2(1). The subordinate ethnic status of Canada's non-English and non-French minorities is reinforced by the weaker *negative, un-*

specified protections afforded their *undefined* collective rights under s.16 of the Accord.

Even less support is afforded under the Accord for the rights of non-ethnic minorities whose minority rights are not only *unspecified* and *undefined*, but, indeed, are nowhere mentioned. Probably the most telling comment on the Accord-endorsed minority 'pecking order' is that Canada's most vulnerable minorities—those disadvantaged by multiple minority status and those most clearly in need of *positive, specified* human-rights protections—are those whose human rights are most seriously violated through omission.

CONCLUDING COMMENTS

The main thrust of this paper has been to demonstrate that constitutional protections for minority rights in the Charter and in the Accord perpetuate and reinforce a long-established hierarchy of ethnic and non-ethnic minorities in Canada. However, this is not to suggest that the outcome has been a constitutionalization of the ethnic status quo. With regard to the Charter, I have shown that new protections for minority rights have been secured under its provisions. However, with regard to the potential impact of the Accord on Charter-endorsed minority rights, my analysis has shown that the provisions of the Accord undermine and thereby weaken the Charter's protections for minority rights. This position currently is strongly supported by a number of legal scholars (Mackay, 1987; Smith, 1987; Swinton, 1987). Accordingly, in conclusion, I submit that the Accord may be interpreted as a retrogressive amendment that harks back to the constitutional priorities behind Canada, vintage 1867.

NOTES

This paper is an adapted and expanded version of the author's earlier paper *The Meech Lake Accord: Entrenching a Pecking Order of Minority Rights* published in *Canadian Public Policy* 14 supplement: *The Meech Lake Accord*, September 1988.

[1]The minority concept is employed in this paper in the accepted sociological sense rather than in a numerical (or political) sense. *Minorities* are social categories whose members occupy a subordinate political, economic, and/or social status in the society in *relation to* the dominant status of corresponding majority categories. The concept focuses on power disparities among social categories, not on differential population numbers.

[2]This typology was originally developed in Kallen, 1982a: 75-7.

[3]The author's typology draws upon legal and broader, socio-political interpretations of Charter provisions put forward by a number of different authors. Particularly relevant sources include Tarnopolsky (1982); Eberts, Flanagan, Gibson, and Morton (all *in* Nevitte and Kornberg [1985]); and Beckton and Magnet (1987).

[4]It should be noted, however, that other voices have been raised. Atcheson (1987) has pointed out that some women in Quebec disagree.

[5]*CHRA*, Sept. 1987. The term 'pecking order' is borrowed from the headline of this issue of the *CHRA*: 'Constitutional Amendment Opens Door to Pecking Order on Human Rights'.

REFERENCES

Abella, Judge Rosalie
1984 *Equality in Employment: A Royal Commission Report*. Supply and Services Canada.

Atcheson, Beth
1987 Commentator on *The Meech Lake Accord* Panel Discussion, Osgoode Hall Law School, York University, North York, 23 November 1987.

Beckton, Clare F.
1987 'Section 27 and Section 15 of the Charter'. In Canadian Human Rights Foundation (CHRF) (1987).

Berger, Thomas R.
1981 *Fragile Freedoms: Human Rights and Dissent in Canada*. Toronto: Clarke, Irwin.

Canadian Human Rights Foundation (CHRF)
1987 *Multiculturalism and the Charter: A Legal Perspective*. Toronto: Carswell.

Daudlin, Bob
1984 *Equality Now*! Report of the Special Committee on Visible Minorities in Canadian Society, House of Commons, 8 March 1984.

Eberts, Mary
1985 'The Use of Litigation Under the Canadian Charter of Rights and Freedoms as a Strategy for Achieving Change'. In Nevitte and Kornberg (1985).

Flanagan, Thomas
1985 'The Manufacture of Minorities'. In Nevitte and Kornberg (1985).

Gibson, Dale
1985 'Protection of Minority Rights Under the Canadian Charter of Rights and Freedoms: Can Politicians and Judges Sing Harmony?' In Nevitte and Kornberg (1985).

Kallen, Evelyn
1982a *Ethnicity and Human Rights in Canada*. Agincourt, Ont.: Gage.
1982b 'Multiculturalism: Ideology, Policy and Reality'. *Journal of Canadian Studies*, 17 (1): 51-63.

1987 'Multiculturalism, Minorities and Motherhood: A Social Scientific Critique of Section 27'. In CHRF (1987).

MacKay, Wayne A.
1987 'Linguistic Duality in Canada and Distinct Society in Quebec.' Paper presented to the Conference on the Meech Lake Accord, University of Toronto, 30 October.

Magnet, Joseph E.
1987 'Interpreting Multiculturalism'. In CHRF (1987).

Morton, F.L.
1985 'Group Rights Versus Individual Rights in the Charter: The Special Cases of Natives and Quebecois'. In Nevitte and Kornberg (1985).

Nevitte, Neil, and Allan Kornberg, eds
1985 *Minorities and the Canadian State*. Oakville, Ont: Mosaic Press.

Smith, Lynn
1987 'The Effect of the "Distinct Society" Clause on Charter Equality Rights for Women in Canada'. Paper presented to the conference on the Meech Lake Accord, University of Toronto, 30 Oct.

Swinton, Katherine
1987 'Competing Visions of Constitutionalism: Of Federalism and Rights'. Paper presented to the conference on the Meech Lake Accord, University of Toronto, 30 Oct.

Tarnopolsky, W.S.
1982 'The Equality Rights'. In Tarnopolsky and G.A. Beaudoin, eds, *The Canadian Charter of Rights and Freedoms: Commentary* Toronto: Carswell.

FIVE

POLICIES ON INDIAN PEOPLE IN CANADA

JAMES S. FRIDERES

INTRODUCTION

The current position of Native people in Canadian society is a result of external and internal pressures that have come to bear upon them over the past two centuries. These pressures are the result of policy directly and indirectly established and enacted by both provincial and federal governments. However, the present paper will look only at those federal policies that have been put in place since the turn of the century, and because of space limitations we will only examine four policy components which have significantly affected Native people: self-government, land claims, education, and economic development.

When Indian policy was first established in Canada (New France), the overriding thrust of the policy was one of 'wardship' that would protect Indians from the white settlers and allow for close control over the former (Tanner, 1983). Since the nineteenth century, specific policies and an administrative bureaucracy to implement these policies have been established. At the outset, policies such as defining specific groups of Indians as either friends or enemies were enacted by the colonial military authorities. By 1830 military jurisdiction over Indians was transferred to civil authorities, who began to develop policies to 'civilize' Indians either through isolation (creation of reserves) or through assimilation by close day-to-day contact with non-Indians.[1] The new assimilationist policy was clear in one goal; there must be a complete destruction of traditional Indian culture that would interfere with the burgeoning capitalistic economic system. This meant that any Indian behaviour, values, or ideologies that were opposed to, antagonistic to, or did not promote capitalism had to be destroyed. As such, political and economic systems of Indians were summarily done away with, as were their traditional religious and kinship systems.

By the mid-1800s a new 'protective' policy enveloping the assimilationist policy gave government further justification for adopting additional and more pervasive policies that would affect Indians in every sphere of their life. To fully 'protect' them, a reserve system was implemented that forced Indians to reside in a specific geographical area and allowed more complete control over their everyday affairs.[2] Under this new policy, the wardship system was complete. It was assumed that under such controlled conditions, government could implement specific policies so that Indians would see the wisdom of leaving the reserves and assimilating into the larger social system. All of these policies were eventually codified in the Indian Act (1876), which has been slightly modified over the years.

The above policy was pursued until the 1950s, when a new 'democratic' ideology emerged in government that acknowledged cultural pluralism as a structural condition of Canadian society; Indian people were not going to disappear.[3] However, the perspective and ideology of assimilation of Indians has, over the past two centuries, become so entrenched in government that it has been extremely difficult for the Department of Indian Affairs to embark upon a new direction. For example, in 1947 the Parliamentary Joint Committee publicly announced its policy of assimilation and elimination of Indian status. The federal government has consistently acted on this policy notwithstanding their rhetoric of equality and full participation in Canadian society. This policy was most forcefully noted recently in the 1969 White Paper, which explicitly rejected any special status for Indians.[4]

The introduction of the multiculturalism policy in 1971 ostensibly represented a shift in the way ethnic groups would be dealt with in Canadian society, how they would be integrated into the social and economic fabric of society, and how they would participate in the political events of Canadian society. Yet it is clear that the Department of Indian Affairs has been able to operate independently of multiculturalism; it is still able to implement policy at variance with other government policy. Change has been slow, although there has been some shift by the federal government towards dealing with Indians in a more pluralistic fashion. New policies are being developed, some are being enacted and others are being replaced. But, as most policy analysts know, once policy is enacted it is rarely removed; rather, it falls into disuse as new policy supercedes the old. This is the case for Indian Affairs. Few policies have been actively removed, although the removal of section 6.1.b of the Indian Act is one significant exception. (This section stated that Indian women who married non-Indian men would automatically lose their Indian status; their children would also be considered non-Indian.) Usually, new policies are implemented to deal with new conditions brought about through Indian lobbying or legal challenges, or in response to societal changes in values and/or ideologies.

As noted above, we will focus on four specific policies that seem to be central to Indians today. These not only affect Indians' identity, their self esteem, and their locus of control, but also determine their inter-relations with non-Indians and their position in Canadian society, as well as their ability to deal with the larger society. We will begin by identifying the role of the provincial governments in Indian policy and how this is changing. As we explore each policy, we will present a brief historical review and then, in more depth, discuss the current policy and its implications for Indians in Canadian society.

THE ROLE OF PROVINCIAL GOVERNMENTS

Prior to the Second World War, the provinces played a minor role in dealing with Indians: they acted as agents for the federal government in enforcing Canadian law on Indians. However, in the past thirty years there has been a shift in policy regarding the role of provincial governments in Indian affairs. Because of rising costs ($900 million in 1970 to over $3 billion in 1987) in implementing Indian policy, the federal government has tried to force the provincial governments into assuming a greater role. Until recently it has not been successful. Indians, the object of discussion, find themselves in a dilemma. They realize that the federal government (Indian and Northern Affairs Canada) has reached its funding limits, and that if additional funds are to be obtained they will have to come from private industry or provincial governments. At the same time, they realize that a historic relationship exists between themselves and the federal government, as laid down in section 91(24) of the Constitution Act, 1867. And, while the relationship is not totally satisfactory, at least they have understood the ground rules and the perspectives of the major actors. To now change these rules would involve new actors, new perspectives, and the possibility that aboriginal, treaty, land, and other Indian rights might be jeopardized—after considerable effort has been put forth to obtain their recognition (Long and Boldt, 1988). This concern was given some credence after the failure of four First Ministers' Conferences (1983, '84, '85, '87) to act upon Indian initiatives. Indians also point to junctures where the provinces have entered Indian lives—in education, in child welfare—with disastrous results.

Today the federal government has adopted a position that reflects its belief that while it has a special relationship with Indians, this relationship should not be an exclusive one (Rawson, 1988). It has not, however, developed a coherent policy on provincial responsibility for services to Indians. Nevertheless, the federal government has begun enacting a series of policies that have not only forced the provincial governments to develop Indian policy, but have forced Indians to look at provincial governments as major actors in their lives. The federal government has reduced its involvement in providing special services for Indians and has transferred greater amounts of its budget to Indian communities. In 1970, about 20 per cent of the service expenditures were handled by Indians; by 1985 this had increased to nearly 60 per cent. Ottawa is integrating provincial standards into remaining federal programs, thus preparing the way for integration of Indian programs into provincial policies (Boldt and Long, 1988). It has also reduced its staff dealing with Indians. In the 1970s Indian Affairs had nearly ten thousand employees, today it has fewer than four thousand. Simultaneously, the Constitution Act, 1982 (Section 15 of the Charter of Rights and Freedoms) has put additional pressure on the provinces to accept greater responsibility for Indians. The tripartite (federal-provincial-Indian) consultations that have been entered into have also thrust provincial governments into Indian affairs. As a result, provinces have reluctantly become more and more involved in Indian affairs. Today, each province has been forced to create a special structure or agency to deal with Indian affairs. This shift in provincial responsibility is just one example of a larger pattern that is fundamentally changing the role of provinces in Canada's society: there has been a significant shift from federal-government dominance and control to greater provincial autonomy and power (Boldt and Long, 1988). The incorporation of Indians into the affairs of provincial governments is not the result of any Indian request. It is the structural shift in Canadian society that has brought about these changes, which will continue to impose themselves on the historic relationship between the federal government and Indians.

SELF-GOVERNMENT

Indians have long asserted their sovereignty and right to self-determination. This stance was evident in the early Atlantic Treaties of Peace and Friendship, and has been echoed by other Indians over the past century, but Canadian law would not sanction such a position. The crack in the legal position emerged in 1973 when the Supreme

Court ruled that Indians did have aboriginal rights, and shortly after this decision, the Prime Minister of Canada conceded that perhaps Indians did have more rights than the government was prepared to acknowledge.

Concerted lobbying efforts by Natives took place in Canada and in Britain throughout the late 1970s and early 1980s. In 1980 the 'Constitutional Express' crossed western Canada and then deposited over a thousand Natives on Parliament Hill to demonstrate for Native rights. When Canada's Constitution finally was enacted in 1982, Canadians' awareness of Indian rights and grievances became part of the public discourse (Canada, 1987a).

The Constitution Act of 1982 includes a statement that 'the existing aboriginal and treaty rights of the aboriginal peoples of Canada are hereby recognized and affirmed.' This also set in motion the four First Ministers' Conferences, which were to discuss and develop a national policy on Native rights and self-government. The last conference focused specifically on a federal proposal for a self-government amendment to the Constitution but, like the previous three, was unsuccessful in enacting any change.[5] Nevertheless, the above events set in motion a number of other initiatives to bring about Indian self-government. For example, a concomitant move was made by Indian and Northern Affairs Canada to reduce its size and structure, with commensurate shifts to local Indian communities.

It would not be until 1983 that an all-party report (the Penner Report) of the Special House of Commons Committee on Indian self-government recommended the development of a new relationship between Indians and the federal government. This new relationship would remove the wardship/protectorate role of government and place Indian people in charge of change affecting their lives. Specifically, this committee endorsed constitutional entrenchment of a right to self-determination. The Prime Minister endorsed this position at the First Ministers' Conference on Aboriginal Constitutional Affairs in 1985. In 1987 he reiterated that Indian self-government was a major theme and priority of Indian and Northern Affairs Canada and attempted, with no success, to have this policy enshrined in the Canadian Constitution.

Even though this policy was not made part of the constitution, a number of attempts have been made to implement it. Two major positions have emerged with regard to how self-government will be achieved. Some have argued that more Indian autonomy and control can be achieved by developing policies that emerge out of the Indian Act: for example, an enhanced capacity for Indians to make their own by-laws could be used to develop self-government. In other cases, actual amendments of the Indian Act could create alternative funding arrangements and promote economic development; for instance, to allow bands to levy local property taxes on their land (Canada 1987d). There is also a push for increased band responsibility for the delivery of various social and economic programs under the existing Indian Act. Bands or Indian corporations could be made responsible for one or more sectors, such as medical services, policing, education, and child welfare services. In addition to delivery, Indians could be made accountable for their expenditures in each sector, in which case their local control would increase as they would decide how they wanted to deliver the service(s) and allocate their funds. Tripartite agreements (federal-provincial-Indian) utilizing the existing Indian Act have also be achieved in the area of child welfare in Nova Scotia and New Brunswick.

Finally, initiatives supporting small-business development are being pursued actively with Indian communities within the confines of the Indian Act in order to increase the independence of Indian communities. While economic independence will not directly bring about self determination, it will increase a community's independence and allow its members to begin the process of control over their lives.

Others argue that self control cannot be achieved by remaining within the confines of the Indian Act. Therefore they recommend that in order to achieve self-government, Indians will have to move beyond its limits. (Proposals that call for new arrangements beyond the present Indian Act are called 'community negotiations'.) These proponents of community-based self-government have submitted proposals that would allow them to determine membership and give them jurisdiction over land and resources, the environment, culture, education, health, and social services.[6] In an attempt to deal with their suggestions, the government has created a bureaucratic structure to implement this policy. Proposals for self-government that move beyond the Indian Act are assessed by the new self-government branch of Indian Affairs. Each proposal is evaluated in terms of its quality, the level of community support it has, its consistency with the government's mandate for self-government, its financial viability, the scope of power within the parameters of the Canadian constitutional principles, and its feasibility (Crombie, 1986).

Community-based negotiations are a distinct policy initiative intended to achieve practical benefits for individual Indian communities that circumvent the Indian Act. In facilitating these community-based negotiations, the federal government does not intend to impose self-government models on Indian communities. The diversity of aspirations and the unique geographical, social, cultural, political, and economic circumstances of Indian communities will mean that a variety of self-government arrangements will emerge (Canada, n.d.).

The new policy accepts the premise that Indians are in the best position to determine the direction and pace of their progress towards self-government. Thus the role of the Department of Indian Affairs is to respond to community-based initiatives, to assist with the refinement and elaboration of proposals where requested, and to help identify and overcome current obstacles in the path of self-government. It is hoped that the development of self-government proposals from a variety of communities will provide the experience needed to establish a greater understanding of what self-government can mean to Indian peoples.

Whichever strategy is pursued, the overall objective of this policy is to develop new self-government arrangements within the existing constitutional framework either within or outside the Indian Act.[7] The community negotiations process is meant to complement the constitutional process and is viewed as a transitional phase from the existing legal framework towards a fuller exercise of Indian self-government. This self-government policy does not involve increasing funding to Indian communities. It does mean that the government will negotiate arrangements with other government agencies in order to provide for a greater degree of autonomy for Indian communities to manage their own affairs and to govern themselves working with funds currently budgeted.

In summary, the new policy has fundamentally changed the explicit role of the Department of Indian Affairs. Departmental officials co-ordinate, in partnership with the community, the involvement of other federal departments. They may also facilitate discussions with provincial and/or municipal governments, if required.[8]

As Indian communities assert greater autonomy, they will be forced to deal directly with other levels of government without involving the federal bureaucracy. It is the federal government's hope that all parties will take this opportunity to create new and practical arrangements for the satisfactory resolution of inter-jurisdictional issues. However, provincial participation will depend on the agreement of each Indian community and provincial government involved.

The process of developing and negotiating self-government arrangements requires a great deal of commitment on the part of Indian communities and governments alike.[9] Many communities will have more pressing needs in the short term and will prefer to pursue self-government over the longer term. Others may wish to embark on the process now. The new policy makes it possible for the Department of

Indian Affairs to work with any of those communities that wish to further the development of Indian self-government.

The Sechelt of British Columbia were the first to negotiate a self-government agreement; the Sechelt Indian Band Self-Government Act (Bill C-93) was enacted in late 1986. It allows the Sechelt Band to assume control over their lands, resources, health and social services, education, and local taxation. Since then, the government of British Columbia has enacted companion provincial legislation that supports Bill C-93. The response to the federal government's self-government policy is growing, with more than 70 proposals for self-government from Indian communities involving approximately 240 bands. Nearly two-thirds of these proposals are actively involved in some stage of the negotiating process (McKnight, 1988).

In summary, the goal of self-government is to increase local community control and decision-making capability, which will lead to greater accountability by Indians to their own constituency. Self-government will also ensure involvement at the grassroots and bring about changes in Indian life that will fundamentally affect their quality of life.

LAND CLAIMS

The first and perhaps still one of the major land settlements affecting Indians was the Royal Proclamation of 1763. This proclamation reserved specific lands for the use of Indians and established a procedure, which required the consent of Indians, by which the federal government could obtain clear title to these lands. During the period of 1764 to 1923, specific treaties were put in force by the federal government in which it obtained land from Indians. After 1927 no major land claims or settlements were carried out by the federal government because it had already taken most of the land it required for orderly settlement of the country, and because it defined Indian land grievances or claims as illegitimate. In short, the federal government consistently took the position that 'aboriginal land claims' were non-existent. This position was steadfastly maintained by political leaders and supported by the legal system, which took a very rigid and narrow interpretation of the law when it dealt with Indian issues (Canada, 1987c).

It was not until 1973 when the Supreme Court of Canada enunciated its now historical and far-reaching decision on the Nishga Indian land claim in British Columbia (*Calder v. the Attorney General of BC*). While the court did not rule in favour of the Nishga claim, it did, for the first time, specify that Indians had aboriginal rights. The new question was whether or not those aboriginal rights had been extinguished. One year later, the federal government announced a major policy stating that it was prepared to negotiate with Indians who had not previously given up their land rights. An Office of Native Claims was established to implement this new policy.

Since the court decision, the federal government has accepted well over two hundred land claims, which it has tried to resolve without resorting to the courts. It has enacted specific policy and bureaucratic procedures to deal with two types of land claims: comprehensive and specific. Comprehensive claims are based on claims to aboriginal title arising from traditional use and occupancy of land. These claims have arisen in areas of Canada that have not been previously 'treatied out': for example, Yukon, Labrador, most of British Columbia, Northern Quebec, and much of the Northwest Territories. Major reviews of this policy were undertaken in 1981 and more recently in 1986. This latter revised policy continues the goal of negotiated settlements of comprehensive claims. One of the major revisions made to the policy on comprehensive claims in 1986 was to introduce alternatives to earlier policy, which required that aboriginal groups agree to the extinguishment of *all* aboriginal rights and title as part of the claims settlement. The new policy identifies alternative options that may be involved.[10] Under the existing comprehensive-claims policy, only land-related rights are at issue in negotiations; any other rights that may exist will remain unaffected (Canada, 1986a). Other changes focus on providing certainty and clarity of rights to ownership as well as the use of land and resources, and on linking land settlements to enhanced self-reliance and economic development for Indian communities. Finally, under the new policy the participation of provincial governments in the negotiations is encouraged.

In negotiating comprehensive land policy, the federal government is prepared to deal with a number of issues such as land selection, self-government, environmental managements, sharing of resource revenue, hunting, and fishing, as well as other topics. The actual topics that will be discussed in any negotiations and the parameters of these negotiations are to be identified in each individual case.

Prior to the implementation of self-government policies, the federal government used comprehensive claims—the James Bay and Northern Quebec Agreement (1975), the Northeastern Quebec Agreement (1978), and the Inuvialuit Final Agreement (1984)—to implement a limited range of local institutions (self-government) that could be created by existing statutory means in the settlement area. Today, with the new comprehensive land-claims policy, aboriginal self-government can openly be negotiated in this context. In 1988, the federal government negotiated three major agreement-in-principle comprehensive claims: the Dene/Métis Northwest Territories, Council for Yukon Indians, and Conseil Attkamek-Montagnais claims.

Specific claims are focused upon some single aspect that arises out of non-fulfilment of a treaty, illegal administration of Indian lands or resources, or some misadministration by officials, whether in Indian Affairs or in some other area of government. These claims may focus on specific land losses, such as cut off lands, but are more often directed to an administrative procedure inappropriately or illegally carried out by the federal government that impacted on lands held by Indians.

In interpreting treaties and other documents negotiated by Indians and the federal government, the courts have, until recently, taken the 'ordinary meaning' approach. For example, in the case of a treaty stating that a medicine chest shall be provided to Indians, the term 'medicine chest' was defined as meaning no more than the words clearly convey: an undertaking by the Crown to keep at the house of the Indian Agent a medicine chest for the use and benefit of the Indians at the direction of the Agent. In addition, the courts have been very reluctant to look beyond the written terms of agreements. All of this has led to a very narrow interpretation of the law and has, in almost all cases, gone against Indian claims (Bartlett, 1987).

Recent decisions suggest a different judicial analysis. The Supreme Court of Canada has recently stated that the old approach might not always be appropriate. Instead, the courts are now leaning towards a method of interpretation that would not depend solely on the technical meaning of the words, but would consider the sense in which these words would naturally be understood by the Indians. In addition, the courts have now begun to accept as evidence oral assurances that go beyond the written document (Bartlett, 1987). One tangible outcome of this shift has been the number of claims that have been settled. In 1986-87, for example, twelve specific claims were settled involving a total of $25.5 million and over 19 thousand hectares of land returned to Indians.

EDUCATION

Education has been viewed by the government as the primary vehicle for assimilating ethnic minority groups. It also has been one of the most important themes in the ideology of our school system, although developments over the past decade have, to some degree, been tending towards the acceptance of cultural pluralism.

Indian Affairs and Northern Development is responsible for the elementary and secondary education of Indian children who reside on the reserve. The provision of elementary and secondary educational services and finances for Indians is authorized by section 114 to 119 and 121 to 123 of the Indian Act, as well as by specific order in council.

Education provided to Indians in the early twentieth century focused on the military and religious groups on reserves. It was not until after the Second World War that secular education became the primary thrust of Indian education. This same period marked a shift in policy, from educating Indians on the reserve to moving them off for schooling. This new policy meant that Indian children were to be integrated into provincial schools and that on-reserve elementary and secondary schools were to be systematically closed. Most secondary schools were closed by the later 1970s, but this trend was reversed as we moved into the 1980s and joint-integrated education agreements were curtailed. For example, in the mid-1970s over two-thirds of the 80,000 Indian students in Canada were being educated in provincial schools. By 1987, two-thirds of the 84,000 Indian students then enrolled were being educated on the reserve, nearly half of them in band-controlled schools. There has been a substantial shift in the policy that has directed Indian education since the turn of the century. Today, the trend is towards local control (band-operated schools) and acceptance of the idea that local communities can develop their own curricula and programs as long as they stay within the boundaries of the provincial educational guidelines.

The formal educational achievements of Indians in Canada are considerably less than those of the non-Indian population. For example, the retention rate (30 per cent), the proportion attaining some high school (20 per cent), and the proportion having a high-school diploma (25 per cent) are less than half the rates for the non-Native population. Nevertheless, these figures show that over the past twenty years Indians' educational achievements have increased substantially.

To fulfil the mandate of Indian Affairs' educational policy, 400 schools have been built and maintained by that department. The concept of Indian control (which is part of the policy of self-government), is being put into practice as local Indians take control of educational services. Recently, two policies (School Space Accommodation Standards and the Policy for the Provision of Education Facilities) have been implemented to establish a system of priorities for such factors as overcrowding, curriculum requirements, and transfer from provincial schools. In addition, the department provides a policy for the construction, renovation, and replacement of Indian schools.

The government's responsibility with regard to post-secondary education is less clear, more recent, and currently in flux. In the 1950s Treasury Board gave Indian Affairs limited authority to provide some post-secondary education to Indians and Inuit. This program evolved and increased its scope throughout the 1960s. By 1972 Indian and

Northern Affairs Canada was able to make a contribution to band councils specifically for the provision of post-secondary education services. Three years later, circular E-12 spelled out the formal policy.[11] By 1979 Indian and Northern Affairs Canada had established its own scale of student living and transportation allowances (Canada, 1988), under which Indian students received funding for up to 96 months.

The goal of the student-assistance policy was to help Indians gain access to post-secondary education and to graduate with the skills needed to pursue careers that would enhance Indian self-government and economic self-reliance (Rayner, 1988). The program has been very successful: with fewer than 500 post-secondary students enrolled in 1967, the number has increased to 15,000 in 1988-89. This increase has also resulted in a phenomenal increase in budgetary allocation, with the 1988-89 budget close to $130 million ($9,000 per student per year). As a result of this increase, in 1989 the federal government decided to change its policy toward providing post-secondary education for Indians. The new policy has reduced the time limit to 48 months, adjusted the rate of assistance, and created a scholarship fund. It does not, however, recognize post-secondary education as a right guaranteed by treaty. The implications are that the budget will be capped, and that if the number of Indian students continues to increase, they will be forced to rely on the same kinds of support available to other Canadians.

The increasing number of Indian students and the higher levels of educational achievement are partially the result of the new policy changes that have been implemented over the past two decades. The introduction of a curriculum more relevant to Indians, the hiring of Indian teachers and teacher aids, and, in some cases, the use of an Indian language in the classroom have all brought about the changes. Perhaps the most important change has been the involvement of adults in the education of their children. However, the impact of increased educational achievements will be influenced by the extent to which children are able to improve their income and/or occupation on or off the reserve. If the skills provided to children are obsolete or in limited demand, then education will not be seen to be important and will fall into disfavour. However, thus far education is viewed positively, and government policy continues to reinforce the idea that Indian-controlled education on the reserve is preferable to provincial integrated schools.

ECONOMIC DEVELOPMENT

The economic development of Indians has been a long-standing goal of Indian Affairs. Having noted this, one can also point out that the attainment of this goal has eluded Indian Affairs for well over a century. The number of Indians living above the poverty line has never exceeded 40 per cent. In many communities, unemployment rates exceed 90 per cent. Most Indians are underemployed, seasonal, or part-time workers. Few reserves have any viable industrial activities. As a result, Indians occupy a position of domestic dependency, although they have become integrated, over time, into the larger national market as a dependent component.[12]

The Department of Indian Affairs and Northern Development Act (1970) since amended defines and limits the scope of the department's responsibilities. The Indian Act (1970) is the legislative basis for all departmental action and, along with the Indian Economic Development Regulations, set down the critical regulations that affect Indian Economic Development policy. Other federal and provincial policies are important insofar as they indirectly impinge upon the authority of the Indian Act. Within the Department of Indian and Native Affairs, five programs have been established, of which three are particularly relevant to economic development; the Indian and Inuit Affairs Program, the Northern Affairs Program, and the Native Claims Program.[13]

Historically, Indian Affairs was the only government department that dealt with Indian people. Today, while it is still one of the most important actors, other federal departments and agencies also have policy and programs targeted for Indian people. The Department of Indian and Northern Affairs' expenditures for all aboriginal peoples in 1987-88 amounted to approximately three-quarters of the total five billion dollars that the federal government had targeted directly for aboriginal people. Other agencies such as the Department for Regional and Industrial Expansion, the Secretary of State, and Canadian Employment and Immigration Commission also have programs directed towards aboriginal people that make up the difference. In addition, Indian and Northern Affairs Canada works in close co-operation with other federal government departments such as National Health and Welfare, the Department of Justice, and the Canada Mortgage and Housing Corporation in order to provide training, advice, and technical expertise and to carry on negotiations with federal, provincial, and municipal governments for the delivery of services. Additional funds are spent on Indian people by provincial governments, although the exact amount is hard to assess (Canada, 1987b).

The economic policy directed towards Indians for the first half of this century focused on developing agricultural pursuits. Because Indians were rural, subsistence peoples, this policy best fitted Indian Affairs' overall strategy for directing Indian economic activities. It was not until the 1960s that the federal government began to change its policy from an agricultural focus to one of developing a modern industrial base on the reserve. Initially the new policy directed economic investments into mega-projects on the reserve. It was hoped that large investments of cash in these mega-projects would increase employment for Indians, enhance their incomes, and, eventually, influence their behaviour by putting non-Indian industrial workers on the reserve as models. However, it became clear within a few years that this strategy was not workable: the high default rate of these investments attests to its failure. The result was a new policy premised on the belief that industrial development must take place in urban areas, and that if economic development on the reserves were to take place, it would have to be in the form of job-training, job-development, and self-sustaining activities. In some cases, if possible, resource development programs would be implemented to exploit the natural resources on a reserve (Canada, 1987; Anders, 1980).

This shift in policy reaffirmed the intention of Indian Affairs to force Indians to leave the reserve and move to the city. Job opportunities are found in urban individual areas and modern technological skills can be employed only in this context. Although in some cases small employment projects are encouraged on the reserve, they are meant only to deal with those who refuse to leave in pursuit of 'real' jobs in the city (Canada, 1986). In many cases the economic developments taking place on the reserve are in reality community-support programs. In addition, the small-business projects developed by Indians generally have insufficient equity and inadequate returns on their initial investment for them to become viable economic undertakings.

In 1985 a new policy was enacted in an attempt to facilitate economic development. The federal government's Alternative Funding Arrangements plan was to provide a way for Indian councils to expand their authority to manage the affairs of Indian people. In addition, Cabinet approved a policy enabling Indian councils to take on a greater role in operating and managing federal programs. Under these new arrangements, Indian councils have expanded authority to develop policies that reflect their own needs and the values of the local community. Bands also have flexibility to allocate funds in accordance with their own community priorities, and can use funds at their own discretion (Asch, 1987).

Today economic-development assistance is available to Indian people under a variety of programs, of which the most important are operated by the Department of Indian and Northern Affairs Canada and the Department for Regional Industrial Expansion. The Department of Indian Affairs' major economic activity is the Economic Development Program, which has existed since the Second World War. It provides advice, assistance, funds, and training in the areas of business development, employment and employability development, and institutional development. Its mandate is to foster Indian economic development through entrepreneurial market participation, removing structural barriers to Indian economic growth and business-skills development, and promoting self-reliance.

The second major actor involved in Indian economic development is the Department of Regional Industrial Expansion. The Department provides direct financial assistance to Natives for viable business and economic-development initiatives. It also plays a co-ordinating role within government to improve the access of aboriginal peoples to other federal programs. Money is provided to Natives under several programs that fund the establishment or acquisition (or modernization) of viable aboriginal business enterprises and offer selected training, innovation, and marketing initiatives. The specific economic-development programs that are presently in force and directed towards Indian communities can be divided into four components: economic development, training and job development, regional development, and major resource development.

In our assessment of Indian economic development, several problems in implementing economic projects have been noted. A clear distinction has not been drawn between economic-development programs and community-support programs; economic-development programs are scattered among numerous departments and, within them, many agencies, few of which have any clear criteria for deciding whether or not to support an Indian enterprise. Our analysis of economic development also points out that while money is provided for Indian business formation, ongoing projects are quickly abandoned. Those small-business projects developed by Indians generally have insufficient equity and inadequate potential return on the initial investment. In addition, because many of these Indian business ventures simultaneously try to provide a community non-profit service, give experience to workers, and produce a product or service for profit, they generally fail (Hunter, 1977; Myint, 1972).

Underlying all these policies and programs is a strong belief in private entrepreneurship, profit, and keeping the public sector out of business decisions. The federal government's economic policy continues to value large-scale production, homogeneity of style, specialized skills, and tolerance for ever-declining standards of our environment. These values fit within the overall parameters of the modern industrial economy in which corporate hierarchies harness labour, energy, and capital in the cause of production and profit. The industrial economy focuses primarily on manufacturing and on primary resource extraction supported by large government bureaucracies that exist to manage transfer payment programs (Pretes and Robinson, 1988).

In summary, despite the efforts of both the federal and provincial governments, the poor economic position of most Native communities continues to be a persistent feature of Canadian life. The impact of government direction of both the social and the economic development of Native people over the past century has been marginal. After two centuries of involvement with the non-Native world economy, most communities have a kind of 'dual allegiance' to both a modified subsistence economy and a modern industrial world economy. The adaptations that Indian communities have made have been primarily the result of non-directed adjustments by local people to opportunities made available by intruding Euro-Canadians (Langdon, 1986). Other community adaptations have been a result of Native population decline, resource decimation, and forced relocation by government. Despite constant innovations in programs, only a few isolated communities find themselves in a better socio-economic position today than a quarter of a century ago. The result has been the creation of an artificial world on Indian reserves, where reliance on government is almost total (Canada, 1986; Wien, 1986). An artificial economy has been created on the reserve that is based upon continued government subsidies, and is one in which the community residents have a difficult time distinguishing between productive and non-productive employment activity.

CONCLUSION

The federal government is currently in the process of phasing out the parallel structures created by Indian and Northern Affairs Canada and thus forcing Indians to become integrated into the dominant society's institution. As a result, the Indian institutions unique to them and facilitating their own cultural system will be phased out. As Boldt and Long (1988: 43) point out:

> The assimilation of Indians into Canada's legal institutions began when Indians were under federal law . . . when the federal government vacated certain areas of jurisdiction and allowed the provinces to pass laws governing Indians on reserves.

The most important policy has been the one dealing with comprehensive claims. In each case, Indians have been forced to create corporations through which they can meet the conditions outlined in the settlement. This has the effect of integrating them into the dominant society and destroying indigenous Indian structures so that there is no returning to traditional institutions.

The provincial governments have been willing participants in the above strategy. However, their acceptance has been tempered by cost consideration. The grounds on which they have resisted the policy are not ideological but financial. Nevertheless, as the federal government withdraws from certain activities, and the consequences of its withdrawal become the responsibility of provincial governments, the latter are becoming more willing to take charge of Indians and Indian issues.

How will the provinces take over Indian issues and relate to Indian communities? Thus far, the provincial procedure has been to assign each reserve municipal status. Such status fits into the existing legal structure of Canadian society, and the provinces have had considerable experience with municipal governments. Finally, such changes remove the special status that Indians have had and relegate them to the status of ordinary citizens.

The federal government's strategy in developing Indian economic policy has been unbalanced. Ottawa has argued that a preponderance of funds has to be invested in health, social welfare, and education before much money can be directed towards economic development and other institutional sectors. They have also argued that it is too costly to develop all sectors of the economy equally within a short period of time, and that, given that most developed economies are unbalanced, this is not the appropriate strategy (Hoselity, 1972; Henriot, 1977).

The federal and provincial governments agree that Indians must move off the reserve in order to fully participate in the socio-political and economic structures of modern society. Jobs exist in the urban areas and cannot be cost-effective if they are forced to move into the rural countryside. At the same time, Indian communities cannot undertake large-scale economic developments on their own. The capital requirements are too high, and community members do not have the occupational skills to operate the modern technology required.

The federal government and Indians have agreed, for different reasons, that land claims, self-government, and economic development are all desirable goals. Indians argue that the settlement of land claims will result in economic development which will lead to and strengthen self-government,[14] which in turn will bring about the preservation of their culture, their spiritual perspective, and their oneness with the land (Dickerson, 1989). Figure 5.1 depicts the relationship between the major issues now facing Indian people and its linkage to cultural preservation.

The federal and provincial governments agree with the importance

Figure 5.1 Current Policy Concerns and their Interrelationships

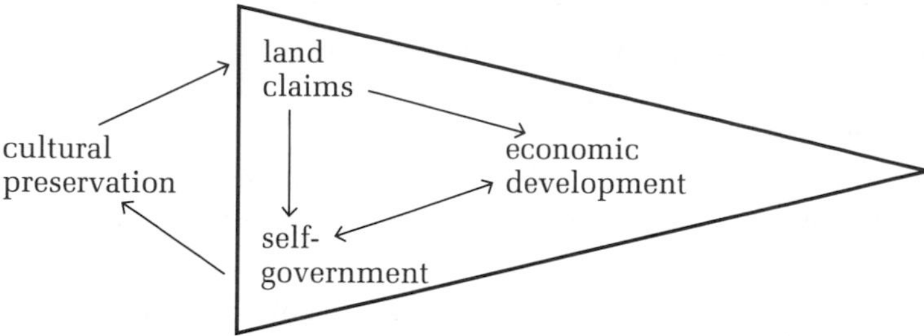

of the three factors within the large triangle. However, they hope that under controlled conditions, the outcome will not be cultural preservation but cultural obliteration. For example, governments have been very careful in terms of comprehensive land claims, the type and structure of the economic development that can take place, and the form of self-government that is allowed (LaRusic and Bouchard, 1979). In short, given the type of control that is exerted by government in these three policy areas, cultural retention will not result. When Indians are provided an education similar to that of the dominant society, local ties are eroded, kinship becomes devalued, and secular views predominate; a rational ideology becomes the basis for action. Government apparently hopes that incorporation into the larger economic system, acceptance of the rules of the political structure, and control over their land will make Indians like other citizens of Canada. Boldt and Long (1988) point this out when they note that the federal government has shifted its policy from cultural assimilation to institutional assimilation. The current policy has focused on the elimination of administrative, political, legal, and economic arrangements that set Indians apart from other Canadians. Given the experience that other minorities in other countries have had, it is likely that the fate of Indians in southern Canada is now sealed.

NOTES

[1]Both strategies were employed in an attempt to ascertain which strategy would more quickly and thoroughly assimilate Indians.

[2]Most reserves were too small to allow for self-sufficiency to be established. In addition, over time large tracts of land originally designated as reserves were sold off by the federal government.

[3]The 1969 White Paper is a recent example of this assimilation policy resurrected.

[4]Boldt and Long (1988) argue that today the federal and provincial govern-

ments are pursuing the same goal through the gradual assimilation of Indians into Canadian institutional structures.

[5]An amendment to the Constitution can be made only when the federal government and seven provinces representing 50 per cent of the Canadian population support a change.

[6]The federal government has created an Indian Self-Government Branch as part of a reorganization of the Indian and Inuit Affairs program and related units.

[7]All negotiations are conducted without prejudice to existing aboriginal and treaty rights or the outcome of any discussions on constitutional matters. While treaty matters may be discussed, the government does not intend to renegotiate or redefine the treaties in this process.

[8]The Department of Indian Affairs and Northern Development must seek legal advice from the Department of Justice, particularly as discussions become more specific. The involvement of other federal departments is determined by the areas of jurisdiction that each community wishes to develop.

[9]Any community-based proposal must be accompanied by a band council resolution supporting the proposal. After a preliminary assessment by the Indian Self-Government Branch and regional officials, the proposal is discussed with the community. After these consultations, the community negotiation staff may recommend proceeding with the proposal, recommend additional work on the proposal, or reject the proposal on the basis that it falls outside the general mandate for self-government. If the proposal is accepted, the community then develops a framework for negotiations. Specifically, it identifies the proposed changes to the operation of the community's present government, where new authorities beyond the Indian Act would be required, a ratification process, and a proposed schedule and agenda. After the proposal has been completed, it is reviewed by regional officials as well as by the community. Any community concerns are taken into account so that the document sent to senior Indian Affairs officials for approval is mutually acceptable.

Based on this discussion paper, a draft agreement is prepared for signature by the Minister of Indian Affairs and Northern Development. At the same time, the community will have to secure a mandate from its members. At this time, substantive negotiations are entered into and the negotiations take place on all areas of dispute. If negotiations are successful, an Agreement in Principle is initiated by the two parties. If the community ratifies the Agreement in Principle, the document will be signed by the two parties and implementation will take place.

[10]Acceptable options are: (a) the cession and surrender of aboriginal land title throughout the settlement area in return for the grant to the beneficiaries of defined rights in specified or reserved areas and other defined rights applicable to the entire settlement area; or (b) the cession and surrender of aboriginal title in non-reserved areas, while allowing any aboriginal title

that exists to continue in specified or reserved areas; granting to beneficiaries defined rights applicable to the entire settlement area.

[11]The E-12 guidelines were discussed extensively by over 500 bands, organizations, and associations for over six months in 1988.

[12]Some have argued that this dependency is encouraged by major businesses because they benefit from such an arrangement. Indians are consumers, not producers.

[13]The remaining programs, Transfer Payments to the NWT Program and the Administration Program, are also an important part of the Department of Indian and Northern Affairs but are not directly targeted toward Indian people.

[14]The double-headed arrows reflect that the relationship between the two variables is reciprocal.

REFERENCES

Anders, G.

1980 'Indians, Energy and Economic Development'. *Journal of Contemporary Business* 9: 57-74.

Asch, M.

1987 'Capital and Economic Development: A Critical Appraisal of the Recommendations of the Mackenzie Valley Pipeline Commission.' In B. Cox, ed., *Native People, Native Lands*. Ottawa: Carleton University Press.

Bartlett, Richard H.

1987 *Indians and Taxation in Canada*. University of Saskatchewan, Native Law Centre.

Boldt, M., and J. Long

1988 'Native Indian Self-Government: Instrument of Autonomy or Assimilation?' In Long and Boldt, eds, *Governments in Conflict*. Toronto: University Toronto Press.

Canada

1986 *Task Force on Indian Economic Development*; Report to the Deputy Minister, Indian and Northern Affairs. Ottawa: Indian and Northern Affairs.

1986a *Comprehensive Land Claims in Canada*. Indian and Northern Affairs, Information Sheet #1. Ottawa: September.

1987 *Federal Programs and Services to Aboriginal People*. First Ministers' Conference, Aboriginal Constitutional Matters, Ottawa.

1987a *A Record of Aboriginal Constitutional Reform*. First Ministers' Conference, Aboriginal Constitutional Matters, Ottawa.

1987b *Economic Development: Program Description*. Evaluation Directorate. Ottawa: Indian and Northern Affairs.

1987c *Aboriginal Land Claims in Canada*. Indian and Northern Affairs, Information Sheet #1. Ottawa: September.

1987d *Aboriginal Self-government*. Indian and Northern Affairs, Information Sheet #1. Ottawa: September.

1988 *Indian School Policy Responds to Indian Concerns*. Communique INAC, Ottawa, 14 July.

n.d. *Indian Self-Government Community Negotiations: Process, General Information, Guidelines*. Ottawa: Indian and Northern Affairs.

Crombie, D.

1986 'Policy Statement on Indian Self-Government in Canada'. Ottawa: Minister of Indian Affairs and Northern Development.

Dickerson, M.

1989 'Issues in Self-Government'. Presentation at The Arctic Institute of North America, Calgary, Alberta, 15 April 1989.

Henriot, P.

1977 'Development Alternatives: Problems, Strategies, Values'. In C. Wilber, ed., *The Political Economy of Development and Underdevelopment*. New York: Random House.

Hoselity, Bert

1972 'Social Implications of Economic Development: General Considerations'. Ottawa: Indian and Northern Affairs.

Hunter, D.

1977 'Legal Principles and Economic Development: General Considerations'. Ottawa: Indian and Northern Affairs.

Langdon, S., ed.

1986 *Contemporary Alaskan Native Economies*. New York: University Press of America.

LaRusic, I., and S. Bouchard

1979 *Negotiating a Way of Life*. Research Branch, Corporate Policy. Ottawa: Department of Indian and Northern Affairs.

Long, J.A., and M. Boldt, eds

1988 *Governments in Conflict?* Toronto: University of Toronto Press.

McKnight, B.

1988 'Notes for Remarks to the Cree General Assembly'. Chisasibi, Quebec. Ottawa: Minister of Indian Affairs and Northern Development.

Myint, A.

1972 'The Demand Approach to Economic Development'. Pp. 218-29 in W. Johnson and D. Kamerschen, eds, *Readings in Economic Development*. Cincinnati: South-Western Publishing.

Pretes, M., and M. Robinson

1988 *Beyond Boom and Bust*. Calgary: Arctic Institute of North America.

Rawson, B.

1988 'Federal Perspectives on Indian-Provincial Relations'. In Long and Boldt (1988).

Rayner, J.

1988 'Developments in Education Policy'. *Transition* 1 (2): 1-2.

Tanner, H., ed.

1983 'Introduction: Canadian Indians and the Politics of Dependency'. In *The Politics of Indianness*, Institute of Social and Economic Research, Memorial University of Newfoundland, St John's.

Wien, F.
1986 *Rebuilding the Economic Base of Indian Communities*. Montreal: Institute for Research on Public Policy.

SIX

MULTICULTURALISM IN CANADA: A SOCIOLOGICAL PERSPECTIVE

LANCE W. ROBERTS AND RODNEY A. CLIFTON

INTRODUCTION

Less than two decades old, Canada's official multiculturalism policy contains a rich and complicated set of ideas, ideals, programs, and policies. Despite the proliferation of research on particular ethnic groups, comparatively little investigation has addressed the public policy of multiculturalism. This is a serious deficiency, since multiculturalism forms the backdrop against which much of the current research in ethnic studies becomes meaningful. This paper discusses the meanings and implications of multiculturalism from a sociological perspective, with the goal of contributing to a critically informed appreciation of this public policy.

We will begin by noting the degree of ethnic diversity in our nation and the fundamental sociological problem that this variety creates. Following this sociological perspective, we will introduce some conceptual tools necessary for understanding multiculturalism, in particular the ideas of culture and social structure. Next, a typology of multiculturalism is developed in an effort to conceptualize the sociological meanings of this term. After identifying three ideal types of multiculturalism (institutionalized, symbolic, and ritualistic) we will briefly elaborate on the kind of commitment that each form of multiculturalism demands of ethnic-group members. We will then turn to the government's perspective and discuss some policy implications—in particular, the social-structural requirements of the three ideal types of multiculturalism—and attempt to assess the government's willingness to underwrite these requirements. The chapter then shifts from formal policy concerns to address some substantive issues, and concludes with comments directed at the relationship of multiculturalism to self-respect, freedom, and rational social policy.

ETHNIC PLURALISM AND MODERNITY

Any review of the statistics on self-reported ethnic-group membership makes it clear that Canada is a 'multi-ethnic society'. This evident ethnic pluralism is a feature that Canada shares with other nations (Vallee, 1988), and one that distinguishes Canada as a 'modern' society. It is worth saying a word about how ethnic pluralism is generally related to the modernization process, since this linkage helps to set the stage for the classical sociological problem that multiculturalism policy is intended to address.

For roughly two centuries, since the French and industrial revolutions (Nisbet, 1966), nations in the Western world have experienced a widely shared set of social changes identified as 'modernization'. Although academics debate the specific features to be included in its definition (Mayes, 1982), there is general agreement that a salient feature of 'modernity' is the recognition and promotion of 'pluralism'. The diversity associated with pluralism is manifest in three domains: cultural, social-structural, and psychological. For example, compared to more homogeneous, small-scale societies, modern (complex) societies exhibit more extensive, rationalized divisions of labour (social differentiation); contain a more diversified set of values and belief systems (world views); and socialize individuals to display greater intellectual flexibility (cognitive complexity) (Berger, 1971; Inkeles and Smith, 1974; Kohn and Schooler, 1979).[1]

From this perspective, ethnic pluralism appears as just one manifestation of the extensive ideological, political, economic, and psychological 'pluralism' that pervades modern societies like Canada. From a sociological viewpoint, the heterogeneity associated with the various kinds of pluralism creates an organizational problem that can be identified as the conflict between adaptation and integration. It is important to appreciate this dilemma, since it is the central organizational issue that a multiculturalism policy must address.

Adaptation and integration

The concept of pluralism highlights variety and heterogeneity among the components or units of a system. From a sociological perspective, Canadian society can be viewed as a social system composed, as all systems are, of a set of 'components' and 'relationships' that connect the components. For present purposes, the 'components' of interest are the various ethnic groups and their members, while the term 'relationships' refers to the interactions both between members within any ethnic group and between different ethnic groups. Conceptualized in this way, the ethnic diversity in Canada presents an organizational challenge that can be stated as follows: What systemic arrangement optimizes the autonomy of ethnic groups to pursue their interests while maintaining social order? Addressing this question requires consideration of the notions of adaptation and integration.

The concept of 'adaptation' focuses on the 'components' of a social system and stresses the processes through which these parts attempt to meet their needs by adjusting to the surrounding environment. By contrast, the notion of 'integration' looks at the system as a whole and emphasizes the processes by which the components are able to co-ordinate their actions. In other words, adaptation highlights the autonomy of the components, while integration highlights their interdependence (Bredemeier and Stephenson, 1962: 47-59). Under conditions of ethnic pluralism, 'adaptation' refers to the attempts of particular ethnic groups to organize themselves and act in ways that optimize their individual and collective interests. 'Integration' refers to whatever adjustments ethnic groups and their members must make to accommodate the interests of other ethnic groups who, like themselves, are using their resources to adapt as well as they can.[2]

Recognizing the distinction between adaptation and integration allows us to appreciate the nature of multiculturalism policy and the sociological problem that it addresses. As a modern society, Canada is composed of a heterogeneous mixture of groups, of which ethnic groups are an important category. These ethnic groups have distinctive interests, and some means must exist for co-ordinating potential conflicts in interest.[3] Ethnic pluralism, in short, makes integration more problematic. As an institution concerned with managing the collective interest through the development of means for integrating individual interests, the government has responded to ethnic pluralism with a policy of multiculturalism.

Culture and social structure

Our first task entails coming to terms with the meaning of 'multiculturalism'. As Lachenmeyer (1971) notes, the language of sociology is notorious for its vagueness and ambiguity, a fact that results in both misunderstanding and problems with the conceptual development of the discipline. This conceptual confusion extends to the concept of multiculturalism. As Mazurek (1987: 146) notes: 'As with "justice", "beauty", and "love", everyone seems to approve of multiculturalism, everyone seems to know what it is, yet everyone seems to define and practice it differently . . . we have yet to settle upon agreement of what, exactly, multiculturalism is.' Similarly, Smith (1983: 266) notes: 'multiculturalism in Canada means different things to different people, and consequently means nothing.' It follows from these comments that any discussion of the policy of multiculturalism and its practical importance must begin with the recognition that multiculturalism does not have a single, unitary conceptualization. Nevertheless, the concept does have meaning. Grasping the multiple referents of the term becomes a critical first task.

To begin, it is necessary to understand the distinction that sociologists make between 'culture' and 'social structure' (Kroeber and Parsons, 1958; Kornhauser, 1978; Geertz, 1973). These concepts distinguish two important components of a social system.[4]

There is considerable disagreement among social scientists on the specific meanings of the terms 'culture' and 'social structure'. Nonetheless, as Wallace's (1983: 47) review notes, 'with few exceptions, both anthropologists and sociologists have long intended, wanted, implied, and very nearly explicitly stated, a distinction between those interorganism behaviour regularities that consist of physical behaviours and those that consist of psychical regularities.' Following this consensus, we have adopted House's (1981) characterization of culture as 'a set of cognitive and evaluative beliefs . . . that are shared by members of a social system and transmitted to new members'. Social structure, in turn, is defined as a '*persisting* and bounded *pattern* of social relationships (or pattern of behavioral interaction) among the units (that is, persons or positions) in a social system' (House, 1981: 542; emphasis in original).

These distinctions emphasize the importance of distinguishing between the shared sets of symbols that identify what members of various ethnic groups believe (culture) and their collective patterns of conduct (social structure). 'Culture' represents the shared symbolic blueprint that guides action along an ideal course and gives life meaning. 'Social structure', by contrast, signifies the constraints on individual action arising from the connections and dependencies existing in all organized systems. Of course, culture and social structure are intimately and reciprocally linked in actual experience. Nonetheless, it remains relevant to distinguish 'between what members of a social system believe and what they collectively do' (House, 1981: 543).

It follows from the analytical distinctions between culture and social structure that these properties are variables that can be related in different ways. To say that culture and social structure are 'variables' is to underline the fact that cognitive and affective orientations of ethnic-group members, as well as their collective patterns of conduct, can change over time. This point is relevant to the notion of 'assimilation', which will be introduced shortly. Moreover, to note the potential independence of the cultural and social-structural components of an ethnic social system is to appreciate the varieties of interdependence that can occur between these variables.

'Assimilation' refers to the process of 'becoming alike' that is illustrated by the image of the 'melting pot'. Ethnic pluralism, underwritten by the policy of multiculturalism, is typically seen as a condition opposite to that of assimilation, in which ethnic groups retain their distinctiveness. However, the situation is not as simple as this dichotomy suggests. Although assimilation and ethnic pluralism stand in contrast to one another, the fact that the cultural and social-structural dimensions of an ethnic group's social system are separate *variables* suggests that 'multiculturalism' can take several forms. In short, multiculturalism has several referents, and to invoke the term without specifying a particular meaning is to invite confusion.

A TYPOLOGY OF MULTICULTURALISM

It follows from this understanding of the notions of culture and social structure that ethnic diversity may be maintained on at least two levels. One is the level of cognitive and affective orientations (cultural); the other is the level of shared behaviour/conduct (social-structural). By charting the various points at which these two dimensions, the symbolic and the behavioural, may intersect, it is possible to identify several ideal types of multiculturalism.

Figure 6.1 portrays the cultural and social structural dimensions of a social system and illustrates three ideal types of multiculturalism as they contrast with assimilation. This figure takes the variable nature of culture and social structure and, for purposes of discussion, labels the extreme attributes of each of these dimensions. It presents the situation from the viewpoint of a particular ethnic group interested in maintaining its cultural distinctiveness from the surrounding society. For instance, the intersection of the column and row labelled with a '+' sign indicates an ethnic social system that, in terms of culture, has successfully internalized its value and belief systems in its members and, in terms of structure, has social arrangements that encourage members to act in accordance with the distinctive social expectations of the group.

Besides the ideal types, the body of this figure contains cells indicating the variable degrees of an ethnic group's success in maintaining its cultural and social-structural distinctiveness. In this way the figure represents the potential empirical diversity of actual ethnic groups. The cell labelled '4' indicates a lack of success by the ethnic

Figure 6.1 Culturally and Structurally Based Ideal Types of Multiculturalism

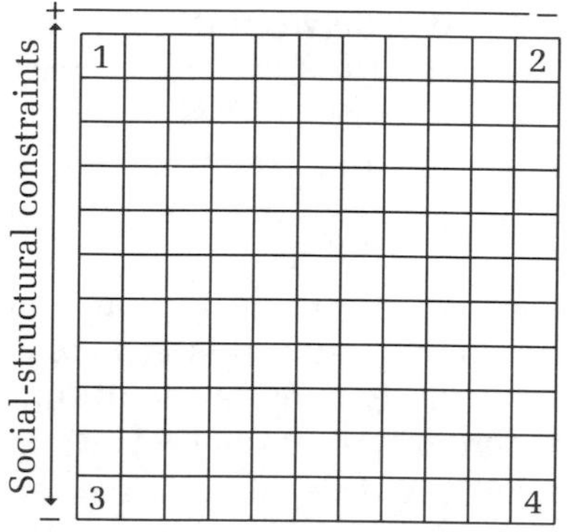

group on both the cultural and social structural dimensions, and therefore is identified 'assimilation'. The other three labelled cells in this figure identify variants of the notion of multiculturalism.[5]

In direct contrast to 'assimilation' is the cell labelled '1', 'institutionalized multiculturalism'. Under these conditions, an ethnic group is able to command conformity from its members to the group's normative expectations in terms of their thoughts, feelings, and actions. The label 'institutionalized multiculturalism' indicates a close alignment between the group's distinctive ethnic ideals and the conduct of its members. This strong form of multiculturalism is presumably evident in ethnic enclaves, such as the Hutterites, that exhibit a high degree of control over their members.

Cell '2', 'ritualistic multiculturalism', indicates a different ideal form of multiculturalism. In this form the group is still able to command behavioural conformity, but is less successful in instilling the culture's distinctive values and beliefs in its members. Here, conformity with the group's expectations is therefore due not to internalized ideals, but to the instrumental contingencies that the group is able to mount in the form of rewards and punishments. The label 'ritualistic multiculturalism' indicates that this conformity is not inspired or informed by cultural ideals. An ethnic group whose members participate in religious ceremonies, or some political process unique to that group, without understanding the symbolic meaning of these activities would be an expression of this form of multiculturalism.

The remaining ideal form of multiculturalism, labelled 'symbolic', is found in cell '3'. In this situation ethnic members identify cognitively and affectively with the symbolic system of the group but are not behaviourally constrained by its social structure. In other words, instrumental structures of rewards and punishments other than those under the group's control play a significant role in shaping their conduct, even though the members remain aware of and sympathetic to the values and beliefs of the ethnic group.

To summarize, following from the distinction between the cultural and social structural components of a socio-cultural system, at least three ideal forms of multiculturalism can be distinguished from the circumstance of complete assimilation. These forms are identified by the degree of alignment between the ethnic group's 'hold' on both the cognitive and affective as well as the behavioural dimensions of conduct. Given these distinctions, it is important to be clear about the type of multiculturalism one is talking about. Using this typology, the following section elaborates on each ideal type of multiculturalism. Since, as we have noted, an ethnic group's interests lie more in the direction of adaptation, the issues discussed in the next section centre on the question of generating commitment from ethnic-group members in order to further the group's interests.

Figure 6.1 serves to remind us that if ethnic groups are going to maintain their distinctiveness they must, in one fashion or another, constrain the conduct of their members. In modern societies most people have what sociologists call 'complex status sets'; that is, they occupy a variety of positions connected with various institutional sectors. As Coser (1974: 2) puts it, 'in the modern world . . . the individual lives at the intersection of many social circles'. Occupying this variety of positions means, in turn, that individuals are expected to develop and play a wide range of social roles and respond to many different expectations. In short, the expectations of ethnic-group membership are in competition with the demands suggested or imposed by friendships, occupations, educational organizations, and the like. The organizational question then becomes: In what ways, or through what mechanisms, can an ethnic organizational structure command the allegiance of its members in order to maintain its distinctiveness as an ethnic group? The following elaboration of the three ideal types of multiculturalism attempts to outline the different ways through which such allegiance can be maintained.

Commitment mechanisms

Symbolic multiculturalism. In its ideal form, this form of multiculturalism is characterized by a high degree of cultural constraint coupled with a low degree of social-structural constraint. In this case, members of an ethnic group have considerable cognitive understanding of and affection for the shared symbol system that is characteristic of their ethnic group, yet display little of this distinctiveness in their conduct. The reasons for this disjunction between cognition and affect on the one hand and behaviour on the other are many, and beyond the scope of this paper. However, it is quite possible to imagine a situation in which ethnic-group members might find the rewards for conforming to a set of employment practices not aligned with the expectations of their ethnic group sufficiently attractive that they would orient their behaviour in that direction. This kind of multiculturalism is labelled 'symbolic' because it depends on a set of shared, commonly defined symbols that constitute 'culture'. The symbolic label is also appropriate because it parallels what Gans describes as symbolic ethnicity, the 'nostalgic allegiance to the culture of the immigrant generation . . . a love for and pride in a tradition that *can be felt without having to be incorporated in everyday behaviour*' (1979: 9; emphasis added). In addition, it falls in line with W.W. Isajiw's ideas about the 'rediscovery' of ethnic identity among the children of original immigrants (i.e., the 'new ethnicity'): 'if they want to retain any traditions, they are those which are most meaningful to their own life in society as a whole. The consecutive generations are to a high degree culturally assimilated into the total society. They, nonetheless, have the ability to turn to the ancestral past and pick from it those cultural patterns in which they find meaning' (quoted in Anderson and Frideres, 1981: 105).

In practice, in symbolic multiculturalism an ethnic group exerts its force over its members through the process of identification. Members possess a sense of solidarity or cohesion based on a sympathy with and for the distinctive elements of their ethnic culture. In this sense, the conformity shown by ethnic-group members under symbolic multiculturalism is similar to what Coser calls 'doctrinal conformity', which occurs when persons 'state institutionalized beliefs to others' (Coser, 1961: 29).

Ritualistic multiculturalism. In its ideal form, ritualistic multiculturalism is the opposite of symbolic multiculturalism in that it represents low cultural and high social-structural constraints by an ethnic group. In this case, members have little knowledge of or affection for the distinctive beliefs, norms, and values that comprise their ethnic culture; nonetheless, they act in a manner that is consistent with these cultural symbols. Again, the reasons for this misalignment between culture and conduct are multiple, but for this condition to exist, the ethnic group must be able to constrain its members' conduct so that, independent of their thoughts and feelings, they act in accord with the group's expectations.

As the adjective 'ritualistic' suggests, in this form of multiculturalism ethnic-group members 'go through the motions'; and thus appear outwardly ethnic while possessing little or no internal commitment to the group's cultural symbol system. To gain the outward compliance of group members, this kind of multiculturalism operates on the basis of instrumental considerations and involves a kind of cognitive/rational commitment based on a calculation of rewards and punishments. Kanter (1968: 500) calls this arrangement 'continuance commitment': 'when profits and costs are considered, participants find that the cost of leaving the system would be greater than the cost of remaining: "profit" compels continued participation'. The kind of conduct expected under conditions of ritualistic multiculturalism is what Coser (1961: 29) calls 'behavioral conformity', defined as the circumstance where 'whatever their attitudinal position, they [members] act in accord with values and norms'.

Institutionalized multiculturalism. Figure 6.1 identifies this strong ideal form of multiculturalism as the combination of both high cultural and high social-structural constraints in an ethnic community. The 'institutionalized' label points to a clear alignment between the ethnic members' acceptance of the cultural beliefs, norms, and values of the group, and their practice of the distinctive ethnic expectations based on these cultural symbols; this dovetails with the sociological understanding of institutionalization as 'the development of stable patterns of social interaction [social system] based on formalized rules, laws, customs and rituals [cultural system]' (Theodorson and Theodorson, 1969: 208).

Such cultural and social-structural arrangements enable ethnic communities to exert strong control over their members, since conformity is primarily based not on sentiment (as it is in symbolic forms) or instrumental considerations (as it is in ritualistic forms), but on a set of internalized commitments that result in the view that the 'demands made by the system are evaluated as right, as moral, as just, as expressing one's own values, so that obedience to these demands is a normative necessity, and sanctioning by the system is regarded as appropriate' (Kanter, 1968: 501). Under the conditions of institutionalized multiculturalism, we expect to find 'attitudinal conformity [which occurs] when individuals grant legitimacy to designated institutional values and norms' (Coser, 1961: 29); there is both private acceptance of and public compliance with the cultural beliefs, norms, and values of the ethnic group.

To summarize, different ideal forms of multiculturalism present alternative visions regarding the place and character of ethnic communities. In turn, different forms of multiculturalism encourage ethnic groups to use different strategies to commit and mobilize their membership in the adaptation process. Institutionalized multiculturalism, for instance, rests on commitment generated by the internalization of distinct ethnic values and beliefs, while ritualistic multiculturalism rests upon the power of instrumental considerations, and symbolic multiculturalism on identification processes. In short, different types of multiculturalism carry very different implications for the expression of ethnicity. These different forms of ethnic expression must to be taken into account by public policies aimed at co-ordinating ethnic groups in order to address the issue of integration.

POLICY IMPLICATIONS

So far we have generated three theoretically plausible ideal types of multiculturalism by cross-classifying two properties generic to the sociological perspective: culture and social structure. We have also touched on the different implications these ideal types have for generating the commitment of ethnic-group members. We now turn our attention to some of the policy implications associated with these ideal types of multiculturalism.

Institutionalized multiculturalism

Institutionalized multiculturalism is the 'fullest' expression of multiculturalism, first, because it involves a distinctive set of shared symbols. It is also fullest in the sense that the conduct of ethnic-group members is most completely constrained. In this form of multiculturalism, the ethnic group's promotion of its distinctive ideas and ideals is accomplished through a system of social arrangements with sufficient surveillance and sanctions to assure that the group's cultural orientations are put into practice.

The first policy consideration relevant to institutionalized multiculturalism is that ethnic groups require a sufficiently developed social structure to perpetuate a coherent cultural heritage. J.F. Scott (1971) made this point cogently when he noted that expecting people to follow cultural constraints without the support and constraint of social sanctions is to rely on a 'sociological anomaly'. In other words, the internalization of ethnic beliefs and values requires the support of ethnic social structures. This is especially the case when institutionalized multiculturalism is promoted in a country like Canada, where the culture of an ethnic group is in competition with the democratic-liberalism ethos of the surrounding society (Brotz, 1980). It follows that ethnic groups must have some social-structural means of controlling the conduct of their members, so that the latter's actions are aligned with the cultural expectations of the group, which in turn are distinct from those of the surrounding culture. This, for example, is the sociological reasoning behind the development of laws, such as Bill 101 and Bill 178, that work to constrain the social, economic, and cultural character of Quebec in order to maintain the province's 'French face'.

The social-structural foundation of the internalization of norms comes in the form of a set of parallel ethnic institutions that are complete enough to satisfy the needs of ethnic-group members and shape their conduct. Breton's (1964) work on the nature of institutional completeness of ethnic groups addresses this point. He argues that the maintenance of an ethnic group's identity is directly related to the group's ability to maintain its boundaries, and that these boundaries in turn depend on the range of ethnic organizational structures that the community manages to operate, including such things as schools, churches, newspapers, and employment agencies.

Roberts and Boldt (1979) have extended the idea of institutional completeness. They criticize Breton's essentially 'enumerative' approach to institutional completeness for ignoring the possibility that some ethnic organizations may have particular characteristics that make them significantly more effective for boundary maintenance. Their point is that the *quality* of ethnic institutions is as important to boundary maintenance as their *quantity*. In particular, Roberts and Boldt stress that, for successful boundary maintenance, ethnic institutions need to be able to 'impose', rather than merely 'propose', role expectations on members of their ethnic community. They label this quality 'structural tightness'. In their words:

> the more extensively and effectively an ethnic group's institutions can 'impose' rather than merely 'propose' normative constraints on individual members, the greater the degree of control it has over them. By imposing expectations the discretionary element of role behaviour is reduced. On the other hand, where ethnic institutions are only able to propose role expectations, individual autonomy will be enhanced since individual interpretation of performance requirements is allowed and perhaps even encouraged. Under such conditions, ethnic groups will be significantly more susceptible to external influence and the risk of assimilation will be increased. (Roberts and Boldt, 1979: 105-6)

Where Breton's understanding of institutional completeness is primarily quantitative, Roberts and Boldt stress the qualitative dimension. Taken together, these conceptualizations are complementary and suggest that, for effective boundary maintenance to occur, ethnic groups require organizational structures that are both *extensive* (quantitatively complete) and *pervasive* (qualitatively complete or 'tight'). In both of these senses, 'institutional completeness' is a variable property, which is precisely what the vertical axis of Figure 6.1 shows.

The greater the institutional completeness of an ethnic group, the greater its ability to command the allegiance of its members in cultivating and practising an orientation that is distinctive.

The prototypical example of this sort of ethnic community in Canada is the Hutterites, who have successfully maintained an ethnic enclave that promotes both cultural vision and practice (Boldt, 1989). The policy questions that arise regarding institutionalized multiculturalism are, first, whether this is a model that the government wishes to support, and, second, whether it is a model that many ethnic groups can reasonably maintain. On both counts, we suggest that the answer is probably no.

The reason for government's reluctance to promote this form of multiculturalism is related to the 'adaptation versus integration' issue introduced earlier in this paper. It may be that, through the formation of enclavic communities of the sort associated with institutionalized multiculturalism, members of these communities are insulated from many of the problems associated with modern life, and hence are able to lead more meaningful lives and maintain a higher quality of life. In short, institutionalized multiculturalism may help the members of ethnic groups to *adapt* to life in a modern societies, largely through the development of what Berger and Neuhaus (1977) call 'mediating institutions'. This goal, however, is not likely to be of *primary* concern to governments. That is not to say that governments are unconcerned about the adaptation of members in a particular ethnic community; however, this is not their principal concern. The primary aim of government in developing a multiculturalism policy is to respond to the demands of most ethnic communities. From the government's viewpoint, the central issue is *integration*; that is, co-ordinating and accommodating the disparate interests of different ethnic groups. The government typically describes this interest as a concern for 'national unity'. Given this concern with integration over adaptation, it is reasonable to think that governments would not promote institutionalized multiculturalism. The sociological reasoning behind this position is cogently set out by Patterson (1977), whose argument takes the following form.

An inevitable trade-off occurs between the freedom of individuals and the constraint of social groups. In the ideal case of institutionalized multiculturalism, an ethnic community is able to institutionalize its culture in the form of a set of social structures that can effectively exert control in the direction of institutional expectations. To the extent that a society is ethnically diverse, successful institutionalized multiculturalism will mean that growing numbers of communities will be established that aspire to different goals (because of their different ethnic values, believe in alternative means (by virtue of their distinctive norms), are committed to alternate truths (stemming from their diverse belief systems), and, as important, are prepared to *act* on the basis of these distinctive orientations. At some point, co-ordinating relations between these ethnic groups is bound to present problems, since there is no reason to believe that at least some of these groups, and perhaps many of them, will not be highly ethnocentric, with all the interactional difficulties this quality entails. That is, different ethnic groups are bound to relate to the surrounding society, including other ethnic groups, in fundamentally different ways, and this may cause serious political problems. This is likely to be the case, even though some advocates of multiculturalism claim 'it is to our advantage to allow alternative forms of social organization and life styles to exist as experiments [since they] ultimately provide for the enrichment and well-being of the greater community' (Appleton, 1982: 157). No matter how desirable such an attitude may be, this position is unlikely to be sustained by governments consumed by short-term concerns for integration and co-ordination.

In summary, if governments were to encourage the strong, unified ethnic groups envisioned by institutionalized multiculturalism, they would be exaggerating the problem of integration, which runs counter to one of their primary interests. It is this line of reasoning that makes sense of the government's reluctance to display commitment to the establishment of institutionalized ethnic communities with parallel, relatively complete social structures through which distinctive cultural systems can be perpetuated. This is just the kind of model underlying the claims of Native groups to greater self-determination through land claims and self-government, or of those Québécois who want stronger control of language and other aspects of their 'distinct society'. In both of these examples, arguments can be advanced that if these developments were encouraged they would assist the adaptation of the groups concerned. The federal government, however, generally resists these movements to some degree because, although they may make the parts of the ethnic mosaic stronger, in doing so they exacerbate the short-term problems of unification.

But federal government resistance is only one reason for doubting that institutionalized multiculturalism will be an important feature of Canadian society. Another reason relates to the composition of ethnic groups. As we mentioned earlier, the 'pluralism' characteristic of modern societies is not just ethnic but pervades other sectors, including those of ideology, politics, and religion. Pluralism is also evident in the social and social-psychological domains, where its presence makes the implementation of institutionalized multiculturalism difficult.

Recall that one characteristic of institutionalized multiculturalism is that ethnic-group members are likely to have behavioural allegiance as well as cognitive and affective commitment. The greater the commitment of ethnic-group members, the more successful the institutionalization of the group's culture. In other words, under conditions of institutionalized multiculturalism the ethnic communities are able to act as 'greedy institutions'; they are able to 'seek exclusive and undivided loyalty and they attempt to reduce the claims of competing roles and status positions on those they wish to encompass within their boundaries. Their demands on the person are omnivorous' (Coser, 1974: 4).

This accomplishment of institutionalized multiculturalism is no mean sociological feat. People in modern societies typically have complex status and role sets, which means that they are members of diverse associations, all of which compete for their attention and resources and, in doing so, generate considerable role conflict that needs to be managed (Coser, 1975). In addition, such people place a high value on individualism and freedom. This combination of social and psychological complexity makes it unlikely that an ethnic group will be able to garner the considerable social resources necessary to build a relatively complete set of alternative ethnic institutions—legal, economic, religious, educational, and so on. Moreover, even if such a set of institutions were in place, it is also unlikely that they would be capable of imposing conformity to ethnic expectations in the face of the alternatives available to modern people, since the value placed on autonomy would probably mean considerable resistance to such impositions.

To state these qualifications is not to rule out the possibility of institutionalized multiculturalism. There are examples, such as the Hutterites (Roberts and Boldt, 1979), some native communities, and some Chinatowns (Kwong, 1987), that approximate these conditions and other collectivities, such as separatist-minded western Canadians and Québécois, who aspire to this condition. However, these qualifications do point out that the circumstance of institutionalized multiculturalism is atypical and is likely to remain so in the near future, given the federal government's concern with integration and the considerable individual autonomy desired by ethnic members.

Ceremonial multiculturalism: ritualistic and symbolic forms

For the purposes of policy discussion, here we will group the ideal types of ritualistic and symbolic multiculturalism into a broader category: ceremonial multiculturalism. Although, as the previous discussion indicated, these are very different types, they both have *either* strong social structural supports *or* strong cultural supports. As the term 'ceremonial' suggests, these forms are less complete than institutional multiculturalism, for they lack either cultural or social-structural substance.

The social and psychological constraints on most Canadians make the ritualistic or symbolic forms of multiculturalism more likely to persist than the institutionalized kind. In contrast to the 'tight' sociocultural conditions required by institutionalized multiculturalism, the situation of most people in modern societies can be described as 'loose'. Not only do modern people value individual autonomy and have complicated status and role sets, but the collective expectations for performance within an ethnic group are not very binding. In terms of institutional completeness, the 'loose' designation implies that ethnic groups suggest (rather than impose) performance guidelines, which in turn are interpreted by individual members in the ways that they find most useful for their individual interests (Boldt and Roberts, 1979). It is through such a process that people living in complex social circumstances are able to articulate their roles so that they can manage the role conflicts that their circumstances entail (Coser, 1975).

Associated with the conditions of modern society are the problems of powerlessness and meaninglessness, or 'alienation'. It therefore makes sense that a connection or anchorage with an ethnic group, encouraged through a policy of multiculturalism, could help to restore some of the continuity, direction, and meaning that are apparently lacking in so many modern lives. After all, whatever meaning life has for us, it is gained through an interactive connection with some culture. However, this sense of culture and heritage must be packaged in a form that is adapted to modern people. This is exactly what symbolic multiculturalism is able to accomplish.

Symbolic multiculturalism allows members of an ethnic group to participate and benefit as members of a complex industrial society while retaining the sense that they belong to a smaller, more intimate community. In other words, members have a psychological attachment to an ethnic group that they can use as a reference group, without being constrained by full-fledged membership in it. Thus symbolic multiculturalism permits the flexibility associated with identification to an ethnic enclave without the commitment necessary for institutionalized multiculturalism. In this way members can respect their ethnic heritage without having to display behavioural allegiance to it.

Symbolic multiculturalism allows flexibility because its basis is psychological rather than social; it serves individual rather than community needs and is therefore less subject to forces beyond an individual's control. Under conditions of symbolic multiculturalism, ethnic members need not belong to a structured community that is capable of exerting systematic pressure for conformity to community standards. The important feature of symbolic multiculturalism is its voluntary quality; it can be taken or left as preference dictates. This adaptability, which exists because the connection to the ethnic heritage is symbolic rather than firmly grounded in a social structure, distinguishes symbolic from institutionalized multiculturalism. This does not mean that symbolic multiculturalism is unimportant, but it does suggest that because its expression is not embedded in a social structure, it may be less consistently displayed than is the case for institutionalized multiculturalism.

Our reading of existing multiculturalism policy suggests that symbolic multiculturalism not only is what the federal government favours but, in many instances, is all that members of ethnic groups desire. The federal government's preference for symbolic multiculturalism can be seen in the recent Act For The Preservation and Enhancement of Multiculturalism in Canada, which states that 'a policy of multiculturalism [is] designed to preserve and enhance the multicultural heritage of Canadians while working to achieve the equality of all Canadians in the economic, social, cultural and political life of Canada', and is intended to ensure 'that all individuals receive equal treatment and equal protection under the law, while respecting and valuing their diversity' (Canada, 1988). On at least two counts this statement shows a preference for symbolic multiculturalism. First, notice the emphasis on individuals (not groups), which is aligned with the modern values of individual autonomy and freedom of choice and is congruent with the Charter of Rights and Freedoms, which preserves individual rights. On the other hand, this emphasis is in direct contrast to the social-structural requirements of institutionalized multiculturalism, which emphasizes collective interests over individual ones. Second, this policy encourages the cultural dimension (i.e., 'multicultural heritage') while assuming that members of ethnic groups will participate in the dominant social structures of Canadian society (i.e., 'economic, social, cultural and political life'). Again, this is in direct contrast to the necessity of parallel social structures emphasized by institutionalized multiculturalism.

Considerable government sponsorship goes into ethnic conferences, festivals, presses, and the like, all of which are expressions of symbolic multiculturalism. These activities perpetuate the cognitive and evaluative beliefs of various cultures in such a way that members of those groups can identify with their heritages if they wish to—if they find it appropriate for adapting to non-ethnic dimensions of Canadian society. While permitting this form of adaptation by members of ethnic groups, government sponsorship of symbolic multiculturalism is not exaggerating the problem of integration. At present, support is not being given to the social structures that would give ethnic groups the permanence and organizational strength that in turn might permit them to mobilize their resources in ways that could challenge the interests either of other ethnic groups or of the country as a whole. For this reason some observers doubt the motives behind Canada's multiculturalism policy, seeing it as just another component of the government-defined social agenda (cf Peter, 1981).

In summary, given the federal government's prior interest in integration over adaptation, coupled with the interests of many ethnic group members who are more inclined to respect their culture than pay allegiance to it, it follows that, in general, symbolic multiculturalism should be given a higher policy profile than institutionalized forms. With respect to ritualistic multiculturalism the government's orientation is more complicated. Government policies toward this form of multiculturalism differ depending on whether the ritualism is active or reactive. In the 'active' case, the development of allegiance to ethnic social organizations is the principal aim of the ethnic group. This occurs, for example, where an ethnic group is actively recruiting and socializing new members. In this case it may be inducing recruits to follow the interaction patterns of the community even before the larger symbolic significance of these activities is clear to these potential new members. This active orientation on the part of an ethnic community is likely to receive a neutral response in terms of multiculturalism policy. That is, although the government is unlikely to sponsor the development of parallel ethnic organizations, it does not discourage such development and allegiance when the initiative and resources are generated by the ethnic group itself.

But the policy of multiculturalism engenders a different response when ritualism in ethnic communities is reactive in nature. One way to conceptualize ritualistic multiculturalism is to think of it as a disjunction between an individual's membership and reference groups; that is, ritualistic multiculturalism occurs when people participate in an ethnic group (i.e., have membership) but cognitively and affectively orient themselves to some non-ethnic (i.e., reference) group. When this situation occurs for reactive reasons—when it is not the intention of the ethnic group but occurs as a reaction to the social-structural circumstances in which it is embedded—multiculturalism policy strongly discourages the result. A classic instance of this is segregation based on prejudice and discrimination towards an ethnic group on the part of the surrounding culture. Under these circumstances the ethnic group remains bound within its own organizational structures, even though it would prefer not to be. It is this reactive, ritualistic multiculturalism that the government's policy disapproves of in its goal to 'promote the full and equitable participation of individuals and communities of all origins in the continuing evolution and shaping of all aspects of Canadian society and assist them in the elimination of any barrier to such participation' (Canada, 1988, 3(1)C). To summarize, in neither the active nor the reactive instances of ritualistic multiculturalism is the government's policy supportive. However, it shows more tolerance of active, ritualistic multiculturalism (by remaining neutral) than it does of reactive forms, which it seeks to sanction.

SOME RELATED IMPLICATIONS

So far we have used the sociological concepts of culture and social structure to generate three ideal types of multiculturalism, each of which we have discussed in terms of adaptation and integration. The issue of adaptation has been addressed in terms of the kinds of commitment mechanisms an ethnic group would employ, under each ideal type of multiculturalism, in order to mobilize its community and perpetuate its heritage. By contrast, the integration issue is the government's principal concern, and therefore each type of multiculturalism has been addressed in terms of the policy implications it has for this issue. In this final section we will discuss substantive issues, specifically the relations between multiculturalism and freedom, self-respect, and instrumental/expressive policy orientations.

Multiculturalism and freedom

In 1971, under Pierre Trudeau's leadership, Canada announced its policy of 'multiculturalism within a bilingual framework'. From the outset this policy was tied to the value of 'freedom', as indicated by the following excerpts from the Prime Minister's statement to the House of Commons: 'A policy of multiculturalism within a bilingual framework commends itself to the government as the most suitable means of assuring the cultural freedom of Canadians. Such a policy should help break down discriminatory attitudes and cultural jealousies . . . the government will assist members of all cultural groups to overcome cultural barriers to full participation in Canadian society' (Trudeau, 1971). This concern with freedom endures in Bill C-93, the Multiculturalism Act, which 'reflects the cultural and racial diversity of Canadian society and acknowledges the freedom of all members of Canadian society to preserve, enhance, and share their cultural heritage' (Canada, 1988). The conclusion we reached, that the federal government is more concerned with symbolic than institutionalized multiculturalism, is supported by these expressions of how the government has intended multiculturalism to relate to freedom.

To appreciate this linkage we need to think in terms of two distinctive characterizations of freedom, labelled 'negative' and 'positive' (Nettler, 1989: 231). These traditional conceptions of freedom, in turn, can be translated into statements about rights and obligations. In the case of multiculturalism, it is useful to examine the issue from the viewpoint of 'obligations' on the part of the government and 'rights' on the part of members of ethnic groups.

Negative freedom, sometimes conceptualized as 'freedom from', has to do with liberating people from unjust or discriminatory treatment; preventing discriminatory hiring practices is an example. In this type of freedom the government has a 'negative obligation' and ethnic groups have 'negative rights'. The government's obligations are 'negative' in the sense that it is government's duty to prevent certain things from occurring—in this instance, unjust hiring. From the ethnic groups' viewpoint, their reciprocal right is negative in that they can demand that such discriminatory practices desist. In short, negative rights and obligations centre on doing away with certain undesirable things.

Building upon the minimalist requirements of negative freedom, positive freedom has to do with enabling or assisting people to pursue their interests; that is, with positive rights and obligations.[6] A multiculturalism policy concerned with this type of freedom would obligate government to provide resources that would empower ethnic groups to pursue and express their interests and, in turn, ethnic groups would have a positive right to claim such resources. It is in this sense that positive freedom becomes synonymous with the provision of what is needed to pursue distinctive cultural orientations.

The Canadian government's policy statements on multiculturalism seem to express a greater concern with negative than with positive freedom; they suggest that the government is interested in assuring that ethnic groups and their members are not inhibited from expressing their cultural orientations, as long as these orientations are consistent with the existing institutionalized social structures. This negative freedom is interpreted by the government as extending into both the cultural and social structural domains. That is, within certain broad limits, the government sees itself as obligated to ensure not only that the expression of a wide range of different values, norms, beliefs, and behaviours is permitted, but that it is made clear to ethnic-group members that they have these negative rights.

In contrast, the government's commitment to positive freedom is not nearly so unqualified. In the relevant policy statements the implicit understanding is that multiculturalism does not extend to positive obligations and rights in either the cultural or the social-structural domains. At most, the government's position appears to be that its positive obligation extends only into the sponsorship of cultural activities. In words and deeds it is much more reluctant to accept a positive obligation to underwrite such things as ethnically based political, health-care, or educational systems. There are few instances in which the government has perceived an obligation to supply the resources that an ethnic group requires in order to mobilize its community. In short, the government does not see its responsibility as extending to providing extensive support to ethnic social structures. It is this downplaying of social-structural obligations that suggests that the government is more committed to symbolic than to institutionalized forms of multiculturalism. If this assessment is correct, we would expect to see the government both allowing and underwriting ethnic cultural expressions, but only allowing (not supporting) the development of ethnic organizations. Of course, this conclusion is not likely to be shared by members of those ethnic groups in which institutionalized multiculturalism is the goal. Members of these groups would be expected to, and do, interpret the multiculturalism policy as extending to positive rights in both the cultural and social-structural realms.

Multiculturalism and self-respect

As we noted, Canada is a modern, pluralistic society. One particular social issue associated with many pluralistic societies is a sense of alienation among significant proportions of citizens. Complex societies are characterized by powerful, large-scale public institutions that dominate individuals. Given such institutional arrangements, many people feel detached or estranged from the society's institutional structures, whether government agencies, private corporations, or educational institutions. This alienation expresses itself in the well-documented forms of powerlessness, meaninglessness, normlessness, isolation, and self-estrangement (Seeman, 1959). The scale of organizational arrangements in complex societies is further complicated by the ethos of competitive individualism that underwrites much of their institutional activity. Taken together, the competitive megastructures of modern society breed widespread feelings of alienation that, in turn, make the maintenance of self-respect difficult (Roberts, 1985).

Self-respect—a person's feelings of worthiness or value—is a fundamental human attribute (Rawls, 1971), founded in the character of our interaction with those around us. When people are unable to relate meaningfully to the social structure and culture in which their activity takes place, feelings of alienation increase and self-respect becomes more difficult to maintain. The policy of multiculturalism may enhance individual self-respect, since ethnic groups and organizations constitute 'mediating institutions', which 'stand between the individual in his private life and the larger institutions of public life' (Berger and Neuhaus, 1977: 2). They are of a size such that people can both contribute to them and be directly influenced by their activity. People can 'make a difference' to organizations of this scale, and because members are sympathetic to the values that underlie them, they provide ample opportunity to become engaged, to feel less alienated, and to participate in a community supporting their self-respect. This result becomes possible because we are social creatures whose mutual interdependence has important implications for the creation and preservation of self-respect. Our images of ourselves are constructed, in large part, from the information provided us by others, and the respect of others is a symbolic reward that is provided when they value us and think we matter.

In short, by encouraging any or all of the three ideal types of multiculturalism, multiculturalism policy provides opportunities for the enhancement of self-respect. By encouraging self-respect, multiculturalism also promotes more tolerant inter-group relations. As Rawls (1971: 441) notes: 'The more someone experiences his own way of life as . . . fulfilling, the more likely he is to welcome attainments by others.' In short, security about one's self-respect is a prerequisite for supporting the self-respect of others through appreciation of their beliefs and behaviours. To the extent that members of ethnic groups can engender the latter, they add to the 'social capital' (Coleman, 1988) that makes society operate more successfully.

Multiculturalism as instrumental or expressive social policy

As noted previously, there are many interpretations of what the government policy of multiculturalism means, leading many observers to conclude that this policy is vague. This vagueness has given rise to considerable speculation about the 'true' agenda that the federal government has in sponsoring this policy. To understand, and join, this debate, it helps to appreciate the distinction between instrumental and expressive actions.

Government policy is a form of action that, like others, can vary on a continuum ranging from instrumental to expressive. Instrumental actions are 'rational' to the extent that they are concerned with the efficiency and effectiveness of achieving some identifiable goals. By contrast, expressive actions are guided by considerations of affect and value, and consequently are directed at expressing moral sentiments (Roberts, forthcoming).

To date, considerable criticism of multiculturalism policy has been developed from the assumption that this policy is an instrumental form of action. One strand of this criticism is forwarded by neo-Marxist observers (among others), who note that a vague policy couched in ambiguous language easily diverts attention from more salient social concerns, and allows the government a degree of freedom to pursue a hidden agenda. Some observers claim, for instance, that keeping the goals of the policy intentionally vague permits the government to interpret and reinterpret the policy at will, and thus allows it to placate and manipulate ethnic groups for their own purposes. As Kallen (1982: 55) reports: 'the policy served as a technique of domination which legitimated and entrenched powers of the ruling Anglo elite when its super-ordinate national position was threatened by Quebec's claim to political power, on the one hand, and by the growing numerical and economic strength and increasing cultural vitality of immigrant ethnic collectives, on the other hand.' Although this kind of interpretation has a lengthy history, dating back at least to René Lévesque's vehement attacks on the policy, it is not the only way to account for the policy's ambiguity. Two other interpretations, one instrumental and one expressive, also deserve mention.

An alternative instrumental interpretation of the ambiguity of multiculturalism policy is that the government required a statement that would capture the nature of the existing cultural realities. In other words, it may be that the existing forms of ethnic expression in Canada were sufficiently diverse that any commitment to a particular kind of multiculturalism would risk alienating some groups. After all, when the policy was formulated some ethnic groups were assimilated to a considerable degree, while others, like the Hutterites, retained considerable institutionalized multiculturalism, and others still exhibited symbolic and ritualistic multiculturalism. It may be that in an honest effort to develop a policy that would accommodate such a broad array of ethnic expressions, a vague statement emerged.

This observation does not, of course, place the ambiguity of the present policy beyond criticism, especially by those (like ourselves) who believe that government policies should specify objectives, for the simple reason that evaluation becomes impossible without such specification. This benign interpretation does, however, help us to understand the potential political prudence behind the form that the policy has taken, without imputing a cynical motive to the government's action.

Finally, it may be that to see the government's multiculturalism policy in means/ends terms is less appropriate than to view it in expressive terms. Following the distinction between instrumental and expressive actions, it may be that the government did not ever have a specific set of goals that it wanted to achieve with this policy. Perhaps it only desired to 'make a statement' proclaiming the virtue of multiculturalism. Just as it is fruitless to try to make rational sense of a person who is, for example, 'jumping for joy', perhaps it is similarly inappropriate to try and understand what the government is 'trying to achieve' with this policy. If the policy is indeed principally expressive, we would expect it to appear vague and ambiguous from an instrumental perspective.

Again, the point here is not to suggest which interpretation, instrumental or expressive, is correct. It is clear that Canada's multicultural policy is ambiguous and, barring further clarification by the government, will remain subject to alternative interpretations. Our point is to underline that reasonable differences of opinion about the intention of this policy are possible, and consequently no single interpretation can legitimately claim priority.

CONCLUSION

In this paper we have used a sociological perspective to examine the policy of multiculturalism in Canada. In closing we wish to note the distinction between the ideas of cultural diversity (cultural pluralism) and multiculturalism. Cultural pluralism is a descriptive concept, while multiculturalism is an evaluative one. Where the signs of ethnic diversity are to be found in empirical enumerations of the number and size of various ethnic groups, the referents of multiculturalism are ideological. In Magsino and Singh's (1986: 80) terms, 'multiculturalism . . . as an *ism* can be literally defined as "adherence to a system or a theory which values having many cultures within a society". As such it conceptually incorporates the component of valuing of or a preference for the existence, maintenance, and extension of individual cultures.' The relevance of this distinction is that it reminds us that just because Canada is ethnically diverse, it does not follow that it is a multicultural society. Multiculturalism involves a policy commitment supported by sponsorship of programs. One thing we have suggested in this paper is that the policy commitment may be conceptualized in terms of the three ideal types of multiculturalism. Moreover, the various forms of multiculturalism have quite different meanings that, in turn, imply different sorts of commitment on the part of both the ethnic groups and the government.

It follows that to judge whether or how well multiculturalism is working in Canada is difficult, since it involves specifying the type of multiculturalism in question. In Canada it seems that all forms of multiculturalism, as well as assimilation, are in operation, some with greater vigour than others. Our reading of government policy statements, including the new Multiculturalism Act, is that the government does not have a singular commitment to one form of multiculturalism. It does appear, however, to set a lower priority on 'institutionalized multiculturalism' than on other types.

Our goal has been to outline a typology useful for the understanding and critical appraisal of Canadian multiculturalism. This framework is clearly only a first approximation and excludes many relevant variables and considerations. However, we believe it represents a useful starting point for comprehending what the government proudly asserts is 'the first national multiculturalism act anywhere . . . one of our finest achievements' (Weiner, n.d.). It may be the first act of its kind, but whether the inter-ethnic reality it seeks to shape is 'one of our finest achievements' remains a question that should be determined by informed appraisal—not left to government declaration.

NOTES

The authors acknowledge the careful reading and contribution of E.D. Boldt, B. Ferguson, J. Young, and the editor to the development of this chapter.

[1]This abbreviated comparison of simple and complex societies is descriptive, not evaluative. That is, these contrasts say nothing about the correlation between modernization and the quality of life in the society. In fact, the roster of social problems and psychological dissatisfactions in modern societies is so long that some students of society suggest that the relationship between quality of life and social complexity is inverse.

[2]This conceptualization of adaptation and integration is simply a restatement of the 'order problem' that underlies sociological thinking. This issue recognizes that people are *both* independent (free, autonomous) *and* interdependent (constrained). Given these conditions of existence, it is impossible to 'maximize' either individual freedom or social order, since doing so fails to recognize the simultaneous existence of both these social facts. Instead, the appropriate course is to find a means of 'optimizing' (i.e., getting enough of) both individual freedom and social order. Breton, Reitz, and Valentine (1980) provide a Canadian assessment of this fundamental issue as it applies to ethnicity.

[3]The importance of the integration issue is highlighted by the social disorder that occurs in pluralistic societies when ethnic groups pursue their interests without regard for others (e.g., Spain, South Africa, etc.).

[4]'Social system', or 'sociocultural system', as it is sometimes called—refers to the regularized patterns of interaction displayed by persons occupying social statuses and playing social roles. The 'regularity' or 'pattern' observed

in such systems is attributed to both the 'cultural' and the 'social structural' features of the system.

[5]Restricting the labels and discussion of Figure 6.1 to the four identified types is done for heuristic purposes, following the notion of 'ideal types'. The empirical types of ethnic groups can, as the figure suggests, occur anywhere within this conceptual space.

[6]Narveson (1988: 60) provides the following succinct distinction between negative and positive rights: '(1) if person A has a negative right to do X, then others have a correlative duty to refrain from interfering with A's doing X. . . . By contrast, (2) if person A has a positive right to do X, then others have a correlative duty not merely to refrain from doing things prohibited by (1) but also to do something to help A to do X, if A is unable to do X unaided.'

REFERENCES

Anderson, Alan B., and James S. Frideres
1981 *Ethnicity in Canada: Theoretical Perspectives*. Toronto: Butterworths.

Appleton, N.
1982 'Democracy and Cultural Pluralism'. In D. Kerr, ed., *Proceedings of the 38th Annual Meeting of the Philosophy of Education Society (US)*

Berger, Brigitte
1971 *Societies In Change: An Introduction to Comparative Sociology*. New York: Basic Books.

Berger, Peter, and Richard Neuhaus
1977 *To Empower People: The Role of Mediating Structures in Public Policy*. Washington, DC: American Enterprise Institute.

Boldt, Edward
1989 'The Hutterites: Current Developments and Future Prospects'. Pp.57-71 in James S. Friederes, ed., *Multiculturalism and Intergroup Relations*. New York: Greenwood Press.

Boldt, Edward D., and Lance W. Roberts
1979 'Structural Tightness and Social Conformity'. *Journal of Cross-Cultural Psychology* 10 (2): 221-30.

Bredemeier, Harry C., and Richard M. Stephenson
1962 *The Analysis of Social Systems*. New York: Holt, Rinehart, and Winston.

Breton, Raymond
1964 'Institutional Completeness of Ethnic Communities and the Personal Relations of Immigrants'. *American Journal of Sociology* 70: 193-205.

Breton, Raymond, Jeffrey G. Reitz, and Victor Valentine
1980 *Cultural Boundaries and the Cohesion of Canada*. Montreal: Institute For Research on Public Policy.

Brotz, Howard
1980 'Multiculturalism in Canada: A Muddle'. *Canadian Public Policy* (1): 41-6.

Canada
1988 The House of Commons of Canada, Bill C-93, The Multiculturalism Act, July 12, 1988.

Coleman, James S.
1988 'Social Capital in the Creation of Human Capital'. *American Journal of Sociology* 94 Supplement: S95-S120.

Coser, Lewis A.
1974 *Greedy Institutions: Patterns of Undivided Commitment*. New York: Free Press.

Coser, Rose Laub
1961 'Insulation from Observability and Types of Social Conformity'. *American Sociological Review* 26: 28-39.
1975 'The Complexity of Roles as a Seedbed of Individual Autonomy'. Pp. 237-63 in Lewis A. Coser, ed., *The Idea of Social Structure*. New York: Harcourt, Brace and Jovanovich.

Gans, Herbert
1979 'Symbolic Ethnicity: The Future of Ethnic Groups Cultures in America.' *Ethnic and Racial Studies* 2 (1): 1-20.

Geertz, Clifford
1973 *The Interpretation of Cultures*. New York: Basic Books.

House, James S.
1981 'Social Structure and Personality'. Pp. 525-61 in M. Rosenberg and R.H. Turner, eds, *Social Psychology: Sociological Perspectives*. New York: Basic Books.

Inkeles, Alex, and D. Smith
1974 *Becoming Modern: Individual Change in Six Developing Countries*. Cambridge, Mass: Harvard University Press.

Kallen, E.
1982 'Multiculturalism: Ideology, Policy and Reality'. *Journal of Canadian Studies* 17 (1): 51-63.

Kanter, Rosabeth M.
1968 'Commitment and Social Organization: A Study of Commitment Mechanisms in Utopian Societies'. *American Sociological Review* 33 (4): 499-517.

Kohn, M.L., and C. Schooler
1979 'The Reciprocal Effects of the Substantive Complexity of Work and Intellectual Flexibility: A Longitudinal Assessment'. *American Journal of Sociology* 84: 24-52.

Kornhauser, Ruth R.
1978 *Social Sources of Delinquency: An Analytic Appraisal of Models*. Chicago: University of Chicago Press.

Kroeber, A.L., and T. Parsons
1958 'The Concepts of Culture and of Social System'. *American Sociological Review* 23: 582-3.

Kwong, Peter
1987 *The New Chinatown*. New York: Hill & Wang.
Lachenmeyer, Charles W.
1971 *The Language of Sociology*. New York: Columbia University Press.
Magsino, Romulo, and A. Singh
1986 *Toward Multicultural Education in Newfoundland and Labrador*. Phase I Report for the Secretary of State Department.
Mayes, Robert G.
1982 'Contemporary Inuit Society'. *Musk-Ox* 30: 36-47.
Mazurek, Kas
1987 'Multiculturalism, Education and the Ideology of Meritocracy'. Pp.141-63 in Terry Wotherspoon, ed., *The Political Economy of Canadian Schooling*. Toronto: Methuen.
Narveson, Jan
1988 'Liberalism and Public Education'. *Interchange* 19 (1): 60-9.
Nettler, Gwynne
1989 *Criminology Lessons*. Cincinnati, Ohio: Anderson Publishing.
Nisbet, Robert
1966 *The Sociological Tradition*. New York: Basic Books.
Patterson, Orlando
1977 *Ethnic Chauvinism: The Reactionary Impulse*. New York: Stein and Day.
Peter, Karl
1981 'The Myth of Multiculturalism and Other Political Fables.' Pp. 56-67 in J. Dahlie and T.Fernando, eds, *Ethnicity, Power and Politics in Canada*. Toronto: Methuen.
Rawls, John
1971 *A Theory of Justice*. Cambridge: Harvard University Press.
Roberts, Lance W.
1985 'Social Change and Self-respect: A Case for Multiculturalism'. *Canadian Home Economics Journal* 35 (4): 184-94.
'Clinical Sociology with Individuals and Families'. In J.G. Bruhn and H. Rebach, eds, *Handbook of Clinical Sociology*. New York: Plenum (forthcoming).
Roberts, Lance W., and Edward D. Boldt
1979 'Institutional Completeness and Ethnic Assimilation'. *Journal of Ethnic Studies* 7 (2): 103-8.
Scott, John F.
1971 *Internalization of Norms: A Sociological Theory of Moral Commitment*. Englewood Cliffs, NJ: Prentice Hall.
Seeman, Melvin
1959 'On the Meaning of Alienation.' *American Sociological Review* 24 (6): 783-91.
Smith, Earl J.
1983 'Canadian Multiculturalism: The Solution or the Problem'. Pp. 260-75 in Dan Landis and Richard W. Brislin, eds, *Handbook of Intercultural Training*. Vol. 3. Willowdale, Ont.: Pergammon Press.

Tepperman, Lorne
1989 *Choices and Chances*. Toronto: Holt, Rinehart and Winston.

Theodorson, G.A., and A.G. Theodorson
1969 *A Modern Dictionary of Sociology*. New York: Barnes and Noble.

Trudeau, Pierre E.
1971 Statement by the Prime Minister in the House of Commons. 8 October 1971. Reprinted pp. 518-20 in J.R. Mallea and J.C. Young, eds, *Cultural Diversity and Canadian Education: Issues and Innovations*. Ottawa: Carleton University Press.

Vallee, Frank
1988 'Inequality and Identity in Multiethnic Societies'. In D. Forcese and S. Richer, eds, *Social Issues: Sociological Views of Canada*. Scarborough, Ont.: Prentice-Hall Inc.

Wallace, Walter L.
1983 *Principles of Scientific Sociology*. New York: Aldine.

Weiner, Gerry
n.d. Message from Gerry Weiner, Minister of State For Multiculturalism.

SEVEN

THE POLITICS OF LANGUAGE

WILFRID B. DENIS

INTRODUCTION

Cleavages of class, gender, and race or ethnicity probably underlie nearly all of the most salient social tensions and conflicts in Canada's history, including those over language. Given Canada's historical origins and development, language issues and subsequent policies have been primarily Eurocentric. Except for an earlier interlude of Nordic languages in Newfoundland, French and English were the first non-aboriginal languages in what is now Canada, and though occasionally aboriginal languages and other non-French/non-English languages surface in language policy, their claims remain secondary in Canada's history, and in the following pages.

Language issues ultimately revolve around language loss, or assimilation; language laws and policies have generally sought to either impose or prevent language transfer among one group or another. The fact that language has now replaced religion as the focal point in English-French relations (McCrae, 1974) emphasizes that underlying the question of language is the more fundamental and encompassing question of cultural survival. The recognition of language rights implies the right to exist as an ethno-cultural entity with the protection of law and with government authority and support; conversely, rejection of the first as a right implies rejection of the second as well.

This explains why most sociological literature on language groups attaches so much importance to questions of language shift and language maintenance. However, these phenomena are also influenced by class. (An even more complete analysis should also consider gender, although this will not be attempted here.) Social class as an explanatory factor poses problems for the prevailing view of a symmetrical relationship between Canada's major linguistic groups, in which a French numerical majority with an anglophone minority in Quebec is the counterpart to an English majority with a francophone minority in the rest of Canada.[1] Examination of the class structure of these four groups is essential in explaining the nature and outcome of language conflicts, and reveals that the symmetrical view of Canada is primarily a convenient ideological distortion.

HISTORICAL ORIGINS OF LANGUAGE ISSUES

1. *Aboriginal languages*

Canadian aboriginal languages received very little legal or juridical recognition, if any, until the 1970s. From their earliest contact, interest in aboriginal languages among European settlers has generally been limited to the transmission of Christian religious beliefs, or to obtaining access to natural resources and cheap labour. The implicit, and very often explicit, policy on Native languages by white government, religious organizations, and private firms has been that of total assimilation to either English or French. White recognition and use of aboriginal languages was intended primarily to facilitate missionary activity and to further all forms of subjugation of these people. This was clearly a policy of cultural genocide. Aboriginal languages in the courts were restricted to access to interpreters (Sheppard, 1971: 164-85). It is only in the last ten to fifteen years that they have been recognized as languages of instruction in some schools, as languages worthy of public forums such as the Berger enquiry into the Mackenzie, and for public agreements such as the James Bay and Northern Quebec Agreements in 1975, and as official languages of the Northwest Territories (Braen, 1987: 97; Didier, 1987: 325; Jull, 1983: 37). Consequently aboriginal languages are seldom included in discussions on language rights even today.

2. *Official languages*

If governments, academics, and the private sector rarely focus their attention on aboriginal linguistic rights, however, such has not been the case with European languages. Since Canada was settled initially from France and then England, our linguistic policies have always centred on English and French, and more specifically on the survival of the latter. The early economic and military conflicts between these two imperial powers and their allies spilled over to their colonies.

Excluding military confrontations, the first major policy reflecting differences in language and religion occurred at the outset of the Seven Years War. In 1755, the Acadians of what is now Nova Scotia were ruthlessly deported by the English, with subsequent deportations over the next few years from Cape Breton and Isle St Jean (Prince Edward Island), and the transfer of Acadian property to English settlers. From 1749 to the 1970s, English was the only official language of the Maritimes including Newfoundland, as well as British Columbia, except for the federal courts under section 133 of the BNA Act of 1867 (Sheppard, 1971: 5-8, 90-1, 303).

Other Franco-English military conflicts along the St Lawrence valley and the Great Lakes culminated in the famous battle of the Plains of Abraham in 1759 and the Treaty of Paris of 1763. The period of military rule from 1760 to 1763 set out the basis for the linguistic and religious tensions that persist to the present. A handful of British merchants and some colonial officials demanded that the Catholic religion, the French language, and all French institutions be replaced with those of England. Thus the Proclamation of 1763 and the subsequent Ordinances were a deliberate policy of religious and linguistic assimilation against the Canadiens. However, Canadien resistance, the persistence of French institutions, the failure to attract large numbers of English settlers, and the pragmatic considerations of administering 80,000 Canadiens with less than a few hundred English citizens led to the formal abandonment of such policies in the Quebec Act of 1774. This act repealed the Proclamation of 1763, recognized French property and civil law along with English criminal law, removed restrictions to the admission of Catholics to official positions, and implicitly recognized the continued use of French in the courts and the publication of Ordinances in both English and French (ibid.: 15)

The Constitutional Act of 1791, which separated Lower and Upper Canada following the large-scale immigration of American Loyalists, had little impact on the use of and recognition of French in Lower Canada, although it recognized English as the language of justice and government for Upper Canada. Nevertheless, the increasing numbers of English-speaking settlers fostered renewed calls for assimilation of the Canadiens.

Continued discord in the Canadas, culminating in the Rebellions of Lower and Upper Canada in 1837-38, led to the suspension of the Legislative Assembly of Lower Canada and its replacement by an appointed Special Council composed of English members. Another outcome was the appointment of Lord Durham to investigate the situation. His report called upon Britain to institute responsible government (i.e., to make the executive responsible to the legislature), to unite the two Canadas with the express purpose of anglicizing the French Canadians, 'and to establish an English population, with English laws and language in this Province [i.e., Lower Canada], and to trust its government to none but a decidedly English Legislature' (in Sheppard, 1971: 55).

Durham's report lead to the Act of Union of 1840, which reunited the two Canadas under a new common legislature. In an action reminiscent of the 1763 Proclamation, this act imposed English as the only language of the legislature, although the courts remained unaffected. However, even in the legislature the French fought back over many years to reintroduce official bilingualism, and to have the offending section 41 of the act repealed. These efforts culminated in the official recognition of French in the British North America Act of 1867, whose section 133 allows the use of French or English in the federal Parliament and the Legislature of Quebec, in all federal courts as well as in those of Quebec, and requires that the laws, records, and journals of both these Houses be printed in both languages. Section 133 reverses the intent of the Act of Union by recognizing in fact the usage of French. It is also an indirect acknowledgment of French Canadian resistance and resilience since 1759 in spite of several very conscious and determined efforts to make them disappear (ibid.: 55-69).

After 1867 there were few attempts to deal with language through legislation in Quebec. In 1910 the Lavergne Law required 'public utility companies to place the French version alongside the English one in printed matter sent to customers', and in 1937 the Duplessis Law granted priority to French in interpreting certain laws, but the outcry by anglophones was such that the law was rescinded the following year (Laporte, 1983: 92). There was no further movement on language until 1961.

In Ontario the impact of section 133 was minimal. For francophones in Ontario or anywhere else outside Quebec, education has been the major area of concern, and under the BNA Act, it falls under provincial jurisdiction. Francophones in Ontario expressed other preoccupations regarding language apart from education, but little movement was obtained from provincial governments until the 1970s and after.

Manitoba was created in 1870 following the armed resistance of the Red River Métis, who were in majority French Catholic. Section 23 of the Manitoba Act was analogous to section 133 of the BNA Act. In spite of this official recognition of French, the Manitoba Legislature 'adopted in 1890 an Act declaring English to be the only official language of legislation and the courts (Braen, 1987: 28).

Political and juridical structures for the remainder of the North-

West Territories were officially established with the North-West Territories Act of 1875, where no mention is made of language. An amendment in 1877, which became section 110, allowed for the use of both French and English in the Council, the courts, and in the journals and records of the Council, and required the Ordinances to be printed in both languages. In 1892, an amendment proposed by F. Haultain was passed, in spite of opposition, to record and publish the proceedings of the Legislative Assembly in English only. Although this resolution never received royal assent, so that in effect it has been without force, and in spite of the fact that the amendment touched only on the publication of Assembly proceedings, in practice the Territorial government and the subsequent governments of Alberta and Saskatchewan prevented the use of French in the provincial courts, the Legislature, and its records from 1892 to 1988 (Denis and Li, 1988). Much the same situation prevailed in the North-West Territories and the Yukon, although French could be required in the courts, since these were under federal jurisdiction (see Sheppard, 1971: 303-4; 312).

After reviewing extensively language jurisdiction and law in Canada, from the 1700s to the 1960s, for the Bilingualism and Biculturalism Commission, Sheppard (1971: 105) stated:

> The BNA Act itself is totally unsatisfactory and does not even provide minimum guarantees to either the French or the English minorities in Canada. Such linguistic rights as exist . . . will be found to be based on custom, practical considerations, or political expediency. When they are embodied in provincial or federal statutes, they can be abrogated at will.

He concluded (ibid.: 313):

> there are only two jurisdictions in which there is no doubt that both languages enjoy almost equal official status: the federal and Quebec jurisdictions . . . it just does not make sense that New Brunswick, 35.2 percent of whose population is French-speaking, should be unilingually English while Quebec, whose English population is only 13.26% of the total and mainly centered on the island of Montreal, is totally bilingual.

3. *Education*

After official recognition in statutes, the legislature, and the judiciary, education is the most controversial area of language use. Initially, education issues centred around religion, although implicitly 'Catholic' meant French as well, and 'Protestant' meant English.

Prior to 1867, denominational Catholic and Protestant schools had been established in Upper and Lower Canada, and section 93 of the BNA Act recognized the rights of denominational schools in existence when a province joined Confederation. In Quebec language and religion coincided to a great extent, so that religious protection *de jure* also produced linguistic protection in fact. But in other provinces this was less the case, although the argument was made that linguistic rights were implicit in section 93. In 1917 the Privy Council ruled 'that the separate schools were based on denominational and not linguistic differences' and that consequently confessional schools could not guarantee any particular language (Sheppard, 1971: 68). From 1917 to 1982, language rights in education were relegated to provincial jurisdiction.

In Quebec two fairly autonomous education systems developed fairly early in the 1850s (Laurendeau and Dunton, 1968: 25-38). From then up to 1964, separate Protestant and Catholic education committees each reported directly to cabinet, although there were some variations in this structure for rather brief periods. The committees' autonomy allowed the Protestant population to control programming, teacher training, taxation rates, and all other matters pertinent to their education needs. As a result, 'an impressive English-language minority school system has been established in Quebec, through the public schools out of tax funds. It has been administered by English-speaking Protestants for English-speaking children in the province, and has thus reflected the aims and aspirations of the minority. Protestant boards even benefitted from the taxes from most non-Catholic ratepayers, whether they were Protestant or not' (ibid.: 32-3). The Catholic system also served the English Catholics although English was used as the language of instruction in their schools and the Catholic school inspectors were vigilant in ensuring fair treatment of this linguistic minority (ibid.: 34)

In the Maritimes, after the Acadians returned, French was tolerated generally but not officially recognized as a language of instruction; nor did it receive any specific administrative support. In some instances an Acadian school inspector might be appointed, but up to the 1960s Acadian education suffered from a lack of official recognition and legislative protection, as well as adequate funding, programs, teacher training, and administrative support (ibid.: 98-114). Only in 1968 were some reforms on the horizon, especially in New Brunswick, but it will take years and countless efforts by Acadians for these to materialize.

In Ontario anti-French and anti-Catholic sentiment led the government in 1912 to adopt Regulation 17, which reduced the use of French as a language of instruction to insignificance. Although the regulation was revoked in 1927, the lack of access, of quality, of financing, and of control over francophone education remained a major source of controversy well into the 1980s.

In 1871 Manitoba had set up a dual system of education similar to

Quebec's, with separate Catholic and Protestant sections each under its own superintendent (ibid.: 45). But twenty years later anti-French and anti-Catholic sentiment pushed for one national school system. 'Accordingly, in 1890, at the same time as the official use of the French language was abolished in the legislative assembly, the civil service, and the courts, the dual system of education was replaced by a non-denominational system under a single board of Education' (ibid.). The ensuing controversy over the next few years produced the Laurier-Greenway compromise in 1897, which did not change the system but allowed for the hiring of Roman Catholic teachers to teach Roman Catholic students. It also allowed religious instruction after regular school hours, and some predominantly Catholic schools were able to obtain government and municipal funding, although this proved to be more of a problem for English Catholic schools in Winnipeg (Comeault, 1979; Staples, 1974). Since this compromise had also allowed the use of French or any other language along with English as languages of instruction, the influx of large numbers of immigrants seemed to strain the education system considerably. Consequently, the government unilaterally abolished the use of any language other than English in Manitoba schools in 1916.

Saskatchewan and Alberta followed much the same path. From a situation where French was accepted as a language of instruction on the same basis as English in the Territories in the 1870s, this recognition was gradually reduced over the years as controversies flared up and died. In Saskatchewan English became the only language of instruction in 1918 except for schools where the local board approved the use of French for grade one and for one hour in other grades. In 1931 English was made the sole language of instruction, although French could still be taught as a subject for one hour a day. This situation remained largely unchanged until 1968 in both Saskatchewan (Denis and Li, 1988) and Alberta (Laurendeau and Dunton, 1968: 118).

In British Columbia, the lack of denominational schools meant that French-Canadians could not regroup within Catholic institutions. Instead, they opted for their own private schools, a common arrangement in other provinces as well.

4. *Minority reaction*

Anglophones in Quebec can hardly be considered a minority during this period. The presence and support of Great Britain's imperial government gave the small number of English citizens a tremendous amount of political power, a power that gradually congealed into economic power as well. It is true that the Durhamites did not obtain the exclusive use of English institutions and language. But failure to obtain such imperialistic and genocidal policies does not reduce their proponents to minority status. The fact that as late as 1937 anglophone protest forced the Quebec government to back down from some very mild language legislation indicates the political power of a dominant group, not that of a minority.

The reaction of francophones to their loss of linguistic rights was as strong as it could be, given their minority status and very often their lack of support from the federal government or other major institutions including, in some instances, the Catholic Church. Without going into detail for each province, certain common forms of action appear. First, associations were created to try to defend minority rights at the provincial level. As new needs were identified, new organizations were established, whether for school trustees, to train or recruit teachers, or to foster economic or cultural development. French organizations assumed the responsibility of providing a French school curriculum from grades one to twelve, since the provincial authorities were unwilling to do so. Where necessary and possible, private schools were established. Alliances were formed with other minorities to defend religious and other rights. Francophones also tried to defend their rights in the courts. However, court cases, even if successful in the first instance, had no long-term or global effect on the official status of French, as provincial governments refused to acknowledge any such claim (Blay, 1989: 188-9; Denis and Li, 1988: 357). Francophones also established their own newspapers and communications systems, including radio stations. And of course they lobbied governments continously with petitions, letters, briefs, meetings, and attempts to get members on appropriate government bodies (Blay, 1989; Comeault, 1979; Denis and Li, 1988). On occasion, more spectacular actions—such as withdrawing children from school for several days in protest against school-board decisions—were required to obtain results (Denis and Li, 1988: 359-60). But all in all, the period from 1890 to 1970 was one of endless defensive struggle, with meagre resources and little economic or political power to prevent further erosion of minority rights and guarantee access to French institutions and language. Ultimately, the lack of adequate minority education facilities and services proved especially detrimental to francophones (Laurendeau and Dunton, 1968: 39-52,73-127). Without a changing climate in the dominant society, francophone minorities alone would not have succeeded in bringing about significant change.

The cost of these assimilationist policies was very high for most of the French Canadian minorities outside Quebec. Their assimilation rate increased significantly over the years. The Bilingualism and Biculturalism Commission reported that these rates varied from a low of 5 per cent in New Brunswick to a high of 50 per cent in British Columbia in 1931, but that by 1961 they had increased to 12 per cent and 65 per cent respectively, with Newfoundland reporting the highest rate of language loss at 85 per cent (Laurendeau and Dunton, 1967: 33, Table 7).

However, according to Joy (1971: 35) even these figures were much too optimistic since they focused on the apparent rather than the actual rate of language loss, thus hiding generational differences. If one considers the youngest age group, 0 - 4 years, who will carry the mother tongue into the next generation, the rate of language loss for British Columbia was 70 per cent in 1931 and 88 per cent by 1961, with Newfoundland still coming out at the top at 94 per cent. The Prairies are all in the 50 -70 per cent range, as are Ontario, PEI, and Nova Scotia. Only New Brunswick retains a low rate of 14 per cent, in 1961. These figures led Joy (1971: 23) to conclude that French is destined to disappear outside Quebec except in the corridor stretching from Sault St Marie through Ottawa and Cornwall in Ontario and Edmunston and Moncton in New Brunswick. He attributed this disappearance to the development of mass media, especially television and radio, the rise of highway transportation, the loss of isolation, and the rising costs of maintaining minority institutions, especially for communities with a low resource base at the outset (ibid.: 36). Interestingly enough, in discussing the situation in Ontario, he argued that statutes had had little impact on assimilation rates (ibid.: 32). Obviously, he overlooked the implications that statutes have for developing and maintaining the minority institutions that allow minority communities to survive and retain their language and culture.

FORMAL EQUALITY OR PATERNALISM? THE CHANGING 1960s AND 1970s

As Canada approached its centennial, the rise of nationalism in Quebec, and growing discontent among other francophones, raised doubts regarding Canada's national unity and its ability to survive for another hundred years (Laurendeau and Dunton, 1965: 21-4). Accordingly, the federal government undertook a major study of language inequality under the Royal Commission on Bilingualism and Biculturalism in 1963 (ibid.: 13-23). But even before the first volume of its report was released in 1967, other studies such as John Porter's influential *The Vertical Mosaic* and Richard Joy's *Languages in Conflict* were raising serious questions regarding ethnic inequality. Subsequently, the numerous studies of the B. and B. Commission identified major inequities that were seriously detrimental to the

French in all areas of society, and generated many recommendations, some of which were implemented by federal and provincial governments over the next few years.

1. *Federal government*

Acting on some of these recommendations, the federal government undertook some changes to reduce inequities for linguistic groups. The act governing Radio Canada was amended to strengthen its mandate of serving the whole of Francophone Canada. This meant much stronger support and presence in the minority communities outside Quebec. Radio-Canada then proceeded to increase its coverage in the Maritimes and in BC, and purchased the four independent radio stations set up in the late 1940s and early 1950s, by francophones in the Prairies. As well, the Secretary of State's mandate vis-à-vis Canada's linguistic and cultural minorities was made more explicit, and funding for these groups was increased. However, probably the most significant change was the passing, in 1969, of the Official Languages Act, which 'confers official and equal status to the French and English languages within the federal Government.' (Braen, 1987: 34). With a few exceptions, all citizens have the right to communicate with federal institutions in either language, as they choose. Judgements from federal courts and quasi-judicial bodies and all federal documents intended for the public must be in both languages. The federal civil service and federal agencies must become increasingly bilingual and provide equal opportunities for francophones, and French must become an effective language of work in those areas. 'The declared intention is therefore to achieve true equality of the two official languages' (ibid.: 34).

Apart from legislative changes, an office of the Commissioner of Official Languages was established by the 1969 Official Languages Act to oversee implementation of the act. After 1969, the Secretary of State was made specifically responsible for official language minorities. Federal funding to these groups increased over the years from $1.9 million in 1972 to $26 million in 1987 (Secretary of State, 1972, 1987). Although the final figure may seem impressive, the Commissioner of Official Languages complained that from 1969 to 1977, 'budgetary allocations barely kept up with inflation' (Commissioner, 1977: 20). In spite of these initial efforts, it was not until after 1980 that some of the more significant changes at the federal level occurred.

2. *Quebec*

The situation in Quebec not only was different, but in fact was largely responsible for the B. and B. Commission. The rise in French nationalism in the early 1960s left many Québécois feeling that Quebec had to catch up to the rest of North American society, but in French (Rioux, 1973). Quebec had to modernize both its political and economic infrastructures and its education system so as to compete and develop within the Canadian and continental economy. But it also had to improve and protect its French language if it was to retain what made Quebec unique in North America, and what was at the very core of its history and culture. During the 1960s, numerous reforms were introduced that became part of the Quiet Revolution. In 1961, the Parent Royal Commission on Education investigated the whole education system. Its five-volume report was published between 1963 and 1966. Based on the Commission's recommendations, Quebec adopted Bill 60, in 1964, which finally created a Department of Education with its own minister, and proceeded with a massive reorganization of education as a whole, including curriculum, administration, and funding. But even if the autonomy of the Protestant and to a lesser extent the Anglo-Catholic minorities was reduced somewhat, the new act and the ensuing structure recognized the right to Protestant education, to independent schools and school administration, and to services in English, since two deputy ministers of education were to be appointed, one Catholic and the other Protestant (Laurendeau and Dunton, 1968: 55-72).

In 1961 Quebec had already become aware of the increasing need to protect and promote the French language by establishing an Office of the French Language. However, as immigration into Quebec increased and growing numbers of both immigrant and Québécois children obtained their education in English, the question of the survival of the French language itself was raised. As a result, three laws were passed dealing specifically with language. Bill 63, the Act to Promote the French Language, passed in 1969, was supposed to overcome 'language inequalities which maintain French in an inferior position' (Braen, 1987: 38). The ineffectiveness of this first law produced heated debate, with nationalists pushing for much more stringent legislation. A Commission of Inquiry into the Status of French and Linguistic Rights (the Gendron Commission) investigated some of these questions in its report tabled at the end of 1972. Following this report, in 1974 Premier Bourassa's Liberal government finally adopted Bill 22, the Official Languages Act, in which French is declared the official language of Quebec for all purposes pertaining to public administration, public corporations, professions, industry, and commerce, although English versions of all documents are allowed as long as a French version exists. In education, language tests are imposed on those who wish to attend English schools (Delorme, 1974).

The coming to power of the nationalist Parti Québécois on 16 November 1976 gave francophone critics of Bill 22 the opportunity to strengthen protection of the French language. Within a few months of taking office the PQ produced a White Paper on *La politique québécoise de la langue française*, much of which was embodied in Bill 101, the Charter of the French Language adopted in 1977. The Charter declares French to be the official language of Quebec, for the courts, and the legislature. French is compulsory in the public service, in all government-related organizations, in labour relations, commerce, and business. Access to English schools is restricted to children who have one parent educated in English in Quebec. 'The Act creates a supervisory agency and attempts to implement measures to improve the quality of the French language' (Braen, 1987: 39). The Charter remains the strongest legislation yet in Canada to protect and promote the French language, but it is confined to Quebec.

3. *English Canada*

Change in English Canada was nowhere near so dramatic as in Quebec. In 1969, New Brunswick's Official Languages Act recognized French and English as official languages; however, most of its clauses remained without effect until the late 1970s (Commissioner, 1979: 23). Over the next decade or so, most anglophone provinces introduced changes to their education system or laws to allow the use of French as a language of instruction and to provide some support either in the area of programs, teacher training, or others (Chevrier, 1983: 47-55). Prince Edward Island passed Bill 33 in 1980 recognising the right to education in French for francophones. In 1981 Nova Scotia's Bill 65 recognized the right of francophones to schools in their mother tongue, 'where numbers warrant'. New Brunswick law allowed not only the use of French in school but the establishment of homogeneous French schools and school boards to serve the Acadian community. Ontario promised changes for 1982 whereby all francophone children would have access to education in French, and francophones would obtain certain management rights through guaranteed positions on existing anglophone boards. Manitoba changed its legislation in 1970 to allow French as a language of instruction, and in 1980 to permit establishment of French classes, and schools where French is the language of administration. Alberta did allow the use of French in school without making any distinction between French immersion and French as a first language. Since 1979 a new policy on French education in British Columbia has guaranteed the establishment of a French class when requested by the parents of ten students. The success of this approach led BC authorities to open a homogeneous francophone school in Vancouver in September 1983 (ibid.: 44-55). Saskatchewan reinstated French as a language of instruction in 1967 and allowed the designation of schools where French could be used in all subjects except English in 1968 (Denis and Li, 1988: 359).

At first glance such extensive changes seem impressive. However, in many instances changes in laws or regulations did not automatically translate into better access and better-quality education in French at the local level. Without adequate funding and resources, and especially without direct control over the education of their children, francophone parents often had to engage in endless lobbying, even resorting to court actions to force recalcitrant school boards to comply with the law (ibid.: 360; see the section on 'Minorities' in yearly reports of Commissioner). Many decisions pertaining to French education were left to the discretionary power of the Minister of Education, and regulations and implementation schedules were absent or inadequate (Chevrier, 1983: 33-55). On the other hand, even if Ontario has always refused to become officially bilingual, it has offered certain bilingual services in certain districts since 1970. Education, social services, health and welfare, justice, and culture in particular are affected. By 1979, Franco-Ontarians were to have the right to a trial before a French judge or jury for criminal offences, and by 1982, most Franco-Ontarians were to have access to civil trials in French (ibid.: 36). Apart from this, anglophone provinces produced very few, if any, modifications to any other area of legislation, policy, or government service to francophones.

In reality, many of the legislative changes identified above were very slow in showing concrete benefits for francophones at the community level. Most of the modifications touched the internal operations of some federal institutions, but at first had little direct impact on francophone communities. Even the Ontario services remain very uneven, and are often constrained by financial and administrative requirements (ibid.: 36). Yet, even though it produced so few immediate changes to reduce linguistic inequities, the Royal Commission on Bilingualism and Biculturalism proved to be a policy watershed, influencing linguistic policy for many years afterwards.

MINORITY AFFIRMATION OR THE LAST CHANCE? THE 1980s

1. *Federal government*

There were few changes in federal language legislation between 1969 and 1982. But this does not mean that there was no action. Debate over patriation of the Constitution, an amending formula, and protection of citizens' rights in the Canadian Charter of Rights and Freedoms occupied much of the political stage in the late 1970s (FFHQ, 1981: 12-14). As the federal government considered patriation, and the nationalist PQ government in Quebec moved towards its referendum on sovereignty-association on 20 May 1980, language issues remained at the forefront of the political agenda. The Charter of Rights enshrined in the Constitution elements of the Official Languages Act of 1969. Section 16 recognizes French and English as the country's official languages, with equal status, rights, and privileges for Canada and New Brunswick. This applies to debate and publication of statutes, records, and journals of debate for Parliament and the legislature of New Brunswick, to all institutions and courts, and to all services provided to the public from any head or central office of the federal or New Brunswick governments. As well, the Charter retains the previous provisions on language contained in section 133 of the BNA Act and section 23 of the Manitoba Act (Statutes of Canada, 1982: s16 - s21).

Although education is under provincial jurisdiction according to the 1867 Constitution, the Charter sets obligations on provinces to provide adequate educational opportunities for linguistic minorities by defining the rights of the latter (Statutes of Canada, 1982: s23). In an attempt to weaken Quebec's Language Charter (Bill 101) the Canadian Charter extends such educational rights not only to members of the linguistic minority, but also to members of the majority who obtained their education in the language of the minority, or whose children are presently receiving their education in that language. On the other hand, article 23 does recognize that, where numbers warrant, such education is to be made available in 'minority language educational facilities provided out of public funds'. As well, article 24 allows recourse to tribunals to obtain remedial action in case of denial or infringement of rights.

The Charter and the annual reports from the Commissioner of Official Languages, as well as pressure from minority groups, led to the adoption in July 1988 of Bill C-72, a new Official Languages Act. In the words of the Prime Minister, the new act will give the Courts 'legislative guidance to interpret the official languages provisions of the Charter'. Bill C-72 confirms the previous act and provides more explicit directives for its implementation, gives more authority to the Commissioner's Office in its responsibilities of overseeing the act, and to the Treasury Board in its role of policy development and monitoring. The new act provides 'a legislative framework setting out the powers and co-ordinating role of the Secretary of State in promoting the official languages and providing support to official language minority communities' (Commissioner, 1988b: 7). Only actual implementation of this most recent language legislation over the next few years will provide some indication of its positive effects, if any, for official language minorities.

Other changes include amendments to the Criminal Code, introduced in June 1978, that guarantee an accused the right to be heard by a judge or jury in his/her language anywhere in Canada, once these are proclaimed by provincial authorities (Commissioner 1978: 30). By 1987, implementation of these amendments as Part XIV (1) of the Criminal Code permitted such trials in French in Saskatchewan, Nova Scotia, Prince Edward Island (Commissioner, 1987: 156-61), and Alberta (*Le Devoir* 11 Sept. 1987: 4). Of course, since 1867 such trials have been possible in English in Quebec under the BNA Act's section 133.

As to funding to minority groups through the Secretary of State, we indicated above that by 1987 this funding had reached $26 million annually, which in reality amounted to an average allocation per project of only $28,000 (Secretary of State, 1987: 25). When we consider that some of these projects also include funding for national organizations, the amount is far from outlandish. In 1988 the Secretary of State signed a framework agreement with Saskatchewan and a comprehensive agreement with New Brunswick. Other agreements were also signed with Ontario, Prince Edward Island, and the Yukon to promote official languages and develop the official-language minority in these provinces (ibid.: 202). The Saskatchewan agreement should enhance educational opportunities for this francophone minority and may provide a model for financing in the future, as it allows for greater co-ordination of efforts by the federal and provincial governments in consultation with the minority concerned.

One other area of federal funding to assist official-language minorities and to promote official languages has been through the Official Languages in Education Program. By the late 1980s, Ottawa was distributing about $225 million annually to the provinces. However, as we shall see later under 'Minority Reaction', the use made of these funds is far from bringing unanimity among all those concerned.

One final area of federal activity of great significance is the Court Challenges Program, which had been utilized minimally prior to 1982. The program provides financial support for those eligible to seek court rulings to clarify official-language rights under the Charter, sections 93 or 133 of the BNA Act, or section 23 of the Manitoba Act (Secretary of State, 1983: 38-9), or to seek recognition and promotion of official-language rights in Canada through the Courts (Canadian Council on Social Development [CCSD], 1986-87: 34). In 1982-83, funding was provided for two cases. The following year the numbers had already increased to five cases before the courts, and support for preparing a case to five others. In 1985 the Secretary of State entered a five-year agreement to have the fund administered independently by the Canadian Council on Social Development. Over the years, the number of requests has increased, from 22 in 1985 to 32 in 1986 and 35 in 1987, although not all requests get funding, and the same case may submit a number of requests as it proceeds through the various levels of the judiciary. Between 1985 and 1989, the CCSD has approved $1.2 million for linguistic court challenges. This program has allowed minorities to defend their rights more effectively through the courts than was ever possible in the past. This program has had a major impact on provincial activities and legislation both in Quebec and in English Canada, as most of the court challenges of provincial legislation, whether education acts in English Canada or Bill 101 in Quebec, were funded in part by this program.

2. Quebec: Anglo Quebec as a 'minority'

As stated earlier, Quebec passed Bill 101, the Charter of the French Language, in 1977, making French compulsory in the legislature and the courts, in education except for those of anglophone origin, in public institutions and services, and in signage of places of business. The basis for the Charter is that the Québécois remain a minority within both Canada and the continent, and that the influx of immigrants who assimilate into the anglophone language and culture, coupled with the drastic drop in francophone fertility, would in the long run transform them into a numerical minority within their own territory. Strong protection is required, not to assimilate anglophones and deprive them of their rights, but to protect the French language. Some of its clauses have provoked very strong reactions among anglophones, but other clauses and laws such as sections 93 and 133 of the BNA Act, do provide protection for them. Also in 1986, Quebec adopted Bill 142, which guarantees health and social services in English, although some regional health councils are accused of being slow in developing access plans (Commissioner, 1988a: 225). Even Bill 101 recognizes for anglophones the right of access to their own educational system and to education in their language.

The shift from religion to language as the central ethno-cultural trait in Canada is perhaps best exemplified by Quebec's Bill 107. After several attempts since 1960, this law replaces denominational school boards with linguistic ones, although French Catholic and English Protestant boards will remain in place in Montréal and Québec city in keeping with section 133 of the BNA Act. Over the years, Catholic boards have increased the number of Anglo-Catholic schools operating under an essentially francophone administrative structure, whereas Protestant boards have significantly increased the number of French schools they operate to accommodate the non-Catholic immigrants who, after Bill 101, have to enrol in French schools (Bissonnette, 1982).

The anglophone 'minority' in Quebec is nevertheless quite well served by its institutions. It has its own schools and school boards, which cover the whole Quebec territory. In 1982 there were 4 anglophone and 2 bilingual CEGEPs to 40 francophone ones (Schachter, 1982: 161-70). By 1989 there were 7 anglophone CEGEPs and 2 bilingual ones out of a total of 47 (Vastel, 1989a). Established since 1967, these schools provide pre-university technical and professional training. There are three universities, of which McGill is one of the most prestigious in Canada. In 1989 these universities carried 28.2 per cent of university enrolments, but granted 31.2 per cent of MA degrees and 38.6 per cent of PhDs in Quebec (ibid.). In the area of health care and social services, in 1982 there were 27 hospitals out of 203 for the whole province; 6 anglophone community health centers out of 81; one English and one Jewish social service center out of 14; 15 senior citizens' homes, 8 centres for mentally and physically handicapped, 4 centres of rehabilitation for socially maladjusted youth and one centre for juvenile delinquents (Schachter, 1982: 179-210). In 1989, some 79 health establishments are required to provide services in English (Vastel, 1989a).

Anglophone media in 1982 included one large daily, the *Montreal Gazette*, 12 weeklies, 15 regional papers, 7 AM and 4 FM radio stations, and 2 television stations. Quebec anglophones also have access to the national network of the English CBC (Schachter, 1982: 235-296). In 1989 there were 3 dailies (28.1 per cent of Montreal's circulation), 18 weeklies, 11 radio stations (36 per cent of the audience), and 3 television stations, with access to 30 other stations including all American networks on cable. Some 46 per cent of movie-goers see films in English and 32 per cent of rented video cassettes are in English (Vastel, 1989a). There are anglophone museums, libraries, and theatres, and a variety of community organizations including YMCAs and YWCAs (Schachter, 1982: 235-96). Another aspect of the anglophone institutional structure is that many of their institutions have been solidly established for many years. McGill University received its charter in 1821 and Bishop's University in 1853; Montreal General Hospital was founded in 1821, and the Royal Victoria Hospital in 1894, among others (ibid.: 166, 210).

Such an institutional infrastructure is not without its problems. Shortages of qualified personnel reduce the availability of service in English, especially in outlying areas. Declining population requires reorganization and jeopardizes the survival of some institutions, and even some anglophone communities (Commissioner, 1988a: 224). Legislative and administrative changes affect these institutions as well. For example, Bill 101's French-language requirements for public institutions and professionals do create problems of adaptation for some. But for the institutions themselves the 'overall result of the language legislation has not seriously damaged the ease with which English-speaking citizens can be served in their mother tongue on the Island of Montreal' (Schachter, 1982: 189). If we add to these institutions the churches, some municipal governments, and the private-sector institutions including commerce, finance, industry, and services, owned by Anglophones and providing service in English, the anglophone 'minority' in Quebec is seen by some as 'one of the best served in the world' (Vastel, 1989a), especially in contrast to the francophone minority outside Quebec.

Thus the recent Bill 178, which maintains French signage on business places, as required by Bill 101, although an obvious irritant, should be placed in its proper context. The Supreme Court of Canada ruled that the articles on French-only business signs in Quebec were against the Quebec and Canada Charter of Rights but that given the 'recognized need to protect the French language' in North America, Quebec could use section 1 of the Charter, the 'notwithstanding clause', to impose collective rights over individual rights (Commissioner, 1988a: 227). It is doubtful that Bourassa's solution of French signs outside businesses and bilingual signs inside is the best way of preserving the French language in Quebec while respecting anglophone rights. On the other hand, the defiance by some English business and their overt refusal to comply with the spirit of Bill 101, which in some cases became overt provocation against francophones, did force the Quebec government to take a very firm line on the issue.

3. *English Canada: Franco-minorities*

By the time the relevant articles of the Charter of Rights were enacted in April 1985, parents in Nova Scotia, PEI, Ontario, Manitoba, Saskatchewan, Alberta, and BC were already considering court proceedings against their respective governments to obtain recognition of their educational rights. The judgements have varied from province to province, with Nova Scotia courts providing the most retrograde positions by removing from the Charter pre-existing legislation incompatible with it (Commissioner, 1988a: 46-7). In the other provinces, the rights of official-language minorities have been recognized, although through different interpretations with different implications (Faucher, 1987: 263-97). The general outcome of these judgements is the recognition that section 23 means that the official-language minority has the right to instruction in their mother tongue, the right to autonomous homogeneous school facilities, and the right to the management and control of these schools. In another important decision in *SANB et al. vs. the Association of Parents for Fairness in Education et al.*, Judge Richard ruled that 'immersion classes cannot be held equivalent of French language instruction for the purposes of the minority education rights guaranteed in the Charter' (Commissioner, 1987: 162). Further, the 1987 decision by Judge Proudfoot in BC also specified that under section 23 anglophone parents have no constitutional right to immersion education. For these parents education in the second language remains a privilege (ibid.: 163).

Most judgements recognize existing provincial legislation in this area as being unconstitutional. In practice, anglophone provinces often refuse to francophones what they provide for anglophones, such as small classes, small schools, multi-grade classrooms, and school boards covering a broad territory. All are awaiting what is hoped will be a definitive statement regarding the different interpretations of the rights included in section 23, expected to be delivered by the Supreme Court of Canada on Alberta's Mahé case in 1989 (Commissioner, 1988: 44-8).

Court challenges of provincial education laws have not been the only area of activity. In 1981 New Brunswick passed Bill 88, which calls for a bilingual civil service and for effective equality between the two linguistic groups (Chevrier, 1983: 39). Implementation of the legislation is not as rapid as the Acadians would like, however.

In Ontario, minor amendments were introduced to existing legislation over the years, including Bill 8, in 1986, which is to provide provincial government services in French in certain regions of the province (Statutes of Ontario, 1986: c.45; *Le Devoir* 24 Nov. 1986: 1). But probably the most significant legislative and administrative change in the last decade was the passing of Bill 109, in 1988, which creates a francophone school board for the Ottawa-Carleton district, with 1,000 teachers, 18,000 students and an operating budget of $100 million. A public francophone school board was also established for Toronto and for Prescott-Russell (Secretary of State, 1988: 221). The Ottawa-Carleton board had been recommended by a provincial commission in 1976 and had, at that time, support from 'the English boards, the local press, and French and English community leaders' (Commissioner, 1979: 32). One is reluctant to consider how long it would have taken the provincial government to act if there had been strong local opposition.

The situation in Manitoba was different, since a court case that eventually reached the Supreme Court in 1979 re-established official bilingualism as set out in section 23 of the Manitoba Act of 1870

(Forest Case). Since then, however, no significant progress has been made in providing services in French or changing legislation.

Another important language judgement for Prairie francophones was rendered by the Supreme Court of Canada in February 1988. Issued an English-only speeding ticket in 1980, Father Mercure of the North Battleford (Sask.) district argued that under the old section 110 of the North-West Territories Act, he had the right to a trial in French. Eight years later, the Supreme Court confirmed that parliamentary, judicial, and legislative bilingualism still applied to Saskatchewan, but it also recognized 'that provincial legislators have the authority to amend such language requirements unilaterally, and indeed even to abrogate the language rights that flow from them' (Commissioner, 1988a: 39; Beaudoin, 1988). This decision applies to Alberta as well. Consequently Saskatchewan passed Bill 02 in April 1988, and Alberta passed Bill 60 in July. Both acts recognize English as the only official language of the province, although certain permissive provisions for French are included. For example, in Saskatchewan French may be used in the legislature, but all statutes, regulations, or ordinances are to be published in English, although some may be published in English and French at the discretion of the Lieutenant-Governor in Council. Similarly, French can be used in some form before some provincial courts. All existing statutes, regulations, and ordinances passed in English only are validated retroactively. 'In short, the two statutes comply with the letter of the Supreme Court decision, but hardly with its spirit' (Commissioner, 1988a: 40).

Legislative recognition of French in English Canada has often been proportional to the institutional completeness of francophone minorities in each province. In 1977 the Fédération des Francophones Hors Québec (FFHQ), a new organization that regroups the major provincial francophone organizations at the federal level, published *Les héritiers de Lord Durham*, which outlined the tremendous institutional and legislative obstacles to their survival. This publication was followed by *Deux poids, deux mesures* in 1978, which compared the startling inequalities that exist between the legislative recognition and institutional development of Quebec anglophones and the francophone minorities. In spite of some changes since the late 1970s, the only provinces to recognize some right of management and control by francophones over their school system are New Brunswick, Ontario, and Nova Scotia (Théberge, 1987: 34). In Ontario the first francophone school board required its own specific legislation to be instituted. In Nova Scotia the law remains inoperative, since judges ruled against section 23 of the Charter. Without legislative recognition and protection, therefore, it is almost impossible for a minority to develop any kind of institutional completeness.

In the area of post-secondary education, the number of francophone universities has increased from one to two between 1978 and 1986, and the number of affiliated colleges has increased from three to five, but the number of bilingual universities has decreased from three to two (ibid.: 35). If we spread these out over nine provinces and two territories, countless cities and regions, university education in the French mother tongue is not readily available for many francophones outside Quebec. Homogeneous community colleges have increased from none to four, three of them in New Brunswick, between 1978 and 1986, and the number of bilingual colleges has increased from three to nine, with six of these in Ontario (ibid.: 36).

The reports of the Commissioner of Official Languages repeat, year after year, information on the frailty of francophone media outside Quebec. In 1989 there are two French dailies, one in Ontario and one in New Brunswick, about twenty weeklies on the perpetual brink of closing, due to financial problems, and Radio-Canada's French television and radio. French TV Ontario has existed since 1987, and the regions closest to Quebec can get other French radio and television networks. 'Apart from this, it is a cultural desert' (Vastel, 1989b). While it is true that almost every major francophone community now has access to Radio-Canada, this creates its own problems. Since Radio-Canada has to compete primarily in the Montreal market, francophones outside Quebec, and probably even within the outlying regions of Quebec, find it difficult to identify with and participate in these media.

In other areas such as health, social, and community services little seems to have changed since the FFHQ publications. Some changes have occurred in Ontario and New Brunswick legislation, but implementation at the local level is far from rapid and is usually limited to regions 'where numbers warrant'. None of the other seven provinces has any policies in this area, so that the services provided vary greatly from province to province. Newfoundland francophones, for example, are given a toll-free telephone line to a francophone hospital in Moncton, New Brunswick (ibid.): that is the extent of their health services in French. The three westernmost provinces don't even offer that. Federal services in outlying regions are more readily available in both official languages, but as the Commissioner of Official Languages' annual reports indicate, there is still much work to be done to provide services in French and to make French an effective language of work in federal institutions.

Overall, New Brunswick Acadians seem particularly strong, with their own university, radio and television (Radio-Canada), homogeneous schools and autonomous school boards, and certain religious and economic institutions. They also elect francophone MLAs in sufficient numbers to give them a political presence provincially.

4. *Minority reactions*

Reaction by Quebec anglophones to Bill 101 is quite well known. Over the last years public organizations such as school boards, corporations, and individuals have challenged Bill 101 in the courts, very often successfully. All legislation in Quebec has to be adopted and published in both languages, and both languages can be used in the courts. However, Quebec has the right to restrict English-language programs in its schools, in public signage and public administration. Some anglophone corporations, such as Sun Life Insurance, have very noisily moved their head offices from Montreal to Toronto (Kierans, Brecher, Naylor 1982). Some professionals have done likewise. Anglophone cabinet ministers resigned to protest Bill 178. Of course, Quebec's anglophones have always had access to two crucial instruments to defend their rights and lobby for change: anglophone politicians and cabinet ministers from Quebec in both Ottawa and Québec, and their own media. In recent years more explicit lobby organizations have appeared to promote anglophone linguistic rights within Quebec. In particular Alliance Québec, founded in 1981, has played a very active role in challenging various articles of Bill 101, or in supporting individuals, organizations or companies who do so.

As for francophones outside Quebec, they have used court challenges where possible to obtain changes to provincial legislation and to services or institutions. They have used the Commissioner of Official Languages to obtain better service in French from federal agencies and offices; they have also continued to establish their own institutions where possible, and often against great odds. In Alberta, in 1987, a francophone NDP MLA, Léo Piquette, dared to use French in the legislature; even more outrageous was his refusal to apologize for doing so (*Le Devoir*, 25, 27, 29, 30 June 1987). Francophones have lobbied extensively to obtain federal funding for their communities, organizations, and institutions. As a result they have come to rely extensively on funding and support from the Secretary of State, although this has not been without difficulties.

Ironically, programs that were intended to assist the francophone minority outside Quebec, by being addressed at 'official language minorities', have often provided great assistance to the anglophone group in Quebec. For example, in 1976 Secretary of State grants to minority communities averaged $12,000 for anglophone projects in Quebec, in contrast to $7,000 for francophone projects outside Quebec. In 1977 the figures were $16,700 and $9,300 respectively (Secretary of State, 1976 and 1977: 37-9). Pressure from the francophone minorities forced the Secretary of State's department to revise some of its funding policies so as to be more equitable in its allocations. Unfortunately, no recent data broken down by province is available to indicate which minority is best served by these programs.

In the Official Languages in Education Program, which funds the teaching of French and English as first and second languages, the Secretary of State has increased its annual spending from $57.5 million in 1970 to $201 million in 1986-87. Although an impressive increase at first glance, the 1986-87 figure is in fact lower than the 1970 figure in constant dollars. Part of the problem that the Secretary of State faces in this regard is that of getting the provinces to increase their contributions in this area of education (Commissioner, 1988a: 22-3).

In the first ten years of this program, francophone minorities complained constantly that the federal funds for their education never reached their communities. Often anglophone school boards and provincial governments could not account at the local level for all the federal funds that they claimed to have spent on francophone education. In some cases up to half of the funds earmarked for French minority education was lost between Ottawa and the community school: for example, federal funds were misused in 'building highways for school buses' (FFHQ, 1981: 45-54). Similarly, 67.5 per cent of money spent on special projects outside Quebec in the early 1970s went for French immersion for anglophone children (ibid.: 41). For francophone minorities, probably the most painful aspect of these programs was that Quebec collected nearly 58 per cent of the $1.08 billion spent by Ottawa on these programs between 1970 and 1978 (ibid.: 20b). In some cases Quebec's share was as high as 74 per cent of the federal funds (ibid.: 37). The major reason for this was that anglophones in Quebec already had numerous schools in place, as well as a number of school boards, so that they more easily qualified for funding under these programs. Ironically, the outcome of these programs was that the weaker the minority, and the more oppressed by its local and provincial authorities, the less likely it was to obtain anything from Ottawa, since such groups did not qualify under federal criteria.

The numerous complaints forced Ottawa to impose stronger accounting procedures on provincial governments, and to revise the manner in which funds were allocated. As a result, a growing share went for French education in English Canada, including immersion, rather than to Quebec, although as late as 1982 to 1985, Quebec's share remained as high as 45 to 48 per cent (Task Force, 1985: 221). According to Taylor-Browne (1988: 198) 'more than half of the Secretary of State's funds for bilingualism in education actually go to supporting English language educational programmes in Quebec. Half of the remaining amount supports French language education for non-Francophones outside Quebec. As a result only a tiny amount is available for minority Francophones.' This view may exaggerate slightly the actual distribution, although it is difficult to know exactly how much money is spent through the various programs for each province. In 1988 Ottawa paid $60.2 million for Quebec's 111,862 anglophone students, an average of $538 per student compared to $68.4 million for the 151,063 francophone students outside Quebec, or an average of $453 per student. Anglophone students learning French as a second language received $57.1 million, nearly as much as the francophone minority (Vastel, 1989b).

In spite of the Official Languages Act, the Commissioner of Official Languages, and increased funding through the Secretary of State, the transfer rates from French to English continued to increase from 1971 to 1981 (Commissioner, 1984: 176-7). This is not surprising, since there were few real changes in the provincial institutional and legislative structures. According to Vastel (1989b, my translation), 'the only right that Francophones enjoy all across the country is the right to be sent to jail in one's mother tongue'.

Immediate change in census data is visible only in the decline in the number of anglophones in Quebec since 1941, and the increase in their average age, especially since Bill 101 in 1976. It will probably take years until the above changes have a sufficient impact on language transfer among francophone minorities for differences to appear in census data. Unfortunately, changes in census questions in 1986 make it very difficult to draw direct comparisons of language transfer rates with previous censuses. The total effects of the last ten to twenty years of struggle and change are far from immediately visible in statistics on language loss. The inertia and subordination arising from generations of oppression and denial of rights are very difficult to overcome, and it will probably take ten to twenty years before significant changes in the francophone groups can be measured by census data. So, in spite of the recent furor over signage in Quebec, the earlier comment from the Commissioner of Official Languages (1978: 31) that 'there is no gainsaying the fact Quebec's Anglophones are much better off than their francophone counterparts in other provinces' still seems most accurate.

If the federal language policies of the last twenty years have an impact on bilingualism rates, this should begin to manifest itself in the censuses of 1991 and 1996, as the students from the immersion and the new minority schools reach adulthood. In the meantime, bilingualism remains very much the responsibility of the francophone minorities. Except for New Brunswick and Quebec, the proportion of persons of French mother tongue who speak both English and French range from 84.0 per cent in Ontario to 89.6 per cent in Nova Scotia, whereas bilingual anglophones range from 1.8 per cent in Newfoundland to a high of 6.6 per cent in Ontario. In New Brunswick the percentages are 60.8 per cent for French mother tongue and 8.9 per cent for English, whereas in Quebec the comparative figures are 53.4 per cent and 28.7 per cent (Statistiques Canada, 1985: Table 6). As Lieberson (1970: 13) argues, ability to speak the dominant group's language is a risk factor, since it becomes the first step in language shift. Except in Quebec, the onus to speak the other group's language falls almost entirely on the francophone minority since so few of the dominant group can converse in the minority language. In Quebec the anglophone group has to become increasingly bilingual in many occupations, as required under Bill 101; however, they are also guaranteed access to education, the legislature and judiciary, and to health and social services in English. So even with Bill 101, many Quebec anglophones can go through life in Quebec without learning or using French. Such is not the case for most francophone minorities, and the next ten to twenty years will reveal whether the federal bilingualism policies have in fact strengthened the francophone minorities or hastened their demise.

LANGUAGE AS ETHNICITY

Language loss, or assimilation, in minority groups has been the central focus of much of the literature on minorities. This phenomenon is explained as being the outcome of identity change (Anderson, 1972; Gordon, 1964; Isajiw, 1981; Vallée et al., 1957) or differential access to political institutions (Vallée et al., 1957), changing attitudes among minority members (Denis, 1978) or other cultural aspects (Backeland and Frideres, 1977; Garigue, 1962; Grabb, 1980; Shapiro and Perlman, 1976). Linguists and demographers focus on objective individual characteristics such as ethnic origin, mother tongue, language spoken and others to explain language shifts in reference to demographic and community or institutional constraints (Beaujot, 1978; Castonguay, 1979, 1982; Joy, 1971). The weaker a minority is in a region or community in relation to the dominant society, the more difficulty it faces in maintaining or developing its own institutions by which its identity, culture, and language can be maintained and transmitted (Lieberson, 1970; de Vries and Vallée, 1980). Homogeneity, size, and segregation appear as crucial factors in minority-group maintenance. However, apart from these objective demographic dimensions, the communal and ethnic institutional structure of the collectivity seem equally important. A minority group of a certain size and homogeneity can resist language loss and assimilation by developing its own network of institutions that provide the same services as those of the dominant society while simultaneously transmitting the culture and language of the minority. Therefore an ethnic community consists of individuals who share certain common traits such as origin and language, and a sense of identification to a collectivity, combined with their participation in a network of institutions proper to their particular group. 'Community implies institutions within which individuals can pursue their material interests, express their identity, establish social relations, and live the belief systems which give meaning to their life' (Breton, 1984: 2, my translation). In other words, the level of institutional completeness of a minority is a major factor in determining the group's ability to survive (Breton, 1964). However, the degree of institutional completeness depends on the access to economic, social, and political resources both within the dominant society and within its own group. Internal development within a minority enclave is not a sufficient condition for a minority to survive (Li and Denis, 1983).

Differential legislation, differential economic and political power, and differential access to the other group's language are equally important factors to be considered. The study of differential power bases is usually left to political sociologists and political scientists. Pluralist theory which equates power with voting patterns and lobby groups, argues that the basis for power rests in numbers, organization, leadership, and resources (Dahlie and Tissa, 1981). The latter includes both collective and individual resources such as wealth, education, access to media, and access to powerful positions (Rose, 1967). Although there exists a substantial literature describing the uneven distribution of resources among Canadian ethnic groups (see, for example, Porter, 1965; Curtis and Williams, 1973; Reitz, 1980: 146-203), these writers tend to argue that since minorities are weak in numbers, they also tend to be weak in resources, leadership and organization. It is therefore not surprising that minorities are unable to defend themselves politically and obtain a more equitable distribution of resources. Much as in the demographic-community analysis, the political weakness of minorities is the normal outcome of their weak numbers. The problem with this argument is that it cannot explain the relative success of the anglophone group within Quebec in protecting its language.

The success of this group is explained in part by elite analyses that focus on the holders of power in powerful hierarchies. In Canada this literature has systematically and constantly indicated that in all elites except labour, White Anglo-Saxon Protestant males, the proverbial

WASPs, predominate almost to the exclusion of other groups (Clement, 1975; Kelner, 1970; Olsen, 1980; Porter, 1965). A few French Canadians and 'others' are present, but mostly on the outer fringes, or in the 'strategic elite' as opposed to the inner circles of the 'core elite' (Kelner, 1970). Given that access to positions of power is mostly through sponsorship by those already in power, and given the tendency to select individuals of stronger affinity, exclusion of minorities is the normal outcome of their difference from the dominant group. In a society where inequality of opportunity prevails, assimilation may be the most realistic strategy for members of minority groups. But such elite analyses focus once again on cultural differences between minority and dominant groups to explain the tendancy for minority members to transfer into the culture of the dominant group.

Power differentials are also at the centre of underdevelopment theory (Davis, 1971; Frank, 1967). Within Canada, this framework has generally been applied to the issue of regionalism (Davis, 1971; Williams, 1978). However it also underlies recent analyses of Anglo-Saxon domination of Saskatchewan francophones through repressive legislation (Denis and Li, 1988) and the level of institutional development of francophones outside Quebec and of anglophones in that province (FFHQ, 1977, 1978, 1981).

These analyses recognize the importance of locating a minority group within the political and economic context established by the dominant society. However, they still treat both entities as homogeneous. Discussion tends to focus on political or ideological dimensions only, and even when economic questions are raised, these tend to be absorbed by the other two dimensions (Ravault, 1983).

Class theory has produced very little literature on ethnicity let alone on the specific issue of language policy. Jackson (1977: 66-9) attempts to integrate some of the above elements in his discussion of a political economy of language. Similarly, Archibald (1978: 186-228) provides an extensive discussion of reported social psychological differences of racial, ethnic, and gender groups from the perspective of political economy. Regarding ethnicity, one factor that stands out is that class differences in attitudes and behaviour are usually greater within ethnic groups than between them. Wardaugh (1983: 104-22) also combines demographic data, studies on institutional completeness, and analyses of political power of francophones outside Quebec, although his overview needs much further elaboration.

A criticism made in another context but equally applicable here is that most of the above literature focuses either on ideological aspects of minority groups or on distributive characteristics such as occupation, education, and income (Miles, 1984). One of the few Canadian studies to consider systematically the relationship between ethnicity and class is that of Li (1988: 140-1) who concludes:

> Primordial cultures of ethnic groups have never been the primary force in producing social classes in Canada. Rather, ethnicity and race have served to fragment social class divisions. Our study shows that social class is one of the main determinants of social inequality in Canada, and that ethnicity and race serve as a basis of fractionalizing the class structure. The proper meaning of ethnic inequality cannot be fully understood outside the context of a class society.

But the question remains: is language policy an ethnic or a class issue?

LANGUAGE AND CLASS

The separation between ethnicity and class in most North American sociology is a heuristic but artificial device. Focusing exclusively on one set of relations greatly facilitates description and analysis. Thus it is easy and convenient to study language issues by focusing on language groups as a whole. Such convenience has made language issues central to the sociology of ethnic relations as seen above. However, languages do not exist in a social vacuum. They flourish or die in an institutional context that is either favourable or detrimental to their survival. But the institutional context depends on the political and economic resources that particular groups control and on the underlying structure of society. In a capitalist society, distribution of economic resources depends first on class, in the collective sense. And class has a significant impact on linguistic groups since they are rarely socially homogeneous or identical. Thus most of the studies in the preceding section take on a totally different meaning if class is introduced into their analysis. Language policy and legislation are no longer the outcome of tension and struggle between ethnic groups, but rather of the struggle between ethnic groups with different class composition and subsequent inequality of political and economic power and resources.

Unfortunately, Statistics Canada cannot provide us with data on the class composition of minorities. But we do know from existing studies—whether the elite analyses of Porter, Clement, and others, or the studies on the Canadian capitalist class by Niosi, Brym, Veltmeyer or Sales, or the more popular accounts of the wealthy in Canada such as those of Newman and Francis— that by and large the Canadian bourgeoisie is Anglo-Saxon. A few wealthy French Canadian or other ethnic families do not disprove the rule. Canadian international or multi-national capital is by and large English-speaking.

1. Anglophones in Quebec

Many Canadian fortunes trace their roots to Quebec, the Conquest, and the fur trade. Although regional capitalists exist in almost every region of Canada, large-scale capital is concentrated primarily in the Montreal-Toronto axis. Consequently, much of the economic power, and hence political power, in Quebec has rested in the hands of the largely English-speaking Quebec section of the Canadian bourgeoisie. This bourgeoisie, which developed initially under the political auspices of the British colonial administration imposed its language on the much larger French Canadian population. From 1760 to 1867 there was a constant see-saw movement between the imposition of English and the French resistance to it. The English language rested on political and economic power; the French language on numbers and existing institutions and traditions. From 1867 to the 1960's, English continued to be associated with the areas of activity of the English-speaking capitalist class, and French was relegated to the rest. However, with the rise of French nationalism in the early 1960s, and the development of large-scale francophone institutions, especially in the co-operative and state sectors, the small French regional bourgeoisie began to develop vigorously. With state support, it increased its sphere of activity and made significant gains against weaker fractions of the English-speaking bourgeoisie (eg., Milner and Milner, 1973). By the 1980s some Québécois capitalists had reached multinational stature.

During the earlier period the English-speaking bourgeoisie could use its capital and economic resources to establish its own institutions: universities such as McGill, Concordia, and Bishop's; hospitals; media; education systems; and other services. They could also use their political power to ensure that their language was constitutionally protected both federally and provincially, and to obtain state funding for their institutions. In the last twenty years this position of dominance has been challenged by the development of large scale francophone co-operative, state, and private economic institutions. Language legislation in Quebec during this period has increasingly sought to make French the dominant language in all spheres of activity within the province. This movement, through legislation such as Bill 101, has forced English institutions to become increasingly bilingual. Yet inasmuch as they serve primarily an anglophone clientèle, they remain anglophone institutions. The only real restriction is that of French signage on buildings. Elsewhere, anglophones may have to know French to qualify for certain positions, but they can still work in English and serve anglophone clients in English in anglophone institutions. Once established, these institutions are able to maintain a certain momentum that allows them to persist even when conditions become somewhat less favourable. The anglophone bourgeoisie in Quebec still has access to vast economic resources, both private and public, to maintain their institutions. The figures given above on Secretary of State funding and Quebec's funding of the anglophone education system are clear examples of such access to state funds.

2. *Francophone minorities*

Unfortunately for francophones outside Quebec, their social origins and current situation are far from comparable. Dispossessed Acadian peasants and small fishermen of the 1750s, Métis freighters and hunters, immigrant peasants and artisans, and poor Québécois without access to arable land: such are the origins of most francophones outside Quebec (Wade, 1967). Each community did have a few francophone professionals, clergy, and teachers. But from the 1700s to the 1900s most were independent commodity producers, in either agriculture, fur, lumber, or fishing. As the working-class/bourgeoisie dialectic developed in Canada starting around the 1850s, they became proletarianized. Over the last hundred years, this process has drawn these independent commodity producers into the cities and into anglophone institutions. For many of these, wage labour implies urbanization and loss of mother tongue.

The few francophones who became capitalists—the Allards, Desmarais, and Campeaus—have not been numerous or concentrated enough to generate the kind of institutional structures created by anglophone capitalists in Quebec. Smaller regional francophone capitalists have developed over the last twenty years, but very often competition in anglophone markets in provinces with no legislative or institutional recognition of their language has forced them away from their community of origin. Success in the world of business often requires or fosters attitudes of estrangement from the francophone working-class and independent commodity producers. Thus francophones outside Quebec have lacked the economic resources to develop a comparable institutional framework, and they have also lacked the political power of a strong bourgeoisie to obtain legislative and constitutional protection of their language rights, and the subsequent state support for these institutions.

Since 1969, federal efforts to counter the independence movement in Quebec have forced Ottawa to give much more importance to these minorities. Any federal intervention in support of anglophones and the English language in Quebec at the end of the twentieth century can be justified only through policies of official bilingualism. Thus the artificial symmetry is created: anglophone minority in French Quebec; francophone minority in English Canada. But as the Commissioner of Official Languages' annual reports constantly reflect, official affirmation of French and English language equality in Canada in 1969 does not make these languages equal in fact. Twenty years after the formal right was established, considerable efforts and resources still have to be deployed to provide services to the public in the minority language, and greater employment and promotion opportunities in the federal system for francophones; to make French an actual language of work; and to ensure access to quality education for francophone minorities. A policy of formal equality that fails to take into account the constitutional, historical, and social inequalities between the two so-called minorities results in tremendous inequalities of treatment. Twenty years after the Official Languages Act, Ottawa spends over $60 million a year on anglophone education in Quebec through an education system that has been in place for over a hundred years and that stretches from pre-school to CEGEPs, and to PhD-granting universities. The francophones in eight English provinces are waiting for court decisions to force implementation of their rigths to management and control over their elementary and secondary schools. Francophones in Alberta and Saskatchewan waited for eight years for the Supreme Court of Canada to finally recongize the validity of claims made since 1892, that French was still an official language in their provinces. After eight years—or rather nearly a hundred years of waiting—both their governments wiped out their rights within six months of having them recognized. So ends the symmetry.

CONCLUSION

Language is not a relation of production, although it can be connected to such relations. Consequently there is no congruent relationship between class and language, at least not in Canada. However, insofar as members of an ethnic group are concentrated in one social class, or a social class consists primarily of members of an ethnic group, class has a direct bearing on language issues, and on relations between linguistic groups. The long history of language policies and legislation in Canada is directly related to the changing structure and composition of its social classes.

The rise of a dominant anglophone bourgeoisie in Quebec from 1760 to the 1960s has ensured the place of English in that province/

nation. The absence of a comparable francophone bourgeoisie outside Quebec has left the francophone minorities with few economic or political resources. Isolation, enclosed communities, and small family enterprises allowed them to retain their language and culture for many generations. But proletarianization and urbanization have forced them into environments where they not only work and consume in the dominant language, but where they are deprived of the legitimacy and constitutional protection of their language.

As the French Canadian bourgeoisie in Quebec increases its economic, political, and ideological control over the province, the federal government is increasingly compelled to intervene to protect the Quebec fraction of the English Canadian bourgeoisie. Given the historical pattern established from 1760 to 1867 and enshrined in section 93 and section 133 of the BNA Act, Ottawa can intervene in the language issue in Quebec only under the guise of official bilingualism, which does open the door to federal financial support to francophone minorities. However, given the lack of control over provincial legislation and spending by federal authorities, the anglophone provinces have been able to take advantage of federal funds to the detriment of the francophone minorities and yet thumb their noses at Ottawa regarding minority rights. On the other hand, the federal support that does trickle down to the francophone minorities makes them increasingly dependent on superstructural conditions for their linguistic survival. This leaves them exposed to the vagaries of shifting political winds and makes them subservient to federal bureaucrats who have their own agendas. We are still a long way from the full recognition of minority rights and full democracy, and for most of the francophones outside Quebec, time may have run out.

NOTE

[1]Sociologically, majority and minority are defined by differential power and resources, not by numerical differences. In this chapter, the sociological meaning is implied unless otherwise indicated.

REFERENCES

Anderson, Alan

1972 *Assimilation in the Bloc Settlements of North Central Saskatchewan: A Comparative Study of Identity Change Among Seven Ethno-Religious Groups in a Canadian Prairie Region.* Saskatoon: University of Saskatchewan, unpublished PhD thesis, Sociology.

Archibald, W. Peter
1978 *Social Psychology as Political Economy*. Toronto: McGraw-Hill Ryerson.

Backeland, Lucille, and Frideres, J.S.
1977 'Franco-Manitobans and Cultural Loss: A Fourth Generation'. *Prairie Forum* 2: 1-18.

Bastarache, Michel
1987 *Language Rights in Canada*. Montréal: Éditions Yvon Blais.

Beaudoin, Gerald
1988 'The Matter of Mercure'. *Language and Society*. Ottawa: Commissioner of Official Language; no. 23 (summer): 19-20.

Beaujot, Roderic P.
1978 'Canada's Population: Growth and Dualism'. *Population Bulletin* 33: 2.

Bissonnette, Lise
1982 'La restructuration scolaire de l'Ile de Montréal: une occasion ratée pour les anglophones'. Pp. 291-303 in Caldwell et Waddell (1982).

Blay, Jacqueline
1989 'Les Droits linguistiques au Manitoba: un accident ou une volonté politique'. Pp. 185-201 in *Écriture et politique*. Les actes du septiéme colloque du CEFCO. Edmonton: University of Alberta (Faculté Saint Jean).

Braen, André
1987 'Language Rights'. Pp. 3-63 in Bastarache (1987).

Breton, Raymond
1964 'Institutional Completeness of Ethnic Communities and the Personal Relations of Immigrants'. *American Journal of Sociology* 70 (2) (Sept.): 193-205.
1984 'Les institutions et les réseaux d'organisation des communautés ethnoculturelles'. Présentation au colloque sur la situation de la recherche sur les communautés francophones hors Québec. Ottawa.

Brym, Robert, ed.
1985 *The Structure of the Canadian Capitalist Class*. Toronto: Garamond.

Caldwell, Gary, et Eric Waddell
1982 *Les Anglophones du Québec: de majoritaires à minoritaires*. Québec: Institut Québécois de recherche sur la culture.

Canadian Council on Social Development (CCSD)
1986-7 *Court Challenges Program: Annual Report*. Ottawa: CCSD.
1987-8

Castonguay, Charles
1979 'Exogamie et anglicisation chez les minorités canadiennes-françaises'. *Canadian Review of Sociology and Anthropology* 16: 21-31.
1982 'Intermarriage and Language Shift in Canada, 1971 and 1976'. *Canadian Journal of Sociology* 7: 263-77.

Chevrier, Richard
1983 *Le français au Canada: situation à l'extérieur du Québec*. Québec: Conseil de la langue française.
Clement, Wallace
1975 *The Canadian Corporate Elite*. Toronto: McClelland and Stewart.
Comeault, Gilbert-L.
1979 'La question des écoles du Manitoba—un nouvel éclairage'. *Revue d'histoire de l'Amérique française* 33 (1) (June): 3-23.
Commissioner of Official Languages
1971- 1988a *Annual Report*. Ottawa: Supply and Services.
1988b *Language and Society*. No. 23 (summer). Ottawa: Supply and Services.
Curtis, James, and Scott Williams
1973 *Social Stratification in Canada*. Scarborough, Ont: Prentice Hall.
Dahlie, Jorgen, and Fernando Tissa, eds
1981 *Ethnicity, Power and Politics in Canada*. Toronto: Methuen.
Davis, A.K.
1971 'Canadian Sociology and History as Hinterland vs Metropolis'. Pp. 6-32 in R. Ossenberg, *Canadian Society: Pluralism Change and Conflict*. Scarborough, Ont: Prentice Hall.
Delorme, Léo
1974 *Bill 22: le Waterloo de Bou Bou*. Laval: Éditions de Duvernay.
Denis, Ann B.
1978 'The Relationships Between Ethnicity and Educational Aspiration of Post-Secondary Students in Toronto and Montreal'. *Canadian Plains Studies* 8: 231-42.
Denis, Wilfrid, and Peter S. Li
1988 'The Politics of Language Loss: A Francophone Case from Western Canada'. *Journal of Education Policy* 3 (4): 351-70.
de Vries, John, and Frank Vallée
1980 *Language Use in Canada*. 1971 Census of Canada, Catalogue 99-762E. Ottawa: Statistics Canada.
Didier, Emmanuel
1987 'The Private Law of Language'. Pp. 313-443 in Bastarache (1987).
Faucher, Pierre
1987 'Language Rights and Education'. In Bastarache (1987).
Fédération des Francophones Hors Québec (FFHQ)
1977 *Les héritiers de Lord Durham*. Ottawa: FFHQ.
1978 *Deux poids, deux mesures*. Ottawa: FFHQ.
1981 *A la recherche du milliard*. Ottawa: FFHQ.
Francis, Diane
1986 *Controlling Interest: Who Owns Canada?* Toronto: Macmillan.
Frank, Andre
1967 *Capitalism and Under-Development in Latin America*. New York: Monthly Review Press.
Garigue, Philippe
1962 'Organisation sociale et valeurs culturelles canadiennes-fran-

çaises'. *Canadian Journal of Economics and Political Science* 28: 189-203.

Gordon, Milton
1964 *Assimilation in American Life*. New York: Oxford University Press.

Grabb, Edward G.
1980 'Differences in Sense of Control Among French- and English-Canadian adolescents'. *Canadian Review of Sociology and Anthropology* 17: 169-75.

Isajiw, W.W.
1981 'Ethnic Identity Retention'. Research Paper No. 125, Centre for Urban and Community Studies, University of Toronto.

Jackson, J.D.
1977 'The Functions of Language in Canada: On The Political Economy of Language'. Pp. 59-76 in W. Coons, D.M. Taylor and M.A. Tremblay, eds, *The Individual Language and Society in Canada*. Ottawa: Canada Council.

Joy, Richard
1971 [1967] *Languages in Conflict*. Toronto: McClelland and Stewart.

Jull, Peter
1981 'Aboriginal Peoples and Political Change in the North Atlantic Area'. *Journal of Canadian Studies* 16 (2) (summer); (also pp. 34-47 in J.E. Elliott, ed., *Two Nations, Many Cultures*, Scarborough, Ont.: Prentice Hall).

Kelner, Merrijoy
1970 'Ethnic Penetration into Toronto's Elite Structure'. *Canadian Review of Sociology and Anthropology* 7 (2) (May): 128-37.

Kierans, Eric, Irving Brecher, and Thomas Naylor
1982 'L'affaire de la Sun Life'. Pp. 248-63 in Caldwell and Waddell (1982).

Laporte, Pierre-E.
1983 'Language Planning and The Status of French in Quebec'. Pp. 91-109 in J.E. Elliott, ed., *Two Nations, Many Cultures*. Scarborough, Ont.: Prentice Hall.

Laurendeau, André, and Davidson Dunton
1965 *A Preliminary Report of the Royal Commission on Bilingualism and Biculturalism*. Ottawa: Queen's Printer.
1967 *Report of the Royal Commission on Bilingualism and Biculturalism: Book I The Official Languages*. Ottawa: Queen's Printer.
1968 *Report of the Royal Commission on Bilingualism and Biculturalism: Book II Education*. Ottawa: Queen's Printer.

Le Devoir (Montreal)
1986 'Quand l'Ontario légifère pour son "son visage français"'. 24 Nov.: 1.
1987 'Un député revendique . . .'. 24 June: 1.
1987a 'S'excuser de parler français . . .'. 27 June: A-2.
1987b 'L'affaire Piquette irrite les francophones . . .'. 29 June: 3.
1987c 'Piquette ne veut pas s'excuser'. 30 June: 3.

1987d 'Première francophone en Alberta'. 11 Sept.: 4.
1989a 'La minorité anglophone du Québec . . .'. 25 Jan.: 1.
1989b 'Les services aux francophone . . .'. 26 Jan.: 1.

Li, Peter S.
1988 *Ethnic Inequality in a Class Society*. Toronto: Wall and Thompson.

Li, Peter S., and Wilfrid Denis
1983 'Minority Enclave and Majority Language: The Case of a French Town in Western Canada'. *Canadian Ethnic Studies* 15 (1): 18-32.

Lieberson, Stanley
1970 *Language and Ethnic Relations in Canada*. New York: John Wiley.

McRae, K.D.
1974 'Consociationalism and the Canadian Political System'. Pp. 238-61 in McRae, *Consociational Democracy: Political Accommodation in Segmented Societies*. Toronto: McClelland and Stewart.

Miles, Robert
1984 'Marxism versus the Sociology of Race Relations'. *Ethnic and Racial Studies* 7 (2) (April): 217-37.

Milner, Henry, and Sheilagh Milner
1973 *The Decolonization of Quebec*. Toronto: McClelland and Stewart.

Newman, Peter
1975 *The Canadian Establishment*. Toronto: McClelland and Stewart.

Niosi, Jorge
1978 *The Economy of Canada: Who Controls It?* Montréal: Black Rose.
1985 *Canadian Multinationals*. Toronto: Between the Lines.

Olsen, Dennis
1980 *The State Elites*. Toronto: McClelland and Stewart.

Porter, John
1965 *The Vertical Mosaic*. Toronto: University of Toronto Press.

Ravault, René-Jean
1983 'L'amorce du redressement des Francophones hors Québec: analyse critique des *Héritiers de Lord Durham*, et de *Deux poids, deux mesures*'. Pp. 273-89 in Dean Louder and Eric Waddell, *Du continent perdu à l'archipel retrouvé: le Québec et l'Amérique française*. Quebec: Presses de l'Université Laval.

Reitz, Jeffrey
1980 *The Survival of Ethnic Groups*. Toronto: McGraw-Hill Ryerson.

Rioux, Marcel
1973 'The Development of Ideologies in Quebec'. Pp. 260-79 in G. Gold and M-A Tremblay, *Communities and Culture in French Canada*. Toronto: Holt Rinehart and Winston.

Rose, Arnold
1967 *The Power Structure: The Political Process in American Society*. New York: Oxford University Press.

Sales, Arnaud
1979 *La bourgeoisie industrielle au Québec*. Montreal: Presses de l'Université de Montréal.

Schachter, Susan
1982 *Working Papers on English Language Institutions in Quebec*. Montreal: Alliance Québec.
Secretary of State
1969-1988 *Annual Reports*. Ottawa: Supply and Services.
Shapiro, Lorraine, and Daniel Perlman
1976 'Value Differences Between English and French Canadian High School Students'. *Canadian Ethnic Studies* 8: 50-5.
Sheppard, Claude-Armand
1971 *The Law of Languages: Studies of the Royal Commission on Bilingualism and Biculturalism, vol. 10*. Ottawa: Information Canada.
Staples, Janice
1974 'Consociationalism at Provincial Level: The Erosion of Dualism in Manitoba 1870-1890'. Pp. 288-99 in K. McRae, *Consociational Democracy: Political Accommodation in Segmented Societies*. Toronto: McClelland and Stewart.
Statistiques Canada
1985 *La situation linguistique au Canada (Language in Canada)*. Ottawa (Cat. #99-935).
Task Force on Program Review (Erik Nielson, chair)
1985 *Service to the Public: Education and Research*. Ottawa: Supply and Services.
Taylor-Browne, Karen
1988 'The Francophone Minority'. Pp. 185-200 in Roger Gibbins, *Meech Lake and Canada: Perspectives from the West*. Edmonton: Academic.
Théberge, Raymond
1987 'Scandale nationale: même là où le nombre le justifie'. Commission nationale des parents francophones, Actes du colloque tenu à Montréal le 13-15 novembre, pp. 23-39.
Vallée, Frank, et al.
1957 'Ethnic Assimilation and Differentiation in Canada'. *Canadian Journal of Economics and Political Science* 23 (4) (November): 540-9.
Vastel, Michel
1989a 'La minorité anglophone du Québec est une des mieux servies au monde'. *Le Devoir* (Montréal), 24 Jan.: 1.
1989b 'Les services aux francophones sont négociés au compte-gouttes'. *Le Devoir* (Montréal), 26 Jan.: 1.
Veltmeyer, Henry
1987 *Canadian Corporate Power*. Toronto: Garamond.
Wade, Mason
1967 *The French Canadians, 1760-1945*. Vol. 1. London: Macmillan.
Wardaugh, Ronald
1983 *Language and Nationhood: The Canadian Experience*. Vancouver: New Star.

Williams, Glen
1978 'The National Policy and Import Substitution Industrialization'. Paper presented to the Annual Meeting, Canadian Political Science Association, London, Ont.

PART THREE

PERSPECTIVES ON RACE AND ETHNICITY

EIGHT

THE VERTICAL MOSAIC REVISITED: OCCUPATIONAL DIFFERENTIALS AMONG CANADIAN ETHNIC GROUPS

HUGH LAUTARD AND
NEIL GUPPY

John Porter's portrayal of Canadian society as a vertical mosaic is a powerful metaphor in contemporary social science research (Porter, 1965). Porter's image of the mosaic depicts Canada as a composite of enduring social groups defined principally by class and ethnicity, but also by language and religion. As well as delineating group boundaries, Porter demonstrated the vertical ranking of these communities on a series of inequality dimensions. In the context of ethnicity, the distinctive communities of the mosaic capture the potent force of ethnic identity, whereas the vertical alignment accentuates the hierarchy of ethnic inequality. It is an argument first of social differentiation, and second of social stratification.

The composition of the Canadian population has changed since Porter first wrote, but social cleavages based on ethnicity remain important. In the 1980s the imagery of a vertical mosaic has been reinterpreted in government circles (Abella, 1984; Boyer, 1985), where the subordinate positions of women, the disabled, Native Indians, and visible minorities have been highlighted. Responding to a growing human rights movement, new policies (e.g., the 1986 Employment Equity Act) have been enacted to facilitate equality and erode the vertical mosaic.

Ironically, at a time when governments are reacting to appeals concerning human rights, some sociologists have begun questioning the durability of ethnicity as an organizing principle in the vertical mosaic. Indeed, two decades after publication of *The Vertical Mosaic*, Porter himself co-authored a paper proclaiming 'the collapse of the vertical mosaic' (Pineo and Porter, 1985: 390; see also Pineo, 1976; Darroch, 1979; Denis 1986).[1] This view is at odds with new government policy as well as with other sociological research demonstrating the continuance of intense ethnic antagonism and discriminatory behaviour (Henry and Ginsberg, 1985; Robson and Breems, 1986).

Sorting out the reasons for this divergence of opinion in the current literature is our starting point (see also Reitz, 1988). In reviewing that literature, we pay particular attention to research findings concerned with historical trends in the salience of ethnicity as a central component of the vertical mosaic. We then present new data, affording the longest historical perspective yet available on the association between ethnicity and occupation, using fifty-five years of census data, from 1931 to 1986. As did Porter before us, we stress both social differentiation and social stratification, although clearly the latter is the key to debates about the *vertical* mosaic.

THE DECLINING SIGNIFICANCE OF ETHNICITY?

In *The Vertical Mosaic* Porter offered three distinct observations about ethnic inequality. First, he argued that 'charter status' groups, the French and English, commanded greater power and privilege than did 'entrance status' groups (i.e., other immigrants) arriving later. Second, he noted an asymmetry of power favouring the English over the French. Third, he claimed that among non-charter immigrant groups too, ethnic inequality persisted. These three aspects of inequality he saw as core features in the distribution of power and privilege in Canada.

Porter's most renowned evidence highlighted the economic elite, where he found that 'economic power belong[ed] almost exclusively to those of British origin' (Porter, 1965: 286). While the French were significantly under-represented, members of non-charter minority groups were virtually absent among economic power-brokers. Clement's more recent (1975) sketch of the economic elite suggested a waning of British dominance, although of 775 elite members 86.2 per cent still were English Canadian, 8.4 per cent were French Canadian, and only 5.4 per cent were of other ethnic origins.

Porter (1965) also presented data from the 1931, 1951, and 1961 censuses. Cross-classifying ethnic origin and occupation, he determined the extent to which various groups were over- and under-represented in different job categories. In the 1931 census he found British and Jewish groups ranked high (i.e., over-represented in professional and financial occupations, and under-represented in low-level, unskilled, and primary jobs); and, as he continued (ibid.: 81) the 'French, German, and Dutch would probably rank next, followed by Scandinavian, Eastern European, Italian, Japanese, "Other Central European", Chinese, and Native Indian.' He concluded (ibid.: 90) that by 1961 and 'except for the French [who had slipped], the rough rank order [had] persisted over time.'

Porter offered two complementary, although independent, explanations for the differential representation of ethnic groups by occupation level. First, immigrants compose a significant portion of the Canadian labour force (more than one in five as late as 1971), and traditionally Canada has attracted a polarized population of both the well educated and the poorly educated, with relatively few people in between.[2] New entrants to Canada reinforce traditional patterns of occupational inequality, since one difference between ethnic groups is the occupation level of their immigrants (Porter, 1965: 86; 1985: 40-51). For instance, new British immigrants acquire professional and financial jobs more often then do recent 'Central European' immigrants, who disproportionately take up unskilled, lower-level positions.

Second, Porter also suggested that once in Canada ethnic groups differed in the extent to which they aspired to upward occupational mobility. Some ethnic groups valued achievement less than others, either because of cultural differences (e.g., less emphasis on material reward) or because of perceived or experienced discriminatory barriers (for a recent statement see Pineo and Porter, 1985: 360-1). However, to the extent that ethnic assimilation occurred, Porter reasoned that ethnic origin exerted less impact on individual occupational mobility. Conversely, in the face of continued ethnic affiliations, mobility was limited—a thesis of 'ethnically blocked mobility'.

Darroch (1979) has undertaken an ambitious revision of Porter's original interpretation. He suggests that Porter paid too much attention to the persistence of a 'rough rank order' over the three censuses, and failed to note the diminishing strength of the association between ethnicity and occupation level. Quite simply, Porter was not sensitive enough to the fact that the occupational over- and under-representation of ethnic groups was much less in 1961 than had been the case in 1931. Darroch reviewed other evidence, including data from the 1971 census, to show that the salience of ethnicity for occupational allocation had diminished over time. He concluded (ibid.: 16) that the idea of blocked ethnic mobility had no foundation in fact and that we should be 'skeptical of the idea that ethnic affiliations are a basic factor in generally limiting mobility opportunities in Canada'.

These sentiments were echoed by Winn (1985) in the context of government policy debates. He was sharply critical of the Abella Commission's (1984: 4) call for the introduction of affirmative-action programs to augment mobility prospects for those groups whose progress had remained 'unjustifiably in perpetual slow motion'. Winn (1985: 689) reviewed data from the 1971 and 1981 censuses, concluding that his evidence provided 'no empirical support for the premise that Canadian society is immobile and that visible or low prestige groups cannot make economic progress'. Affirmative action was unnecessary, he said, because the ethnic inequality implied by the vertical mosaic was exaggerated.

A more pessimistic conclusion concerning the continuing salience of ethnicity as a basis for inequality appears in Lautard and Loree (1984). Using more detailed occupation data, they agreed with Darroch's finding that occupational inequality among ethnic groups had declined over time. But whereas Darroch (1979: 22) was willing to conclude that ethnicity was no longer a fundamental source of inequality, Lautard and Loree (1984: 342) maintained that 'occupational inequality is still substantial enough to justify the use of the concept "vertical mosaic" to characterize this aspect of ethnic relations in Canada'.

Porter (1985: 44-51) repeated his earlier analysis with the 1971 census and, agreeing with Lautard and Loree, claimed that 'ethnic stratification has persisted through to 1971' (ibid.: 48). Here he offers no hints about a 'collapse' of the vertical mosaic. The census, however, contains data for both the foreign-born and the native-born, and so it confounds the two explanations that Porter offered for the association between ethnicity and occupation.

Working with Pineo (Pineo and Porter, 1985), Porter demonstrated that the strength of the association between ethnic origin and occupational status had attenuated in recent decades (up to 1973), at least for males from the major European ethnic groups.[3] They also showed that for native-born Canadian men, ethnic origin had no significant influence on individual occupational mobility. This latter finding suggests that the thesis of 'blocked ethnic mobility' does not persist for second- and third-generation Canadian men (from the major European ethnic groups).

If, as these data show, occupational mobility is not limited by ethnic origin for many groups, then of Porter's two explanations for the ethnicity-occupation link, immigration would seem now to be the remaining factor. Boyd's (1985) research on the influence that birthplace exerts on occupational attainment supports this interpretation. For foreign-born men and women, she showed that ethnic origin had a definite effect on occupational attainment, even after controlling for differences in the average age, education, social origin, and place of residence of ethnic groups. For women she found evidence of a double negative for being female and foreign-born. Indeed, she concluded by noting the 'importance of birthplace and sex as factors underlying the Canadian mosaic' (ibid.: 441).

A small part of the dispute over whether an ethnic component to the vertical mosaic has persisted in Canada is captured by the proverbial 'is the glass half-full or half-empty?'. Exactly how much inequality is enough to attribute it 'fundamental' status? However, a far larger part of the dispute turns on matters of both theoretical definition and methodological procedure. For example, both Winn and Porter (in his early work) relied mainly on rank-ordered data, and Darroch was surely correct in contending that the size of the gap between ranks is crucial. But further, as Lautard and Loree insisted, the gap's size depends on the number of occupations considered, and so they improved the quality of evidence by looking at a wider range of occupation levels. In addition, the use of differing ethnic categories (especially notable in survey-based as opposed to census data), makes comparison and definitive conclusion precarious.

Key issues of theoretical and methodological dispute revolve around three aspects: the ethnic groups studied, the occupation levels considered, and the purity of historical comparability. These are reviewed in turn.

Ethnic groups. The definition of ethnicity remains contentious in social-science literature, and this debate touches directly on ethnic inequality and the vertical mosaic. Census data have been among the principal sources of evidence in evaluating the association between ethnic origin and occupation level. However, until 1981 the census definition of ethnicity relied on tracing ancestral male lineage, often a difficult task after several generations, especially given inter-ethnic marriages and historical changes around the world in national boundaries.

In addition, Statistics Canada is reticent about releasing detailed information for relatively small groups, and so ethnic categories have frequently been combined to form groups of mixed origin (e.g., Asian, Scandinavian). Typically the following ethnic categories have been used in the census: British (English, Irish, Scottish), French, German, Italian, Jewish, Dutch, Scandinavian, Eastern European (Polish, Ukrainian), Other European, Asian, and Native Indian.[4]

Occupations. Porter (1965) relied on five broad occupation groups and a residual category for his 1931 to 1961 census analysis: professional and financial, clerical, personal service, primary and unskilled, agriculture, and all others. By 1961 the residual category ('all others') had swollen to 58 per cent of the total. Darroch's (1979) reanalysis was forced to employ these crude groupings, but Lautard and Loree

(1984) began afresh and used more refined occupation distinctions, amounting to hundreds of separate job categories for each census.

Also at issue here is how occupations are seen to be related. Attention can centre on whether or not ethnic groups tend to be concentrated in different occupations (a focus on the ethnic division of labour—i.e., social differentiation). Alternatively, if ethnic groups tend to congregate in different occupations, then there is a concern with the degree of status inequality between ethnic groups (a focus on the occupational prestige hierarchy—i.e., social stratification).

Historical comparability. Changes in the occupation structure and in the countries of origin of immigrants have meant that census procedures have had to be revised over the years. For occupation this has meant both the addition and deletion of job titles (e.g., computer programmer). For ethnicity one crucial change is in reporting procedures; for instance, in the early years when European groups dominated, little detail was made available for such visible minorities as Blacks or Indo-Pakistanis (even though both groups have a long history in Canada). Also, in 1981 the census questions for ethnicity changed (see Kralt, 1980).[5]

Since census definitions of occupations have changed over time there are advantages and disadvantages in the use of both broad and narrow occupation groups. The broad groups maximize comparability over time because most specific jobs are still classified in the same broad categories from one census to the next. However, the broad categories obscure crucial status gradations and are thus more useful in distinguishing social differentiation than social stratification, and the latter is the more important component in the current debate. Using more occupations gives a more refined calibration of inequality at any one point in time, although it does so by sacrificing comparability over time.

METHODS

We begin by reviewing the results reported by Lautard and Loree (1984) for 1931-71. We then present results for 1971, 1981, and 1986, based on unpublished census data, permitting an examination of the seventeen ethnic groups shown in Table 8.1.[6] To enhance comparability for the latter census years, we employ the 1971 occupational classification in both 1981 and 1986.

Although all of the nearly 500 detailed occupations of the 1971 classification are used in our full analysis of differentiation and stratification among ethnic groups, the broad occupational groups shown in Table 8.1 enable us to see persisting aspects of the vertical mosaic.

Table 8.1 Percentage distribution of selected single-origin ethnic groups, by occupational group and gender, Canada, 1986

Occupational group	Total labour force (%)		British (%)		French (%)		German (%)		Dutch (%)		Scandinavian (%)		Italian (%)		Portuguese (%)		Greek (%)		Yugoslav (%)		Ukrainian (%)		Polish (%)		Hungarian (%)		Jewish (%)		Chinese (%)		South Asian (%)		Indian and Métis (%)		Black (%)	
	M	F	M	F	M	F	M	F	M	F	M	F	M	F	M	F	M	F	M	F	M	F	M	F	M	F	M	F	M	F	M	F	M	F	M	F
Managerial and administrative	9	6	11	6	9	6	9	5	9	5	10	7	7	4	3	2	4	3	6	4	10	6	9	5	9	7	21	12	7	5	9	4	5	4	5	4
Natural sciences, engineering, math	5	1	5	1	4	1	4	1	5	1	6	2	4	1	2	1	3	1	6	2	5	1	8	2	7	2	6	2	12	4	9	2	2	1	4	1
Social sciences	1	3	1	3	1	2	1	2	1	3	1	3	1	1	0	1	0	1	1	2	1	2	1	2	1	2	7	7	1	1	1	2	3	7	2	2
Teaching, related	3	6	3	6	3	7	2	5	2	5	3	7	2	4	0	2	1	3	2	4	3	7	3	5	3	5	5	11	2	3	3	3	1	6	3	3
Medicine, health	2	9	2	9	2	9	1	9	1	10	1	10	1	3	0	2	1	2	1	5	2	8	2	8	2	7	8	7	4	6	3	8	1	5	3	17
Artistic, literary, and recreational	2	2	2	1	2	2	1	1	1	1	2	2	1	1	1	1	1	1	1	1	1	1	1	1	2	2	3	4	1	1	1	1	2	1	2	1
Clerical	7	33	7	34	7	33	5	31	5	29	5	33	7	33	5	22	5	23	6	25	6	34	6	29	5	29	7	31	8	28	9	31	4	22	10	28
Sales	10	10	10	10	10	9	9	11	9	11	10	11	10	11	5	6	9	8	7	10	10	11	8	10	8	11	24	18	10	7	9	7	3	5	6	6
Service occupations	10	16	9	15	10	15	7	17	7	15	9	15	12	15	14	25	38	29	9	21	8	15	8	18	8	17	4	4	26	20	10	13	9	26	15	18
Farming and related	6	2	6	2	4	2	14	6	15	8	11	4	2	1	4	2	1	1	3	1	12	5	7	3	8	4	0	0	1	1	2	5	5	2	1	0
Fishing, hunting and trapping	1	0	1	0	0	0	0	0	0	0	1	0	0	0	0	0	0	0	1	0	0	0	0	0	0	0	0	0	0	0	0	0	3	0	0	0
Forestry, logging	1	0	1	0	2	0	1	0	1	0	2	0	0	0	0	0	0	0	1	0	1	0	1	0	0	0	0	0	0	0	0	0	6	0	0	0
Mining, quarrying, incl. oil and gas	1	0	1	0	1	0	1	0	1	0	1	0	0	0	0	0	0	0	1	0	1	0	1	0	1	0	0	0	0	0	0	0	2	0	0	0
Processing	5	2	4	2	6	2	4	2	4	1	3	1	5	3	7	6	4	2	7	4	3	1	5	2	4	2	1	1	4	2	7	3	5	2	5	2
Machining, related	4	0	3	0	4	0	4	0	4	0	2	0	5	0	6	1	3	0	9	1	3	0	6	1	7	1	1	0	2	0	6	1	3	0	6	1
Fabricating, assembling, repairing	10	4	9	2	10	5	10	3	10	2	8	1	12	14	13	20	12	18	15	10	9	2	12	6	13	5	5	1	9	13	12	10	5	3	14	9
Construction trades	10	0	9	0	10	0	13	0	13	0	10	0	18	0	23	1	7	0	13	0	10	0	9	0	10	1	2	0	2	0	3	0	18	1	6	0
Transport equipment operating	6	1	6	1	6	0	5	1	6	1	6	1	4	0	3	0	3	0	3	0	6	1	5	0	5	0	2	0	2	0	4	0	5	1	5	0
Other and not stated	10	6	10	5	10	6	9	5	8	5	9	4	10	7	12	9	7	7	11	8	10	5	10	6	9	6	5	4	9	8	10	10	20	12	12	8
TOTAL[a]	100	100	100	100	100	100	100	100	100	100	100	100	100	100	100	100	100	100	100	100	100	100	100	100	100	100	100	100	100	100	100	100	100	100	100	100

SOURCE: Based on special tabulation of 1986 Census data.

[a]May not equal 100 per cent because of rounding.

For example, British males and Jewish males and females are over-represented in managerial and administrative occupations, whereas Italians, Portuguese, Greeks, Yugoslavs, Chinese, Blacks, Native Indians and Métis, as well as South Asian (Indo-Pakistani) females are under-represented in this same occupational niche. Conversely, the British and the Jews are under-represented in service occupations, where there is an over-representation of Portuguese, Greeks, Chinese, and Blacks, as well as Yugoslav and Native Indian and Métis females.

Although we could continue to scan Table 8.1 for such differences, it is unlikely that doing so would give us a coherent sense of the overall differentials among the ethnic groups shown—there are simply too many possible comparisons. However, if we calculate the total of either the positive or the negative percentage differences between the occupational distribution of an ethnic group and the total labour force, we obtain a figure indicating the percentage of the members of the group who would have to have different occupations for that group's occupational distribution to be the same as that of the total labour force.[7] Called the index of dissimilarity, this measure allows us to compare occupational differentiation among groups.

For example, calculated from the data in Table 8.1, the index of dissimilarity for Black males is approximately 20, indicating that roughly one out of five Black men in the labour force would have to be in a different occupational category for there to be no difference between their occupational distribution and that of the total male labour force. The equivalent proportion for Native Indian and Métis men is approximately 28 per cent, indicating even greater differentiation.

Again, however, the broad occupational categories in Table 8.1 result in lower measures of dissimilarity than do the hundreds of more detailed occupations used for the results presented below. For example, although Table 8.1 shows the percentage of British males in transport-equipment operating occupations is no different than that of the total male labour force, detailed occupational data indicate that British males are over-represented among air pilots and under-represented among taxi drivers.

Finally, measures such as the index of dissimilarity are most appropriately calculated for a group in comparison with the total labour force minus that group, to correct for the presence of the group itself in the total (Duncan and Duncan, 1955: 494). Accordingly, the results presented in the next section indicate the differentials between each ethnic group and the rest of the labour force, rather than between groups and the total labour force (as in the examples given above).

Dissimilarity, however, does not necessarily mean disadvantage. For example, the highest index of dissimilarity that can be calculated from the data in Table 8.1 is for Jewish males, at 43; this is the result of their over-representation in most of the categories in the upper half of the table and their corresponding under-representation in the remaining occupational categories. There is another measure, however—the index of net difference—that may be calculated with occupational data ranked according to socio-economic scales such as those prepared by Blishen (1958) for 1951; Blishen (1967) for 1961; Blishen and McRoberts (1976) and Blishen and Carroll (1978) for males and females, respectively, for 1971; and Blishen et al. (1987) for 1981. Related to the index of dissimilarity but more complicated in its calculation, the index of net difference provides a measure of the overall occupational ranking of a group in relation to the rest of the labour force. Indexes of net difference may be negative as well as positive, with a minus sign indicating comparatively lower occupational status, and a positive sign comparatively higher status; zero would indicate overall equality of occupational status.[8]

We now turn to the results of the analysis of ethnic occupational differentiation and stratification in Canada, using the indexes of dissimilarity and net difference.

RESULTS

Table 8.2 contains Lautard and Loree's (1984) indexes of occupational dissimilarity for the ethnic groups examined by Porter (1965) and Darroch (1979) for the census years 1931 through 1971. These indexes show the decline in occupational differentiation found by Darroch, although the levels of dissimilarity are considerably higher. The indexes for men in 1961, for example, include no values lower than 15 per cent, and the mean (29) is more than double that yielded by Darroch's analysis (14). By 1971 there is one value for men lower than 15 per cent, but again the mean (24) is nearly double that calculated by Darroch (14) for both sexes combined. After 1931, when the average dissimilarity for females is the same as that for males (37 per cent), ethnic differentiation among women in the paid labour force is less than that among men, but even by 1971 only four groups (German, Dutch, Scandinavian, and Polish) have indexes of 15 per cent or less, and all these are above 10 per cent; the mean for women in 1971 is 21 per cent. Thus, on average, in 1971 a quarter of the male labour force and a fifth of the female labour force would have to have had different occupations in order for there to have been no occupational dissimilarity among ethnic groups. It is also evident from Table 8.2 that while the standard deviations, like the means, decline between 1931 and 1971, relative variation (V) undergoes a net increase for both sexes. The rankings of ethnic groups by degree

Table 8.2
Occupational dissimilarity between selected ethnic groups and the rest of the labour force, by sex: 1931, 1951, 1961, and 1971

	Male				Female			
Ethnic group	1931	1951	1961	1971	1931	1951	1961	1971
British	22	20	19	15	27	23	22	16
French	15	17	16	14	26	23	17	17
German[a]	24	23	17	15	20	14	13	11
Italian	48	34	40	35	39	24	45	38
Jewish	65	63	59	51	51	40	34	32
Dutch	21	20	17	17	14	17	15	15
Scandinavian	29	23	18	17	25	13	10	12
Polish	34[b]	23	18	15	45[b]	21	17	14
Ukrainian		28	21	15		22	21	16
Other European[c]	43	21	19	21	49	18	20	23
Asian[d]	61	46	45	36	50	25	20	25
Native Indian[e]	49	57	57	41	59	53	48	31
Mean ($\overline{X}$)	37	31	29	24	37	24	24	21
Std. Dev. (s)	17	16	17	13	15	11	12	9
V ($s/\overline{X}$)	.46	.52	.59	.54	.41	.46	.50	.43
Number of occupations	(388)	(278)	(332)	(496)	(265)	(226)	(277)	(412)

SOURCES: 1931 (Dominion Bureau of Statistics, 1936: Table 49); 1951 (Dominion Bureau of Statistics, 1953: Table 12); 1961 (Dominion Bureau of Statistics, 1964: Table 21); 1971 (Statistics Canada, 1975: Table 4).

[a]Includes Austrian in 1931.
[b]Eastern European (Polish and Ukrainian combined).
[c]Other central European in 1931.
[d]Weighted average of Chinese and Japanese in 1931.
[e]Includes Eskimos in 1951.

Reproduced with permission from Lautard and Loree (1984: 338).

of dissimilarity, moreover, remain remarkably stable, with the Italian, Jewish, Asian, and Native Indian groups tending to be more dissimilar from the rest of the labour force than other groups.

As noted in the previous section, occupational dissimilarity does not necessarily involve inequality of occupational status. Table 8.3 presents Lautard and Loree's (1984) indexes of net difference in occupational status between each ethnic group and the total labour force for 1951 through 1971.[9] The few positive indexes reflect the relatively high occupational rank of the British, Jewish, and, by 1971, Asian groups, as well as a slight advantage in 1951 and 1961 for Scandinavian females. The negative values indicate the relatively low status of the other groups. With one exception (women of Italian origin in 1971), the largest negative indexes are those for Native Indians, for whom even the 1971 indexes exceed −.30 for males and −.20 for females. Between 1951 and 1971, mean ethnic inequality

Table 8.3
Net difference in occupational status between ethnic groups and the total labour force, by sex: 1951, 1961, and 1971

	Male			Female		
Ethnic group	1951	1961	1971	1951	1961	1971
British	.09	.11	.07	.11	.12	.07
French	−.11	−.10	−.04	−.11	−.07	−.01
German	−.03	−.06	−.07	−.13	−.11	−.09
Italian	−.15	−.28	−.21	−.08	−.37	−.34
Jewish	.41	.42	.35	.20	.21	.24
Dutch	−.10	−.09	−.09	−.15	−.12	−.10
Scandinavian	−.04	−.05	−.08	−.01	−.03	−.01
Polish	−.14	−.07	−.07	−.20	−.16	−.12
Ukrainian	−.11	−.10	−.09	−.20	−.19	−.12
Other European	−.12	−.11	−.11	−.17	−.19	−.20
Asian	−.14	−.03	−.10	−.06	−.05	−.01
Native Indian[a]	−.68	−.63	−.34	−.55	−.47	−.23
Mean ($\|\overline{X}\|$)	.18	.17	.14	.16	.17	.13
Std. Dev. (s)	.19	.18	.11	.14	.13	.10
V ($s/\|\overline{X}\|$)	1.06	1.06	.79	.88	.76	.77
Number of occupational ranks[b]	(208)	(298)	(496)	(178)	(252)	(412)

SOURCES: 1951 (Dominion Bureau of Statistics, 1953: Table 12); 1961 (Dominion Bureau of Statistics, 1964: Table 21); 1971 (Statistics Canada, 1975: Table 4).

[a]Includes Eskimo in 1951.
[b]May not equal the number of occupations in Table 8.1 because of ties.

Reproduced with permission from Lautard and Loree (1984: 338).

declined, as did the standard deviations and the relative variation (V), but the latter remains very high for both sexes. The most pronounced shifts in the rank-order of the ethnic groups by relative occupational status include the Asian and Polish men, rising from a tie at third-lowest in 1951 to second- and sixth-highest respectively in 1971; and Italian females dropping from fifth-highest in 1951 to lowest in 1971. Otherwise, the ranking of ethnic groups by relative occupational status is about as stable as that by occupational dissimilarity.

Table 8.4 contains indexes of dissimilarity for sixteen ethnic groups as of 1971, and seventeen as of 1981 and 1986. With the exception of the indexes for German, Dutch, and Polish males and Jewish females (which are slightly higher in 1986 than in 1971), and those for French males and Polish females (which are the same in 1986 as in 1971), the figures in Table 8.4 indicate continuing declines in ethnic occupational differentiation. However, the replacement of 'Other European' with Hungarian, Portuguese, Greek, and Yugoslav, and 'Asian' with Chinese and South Asian, results in higher average dis-

Table 8.4
Occupational dissimilarity[a] between selected ethnic groups and the rest of the labour force, by sex: Canada, 1971, 1981, and 1986

	Male			Female		
Ethnic group	1971	1981	1986	1971	1981	1986
British	15	10	10	16	9	8
French	14	14	14	18	14	14
German	15	15	17	11	9	10
Dutch	16	17	18	15	13	14
Scandinavian	17	18	13	12	12	11
Ukrainian	15	13	14	16	9	11
Polish	15	14	16	14	10	14
Hungarian	21	19	19	20	15	16
Italian	35	26	24	38	25	22
Portuguese	46	42	39	57	48	40
Greek	48	45	42	51	42	37
Yugoslav	33	31	25	35	29	21
Jewish	51	49	49	32	33	34
Chinese	52	44	42	34	30	30
South Asian	46	34	30	31	27	25
Indian and Métis	41	37	38	32	29	30
Black	NI	32	28	NI	30	27
Mean ($\overline{X}$)	30	27	26	27	23	21
Std. Dev. (s)	15	13	12	14	12	10
V (s/$\overline{X}$)	.50	.48	.46	.52	.52	.48
(Number of occupations)	(498)	(496)	(496)	(464)	(495)	(495)

SOURCE: Special tabulations of census data.

[a]Each figure in the table indicates the percentage of the ethnic group that would have to have a different occupation in order for there to be no difference between the occupational distribution of that group and the rest of the labour force.

NI: not included.

similarity for 1971 than in Table 8.2: 30 and 27 per cent, for males and females respectively, compared to 24 and 21 per cent. As of 1986, a quarter of the males and a fifth of the females would have to have a different occupation in order for there to be no occupational differentiation among these ethnic groups. As well, relative variation remains around 50 per cent, with the British, French, Germans, Dutch, Scandinavians, Ukrainians, Polish, and Hungarians below the means, and—except for Italian males and Yugoslavs of both sexes, in 1986—the Italians, Portuguese, Greeks, Yugoslavs, Jews, Chinese, South Asians, Indians, and Métis, and Blacks above the means, for each year under consideration.

Table 8.5 presents indexes of net difference in occupational status between each of the ethnic groups and the rest of the labour force.

Table 8.5
Net difference in occupational status between selected ethnic groups and the rest of the labour force, by sex: Canada, 1971, 1981, and 1986

	Male			Female		
Ethnic group	1971	1981	1986	1971	1981	1986
British	.13	.06	.05	.14	.06	.04
French	−.06	−.04	−.01	−.02	.00	.01
German	−.08	−.02	−.03	−.09	−.04	−.05
Dutch	−.09	−.06	−.05	−.10	−.06	−.05
Scandinavian	−.08	.01	.01	−.01	.03	.06
Ukrainian	−.09	.01	.02	−.13	.00	.01
Polish	−.08	.03	.05	−.12	−.01	−.02
Hungarian	−.06	.03	.04	−.13	−.03	−.02
Italian	−.22	−.12	−.09	−.35	−.19	−.14
Portuguese	−.38	−.33	−.30	−.62	−.40	−.34
Greek	−.27	−.31	−.28	−.48	−.36	−.31
Yugoslav	−.12	−.05	−.03	−.29	−.18	−.11
Jewish	.36	.30	.34	.24	.27	.29
Chinese	−.04	−.08	−.05	−.20	−.14	−.13
South Asian	.26	.09	.03	.19	−.09	−.11
Indian and Métis	−.35	−.25	−.24	−.23	−.18	−.16
Black	NI	−.02	−.11	NI	−.02	−.05
Mean ($\lvert\overline{X}\rvert$)	.17	.11	.10	.21	.12	.11
Std. Dev. (s)	.12	.11	.11	.16	.13	.11
V ($s/\lvert\overline{X}\rvert$)	.71	1.00	1.10	.76	1.08	1.00
(Number of occupational ranks)	(498)	(468)	(468)	(464)	(467)	(468)

SOURCE: Special tabulations of census data.

[a]A negative figure indicates relatively lower overall occupational status, a positive figure relatively higher status. Zero indicates overall equality of occupational status. The greater the absolute size of the index, the greater the inequality.
[b]May not equal the number of occupations in Table 8.4 because of tied ranks.

NI: not included.

The results for 1971 are consistent with those in Table 8.3. With the exception of the indexes for the British, the Jews, and the South Asians of both sexes, all values for 1971 are negative. As well, in 1971, the Italians, Portuguese, Greeks, Yugoslavs, and Native Indians and Métis have lower overall occupational status than the rest of the groups examined. In 1981 and 1986, the pattern is somewhat different, particularly for males. In addition to British and Jewish males, Scandinavian, Ukrainian, Polish, Hungarian, and South Asian males have positive indexes for both 1981 and 1986. The relative occupational status of Black males is comparable to that of German males in 1981, while the overall rank of Chinese males is similar to that of the Dutch in 1981. Finally, Yugoslav males are positioned between

French and Dutch males in 1981 and tied with German males in 1986. Otherwise the basic pattern holds.

Among women, the British and the Jews have positive indexes for both 1981 and 1986, as do the Scandinavians. Overall equality of occupational status vis-à-vis the rest of the labour force in 1981 is indicated for both the French and Ukrainian groups, which are tied at +.01 in 1986. The overall status of Black females falls between that of Polish and Hungarian women in 1981 and is tied with that of both German and Dutch women in 1986. Otherwise, the pattern prevails: Italian, Portuguese, Greek, Yugoslav, Chinese, South Asian, and Indian and Métis women have lower relative occupational status than do women of the other groups under consideration, in both 1981 and 1986. For both sexes, moreover, the Portuguese have the lowest occupational status, and (except for males in 1971) Greeks the second-lowest status, in all three census years. On average, although occupational inequality among ethnic groups appears to have continued to decline between 1971 and 1986, relative variation in occupational status remains very high.

The results considered above are for the country as a whole, and they could merely reflect regional differences in both ethnic composition and economic structures. Analysis of occupational differentiation as of 1986 among ethnic groups by region, however, indicates that occupational dissimilarity among ethnic groups is generally greater than that observed at the national level. Average ethnic occupational dissimilarity in both the male and female labour forces, as of 1986, is higher in the Atlantic region, in Quebec, on the Prairies, and in British Columbia than in the country as a whole, while the means for Ontario are the same as the national averages. Moreover, the rankings of ethnic groups by degree of occupational dissimilarity in most regions are similar to those observed for the country as a whole.[10]

Finally, occupational differentials among ethnic groups could result from educational differences among groups. We do not have educational data for 1986, but we do have such data for 1981 for the British, French, German, Dutch, Scandinavian, Ukrainian, Polish, Italian, Portuguese, Jewish, Chinese, and Native Indian and Métis groups.[11] Average ethnic dissimilarity for men with a high-school education or the equivalent and men with post-secondary education is two points lower than that among all men, while it is four points higher for men with less than high school. Among women, only these with a high-school education or the equivalent show lower mean occupational dissimilarity among ethnic groups (by 3 points) than do all women, while those with post-secondary education have the same average ethnic dissimilarity as all women. Among women with less than high school, mean ethnic occupational dissimilarity is 5 points higher than that for all women. Moreover, at all educational levels and for both sexes, the general ordering of ethnic groups according to degree of occupational dissimilarity follows the now-familiar pattern.

Average ethnic occupational inequality for men with less than high school or the equivalent and men with a post-secondary education is only one point less than that for all men, and only two points less than for those with high school or the equivalent. Among women with less than a high-school education, average ethnic occupational inequality is one point higher than for all women. Only for women with high school or the equivalent and women with post-secondary education is ethnic occupation inequality substantially reduced, by about one-half and nearly two-fifths, respectively. Nevertheless, for both men and women in each educational category, relative variation remains extremely high, and the ranking of ethnic groups by relative occupational status is generally the same as that previously observed. The vertical mosaic, therefore, is based on more than either regional or educational differences.

DISCUSSION

The historical comparison of ethnic inequality, as measured by occupational differences, suggests that between 1931 and 1986 a decline in the significance of ethnicity has occurred. The decline has been moderate, however, and ethnic origin continues to influence occupational destination.

The trend in occupational dissimilarity indicates a reduction in the ethnic division of labour of roughly 50 per cent in 55 years. Social differentiation based on ethnicity is slowly eroding. The comparable results in ethnic occupational stratification reveal a similar degree of reduction, although over a shorter time span (from 1951 to 1986). These historical comparisons are admittedly crude, and we caution that precise calculations are impossible.

Do these results imply a 'collapse' in the vertical mosaic? Using 1971 census data, Porter himself felt that 'ethnic stratification' had persisted. For males Tables 8.4 and 8.5 both reveal very small declines in differentiation and stratification between 1971 and 1986, affording no firm grounds for repudiating Porter's claim. For females the 1971 to 1986 changes have been larger, but by 1986 levels of differentiation and stratification among women of various ethnic groups are still similar to those for men.

An alternative method of illustrating how large or how small the reported differences are is to compare the differentiation and stratification among ethnic groups with similar differences between women and men. Using a comparable classification of occupations for the 1981 census, Fox and Fox (1987) report an index of dissimilarity for the occupational distributions of women and men of 61 per cent. This figure is greater than the 1981 averages we report (27 per cent for men; 23 per cent for women) and indeed is greater than the index figure for any single ethnic group. Still, certain ethnic groups, notably the Jewish, Greek, Chinese, and Portuguese among men, and the Portuguese and Greek among women, have dissimilarity scores approaching the figure for gender.

Using socio-economic status as the dimension that best illustrates the issue of vertical mosaic, the ethnic distribution can once more be compared with differences between women and men. In this case, ethnic inequality is greater than is gender inequality (see e.g., Darroch, 1979: 13). This comparison obscures much of the known inequality between women and men (SES scores combine education and income, and typically women in the labour force are paid less but have higher levels of schooling than men). The index of net difference value for women compared with men is very close to zero in 1986, whereas the average value for ethnicity is .10 among men and .11 among women.

What these two comparisons suggest is that the gendered division of labour is more marked than is the ethnic division of labour. That is, men and women tend to be clustered in 'sex-typed' jobs more often than members of specific ethnic groups are concentrated in 'ethnic-linked' jobs. However, when the comparison is made on the dimension of socio-economic status, inequality is more marked among ethnic groups than it is between the genders (granting, however, the limitations of SES comparisons between women and men).

Porter's 'vertical mosaic' interpretation of Canadian society rested upon far more than ethnic occupational differentiation. As we noted above, the penetration of ethnic members into elite groups, a key element of the vertical mosaic, has remained limited. Nevertheless, some progress has been made here too, as the new 'entrepreneurial' immigration category suggests, and certainly visible minorities have done well in selected occupational niches—among professionals, for example (Lambert, Ledoux, and Pendakur, 1989).

The research design that we have employed prohibits us from investigating which of Porter's two dynamics best explains the continuing level of ethnic inequality: differential immigration or blocked mobility. Our reading of the research literature suggests that immigration continues as the more important factor, especially in terms of visible minorities (McDade, 1988). But even here, the bimodal character of Canadian immigration, to which Porter initially drew attention, continues.

NOTES

The research reported here was supported by an SSHRCC Leave Fellowship and an SSHRCC Research Grant awarded to Hugh Lautard, a Killam Research Fellowship awarded to Neil Guppy, and grants from the University of New Brunswick Research Fund and Faculty of Arts. The authors are grateful for assistance by Dianne Bawn, Nancy Burnham, and Tim MacKinnon.

[1]Porter died before this paper was published and it is unclear whether he saw the concluding section, from which this quotation is taken, before his death.

[2]For much of Canada's history foreign-born workers have had a higher level of education than have native-born Canadians (see Lagacé, 1968; Boyd, 1985). What this average hides, however, is the tendency for immigrants to be either relatively well or relatively poorly educated.

[3]In this particular analysis Porter included the following ethnic groups: English, Irish, Scottish, French, German, Dutch, Italian, Jewish, Polish, Ukrainian, Norwegian, Russian, and a residual ('other') category.

[4]Winn's work is the exception here in that he reports on only 'selected' ethnic groups and so from the 1981 census neither the British nor the Germans (for example) appear.

[5]Prior to 1981 the census question to determine ethnic origin was: 'To which ethnic or cultural group did you or your ancestor (on the male side) belong on coming to this continent?' In 1981 the question was: 'To which ethnic or cultural group did you or your ancestors belong on first coming to this continent?' Notice, especially, how difficult it is for Native Indians to accurately answer this question. Also in 1981, and for the first time, multiple origins were accepted.

[6]Ethnic groups for 1981 and 1986 are based on single responses and exclude those reporting multiple ethnic or cultural origins. In 1981, only 8 per cent of the population reported multiple ethnic origins, but in 1986, 28 per cent did so. The 1986 data used here are more complete than the latter figure would suggest. First, 8 per cent of the population reported two or more British origins (e.g., English and Scottish), and those in the labour force are included in the present study. Similarly, nearly 6,000 persons reported two or more French origins (e.g., French and Québécois), and those in the labour force are included in the present study. As well, our Scandinavian, Yugoslav, South Asian, and Black categories for 1986, although not for 1981, include persons reported multiple origins involving any combination of the respective constituent groups of each of these categories. For example, persons reporting any combination of Danish, Icelandic, Norwegian, Swedish,

or simply 'Scandinavian' are included as Scandinavian, along with persons who included only one such origin. All other multiple origins are excluded, as are single origins too small for the type of analysis undertaken or too costly to include (e.g., Armenian and Czechoslovakian). In all, the groups included represent 81 per cent of the experienced labour force, as of 1986.

[7]The index of dissimilarity may also be obtained by adding all the differences between two percentage distributions, without regard to signs, and dividing the sum by two (Duncan and Duncan, 1955: 494). Each method is subject to rounding, which in the absence of decimals, as in Table 8.1, does present a problem for some groups.

[8]Specifically, a negative index of net difference indicates the extent to which the probability of a member that the ethnic group in question will have a lower occupational rank than a member of the rest of the labour force exceeds the opposite probability, assuming random pairing. A positive value indicates the opposite relation, while zero would indicate that the two probabilities are the same (Lieberson, 1975: 279-80).

[9]Because there is no occupational ranking for 1931, there are no indexes of occupational inequality for that year.

[10]To maximize the numbers of ethnic members in occupation categories, the regional analysis of ethnic occupational dissimilarity was carried out with Statistics Canada's 22 major occupational groups (cf., Table 8.1). As well, because of the small size of the Hungarian, Portuguese, Greek, and Yugoslav groups in the Atlantic region, these groups were excluded from the analysis for this region. Because the socio-economic scales used in the calculation index of net difference require detailed occupational data, a regional analysis of ethnic occupational inequality is not attempted.

[11]Because of the small number of Portuguese and of Native Indians and Métis with post-secondary education, these two groups were excluded from the analysis at this educational level.

REFERENCES

Abella, Rosalie

1984 *Equality in Employment: A Royal Commission Report*. Ottawa: Supply and Services.

Blishen, Bernard R.

1958 'The Construction and Use of an Occupational Class Scale'. *Canadian Journal of Economics and Political Science* 24: 519-31.

1967 'A Socio-economic Index for Occupations in Canada'. *Canadian Review of Sociology and Anthropology* 4:41-53.

Blishen, Bernard R., and William K. Carroll

1978 'Sex Differences in a Socio-economic Index for Occupations in Canada'. *Canadian Review of Sociology and Anthropology* 15: 352-71.

Blishen, Bernard R., and Hugh A. McRoberts
1976 'A Revised Socio-economic Index for Occupations in Canada'. *Canadian Review of Sociology and Anthropology* 13: 71-9.
Blishen, Bernard R., William K. Carroll, and Catherine Moore
1987 'The 1981 Socio-economic Index for Occupations in Canada'. *Canadian Review of Sociology and Anthropology* 24: 465-88.
Boyd, Monica
1985 'Immigration and Occupational Attainment'. Pp. 393-446 in M. Boyd, et al., eds, *Ascription and Attainment: Studies in Mobility and Status Attainment in Canada*. Ottawa: Carleton University Press.
Boyer, J. Patrick
1985 *Equality for All*. Report of the Parliamentary Committee on Equal Rights. Ottawa: Supply and Services.
Clement, Wallace
1975 *The Canadian Corporate Elite*. Toronto: McClelland and Stewart.
Darroch, Gordon
1979 'Another Look at Ethnicity, Stratification and Social Mobility in Canada'. *Canadian Journal of Sociology* 4 (1): 1-25.
Denis, Ann
1986 'Adaptation to Multiple Subordination? Women in the Vertical Mosaic'. *Canadian Ethnic Studies* 18 (3): 61-74.
Duncan, Otis Dudley, and Beverly Duncan
1955 'Residential distribution and occupational stratification'. *American Journal of Sociology* 60: 493-503.
Fox, B., and J. Fox
1987 'Occupational Gender Segregation in the Canadian Labour Force, 1931-1981'. *Canadian Review of Sociology and Anthropology* 24 (3): 374-97.
Henry, Frances, and Effie Ginsberg
1985 *Who Gets the Work?* Toronto: Urban Alliance on Race Relations and the Social Planning Council of Toronto.
Kralt, John
1980 'Ethnic Origin in the Canadian Census: 1871-1981'. In Roman Petryshyn, ed., *Changing Realities: Social Trends Among Ukrainian Canadians*. Edmonton: Canadian Institute of Ukrainian Studies.
Légacé, Michael D.
1968 'Educational Attainment in Canada'. Dominion Bureau of Statistics, Special Labour Force Survey No. 7. Ottawa: Queen's Printer.
Lambert, M., M. Ledoux, and R. Pendakur
1989 'Visible Minorities in Canada 1986: A Graphic Overview'. Policy and Research Unit, Multiculturalism and Citizenship, Ottawa.
Lautard, Hugh, and Donald Loree
1984 'Ethnic Stratification in Canada, 1931-1971'. *Canadian Journal of Sociology* 9 (3): 333-44.
Lieberson, Stanley
1975 'Rank-sum Comparisons between Groups.' Pp. 276-91 in David R. Heise, ed., *Sociological Methodology 1976*. San Francisco: Jossey-Bass.

McDade, Kathryn
1988 'Barriers to Recognition of the Credentials of Immigrants in Canada'. Discussion Paper 88.B.1, Institute for Research on Public Policy, Ottawa.

Pineo, Peter
1976 'Social Mobility in Canada: The Current Picture'. *Sociological Focus* 9 (2): 109-23.

Pineo, Peter, and John Porter
1985 'Ethnic Origin and Occupational Attainment'. Pp. 357-92 in M. Boyd, et al., eds, *Ascription and Attainment: Studies and Status Attainment in Canada*. Ottawa: Carleton University Press.

Porter, John
1965 *The Vertical Mosaic*. Toronto: University of Toronto Press.
1985 'Canada: The Societal Context of Occupational Allocation'. Pp. 29-65 in M. Boyd, et al., eds, *Ascription and Achievement: Studies in Mobility and Status Attainment in Canada*. Ottawa: Carleton University Press.

Reitz, Jeffrey
1988 'Less Racial Discrimination in Canada, or Simply Less Racial Conflict? Implications of Comparisons with Britain'. *Canadian Public Policy* 14 (4): 424-41.

Robson, Reginald, and Brad Breems
1986 *Ethnic Conflict in Vancouver*. Vancouver: British Columbia Civil Liberties Association.

Winn, Conrad
1985 'Affirmative Action and Visible Minorities: Eight Premises in Quest of Evidence'. *Canadian Public Policy* 11 (4): 684-700.

NINE

STUDIES OF ETHNIC IDENTITY AND RACE RELATIONS

K. VICTOR UJIMOTO

STUDIES OF ETHNIC IDENTITY

Since the promulgation of the policy on multiculturalism on 8 October 1971, several studies on various ethnic groups, ethnicity, and ethnic identity have been published. One of the first publications to appear resulted from a symposium held in May 1971 at the University of Ottawa to discuss some of the key issues related to multiculturalism. In *Sounds Canadian, Languages and Cultures in Multi-Ethnic Society* (1975), the book's editor, Paul M. Migus, captures the essence of the symposium, namely those issues associated with education, language, and culture and their impact on ethnicity, ethnic identity, and ethnic survival.

In one of the articles in the book, Simon (1975: 3) argues that differences in language and religion stand out among the factors that generate conflict and tensions. These two factors are also the key variables that serve to reinforce the sense of ethnic identity. Simon's argument takes on significance when we realize that conflict occurs only in the 'wake of progress'. He uses the example of a situation in which language competency becomes important in securing employment in government and other forms of public service. He notes that in pre-industrial, rural, and predominantly illiterate societies, diverse language groups may coexist in harmony and that multilingualism is of little political consequence. Thus in terms of ethnic relations, as long as there is no pressure to learn the language of another ethnic group, conflict can be avoided.

For students of multiculturalism and Canadian society, there is clearly a very important point to be noted in Simon's observations. Conflict can be avoided if there is a lesser degree of political interference and a greater knowledge of each other's language and culture as a natural aspect of the learning process. However, this situation is more of an ideal than a reality, since equal access to language training is not available to all citizens. In multicultural societies such as Canada, where there is a ruling dominant group, there is very little motivation to learn the languages and cultures of the subordinate groups unless one is forced to do so. Thus there is a natural tendency for subordinate groups to attempt to preserve their language and culture. In the process of preservation, survival becomes the operative term; at the same time, however, ethnic-community cohesion and ethnic identity may be further strengthened.

In addition to the role of language in the formation and retention of ethnic identity, Millet (1975: 105) observes that among the institutions that have contributed to the survival of a distinctive culture, the church has served an important function. Using census material and church records, he examined 'religion as a source of perpetuation of ethnic identity'. While Millet's 1968 study indicates that 'Roman Catholics worshipped in twenty-one languages, the United Church in fourteen, the Anglicans in twelve, the Presbyterians in five, the Lutherans in nine, and the Baptists in thirteen', there was a heavy concentration of adherents from the same ethnic group. He concludes that given the number of languages used in the Canadian religious institutions, the church has not only encouraged multilingualism, but also enabled many ethnic communities to survive as a distinct group.

An interesting question raised by Millet (1975: 106) is 'whether the churches' diversity is merely a reflection of Canada's diversity, or whether the churches purposely maintain this diversity'. He argues that the churches are 'a repository of diversity by default' by virtue of the legal fact that the official languages of many of our public institutions are English and French: in most instances, therefore, the church and family environments are the only places where people of various ethnic origins can comfortably express their views. Traditionally, the church has always served as a haven from the stress and tensions of the everyday work world. The church environment that enabled ethnic minorities to participate in religious as well as non-religious activities not only served to strengthen and preserve their members' ethnic identity, but also allowed them to survive as a group with a common language, religious practices, and rituals. The role of the church in assisting in the preservation of ethnic identity as a means of furthering the well-being of the ethnic minority group can be observed today, particularly in those communities consisting of recent immigrants to Canada such as the Vietnamese, Cambodian, Korean, and Latin American refugees.

Although the church as an institution may facilitate the preservation of ethnic identity, the actual process of maintaining that identity is an important aspect to consider. Isajiw (1975: 128) defines ethnic identity as a 'commitment to a social grouping of common ancestry, existing within a larger society of different ancestral origins, and characterized by sharing of some common values, behaviourial patterns or symbols different from those of the larger society'. Such a broad definition allows for both examination of the variety of ways in which people may contribute to the process of commitment to their own ethnic group and identification of the range of values and social behaviour across different ethnic groups. Isajiw argues that differentiation in the forms of ethnic identity is necessary in order to understand the process of its maintenance over generations.

Isajiw (1975: 128) observes that the conventional starting point for the study of ethnic identity maintenance has been the concept of assimilation and the various factors that influence it. The main problem with assimilation theory is that it is extremely difficult to determine empirically exactly what ethnic groups are supposed to be assimilating or acculturating to in a multicultural society. Noting Milton Gordon's distinction between cultural and structural assimilation, Isajiw argues that one may become culturally assimilated, but structurally remain unintegrated. In other words, 'the two forms of assimilation are not necessarily conditioned by one another.'

Isajiw (1975: 132) singles out three patterns of ethnic identity maintenance—(a) the pattern of 'transplantation' of the old culture, (b) the rebellion pattern, and (c) the returning or rediscovery pattern—which he assumes 'are discernible under the conditions of pluralism of ethnic stratification'. As the term implies, the pattern of 'transformation' occurs when the immigrant generation attempts to re-establish the patterns of behaviour or institutional ways of their home country. In the case of the first-generation Japanese immigrants, or *issei*, for example, it was necessary to transplant the institutional ways learned in Japan in order to survive in the politically and socially hostile new country.

The rebellion pattern of ethnic identity maintenance is characteristic of the Canadian-born or the *nisei* (second generation) and *sansei* (third generation). Again using the Japanese Canadian example, it was the *nisei* and *sansei* who provided the leadership to heighten awareness of the cultural, social, and historical background of the Japanese Canadian internment and to pursue the subsequent quest for redress and compensation. As Isajiw (1975: 133) has observed, this type of self-awareness occurs 'as a consequence of the psychological confrontation with the cultural ways and relational structures of the larger society'.

The 'returning or rediscovery' pattern of ethnic identity maintenance occurs with the second, third, and subsequent generations of immigrant groups. These people are essentially socialized in Canadian society and removed from the traditional culture of their immigrant forbears. The search for one's 'cultural roots' appears to be the dominant stimulus in this pattern of ethnic identity maintenance. In this instance, the linkage of the past is not for day to day survival, but for more symbolic reasons.

Subsequent studies on ethnic identity and aspects of ethnic-group survival have been provided by Driedger (1977, 1978, 1987). Examining the 'extent to which various ethnic groups adhere to their own distinctive cultural heritage', Driedger (1978: 14-15) provides the following six ethnic identification factors: (a) identification with an ecological territory; (b) identification with an ethnic culture; (c) identification with ethnic institutions; (d) identification with historic symbols; (e) identification with an ideology; and (f) identification with charismatic leadership. Drawing on previous studies by Joy (1972) and Lieberson (1970), which argued that neither language nor culture can be maintained unless there is a 'sufficiently large number of a given ethnic group concentrated in a given territory' (Driedger, 1978: 16) examined the concentration of Hutterites, Germans, Ukrainians, Poles, and Jews in Canada with respect to the relationship between territory and maintenance of ethnic identity.

If significant numbers of a given ethnic group occupy a given territory, it seems reasonable that certain ethnic institutions may eventually develop. The extent to which ethnic social, educational, economic, and political institutions may flourish has been discussed in terms of 'institutional completeness', a concept developed by Breton (1964). Driedger notes from his examination of territorial, institutional, and cultural-identity factors that these three factors tend to reinforce each other. The development of institutional completeness will, in turn, enable members of the community to celebrate their historical rituals and symbols, thus strengthening their ethnic identity. In those instances where a strong religious or political ideology exists, members of the ethnic community may go beyond their cultural and traditional values to develop a sense of purpose. Driedger concludes that it is charismatic leadership that makes it possible to harness this ideology in order to develop a sense of purpose for current and future situations.

While we have noted several studies on ethnic identity by Canadian scholars such as Driedger and Isajiw, comparative ethnic and multicultural studies in Canada are a relatively recent phenomenon, and therefore many of the theories that are being developed centre on ethnic identity and ethnic relations more than on race relations. Given the policy of multiculturalism in Canada, it may be appropriate to emphasize ethnic relations rather than race relations as in the United States. However, recent events in Canada—such as the sudden arrival of Tamil refugees and Sikhs, the shooting deaths of two Blacks, Lester Donaldson and Michael Wade Lawson, in Toronto by on-duty police officers, and the concomitant public outcry regarding both of these events—suggest that it doesn't take much to kindle racial hatred. Issues related to race and colour are little understood because we have not examined the religious and cultural attributes usually associated with racial or visible minorities. Thus in situations involving survival or competition for scarce resources, conflict and violence are often the ultimate result. While we have not experienced any major racial violence in Canada, perhaps the time has now arrived for serious examination of some of the simmering issues related to both ethnic identity and race relations in Canadian society. Therefore we will now examine some of the issues related to race and race relations.

THE CONCEPT OF 'RACE'

According to Anderson and Frideres (1981: 14), in the past the concept of race as used by physical anthropologists and biologists was simply intended as a way of categorizing groups of people into phenotypes that were statistically identifiable. The characteristics chosen for this categorization apparently bore no relation to culture, personality, or social behaviours. As a result, understanding what the concept meant was extremely difficult. For example, van den Berghe (1967: 9) notes four connotations of the term 'race':

1. As a sub-species of homo sapiens characterized by certain phenotypical and genotypical traits, for example, the 'Mongoloid race' or the 'Negroid race'.
2. As a human group that share certain cultural characteristics such as language or religion, for example the 'French race' or the 'Jewish race'.
3. As a synonym for species, for example, the human race.
4. As a human group that defines itself and/or is defined by other groups as different from other groups by virtue of innate and immutable physical characteristics.

Although many physical anthropologists have characterized race in terms of certain phenotypical and genotypical traits, there is no common agreement. Furthermore, the biological classifications of the human species consists of even more racial taxonomies than they have described.

According to van den Berghe, we consistently use the fourth definition of race noted above: that is, we commonly refer to a group 'that is socially defined but on the basis of physical criteria' (1967: 9). For our purposes, we need not concern ourselves with the first or third definitions. In the Canadian context the second definition, based on certain cultural characteristics, is most applicable to ethnic groups. Since ethnic groups are defined in terms of cultural characteristics, it is often very difficult to differentiate between social definitions based on physical criteria and cultural criteria. As illustrations, consider the following examples provided by van den Berghe (1967: 10):

> Cultural traits are often regarded as genetic and inherited (e.g., body odour, which is a function of diet, cosmetics, and other cultural items); physical appearance can be culturally changed (by scarification, surgery, and cosmetics); and the sensory perception of physical differences is affected by cultural definitions of race (e.g., a rich Negro may be seen as lighter than an equally dark, poor Negro, as suggested by the Brazilian proverb: 'Money bleaches').

The confusion that stems from such a variety of definitions and criteria has led some authors to avoid the term. In the 1930s, for instance, W. Lloyd Warner examined race relations in terms of caste, as 'an endogamous and hierarchized group in which one is born and out of which one cannot move' (van den Berghe, 1967: 10). Thus Warner speaks of the whites and blacks in the United States as 'castes separated by caste line'. Warner's theory of colour-caste was the first American attempt at a theory of race relations (Rex, 1970: 13).

According to Rex (1970: 13), Warner's theory of colour-caste in American society consisted of both class and caste divisions. In order to identify individuals on a stratification system, Warner used both subjective and objective measures. Subjective measures were employed to establish an individual's social status. Commencing with the American stratification system, Warner examined the social mobility of white and non-white minorities in American society, and found that while European or white minority groups were able to move up the stratification system in subsequent generations after migration, Blacks were not; regardless of their objective status, Blacks were denied equal social access and status. Similarities between the Hindu caste system and the social position of American Blacks, such as segregation and various taboos, prompted Warner to draw upon the comparative framework. However, subsequent scholars examining white-Black relations have dismissed the caste analogy.

STUDIES OF RACE RELATIONS

Perhaps one of the most influential approaches to the study of interaction between the whites and Negro migrants in the US is that developed by Robert E. Park at the University of Chicago in 1924 (Richmond, 1973: 1). In his conceptual scheme, illustrated in Figure 9.1, Park represented this interaction as a cycle that began with the initial-contact stage and ended with the assimilation of the minority group into the majority or dominant group. The intermediate stages consisted of competition for scarce resources, eventual conflict, and, as the conflicts that arose from competition for housing, employment, social mobility, and other factors were regulated, gradual accommodation into existing social institutions. According to Park's theory, this accommodation eventually gave way to assimilation.

Although Park's race-relations theory was an important starting point, several sociologists have criticized and made several modifications to it. For example, Lieberson (1980: 68) suggests that a race-relations theory should take into account 'such divergent consequences of contact as racial nationalism and warfare, assimilation

Figure 9.1 Park's Race-Relations Cycle

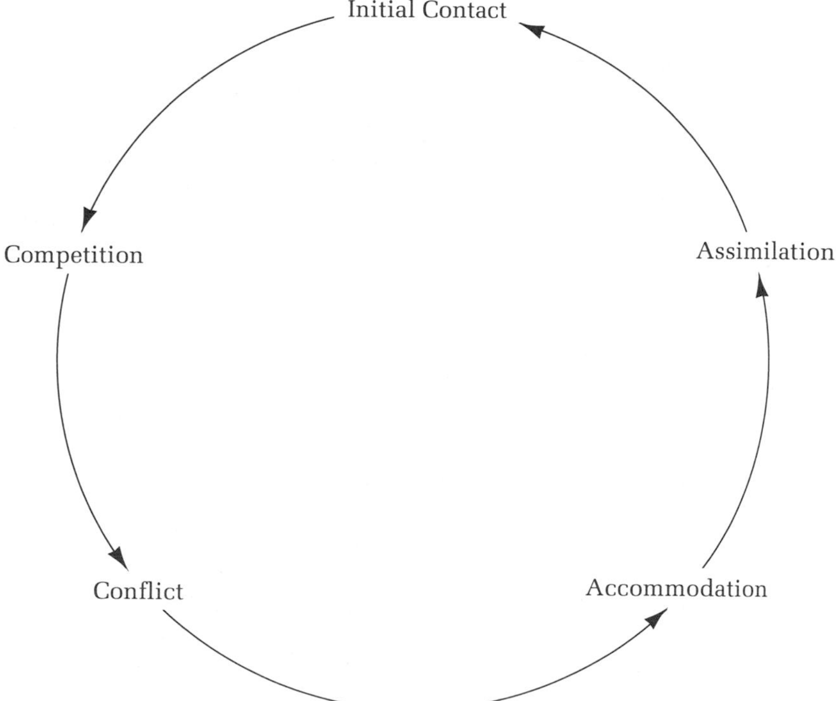

and fusion, and extinction'. He argues that 'the critical problem on a societal level in racial or ethnic contact is initially each population's maintenance and development of a social order compatible with its ways of life prior to contact.' At each phase of the race-relations cycle, therefore, the political, social, and economic institutions must be examined in relation to the overall context of a particular event or 'cycle' (in Park's term). For Lieberson, however, knowledge of the nature of one group's domination over another is 'a necessary but insufficient prerequisite for predicting or interpreting the final and intermediate stages of racial and ethnic contact'. He argues (1980: 68) for a distinction between two major types of contact situations:

1. contacts involving subordination of an indigenous population by a migrant group, for example, Negro-white relations in South Africa, and
2. contacts involving subordination of a migrant population by an indigenous racial or ethnic group, for example, Japanese migrants to the United States.

In the Canadian case, it is worth noting that both of those contact situations did occur. In the first instance, the European explorers came into contact with the indigenous native or aboriginal groups and eventually subordinated them. Over time, the European migrant group became dominant and subsequent immigrants to Canada such as the Chinese and Japanese were maintained in their subordinate positions through discriminatory institutional controls.

As noted earlier, it is essential to understand the socio-political and economic environments in which migrant groups have entered Canada. In the case of the Chinese and Japanese and their initial contact experiences, we must understand the dominant ideology of the time, which was based on colonial domination and the superiority of the white race. The basic ideology of white superiority was a theme perpetuated by the various churches in Canada, particularly those that had missionaries abroad. In their enthusiasm to raise funds, returning missionaries emphasized the racial and cultural differences between Orientals and natives—the 'heathens'—and the superior Westerners. Thus in order to comprehend the anti-Oriental hysteria and the subsequent treatment of the *issei*, or first-generation Japanese, in Canada between 1877 and 1948, it is essential, as noted by Bolaria (1983: 160), 'to draw historical connections between international colonialism, treatment of non-white immigrants as colonial subjects, and the pattern of racial domination and exploitation here'.

As illustrated in Figure 9.1, as long as the conditions of initial contact are maintained and the established relations between the indigenous and migrant, or dominant and subordinate, groups are relatively stable, racial harmony can be maintained. But what happens when the dominant ideology of racial superiority is gradually challenged by the adaptive capacity of the supposedly inferior racial minority? Answers to this question can be found in Canadian history and in the study of various Canadian immigration laws. For example, in the Japanese Canadian case a period of relatively free immigration existed between 1877 and 1907. Then there was a period of controlled immigration between 1908 and 1941. Subsequently, between 1941 and 1948, the Japanese in Canada were deprived of their civil rights, and although the period since 1949 can be characterized as one in which those rights were restored, various issues that stemmed from the preceding period remained unresolved until compensation was legislated on 22 September 1988, some forty-six years after the forced removal of Japanese Canadians from the Pacific coast and the confiscation of their homes and property.

Lieberson draws our attention to the various situations that result in conflict. The form of social organization and the degree of institutional completeness (Breton 1964: 193-205) of the migrant group may be perceived as a threat to the established social order. In the Japanese Canadian case, this perceived threat was based upon aspects of traditional Japanese culture that emphasized frugality and hard work, diligence, perseverance, and co-operation and were manifested in day-to-day activities. As noted by Ujimoto (1983: 126), the social organization of the Japanese immigrant community was centred on a shared need for survival and a sense of group consciousness. This group solidarity was strengthened by the fact that the Japanese were physically and socially segregated in their residential and work environments. The prejudice and discrimination they faced offered very little alternative but to revert to the Japanese system of interdependent social relations based on the principle of social and moral obligations and the traditional practices of mutual assistance, such as *oyabun-kobun* (parent-child) and *sempai-kohai* (senior-junior) relationships.

The extremely high degree of social organization that was developed by the Japanese Canadians in order to survive as a community between 1877 and 1907 was perceived as an economic and political threat; consequently, the dominant group looked for ways to protect itself. In order to control the economic and political outcome to its own advantage, institutional controls were imposed to limit the number of new immigrants to Canada.

Such controls had been imposed on the Chinese as early as 1885, when a head tax of $50 was introduced. A series of attempts to legislate the tax had started in 1872, but it was not until 1885 that the federal government finally bowed to public pressure. This was the first of several measures to be passed by the Dominion government to restrict Asian immigration to Canada. Hostility against the Asian immigrants was most intense in British Columbia, where the Asiatic Exclusion League was formed in Vancouver in the summer of 1907. Because of Japan's special relationship with the British Empire (see Adachi, 1976: 71), the federal government was unable to impose restrictive immigration measures, and thus the provincial pressure groups took the initiative to press for the complete exclusion of Asians from BC. Eventually, anti-Asian sentiments culminated in the Vancouver Anti-Japanese Riots of September 1907 (Sugimoto 1972: 93).

At this juncture, it is necessary to reflect upon Park's race-relations cycle once again. As Lieberson (1980: 69) notes, when two populations begin to share a given territory but do not share the already established order and each group attempts to maintain its own institutional arrangements for whatever reasons, conflict will arise. He states that if groups in contact differ in their capacity to impose changes on the other group, then we may expect to find a 'superordinate' group and a 'subordinate' one. Lieberson argues that 'it is here that efforts at a single cycle of race and ethnic relations must fail. For it is necessary to introduce a distinction in the nature or form of subordination before attempting to predict whether conflict or relatively harmonious assimilation will develop.' This is a very important point that must be underscored with respect to any future aspect of race relations and public policy because, according to Lieberson, the 'race relations cycle in areas where the migrant group is superordinate and indigenous groups subordinate differs sharply from the stages in societies composed of a superordinate indigenous group and subordinate migrants.' Obviously, then, for Canadian society a single race-relations cycle is not tenable, since we have both of the situations noted by Lieberson.

The situation that may be characterized as 'migrant superordination' clearly occurred in early Canadian history when the first Europeans arrived possessing technology that was much superior to that of the natives. In addition, the division of the aborigines or natives into various tribal groups weakened their ability to stand up to the 'superordinate migrants', who were well organized as a social group. Other examples of white invasion of indigenous groups are available in Australia, New Zealand, and the United States, where white conquest has nearly eliminated indigenous populations through warfare and disease.

Lieberson (1980: 70) also alerts us to the fact that 'in addition to the economic and demographic upheavals, the superordinate migrants frequently create political entities that are not at all coterminous with the boundaries existing during the indigenous populations' supremacy prior to contact. He cites the example of the British and Boers in southern Africa, where new political states were established that included traditionally separate and warring groups. Through conquest, the migrant superordinates become the indigenous superordinates for the later wave of migrants.

As already illustrated with the example of Chinese and Japanese immigration and institutional controls in Canada, superordinate populations can limit the numbers and groups coming to the country. Recent Canadian immigration laws as well as pending refugee laws are cases in point. Situations in which migrants trickle into the country gradually will likely create less conflict. But what happens when immigrants are selected on the basis of technological and entrepreneurial skills? Will they in time become the superordinate class? The race-relations cycle may be repeated, but in a different way in that the accommodation stages will become rather blurred, especially in a global environment in which the commonly accepted assimilation and acculturation criteria may no longer apply.

From this account of factors that may culminate in a conflict situation, it is obvious that the conditions necessary to maintain a given social order will vary according to each migrant group and the conditions under which it enters. As is already becoming abundantly clear in Britain and in various parts of Canada, an immigration policy that favours family reunification and the entry of ethnic groups that are socially cohesive frequently leads to a situation in which certain geographic areas are dominated by the new migrants. Subsequently, for various reasons, the indigenous population decreases, and one result is a weakening of existing economic and political organizations. If these demographic shifts are gradual and options are available for geographic mobility, then it is quite possible that racial conflict will not arise. The perception of competition for scarce resources, which include territory and social mobility, may be a much more significant factor in predicting conflict than are other variables. As suggested by Patel (1980: xiii), race-relations and social policies of the future will have to deal with the causal factors of conflict rather than attempt to address simply the conflict itself.

Another aspect of Park's race-relations cycle that has received considerable examination is the concept of assimilation. In 1921, Park and Ernest W. Burgess defined assimilation as 'a process of interpenetration and fusion in which persons and groups acquire the memories, sentiments, and attitudes of other persons or groups, and by sharing their experience and history, are incorporated with them in common cultural life' (Gordon, 1964: 62). Although the key terms in the above definition of assimilation—'sharing their experience' and a 'common cultural life'—seem to suggest accommodation, the literature provides very little evidence of accommodative processes prior to assimilation. The main assumption in Park's race-relations cycle appears to be the notion of sharing not only experiences, but also resources. This is a very naïve assumption, as historical facts inform us otherwise.

A further assumption made by Park and Burgess was that as social contact occurred, appropriate social interaction would result and assimilation would be its final result. However, we have already seen in Figure 9.1 that the linkage between initial contact and accommodation is provided by both competition and conflict. The issue of the form or nature of the initial contact was not examined sufficiently, as Lieberson has already noted, and perhaps too much emphasis was placed on the importance of assimilation as a naturally occurring phenomenon. Ideas related to social exchange and access to available resources were not considered. Gordon (1964: 63) notes that although Park was 'one of the most prolific germinal thinkers' of the time, he appears to have confined his thinking on assimilation to 'the realm of cultural behaviour (with political overtones), and, by implication, to secondary relationships'. He quotes Park's (1930: 281) definition of assimilation as

> the name given to the process by which peoples of diverse racial origins and different cultural heritages, occupying a common territory, achieve a cultural solidarity sufficient at least to sustain a national existence.
>
> In the United States an immigrant is ordinarily considered assimilated as soon as he has acquired the language and the social ritual of the native community and can participate, without encountering prejudice, in the common life, economic and political. The common sense view of the matter is that an immigrant is assimilated as soon as he has shown that he can 'get on in the country'. This implies among other things that in all the ordinary affairs of life he is able to find a place in the community on the basis of his individual merits without invidious or qualifying reference to his racial origin or to his cultural inheritance.

Building on this definition of assimilation, Gordon alerts us to other variables, such as prejudice and discrimination, that should be differentiated. He outlines an 'ideal type' situation in which a complete or 'ultimate form' of assimilation may occur. The seven variables that he suggests are involved in the assimilation process are presented in Table 9.1. Noting that each of these subprocesses may be thought of 'as constituting a particular stage or aspect of the assimilation process', Gordon assigns them terms such as 'structural assimilation' and 'cultural assimilation'. In this sense, he has refined Park's race-relations theory considerably.

These refinements in the definition and the subprocesses involved in the overall assimilation process have enabled subsequent investigators to secure the appropriate empirical data to fit the typology.

Table 9.1
Gordon's Key Assimilation Variables

Subprocess or Condition	Type or Stage of Assimilation	Special Term
Change of cultural patterns to those of host society	Cultural or behavioural assimilation	Acculturation
Large-scale entrance into cliques, clubs, and institutions of host society, on primary group level	Structural assimilation	None
Large-scale intermarriage	Marital assimilation	Amalgamation
Development of sense of peoplehood based exclusively on host society	Indentificational assimilation	None
Absence of prejudice	Attitude receptional assimilation	None
Absence of discrimination	Behaviour receptional assimilation	None
Absence of value and power conflict	Civic assimilation	None

SOURCE: Milton Gordon, *Assimilation in American Life* (New York: Oxford University Press, 1964), p. 71.

However, as Richmond (1973: 2) has noted, others have attempted to refine and criticize the concept of assimilation itself. Given the pluralistic and highly mobile industrial societies of today, Richmond and others strongly doubt that complete assimilation will ever occur.

Further insights into race-relations theory were developed particularly in Britain in the late 1960s, when problems were beginning to emerge in terms of competition for scarce resources, specifically housing (Richmond, 1973: 3). In examining the British situation, Rex (1970: 17) draws upon the insights provided by American race-relations situations. Commenting on how the major problems of social systems are represented in Parsons' (1952: 67) concepts of 'universalism, achievement, particularism and ascription and, in the later language as adaptation, goal attainment, integration and pattern maintenance, and tension management', Rex cogently argues that what this means is that social systems involve some roles. Thus, depending on the stage of development of the society, different priorities are assigned to these roles. To illustrate, Rex notes that the most highly valued role in the American system is adaptation, whereas in the Soviet system it is goal-attainment, and in the Chinese, integration. In terms of race-relations theory, then, Rex argues that the key problem is to determine 'what scale of priorities exist, and then to discover how the assignment of individuals to roles, and of possessions to individuals, varies in accordance with this scale, both in the society at large, and within each institutional context'.

Rex (1970: 18) observes that in reality the actual distribution of roles and rights deviates from the norm because of power. Although various groups are brought together, and some lip services is paid to the value system of each group, there is no 'shared value system on which an agreed pattern of stratification, either of all groups, or of all individuals within society, could be based'. Therefore Rex recognizes that given the variety of race-relations situations, a theory of race relations that is limited to a single frame of reference cannot possibly account for the variety of stratification patterns. We can no longer understand race relations in terms of stratification theory, since the society we are dealing with is plural.

For Rex, race relations in the plural society are a matter of 'neither hierarchically arranged castes, nor classes in conflict, nor a system of roles of some set of ideal values'. What he is concerned about are 'segments which cut across the strata, producing vertical rather than horizontal divisions within the society'. Commenting on Furnivall's description of Burma as a plural society, Rex notes that Furnivall's interpretation of social life is 'what goes on round the camp-fires of the separate communities when they are separated from each other'. There is 'almost total disjunction' (Rex, 1970: 19) between the various groups that make up the society, and contact is limited to the market place. Thus, Rex observes, there is no common will, and no normative order.

One concept that interests Rex is that of cultural pluralism. Quoting Smith (1965: 82), he states that the core of any culture is its institutional system, which includes 'kinship, education, religion, property and economy, recreation and certain sodalities'. He notes, however, that this system does not include government, 'because without a single governmental institution we should not have a society at all', but merely coexisting societies. On the basis of his review of several sociological theories and study of race-relations situations, Rex (1970: 30) defines his own approach to the theory of race relations, which includes the following three key elements:

> 1. a situation of differentiation, inequality and pluralism as between groups;
> 2. the possibility of clearly distinguishing between such groups by their physical appearance, their culture or occasionally merely by their ancestry;
> 3. the justification and explanation of this discrimination in terms of some kind of implicit or explicit theory, frequently but not always of a biological kind.

In order to assess race-relations situations, therefore, it is essential to have a firm understanding of the social-structural properties of a society. Rex's approach (1970: 30) to the study of social structures differs from that of other scholars, noted earlier, in two respects:

> One is that we take the view that, before going on to talk about the structure of society in general, it is important to look at the social relations which characterise the society's productive institutions, since these contribute important meanings to the overall social pattern.
>
> The other is that we draw attention to the fact that the social relations of production, as well as the larger social structure, are based upon coercion of one group by another, a state of affairs which is most likely to come about in conditions where one group on a lower technological level than another is conquered by the other.

Indeed, in order to understand race relations in Canada, Basran (1983: 5) has observed that 'one has to comprehend the nature of capitalism, the role of the Canadian state and the control of the Canadian economy by the United States. Canadian immigration policy has been dictated by these forces.' Basran argues that from a Marxist perspective, 'racism is the function of economic inequality, the class system and our system of production and distribution'. In addition to disucssing racism as a mechanism for exploiting labour, Basran observes that immigration is also used by the ruling class 'to create a reserve army of labour which can be utilized according to their needs and interests'. This aspect of immigration policy—that is, control based on economic conditions—will have severe implications for race relations because non-white immigrants become the scapegoats blamed for any deterioration in the economic condition, which will create a conflict situation.

A recent publication that examines race relations in Canada in terms of the relationships of production and the contributions made by non-whites to the country's economic development is Bolaria and Li's (1985) book on racial oppression in Canada. They argue that previous literature in the field of race and ethnic studies has placed too much emphasis on the cultural aspects of immigrant adaptation and assimilation. The net result, the authors write (1985: 1) is 'the emergence of an orthodoxy in race and ethnic studies that preaches the value of cultural identity, and linguistic retention by way of studying the multicultural mosaic of Canada'. They challenge the assimilation theories on their inability to account for the increasing manifestations of racism and racial phenomena in Canada and the United States.

Bolaria and Li assert that race problems begin as labour problems in which racial encounters are not a matter of cultural differences, but of confrontation based on power relationships between the dominant and subordinate groups. Accordingly, they argue (1985: 1) that racism is not an outcome of cultural misunderstanding, but rather 'a deliberate ideology designed to justify the unjust treatment of the subordinate group for the purpose of exploiting its labour power'. While the Bolaria and Li approach to race relations might more appropriately be called the political economy of race, they argue (1985: 2) that to accept the label of political economy when discussing race relations would be 'conceding legitimacy to the view that race and ethnic studies deal exclusively with cultural theories and issues'. Their theoretical perspective is not entirely new in that there is a large literature dealing with earlier plantation and colonial societies in which racial categorization and slave labour are intertwined. Under such circumstances, it is generally only a matter of time before conflict situations arise.

Race-relations situations in which conflict occurs must be examined in terms of the exact nature of the conflict. Rex (1970: 121) alerts us to at least four different kinds of conflict. In the first example, a conflict situation may arise when the minority group attempts to enter the stratification system. In such cases institutional controls such as the denial of citizenship rights may prevail. In the past, the first-generation Chinese and Japanese in Canada did not challenge this exclusion and meekly accepted their subordinate positions.

A second example is the case of conflict based on the competition for scarce resources—for instance, land or housing. Another such variable might be the competition for consumer markets, examples of which are abundant in the agricultural and fishing industries of British Columbia prior to the Second World War. The third case centres on a competitive situation in which punitive policies are pursued by dominant groups. For example, Japanese Canadian fishermen on the west coast were permitted fishing boats of limited horsepower; however, even that was not enough to stem the tide of economic competition, and all their boats were eventually confiscated.

The fourth example of conflict noted by Rex is the situation in which one group systematically attempts to dominate and exploit the other. This situation usually occurs in the colonial context, and the social and psychological consequences are often long-lasting. An important point to note here with respect to public policy is that conflict situations are very seldom differentiated as to their causes, and very general, blanket policies are most often advanced for short-term political considerations.

While much of the literature noted thus far has concentrated on conflict, we have limited our discussion to conflict based on competition. One very important aspect that requires greater attention is conflict based on differences in the value system. In a pluralistic society, it is urgent that we have a firm grasp of the conflicting value systems before we can advance any meaningful social policy. This aspect of conflict, which is essentially centred on religious and other belief systems, is gradually becoming recognized in the health-science professions.

Our discussion of race relations and conflict will not be complete without reference to the way we should deal with interracial conflict. What have we learned from the literature on race relations in the United States and Britain? Must we wait for violence to erupt before concrete action can be taken? The literature reviewed thus far has been extremely limited in terms of facilitating racial accommodation, and this suggests that greater effort is required to examine the strategies that might be used to avert serious conflict or violence of the kind seen in recent race riots in Britain. As Patel (1980: xiii) has correctly observed, violence is only a symptom of some of the more basic problems in society. Therefore we must identify some of the crucial variables that result in racial conflict.

In the Canadian context, such conflicts usually arise between whites and non-whites, or between Caucasians and visible minorities. Thus there are often differences in the perspectives from which a given phenomenon is assessed. Similarly, when public-policy advocates attempt to analyse racial violence, they too employ their favourite theoretical perspectives. It is important, therefore, to be able to assess the different theoretical perspectives that can be employed in examining race relations in general and racial violence or conflict in particular, as the success of a given policy may well depend on the perspective selected at the outset in assessing the situation.

Patel (1980: 2) provides an overview of the major perspectives often employed in suggesting solutions to racial violence. Each perspective operates at a different level of analysis—for example, at the individual or the group level—and each perspective will also rest on different assumptions about human behaviour. Patel labels these the (a) deviant-individual, (b) social-forces, and (c) institutional-structural perspectives.

The deviant-individual perspective views violence essentially as an aberrant or deviant behaviour. While this may be the case, this perspective is weakened by its assumption that existing institutions are adequate to resolve the underlying problem(s). It fails to assess the causal factors that may have precipitated the deviant behaviour in the first place. The solutions that are advanced are often repressive in nature and of short-term value. The solutions are basically intended to maintain the status-quo. Thus institutional change does not occur.

The social-forces perspective sees collective violence as an inevitable product of certain historical or social conditions that have been neglected, perhaps because of prejudice or racial factors, and that cause the affected group to react with collective violence. Patel notes that in such situations, solutions usually consist of socio-economic reforms that may sometimes be far-reaching, but are most often just token efforts. As in the deviant-individual perspective, the existing political and economic institutions remain untouched.

The institutional-structural perspective views collective violence as purposeful and politically meaningful. This perspective is gaining some currency as a legitimate form of protest, especially in those political environments where leadership is extremely weak and any major thrust for social change must originate from the population at large. If the collective action does not occur, the status quo is maintained unchallenged. As Patel observes, such collective action may serve as a catalyst for social change or as a warning signal of a serious malfunction in the social system. In either case, it signifies dissatisfaction with the existing political leadership.

In concluding this very brief discussion of the various perspectives on racial-conflict resolution, it must be underscored that these perspectives should not be viewed in isolation from each other. Solutions to race-relations issues must be advanced at various levels simultaneously, not independently at the individual, group, or institutional level.

CONCLUSION AND SOME THOUGHTS FOR THE FUTURE

This chapter has attempted to provide an overview of the major writings on ethnic identity and race relations. It is obvious that there is much more race-relations literature that can be examined: for example, the studies by Banton (1967), Richmond (1972), and Rex and Mason (1968). In addition, the Canadian literature on ethnic relations and ethnic studies is a rich one. Recent works by Driedger (1987), Bienvenue and Goldstein (1985), Bolaria and Li (1985), Kallen (1982), Kinloch (1979), and Hughes and Kallen (1974) are all excellent, and serious students of race relations should consult them.

The review of Park's race-relations cycle reminds us that the issues that stem from the subordination of indigenous groups by the migrant groups from Europe are still unresolved today. During the week of 13 October 1987 the Commonwealth leaders met in Vancouver to discuss the racial issues of South Africa. Yet in our very own backyard, Georges Erasmus (Cruikshank, 1987: 8) of the Assembly of First Nations was attempting to get his people's problems on the agenda at the Commonwealth Conference. Unfortunately, the concerns of the Commonwealth's aboriginal peoples were not on the agenda, and instead Prime Minister Brian Mulroney pushed for reforms in South Africa. For our political leaders, the process of accommodation and fair play noted in Park's race-relations cycle is still far off. Mr Erasmus is correct in asserting that Canada could be a leader in addressing aboriginal issues 'if we had the will and courage to move ahead'. As it stands today, the lack of interest shown by our own government has forced the Canadian native peoples to seek assistance from international organizations to advance recognition of their rights. At present, the aboriginal peoples still have not been consulted on the Meech Lake Accord that deals with constitutional matters.

Finally, we should also remember the salient aspects of ethnicity as well as the demographic aspects of ethnic identity. Kalbach (1975: 139) has observed over the years a succession of identity crises and problems associated with the ethnic balance in our immigration. These issues continue to be controversial and will undoubtedly receive more media attention as more and more immigrants come to Canada from the non-traditional source countries in Asia and Latin America. The humanitarian concerns of all Canadians have prompted unprecedented acceptance of refugees from many war-torn countries, and the long-term implications of these developments are yet to be explored in terms of social policy. Moreover, the demographic trend towards a rapidly aging Canadian society provides students of ethnic relations with a challenging and important area for future research.

REFERENCES

Adachi, Ken
1976 *The Enemy That Never Was: A History of the Japanese Canadians*. Toronto: McClelland and Stewart.

Anderson, Alan B., and James S. Frideres
1981 *Ethnicity in Canada: Theoretical Perspectives*. Toronto: Butterworths.

Banton, Michael
1967 *Race Relations*. London: Tavistock.

Basran, Gurcharn S.
1983 'Canadian Immigration Policy and Theories of Racism'. Pp. 3-14 in

Peter S. Li and B. Singh Bolaria, eds, *Racial Minorities in Multicultural Canada*. Toronto: Garamond.

Bienvenue, Rita M., and Jay E. Goldstein
1985 *Ethnicity and Ethnic Relations in Canada*. 2nd ed. Toronto: Butterworths.

Blalock, Hubert M.
1982 *Race and Ethnic Relations*. Englewood Cliffs, NJ: Prentice-Hall.

Bolaria, B. Singh
1983 'Dominant Perspectives and Non-White Minorities'. Pp. 157-70 in Li and Bolaria (1983).

Bolaria, B. Singh, and Peter S. Li
1985 *Racial Oppression in Canada*. Toronto: Garamond.

Breton, Raymond
1964 'Institutional Completeness of Ethnic Communities and Personal Relations to Immigrants'. *American Journal of Sociology* 70: 193-205.

Commission on Wartime Relocation and Internment of Civilians
1982 *Personal Justice Denied*. Report of the Commission on Wartime Relocation and Internment of Civilians. Washington, DC: US Government Printing Office.

Conroy, Hilary, and T. Scott Miyagawa
1972 *East Across the Pacific*. Historical and Sociological Studies of Japanese Immigration and Assimilation. Santa Barbara: Clio Press.

Cruickshank, John
1987 'Aboriginal People Use Conference Backdrop to Gain Ottawa's Ear'. *Globe and Mail*, 13 Oct. 1987: 8.

Driedger, Leo
1977 'Toward a Perspective on Canadian Pluralism: Ethnic Identity in Winnipeg'. *Canadian Journal of Sociology* 2: 77-96.
1978 *The Canadian Ethnic Mosaic*. Toronto: McClelland and Stewart.
1987 *Ethnic Canada: Identities and Inequalities*. Toronto: Copp Clark Pitman.

Globe and Mail
1985 'Canadian Property Lost'. 20 March.

Gordon, Milton M.
1964 *Assimilation in American Life*. New York: Oxford University Press.

Hughes, David R., and Evelyn Kallen
1974 *The Anatomy of Racism: Canadian Dimensions*. Montreal: Harvest House.

Isajiw, Wsevolod W.
1975 'The Process of Maintenance of Ethnic Identity: The Canadian Context'. Pp. 128-38 in Migus (1975).

Joy, R.J.
1972 *Languages in Conflict*. Toronto: McClelland and Stewart.

Kalbach, Warren E.
1975 'Demographic Aspects of Ethnic Identity and Assimilation'. Pp. 139-46 in Migus (1975).

Kallen, Evelyn
1982 *Ethnicity and Human Rights in Canada*. Agincourt, Ont.: Gage.
1987 'Ethnicity and Collective Rights in Canada.' In Driedger (1987).

Kinloch, Graham C.
1979 *The Sociology of Minority Group Relations*. Englewood Cliffs, NJ: Prentice-Hall.

Kitano, Harry H.L.
1974 *Race Relations*. Englewood Cliffs, NJ: Prentice-Hall.

Li, Peter S., and B. Singh Bolaria
1983 *Racial Minorities in Multicultural Canada*. Toronto: Garamond.

Lieberson, Stanley
1970 *Languages and Ethnic Relations in Canada*. New York: John Wiley.
1980 'A Societal Theory of Race and Ethnic Relations'. In Jay E. Goldstein and Rita M. Bienvenue, eds, *Ethnicity and Ethnic Relations in Canada*. Toronto: Butterworths.

Migus, Paul M.
1975 *Sounds Canadian: Languages and Cultures in Multi-Ethnic Society*. Toronto: Peter Martin.

Millet, David
1975 'Religion as a Source of Perpetuation of Ethnic Identity'. In Migus (1975).

Newman, William M.
1973 *American Pluralism: A Study of Minority Groups and Social Theory*. New York: Harper and Row.

Park, Robert E.
1930 'Assimilation, Social'. P. 281 in Edwin R.A. Seligman and Alvin Johnson, eds, *Encyclopedia of the Social Sciences*. Vol. 2. New York: Macmillan.

Parsons, Talcott
1952 *The Social System*. London: Tavistock.

Patel, Dhiru
1980 *Dealing With Interracial Conflict: Policy Alternatives*. Montreal: Institute for Research on Public Policy.

Pettigrew, Thomas F.
1980 *The Sociology of Race Relations*. London: Collier Macmillan.

Rex, John
1970 *Race Relations in Sociological Theory*. New York: Shocken.

Rex, John, and David Mason
1986 *Theories of Race and Ethnic Relations*. London: Cambridge University Press.

Richmond, Anthony H.
1972 *Readings in Race and Ethnic Relations*. Toronto: Pergamon.
1973 *Migration and Race Relations in an English City*. London: Oxford University Press.

Simon, Walter B.
1975 'A Sociological Analysis of Multilingualism'. Pp. 3-22 in Migus (1975).

Scott, Gilbert H.
1987 'Race Relations and Public Policy-Uncharted Course'. Paper presented at the Canadian Political Science Association Conference, McMaster University, 8 June.

Smith, M.G.
1965 *The Plural Society in the British West Indies*. Berkeley: University of California Press.

Stasiulis, Daiva
1987 'Race Relations in Multicultural Policy'. Paper presented at the Canadian Political Science Association Conference, McMaster University, 8 June.

Sugimoto, Howard H.
1972 'The Vancouver Race Riots of 1907: A Canadian Episode'. In Conroy and Miyakawa (1972).

Sunahara, Ann Gomer
1981 *The Politics of Racism*. Toronto: James Lorimer.

Ujimoto, K. Victor
1976 'Contrasts in the Pre-World War II and Post War Japanses Community in British Columbia: Conflict and Change'. *Canadian Review of Sociology and Anthropology* 13 (1).

1982 'Visible Minorities and Multiculturalism: Planned Social Change Strategies for the Next Decade'. *Journal of Canadian Studies* 17 (1).

1983 'Institutional Controls and Their Impact on Japanese Canadian Social Relations: 1877-1977'. In Li and Bolaria (1983).

1987a 'The Ethnic Dimension of Aging in Canada'. In Victor Marshall, ed., *Aging in Canada*. 2nd ed. Toronto: Fitzhenry and Whiteside.

1987b 'Ethnic Relations in an Aging Multicultural Society'. In James S. Frideres, ed., *Multiculturalism and Intergroup Relations*. Westport, Conn.: Greenwood Press.

Ujimoto, K. Victor, and Gordon Hirabayashi
1980 *Visible Minorities and Multiculturalism: Asians in Canada*. Toronto: Butterworths.

van den Berghe, Pierre L.
1967 *Race and Racism: A Comparative Perspective*. New York: John Wiley.

1972 *Intergroup Relations: Sociological Perspectives*. New York: Basic Books.

Warner, W. Lloyd
1936 'American Class and Caste'. *American Journal of Sociology* 62 (September): 234-7.

Weinreich, Peter
1988 'The Operationalization of Ethnic Identity'. Pp. 149-68 in J.W. Berry and R.C. Annis, eds, *Ethnic Psychology: Research and Practice With Immigrants, Refugees, Native Peoples, Ethnic Groups and Sojourners*. Amsterdam: Swets and Zeitlinger.

TEN

LANGUAGE AND ETHNICITY: CANADIAN ASPECTS

JOHN DE VRIES

INTRODUCTION

In this chapter I intend to discuss the linkages between language and ethnicity in a Canadian context. These connections are often not established. Hence we normally encounter two separate lines of research: studies of Canadian ethnicity (which tend to ignore issues of language), and studies of linguistic pluralism in Canada (which generally fail to consider issues relating to ethnicity).

To establish the linkages, I begin with a discussion of some basic concepts: ethnicity, ethnic group, and multi-ethnic society. I then discuss various 'markers' of ethnicity that may be found around the world: language, religion, national origin, and 'race' (i.e., physical characteristics). The main thesis underlying this chapter is that the loss of an ethnic 'marker' inevitably leads to the loss of ethnicity. In addition, when enough members of an ethnic group lose their marker, the ethnic group itself may cease to exist as such. I argue that, for ethnic groups marked by language, the process of language shift is an indication of the weakening and eventual demise of ethnicity.

Among the relevant social factors and processes to be discussed are institutional completeness, ethnic exogamy, residential segregation, and language shift. Canadian census data on ethnic origin and language are also examined with regard to their utility for the study of 'ethnic maintenance'. In the final section I introduce selected data on five Canadian ethnic groups: Finns, Germans, Greeks, Italians, and

Ukrainians. These data are used to illustrate the empirical connections between the various factors linking language and ethnicity in Canada.

SOME CRUCIAL DEFINITIONS

The literature of social science has been blessed with many definitions of the term *ethnicity*. Isajiw (1970) collected over seventy; two decades later, it is likely that the number of definitions has increased considerably. For this chapter I want to follow a line that may be traced back to Schermerhorn (1970), Vallee (1975; 1988), Allardt (1984), and de Vries (1985a). Vallee's most recent statement on ethnicity gives us a good starting point: 'For our usage, ethnicity refers to real or imputed descent from ancestors who shared a common culture or subculture manifested in distinctive ways of speaking and/or acting . . . in all cases, the kinship networks are the crucial bearers of the culture' (1988: 130).

Vallee's subsequent discussion of 'ethnic identification' (by oneself—'Ego'—and by others) suggests that the above definition is incomplete: ethnicity 'exists' only when a person's ethnicity is acknowledged by others as well as by the individual concerned. His discussion thus leads logically into a definition of an *ethnic group* as one 'made up of people who share ethnicity (as previously defined), who share some sense of peoplehood or consciousness of kind, who interact with one another in meaningful ways beyond the elementary family, and who are regarded by others as being in the one ethnic category' (1988: 131).

Finally, Vallee defines a *multi-ethnic society* as 'a political state which contains more than one major ethnic group, as defined above' (131).

In a non-trivial way, it should be clear that 'ethnicity' and 'ethnic group' are only of interest in a multi-ethnic society: in societies containing only one ethnic group, we cannot discuss distinctive ways of speaking and/or acting in a meaningful way; nor does the notion of 'self-identification' make much sense. In the real world, almost all societies are multi-ethnic. Iceland comes to mind as an exception: its citizens belong to one 'ethnic group', which therefore is no ethnic group at all.

Briefly stated, an ethnic group may be said to exist if four necessary conditions are met:

1. group membership must be defined by means of a characteristic normally 'inherited' from one's parents (i.e., by descent). We refer to this as the 'marker' of ethnicity;

2. the group must have a distinct social structure or social organization;
3. the common ethnicity must be recognized by individual group members (we refer here to 'ethnic identity');
4. the common ethnicity must be recognized by others.

Of these four characteristics, the first two are 'objective' ones: that is, once we have provided operational definitions for a specific ethnicity (e.g., all Canadian residents who have Italian as mother tongue) and for a 'distinct social structure' (e.g., the presence of a church in which religious services are regularly conducted in Italian, or the use of a unique set of kinship terms), it is possible for researchers to collect reliable data that are in accord with such definitions. In contrast, the two aspects of 'identification' are 'subjective'. It may be quite possible for members of some groups to 'deny' or 'hide' their ethnic identity. It is also possible that other members of society may fail to identify a given ethnicity correctly, perhaps as a function of having incorrect or incomplete information (e.g., many refugees from Southeast Asia were initially considered to be of Vietnamese ethnicity, but eventually turned out to be ethnically Chinese, despite their previous residence in Vietnam), or as a result of past societal practice.

It is my view that ethnic groups exist only when all of these four conditions are met. One interesting deduction from this statement is that not everyone belongs to an ethnic group; thus a person's loss of a given ethnicity does not automatically mean that a new ethnic identity has been acquired. It is also possible that individuals who initially all belonged to some statistical category (e.g., based on language or religion) may later 'form' an ethnic group. Usually such processes of ethnic-group formation are outcomes of broader societal events or processes. It has been argued, for example, that English-speakers in Quebec 'became' an ethnic group after the election of the Parti Québécois government in November 1976, and the subsequent proclamation of the Charter of the French Language, Bill 101, in 1977.

MARKERS OF ETHNICITY

A quick survey suggests that ethnicity and ethnic groups may be marked by language, religion, national origin or citizenship, and/or physical characteristics (in particular, skin colour). In this last case, we usually refer to such groups as 'racial groups' or even 'races'. Some of these terms are probably not perfectly applicable. For example, 'race' is a somewhat fuzzy concept that does not always pertain strictly to skin colour, but often becomes contaminated by social criteria. The South African government at one point declared Japanese to be 'honorary whites'; in a similar way, Nazi Germany declared some groups to be 'honorary Aryans', and Hispanics in the southern United States were labelled as 'non-whites' in the years before the Second World War. Another point of some dispute is whether or not we should add 'regional origin' to the list: Are Newfoundlanders in Toronto an ethnic group?

We easily recognize that the particular choice of an ethnic marker varies from society to society. In Northern Ireland, Lebanon, and Israel the marker appears to be religion (Protestants versus Roman Catholics; Christians versus Muslims; Jews versus Muslims versus Christians). In South Africa the primary marker is 'race' (mostly, but not exclusively, defined in terms of skin colour). Many societies in Western and Northern Europe define ethnicity in terms of nationality or citizenship (e.g., Belgium has many residents whose parents came from Italy to the Belgian mining regions; despite having been born in Belgium, and functioning in French or Dutch, these people are still regarded as Italians).

In Canada we use two different markers of ethnicity: 'race' and language. The former is used to create a division between Caucasians (= 'whites') and Native Canadians (Inuit, Métis, North American Indians). The fact that the latter category is easily further subdivided into smaller groups on the basis of language (in other words, groups that do *not* share distinct ways of speaking and/or acting with others) seems to have been overlooked by most other Canadians (whites rarely distinguish between Cree, Ojibway, and Micmac, for example). Among Caucasians (often supplemented by various groups of Asiatic origin, such as Chinese and Japanese—our version of honorary Caucasians?) the primary marker is language. Thus Canadians find it natural to refer to such groups as 'francophones' (i.e., people who normally speak French) or Dutch-Canadians (i.e., people now residing in Canada who have some connection with the Dutch language).

This subdivision of the Caucasian segment of the Canadian population into ethnic groups on the basis of language (incidentally suggesting that 'recognition by others' is indeed not uncommon) also presents some problems. For example, immigrants from Italy may have spoken distinct dialects when they first arrived in Canada, such as Friulan and Calabrese; their self-identification may have been based on their dialect and region of origin in Italy (Friuli, Calabria). Other Canadians may not have been able to distinguish these regional differences, and may have regarded all these people as 'Italian'. Social pressures, as well as the limitations of group size, may in fact have forged an 'Italian-Canadian' identity and Italian-Canadian associations, churches, and the like.

Canadian society has stressed the use of language as an ethnic marker for many decades. Many federal and provincial laws provide rights and access to services on the basis of language (beginning with the British North America Act and undoubtedly not ending with the Official Languages Act, the Charter of Human Rights, or Quebec's Bill 178). Even in cases where legal provisions are not made, various levels of government do recognize individual rights to service in various languages (alternatively, the costs of *not* providing services may simply be too high).

I have already noted that individuals could 'lose' their ethnicity without necessarily acquiring a new one. It is possible for a person to 'pass' from one ethnic group into another one by virtue of a change in language behaviour, or for persons to end up without an ethnic identity. In the latter case, they clearly do not belong to an ethnic group. It may be argued that 'English Canadians' outside Quebec are not really an ethnic group in the strict sense, and that members of many immigrant groups eventually become 'non-ethnic' English-speaking Canadians. This point was made more generally by Max Weber, who wrote that 'where these ties are lacking, or once they cease to exist, the sense of ethnic group membership is absent, regardless of how close the kinship may be' (1987: 19).

At this point I wish to recall the subdivision of the four criteria for ethnicity into objective and subjective components. If, indeed, language behaviour changes in such a way that some individuals no longer use a particular language for communication (remember the 'distinctive ways of *speaking* and/or acting'), the objective dimension of ethnicity has of course changed. The *descent* from (real or imputed) ancestry cannot be changed, unless we revise the imputations (the 'Roots' phenomenon, perhaps?). Thus change in language behaviour may well yield individuals who act/speak like the members of the ethnically indistinct majority, without sharing an ancestry with them. Such new 'converts' almost certainly do not have a strong 'sense of peoplehood': thus they have no strong ethnic self-identification and probably an even weaker recognition by others. According to the definition of ethnicity given above, the loss of a specific language thus implies the loss of the associated ethnicity. Such 'loss of language' is usually called 'language shift', defined as 'the change in the habitual use of one language to that of another' (Weinreich, 1953). In Canadian society most cases of language shift yield (habitual) speakers of English outside Quebec and of French or English in Quebec. In such cases we may argue that language shift is a good indicator of a person's assimilation into Canadian society.

The obverse of this argument, I claim, is that 'language maintenance' is a *necessary* condition for the maintenance of ethnicity—though not a *sufficient* condition. Some of the finer points of this argument will reappear later in this chapter.

INDICATORS OF WEAKENING ETHNICITY

The theoretical and empirical tradition in Canadian social science generally holds that ethnic groups maintain themselves (or, if you prefer, their ethnic identity) most successfully if their members are able to live their lives to a large degree in their own language. Raymond Breton has made the point that we can establish the level of 'institutional completeness' for ethnic groups by measuring the number of social institutions providing services specifically in the language associated with that ethnic group (1964: 193-205). The link to our 'distinct social structure' is easily established. In fact, Breton's research on the behaviour of immigrants in Montreal established a significant correlation between the institutional completeness of ethnic groups and the extent to which group members interacted with other members of the group. While it is tempting to interpret this correlation as indicating a *causal* relationship (briefly stated as: high institutional completeness leads to within-group interaction), such an inference is not warranted. It is quite possible that the causal direction is exactly the reverse: groups whose members have strong preferences to interact with other group members are more likely to establish and maintain specific social institutions than are groups in which such in-group preferences are weak or non-existent. Finally, it is also possible that the relationship is a spurious one, explained by such factors as *group size* (larger groups will find it easier than smaller groups to establish social institutions; members have higher chances of meeting other group members), *recency of settlement* (recent arrivals are less likely to speak the majority language), or *residential segregation* (physical proximity may lead to interaction in formal as well as informal settings).

A little bit of work on Breton's (1964) data helps us to appreciate the complexity of these issues. He lists the various ethnic groups, which he divides into 'high' and 'low' levels of institutional completeness. His sample, drawn from a stratum of Montreal census tracts that were characterized by high percentages of residents born outside Canada, pertains to the population of the Montreal metropolitan area in the early 1960s. The population census of 1961 gives us a rough idea of the size of most of the ethnic groups classified by Breton, but we must use approximations, because some of the necessary census data are given only for the entire province of Quebec and some for the total Montreal metropolitan area, while an even smaller set of ethnic-group data is given for the city of Montreal.

The most reliable way to summarize the information is to present *median* group sizes. At all three levels of aggregation, we find that the groups with 'high' institutional completeness are about three times as large as those with 'low' institutional completeness. For the 'high' category the median group sizes are 19,390, 27,110, and 13,858; the corresponding values for the 'low' category are 7,381, 7,138, and 3,640. Such evidence supports the notion that the relationship between institutional completeness and in-group interaction is a spurious one, explained by group size.

Regardless of the proper causal interpretation of such correlations, it may be possible to establish empirically whether there is an association between the decline of institutional completeness and the intensity of language shift (as an indicator of weakening ethnic identity). A second aspect of weakening ethnic identity may be found in the tendency of group members to marry outside their own group (ethnic exogamy). Obviously, if group members adhere strongly to distinct ways of speaking and/or acting, they will find it hard to associate with potential mates who do not share these distinct ways. It is thus reasonable to argue that high levels of exogamy indicate a weakening of adherence to ethnic norms about behaviour and, by implication, a weakening of ethnic identity.

A third factor we could consider is the degree of residential segregation. If a group is highly segregated from other groups, chances are high that physical proximity to other group members (and, by implication, greater distance from outsiders) is associated with high viability for ethnically homogeneous social institutions and a greater tendency for individuals to maintain their language and ethnic identity (consider 'Little Italy' and 'Chinatown'). Declining segregation may thus be taken as a correlate of weakening ethnicity.

Last, there is the phenomenon of language shift. If we use Weinreich's (1953) definition, we could approximate his 'change in habitual language use' by comparing the language(s) used by individuals at two or more points in their life cycle. We will take *identity* in language use as an indicator of language maintenance (and, by implication, of ethnic maintenance) and *differences* in language use as indicating language shift. As with all analyses of status change (be it social, occupational, or residential) we can consider processes of language shift within a generation (pertaining to individuals) or between generations (intergenerational language shift). This latter aspect is an important one, given the assertion at the beginning of this paper that ethnicity is normally reproduced through the kinship system.

But while the foregoing looks intriguing, we run into problems when we try to get empirical support for these suggestions. Given that we lack the resources necessary to collect primary data, we have to resort to existing data, and with these limitations it is impossible to deal adequately with the concept of institutional completeness. After a short excursus into the nature of census data, therefore, the following sections will deal with some evidence regarding ethnic exogamy, residential segregation, and language shift. These analyses will attempt to establish associations between the various aspects of ethnic maintenance and decline.

CANADIAN CENSUS DATA ON LANGUAGE AND ETHNIC ORIGIN

A large proportion of the quantitative research on ethnicity in Canada is based on data from the census of population. A convenient feature of these data is that they have been collected over a long period of time, generally with high levels of consistency. What follows is a very brief discussion of census data and their limitations.

Since 1871 Canadian censuses have contained a question on *ethnic origin*. Before 1951 the question referred to 'racial origin', but the wording of the questions and the response categories listed fit our definition of 'ethnicity'. Through 1971 the questions required the respondents to trace their ancestry *through the paternal line* and identify the racial, cultural, or ethnic-group membership of the first male ancestor to arrive in North America. (Various deviations from these descent criteria have been noted for earlier censuses; see de Vries and Vallee, 1980: 23ff, for examples.)

The reference to paternal ancestry was removed in 1981, allowing respondents to mention more than one ethnic origin, and indeed a large proportion of the population did so. The propensity to give multiple responses to the question on ethnic origin was particularly high for persons born in Canada. Now, if ethnicity is reproduced by descent, it makes sense to argue that multiple ethnic origins are associated with descent from several ethnic groups. Under these circumstances, individuals could have created new 'ethnicities', *or* made a (subjective) choice about their ethnicity, based on one of their ethnic origins, *or* had low or non-existent ethnic identities.

With regard to language two census questions seem to be crucial. The question on *mother tongue* has been asked in most censuses since 1901 (the exceptions were 1911 and 1966). From 1941 on, the question has referred to the 'language first learned in childhood and still understood'. Although the exact wording has differed somewhat from one census to another, it is generally held that mother-tongue data in the censuses from 1941 through 1986 are quite comparable.

A second language question was introduced in 1971 and repeated in 1981 and 1986. This question refers to the individual's *home language*: that is, the language spoken most often by the individual in the home. Various studies discuss the methodological intricacies, the reliability, and the validity of these questions (Demers, 1979; Kralt, 1977; 1980; forthcoming; de Vries, 1985a).

The combination of the questions on mother tongue and home language is of considerable importance for the study of language shift. Census data for 1971, 1981, and 1986 allow for relatively consistent analyses of language shift, by means of the joint analysis of individual responses to the questions on mother tongue (indicating language use in early childhood) and home language (referring to current language use). Such data allow us to estimate the proportion of all people of a given mother tongue who have changed their habitual language behaviour. We have referred to this factor as *current* language shift (see de Vries and Vallee, 1980: 117-34).

Also of interest is the joint consideration of data on ethnic origin and mother tongue. For many ethnic origins there is only one associated value for the 'ethnic' mother tongue (e.g., Italian, Ukrainian), while other ethnic origins used in the Canadian census are associated with two or more languages (e.g., Belgian, Swiss). For the former category we can analyze the data on ethnic origin and mother tongue. As with the analysis of current language shift, we will take consistent (i.e., identical) responses as indicating ethnic-language maintenance, whereas different responses suggest that language shift has taken place. We should understand, however, that such language shift almost certainly occurred in an earlier generation (given that the respondent's mother tongue—the language first learned in early childhood—is already inconsistent with the ethnic origin). We labelled this factor 'ancestral language shift' (de Vries and Vallee, 1980: 101) to indicate that the respondent's ancestors, an unknown number of generations ago, already shifted to a different language. As is the case with current language shift, virtually all of the ancestral language shift in Canada benefitted English and—in Quebec—French.

This discussion of the census questions on *ethnic origin* suggests that they measure something related to, but not identical with, ethnicity as it was defined in the beginning of this paper. The strict wording of the ethnic-origin question appears to emphasize ancestry or descent. Analyses of earlier data on ethnic origin provide credible evidence for the suggestion that this question captures some degree of self-identification. Ryder (1955) showed, for example, that German ethnic origin became less popular at times in history when political relations between Canada and Germany were less than amicable (e.g., 1941), only to re-establish itself after the end of the hostilities. Similar factors have affected other ethnic-origin categories, such as Austrian, Dutch, and Ukrainian (Ryder, 1955; de Vries, 1985b).

However, we have more specific evidence that the Canadian census question on ethnic origin does not do a good job of eliciting the self-identification dimension of ethnicity. The Canadian Mobility Survey of 1973 contained two questions pertaining to ethnicity. One was a straight duplication of the 1971 census question on ethnic origin, while the other one asked the respondent to mention the ethnic group with which he or she identified most strongly. Among the permissible responses to this question were 'Canadian' and 'hyphenated Canadian' (e.g., German-Canadian). A cross-tabulation of the responses to these two questions yielded some interesting results (see Table 10.1).

These data suggest that it is reasonable to take ethnic origin, as measured in the Canadian census, as only a weak indicator of ethnicity. While it measures 'descent' (in a restricted way when respondents were asked to mention only their paternal ancestry), there are only weak connections with self-identification. Furthermore, the data in Table 10.1 suggest that ethnic origins with high proportions born in Canada are very likely to identify as 'Canadian'.

A second indicator of the weakness of the ethnic-origin data as proxies for ethnicity is the prevalence of *multiple* responses. Such multiple responses were tolerated in the 1981 census and encouraged in 1986. Given that the questions in those years no longer specified the *paternal* ancestry, and that many groups had fairly high rates of ethnic exogamy, many Canadians indeed had ancestors from two or more ethnic groups. Kralt (forthcoming) has provided some examples of the prevalence of multiple responses for a small sample of ethnic-origin categories (see Table 10.2).

Such data suggest that high proportions of Canadians of German, Ukrainian, and Italian ethnic origin in fact do not identify strongly (or perhaps at all) with the particular ethnicity. Even in 1981, when

Table 10.1
Percentage of respondents identifying themselves as 'Canadian', by sex and descent group: Canada, 1973

	Males	Females
English	92	91
Irish	88	90
French	87	87
Scottish	87	87
Dutch	87	88
German	86	84
Norwegian	86	84
Polish	73	70
Ukrainian	59	62
Italian	49	47
Don't know	93	94

SOURCE: de Vries, 1985a: 354

Table 10.2
Percentage multiple responses for selected ethnic origins: Canada, 1981 and 1986

	1981	1986
German	34	64
Ukrainian	30	56
Italian	14	30
Jewish	9	28
Philippino	4	13
Chinese	4	13

SOURCE: Kralt, forthcoming, Appendix B.

multiple responses were tolerated rather than encouraged, around one-third of the first two groups mentioned additional ethnic origins.

ETHNIC MAINTENANCE AND ITS CORRELATES

What I have suggested so far is that language maintenance is a necessary condition for the maintenance of ethnic identity (provided, of course, that language was the original marker of ethnicity) and the survival of the ethnic group. The preceding discussion also suggests that we may consider other aspects of behaviour as indicators of 'ethnic' behaviour. Marriage outside the ethnic group suggests that ethnic norms about proper individual behaviour were relaxed; low levels of residential segregation hint at the integration of ethnic-group members into the surrounding community.

The collection of primary data on these indicators is time-consuming and expensive. To put some empirical flesh on the theoretical skeleton, I will present selected data from several Canadian censuses (based on ethnic origin, despite the flaws) and from the 'Non-Official languages survey' conducted in 1973 in five large Canadian metropolitan areas. I have selected five ethnic groups for illustrative purposes: Finns, Greeks, Germans, Italians, and Ukrainians. 'Gaps' in the data that follow are the consequence of specific decisions by census takers about what published data should be produced, and by survey designers about the inclusion or exclusion of particular ethnic groups. These groups have been selected to provide a variety of immigration histories: Germans and Ukrainians arrived earliest, Italians and Greeks most recently. Finns and Greeks are comparatively small groups in comparison to the other three. The groups cover different regions of Europe: North, West, South, and East. Some (Ukrainians, Greeks) are associated with distinct religious affiliations; one (Finns) is associated with a language that does not belong in the Indo-European family of languages. Table 10.3 gives the number of individuals

Table 10.3
Number of persons reporting selected ethnic origins, censuses of 1951-1986

	1951	1961	1971	1981[a]	1986[b]
Finnish	43,745	59,436	59,215	52,315	91,340
German	619,995	1,049,549	1,317,195	1,142,365	2,467,055
Greek	13,966	56,475	124,475	154,360	177,315
Italian	152,245	450,351	730,820	747,970	1,006,915
Ukrainian	395,043	473,337	580,660	592,615	961,310

[a]Single origins only
[b]Single and multiple origins combined

in each of these categories as reported in the censuses of 1951 through 1986. Note that for 1981 only the *single* origins were included.

Table 10.4 presents data on ancestral-language maintenance. Note, again, that 1981 data refer only to *single* ethnic origin responses and therefore contain a much higher proportion of foreign-born respondents than did the other censuses. For the oldest immigrant groups (German, Ukrainian) we see the highest levels of language shift. Italian immigration continued into the early 1960s, so we note a decline in ancestral-language maintenance beginning with 1971. Greek immigration peaked even more recently, with an associated maximum value for ancestral-language maintenance occurring in 1971. The 1986 data suggest that the earliest immigrant groups especially show rather low levels of ancestral-language maintenance.

Table 10.5 shows the effects of nativity and age at immigration unambiguously. Ancestral-language maintenance was quite low for persons born in Canada, universally quite high for those born elsewhere. Persons who immigrated as children (under age 20) were a little less likely to show ancestral-language maintenance than those who immigrated as adults. The differences between the groups diminish tremendously after these controls for nativity. The exception is formed by the Greeks, of whom half of the Canadian-born respon-

Table 10.4
Mother-tongue maintenance as a percentage of ethnic origin: 1951-1986

	1951	1961	1971	1981[a]	1986[b]
Finnish	70	68	56	61	30
German	53	54	36	N/A	21
Greek	58	72	78	79	73
Italian	51	74	70	69	55
Ukrainian	74	64	49	55	29

[a]Based on single ethnic origins only.
[b]Based on single and multiple ethnic origins.

Table 10.5
Percentage of ethnic origin group maintaining ethnic mother tongue, by age at immigration: Canada, 1981

	Born in Canada	Age at Immigration		
		Under 20	20-44	45 and over
Finnish	26	82	90	88
Greek	50	85	93	93
Italian	32	86	95	96
Ukrainian	29	79	90	89

dents indicated that Greek was their mother tongue. The more recent arrival of the Greeks means, of course, that a higher proportion of those born in Canada had foreign-born parents than we find for the other three categories in Table 10.5. Unfortunately, the 1981 census does not provide information about the birthplace of the respondent's parents.

Table 10.6 focuses on *current* language maintenance and shift. To put some of these numbers in words: of all persons of Greek mother tongue in 1971, 76 per cent were using Greek most often at home. In 1981 the percentage had dropped to 71 per cent. (Note that the data for 1981 in this table refer to persons reporting one mother tongue and one home language.) The 1986 data are not comparable to those for the earlier censuses, since they are based on single as well as multiple responses to the questions on mother tongue and home language. Thus we cannot tell whether current language shift increased or decreased between 1981 and 1986.

Regardless of these complications, Table 10.6 shows that here too we can rank the groups by recency of arrival in Canada. Older immigrant groups (Germans, Ukrainians) show low levels of current language maintenance, while the most recent group shows the highest

Table 10.6
Percentage of mother tongue group using ethnic language most often at home: Canada, 1971-1986

	1971	1981[a]	1986[b]
German	35	30	40
Greek	76	71	81
Italian	74	64	73
Ukrainian	42	31	31

[a]Based on single responses to mother tongue only.
[b]Based on single and multiple responses to mother tongue.

level. Current language shift has gone mostly to English outside Quebec, to English and French in Quebec. The data for 1971 and 1981 suggest that, for each of these groups, longer residence in Canada is associated with increasing language shift.

Table 10.7 shows the effects of nativity and age at immigration for 1981. Again we find marked differences between respondents born in Canada and those born abroad. The current maintenance of ethnic languages among the Canadian-born members of these categories is considerably lower than it is among the immigrants. Here again the effects of 'generation' may be at work. High proportions of the people with Greek and Italian as mother tongue will have one or two foreign-born parents. The ethnic mother tongue may thus be used frequently with those parents (and be reported as the language spoken most often at home). In contrast, Finns and Ukrainians are much more likely to have Canadian-born parents and thus to be less in need of maintaining the minority language for use within the home.

With regard to current language maintenance and shift, we see fairly strong similarities between those born in Canada and those who immigrated before the age of 20. These young immigrants almost certainly came to Canada as dependent children, with one or more foreign-born parents. The similarity in current language maintenance between those who arrived in Canada as young people (depending on foreign-born parents) and those who arrived as infants should not surprise us.

Table 10.7 also demonstrates the impact of what one might call the 'relative length of exposure': immigrants who settled in Canada at higher ages had more years of exposure to their mother tongue, and fewer years of exposure to English, than did those who immigrated at lower ages.

The next set of tables uses somewhat finer-grained data from the 1973 Non-Official Languages Survey. The respondents to this survey were selected from ten specified ethnic groups in five large metro-

Table 10.7
Percentage of mother-tongue group using ethnic language most often at home, by age at immigration: Canada, 1981

	Born in Canada	Age at Immigration		
		Under 20	20-44	45 and over
Finnish	18	30	68	76
Greek	64	67	81	96
Italian	47	52	84	97
Ukrainian	21	43	80	92

politan areas. Four of these groups have already been described in the preceding tables: Germans, Greeks, Italians, and Ukrainians.

Table 10.8 picks up on the generational effect suggested in the earlier analyses. The 'first generation' is identical to persons born outside Canada; the 'second generation' refers to Canadian-born respondents with foreign-born parents; 'third generation' (presumably also including generations beyond three) includes Canadian-born respondents with Canadian-born parents.

Table 10.8 refers to fluency (self-evaluated) by respondents of the first, second, and third generations. While the census data for 1971 and 1981 pointed to a fair rate of current language maintenance among persons who arrived at young ages, the data in Table 10.8 suggest that such users of ethnic-minority languages may well be using restricted codes in those languages, and not be capable of speaking their mother tongues perfectly. Somewhat surprisingly, perhaps, not even all of the foreign-born respondents claimed to be fluent in their ethnic mother tongue. This suggestion of declining mother-tongue fluency is strongest for the Ukrainians, most of whom arrived in Canada before the beginning of the Second World War. In all these ethnic groups, later generations apparently could not claim fluency in the ethnic language at all. Data such as those presented in Table 10.8 support the assertion that ethnic-minority languages show relatively little viability beyond the first generation.

Table 10.9 describes the 'domains' in which members of these ethnic groups use the ethnic language at all. Recall, from Table 10.8, that the proportion of fluent speakers in the second and third generations is near zero. The domains in Table 10.9 are ordered by descending percentages using the ethnic languages (generally, highest values in the top left-hand corner of the table, lower values in the bottom right-hand corner). This ordering is nearly perfect.

What shows up is that the rows indicate declining degrees of 'in-

Table 10.8
Percentage fluent in the ethnic language, by ethnic group and generation: Canada, 1973

	First generation	Second generation	Third generation
German	78	5	0
Greek	81	–	–
Italian	72	9	–
Ukrainian	64	19	1

SOURCE: O'Bryan et al., 1976: 46
–: insufficient cases.

Table 10.9
Percentage reporting at least some use of the ethnic language in speaking to various types of persons, by ethnic group: Canada, 1973

	Greek	Italian	Ukrainian	German
Family	94	90	66	62
Close friends	81	67	40	30
Clergy	84	50	41	15
Grocer	37	43	8	7
Doctor	33	33	14	9
Co-workers	33	27	16	9

SOURCE: O'Bryan et al., 1976: 64.

timacy' and 'privacy' as we move from the top to the bottom of the table. They also indicate increasing dependence on institutions in the wider community. 'Family' and 'close friends' are probably the backbone of ethnic communities (recall the assertion that ethnicity was reproduced through the kinship system); members of the clergy may well function as the link between an ethnic community and the outside world. Beyond these three domains we enter into the type of social institution that plays a role in 'institutional completeness'. The data show that only among Greeks and Italians was a sizeable proportion able to maintain the ethnic language in contacts with the world outside: commerce, health care, and work. Such data present a somewhat gloomy picture of the viability of ethnic languages, ethnic communities, and—in the long run—ethnic identity.

Table 10.10 tells us something about the linkages between ethnic identity and language retention. It shows strong correlations between people's identification with a given ethnic group and their attitudes regarding the importance of maintaining the ethnic language. Support for ethnic-language maintenance was strongest among the most recent immigrant groups and weakest in the groups with the longest residence in Canada. Among people who labelled themselves as 'German', only 35 per cent felt that the maintenance of the German

Table 10.10
Relation between ethnic self-identification and attitude towards language retention: percentage responding 'very desirable': Canada, 1973

	Greek	Italian	Ukrainian	German
'Ethnic label'	72	56	–	35
Ethnic-Canadian	48	40	42	32
Canadian	–	16	16	13

language was very desirable. It was only among ethnic Greeks and Italians (i.e., those who labelled themselves as 'Greek' or 'Italian') that a majority rated the retention of the ethnic language as 'very desirable'. The data in Table 10.9 reveal that such attitudes are quite consistent with behaviour: Germans were least likely to use their language in the domains listed, while Greeks were most likely to do so.

Table 10.11 presents some data on ethnic endogamy. This is a rather limited collection of data with regard both to the number of ethnic groups covered and to the number of censuses included. In general, we see declining levels of ethnic endogamy (or increasing levels of ethnic exogamy). The one exception is formed by the Italians, among whom endogamy increased between 1941 and 1961. This somewhat aberrant pattern reflects the fact that much of the Italian immigration occurred in the 1950s (see Table 10.3), much more recently that the German and Ukrainian. The last row in Table 10.11 gives the proportion of males of German, Italian, and Ukrainian mother tongue whose wives had the same mother tongue. The difference in levels of endogamy by ethnic origin and mother tongue points to a weakening of ethnic identity among those who had abandoned the ethnic language as mother tongue.

Table 10.12, finally, reports 1981 levels of residential segregation[1] for selected categories of ethnic origin in three large metropolitan areas. I have included a few additional categories to provide some basis for comparison. Overall, the Germans (in this case joined by the Austrians) had the lowest levels of segregation from the overall population. The Italians and Greeks, much more recent arrivals, were much more segregated from the rest of the population.

Table 10.11
Endogamy ratios by ethnic origin, Canada, 1941-1971, for selected ethnic groups

	German	Italian	Ukrainian
1941 (males)	56	55	80
1951 (males)	52	N/A	75
(females)	52	N/A	71
1961 (males)	52	77	62
(females)	51	82	61
1971 (males)	49	76	54
(females)	51	84	55
1971 MOTHER TONGUE (males)	68	85	69

SOURCE: de Vries and Vallee, 1980: 156, 164.

Table 10.12
Segregation indices between specific ethnic and remainder of the population in Montreal, Toronto, and Vancouver: 1981

	Montreal	Toronto	Vancouver
British	.459	.261	.176
French	.472	.198	.210
German/Austrian	.409	.192	.157
Italian	.565	.506	.448
Greek	.638	.461	.480
Portuguese	.603	.633	.589
Chinese	.595	.447	.502
Mean	.564	.422	.382

SOURCE: Balakrishnan and Kralt, 1987: 151.

SUMMARY

In the initial sections of this chapter I developed the theoretical argument that language maintenance is a necessary condition for the maintenance of ethnic identity. Then I asserted that ethnic identity, as a characteristic of individuals, is an essential condition for the existence of ethnic groups. The brief survey of selected data seems to provide supportive evidence, though it is indirect. Ethnic identity and language maintenance are strongly linked to nativity; behaviour that goes beyond the boundaries of an ethnic community (such as marrying an outsider, dealing with grocers or co-workers, etc.) seems to become more common as time goes on; identification with a specific ethnic group weakens with each generation and in association with declining knowledge of the ethnic language.

Among the five ethnic groups I used for illustration, Germans seem to rank the lowest on various indicators of ethnic maintenance; Greeks, the highest. It is tempting to use 'length of residence' as the explanatory variable, but we should not overlook alternative explanations. In this set of five ethnic groups, Greeks and Ukrainians differ from the other three in two important aspects. Both have their 'own' churches—denominations that are organizationally separate from other religious groupings in Canada; both also happen to use different alphabets from those used by English and French. Thus the written languages *look* different from the official languages in even the most basic way. The role of the written language in the maintenance of immigrant languages and ethnicities has not been explored as yet.

Finally, I should alert the reader to the risk of making incorrect causal inferences. The data presented here show quite credible, sometimes even substantial, correlations. But it is not always possible to provide a single correct causal interpretation of such patterns; often several alternatives can be worked out. To establish empirically 'what causes what' is normally a difficult task—and often an impossible one.

NOTE

[1]The segregation index (also called the index of dissimilarity) measures the extent to which two groups are residentially segregated from each other. It has a range from zero (indicating that there was *no* residential segregation) to one (indicating the the groups being compared were completely segregated from each other). For a more detailed discussion of the index and its computational formula, see Matras, 1977: 388-90.

REFERENCES

Allardt, Erik

1984 'What Constitutes a Language Minority?'. *Journal of Multilingual and Multicultural Development* 5: 195-205.

Balakrishnan, T.R., and John M. Kralt

1987 'Segregation of Visible Minorities in Montreal, Toronto and Vancouver'. Pp. 130-57 in Driedger (1987).

Breton, Raymond

1964 'Institutional Completeness of Ethnic Communities and the Personal Relations of Immigrants'. *American Journal of Sociology* 70: 193-205.

Demers, Linda

1979 'Evaluation de la qualité des informations ethniques et linguistiques fournies par les recensements canadiens 1901 à 1976'. Unpublished MA Thesis, Démographie. Montreal: Université de Montreal.

Driedger, Leo

1987 *Ethnic Canada: Identities and Inequalities*. Toronto: Copp Clark Pitman.

Driedger, Leo, et al., eds

Ethnic Demography. Ottawa: Carleton University Press (forthcoming).

Isajiw, Wsevolod W.

1970 'Definitions of Ethnicity'. *Ethnicity*, 1: 111-24.

Kralt, John M.

1977 'Processing and its Impact on the 1971-1976 Census Mother Tongue Data'. Unpublished working paper. Ottawa: Statistics Canada.

1980 'Guidelines for the Language Variables'. Unpublished working paper. Ottawa: Statistics Canada.

'An Overview of Ethnic Orgins in the Canadian Censuses 1871-1986'. In Driedger et al. (forthcoming).

Kralt, John, et al.
1983 'Evaluation of 1981 Census Data on Métis/Non-Status Indians and Inuit'. Unpublished. Ottawa: Statistics Canada.

Matras, Judah
1977 *Introduction to Population: A Sociological Approach*. Englewood Cliffs, NJ: Prentice-Hall.

O'Bryan, K.D., et al.
1976 *Non-official Languages: A Study in Canadian Multiculturalism*. Ottawa: Minister Responsible for Multiculturalism.

Ryder, Norman B.
1955 'The interpretation of origin statistics'. *Canadian Journal of Economics and Political Science* 21: 466-79.

Schermerhorn, R.A.
1970 *Comparative Ethnic Relations*. New York: Random House.

Vallee, Frank G.
1975 'Multi-ethnic Societies: The Issues of Identity and Inequality'. Pp. 162-202 in Dennis P. Forcese and Stephen Richer, eds, *Issues in Canadian Society: An Introduction to Sociology*. Scarborough, Ont.: Prentice-Hall.
1988 'Inequality and identity in multi-ethnic societies'. Pp. 129-50 in Dennis P. Forcese and Stephen Richer, eds, *Social Issues: Sociological Views of Canada*. Scarborough: Prentice-Hall.

de Vries, John
1985a 'Some Methodological Aspects of Self-report Questions on Language and Ethnicity'. *Journal of Multilingual and Multicultural Development* 6: 347-68.
1985b 'Explorations in the Demography of Language and Ethnicity: The Case of Ukrainians in Canada'. Pp. 111-32 in T. Yedlin, ed., *Central and Eastern European Ethnicity in Canada*. Edmonton: CEESSA.
1986 *Towards a Sociology of Languages in Canada*. Quebec: Presses de l'Université Laval.
'Ethnic language maintenance and shift'. In Driedger et al. (forthcoming)

de Vries, John, and Frank G. Vallee
1980 *Language Use in Canada*. Ottawa: Statistics Canada.

Weber, Max
1987 'Ethnic Groups'. Pp. 14-27 in Driedger (1987).

Weinreich, Uriel
1953 *Languages in Contact*. New York: Linguistic Circle of New York.

ELEVEN

THE POLITICAL ECONOMY OF RACE AND ETHNICITY

VIC SATZEWICH

The headlines are now familiar: 'Clash in Soviet Georgia leaves 16 dead, 200 hurt' (*Globe and Mail*, 1989b); 'Albania riot broken up in fourth day of unrest' (*Globe and Mail*, 1989a); 'Racial issues key to Chicago mayoral vote' (*Globe and Mail*, 1989c); '[Canadian] Native tells story of misery, racism' (*Star Phoenix*, 1989). Within the Soviet Union, the present policy of 'glasnost', or 'openness' appears to have unleashed a new wave of ethnic nationalism that extends from the Baltic republics to Georgia and Armenia. Closer to home, despite a policy of multiculturalism that has been in place in Canada for over ten years, evidence of discrimination and ethnic and 'racial' conflicts appears to be steadily on the increase. In both the Eastern Bloc and the West, it seems that ethnic conflict, nationalism, and racism remain salient aspects of social relations.

The persistence of ethnic and 'racial' phenomena within Canada, and the apparently increasing importance of ethnic nationalism within the world system generally, is taken by some academics to be indicative of the inability of political economy to account for present-day realities (Richmond, 1988: 35, 152-4; Beaujot, Basavarajappa, Verma, 1988: 12). Often, such events are cited in relation to Marx's (1978: 474) claim in the *Communist Manifesto* that with the development of capitalism, the world would become increasingly polarized into two opposing classes: the bourgeoisie and the proletariate. The apparently artificial divisions of the world's working class that have been based on factors like 'race', ethnicity, and gender would, Marx thought, eventually give way to the emergence of a united class engaged in collective struggle against its common oppressor. Thus the retention of ethnic identities and the existence of communal conflict among groups of people is taken as *prima facie* evidence that political economy is inadequate for the challenge of understanding ethnic and racial phenomena.

Marx was incorrect in some of his predictions. Capitalism appears to be much more resilent than he thought, and sections of the working class in the more developed centre formations have achieved increasing levels of material prosperity (although with the present process of global economic restructuring, the jury is still out on this matter). Similarly, his predictions concerning the declining significance of non-class-based differences appear to have been incorrect. But do these observations mean that the political economy tradition has nothing to offer the study of ethnic and 'racial' issues? The short answer is that political economy does have something to offer, and in this paper I will examine some recent contributions that Canadian political economists have made to the study of ethnic and 'racial' phenomenon in the country. I focus on two sets of issues that constitute fundamental points of controversy within political economy: debates surrounding the analysis of racism, and debates surrounding the articulation of 'race' and class (see Solomos, 1987 for a review of these debates in Britain). In so doing, I also want to point to some directions for future research.

POLITICAL ECONOMY AND THE CRITIQUE OF 'RACE-RELATIONS' SOCIOLOGY

Canadians are increasingly being told by politicians and the media that if something is not done, and done soon, it is likely that a 'race-relations' problem will emerge in the country (Svenson, 1978). City councils accross the country are forming 'race-relations' committees to try and prevent a 'problem' from emerging. More soberly, sociologists of 'race relations' tell us that Canada already has a 'race' problem, and that we will probably soon have our own versions of Brixton and Chicago (Reitz, 1988: 141).

The view that Canada has, or is going to have, a 'race-relations' problem is based on the apparently self-evident observation that 'races' of people exist, and that these 'races' have social relations with one another. But does the belief in the existence of 'races' and 'race relations' mean that these are real phenomena that can be the object of social scientific inquiry? This section critically examines the unscientific and common-sense notions of 'race' that inform 'race-relations' sociology and questions the analytical utility of the concepts of 'race' and 'race relations'.

Since 1945, scientists from around the world have increasingly discredited the belief that 'race' is an objective biological category that can be used to describe and explain human differences. Over the years, the United Nations Educational, Scientific and Cultural Organization (UNESCO) has held a number of conferences bringing together respected scientists from the disciplines of anthropology, sociology, population genetics, biology, and physiology to critically discern the meaning of 'race'. It has done so in order to help ensure that the Nazi biological doctrines that legitimized the mass murder of six million Jews would never arise again (Rex, 1983: 1-3). The arguments that have emerged out of the various UNESCO conferences (1950, 1951, 1964, and 1967) are complex, but the basic theme of the discussions has been that the scientific utility of the 'race' concept is extremely limited (see Rex, 1983, and Montagu, 1972, for more details of the UNESCO conferences).

Very broadly, the term 'race' has tended to be defined by reference to either phenotypical or genotypical criteria (Miles, 1982: 9-21). Both definitional strategies are problematic. In attempting to define 'races' of people by reference to phenotypical or physical criteria, scientists are faced with the problem of justifying why certain physical characteristics are taken to be indicative of a 'race' difference and why others are not. On the level of common sense, people tend to think of 'races' as being defined in terms of skin colour, hair texture, lip shape, eye shape, or some combination of these characteristics. But the choice of criteria is ultimately arbitrary and cannot be justified scientifically. The UNESCO conferences have definitively argued that there is no correlation between the physical appearance of groups of people and their social behaviour, or their capacity to engage in certain forms of social behaviour (Montagu, 1972: 9-10). Thus it is as irrational to use skin colour to measure 'race' differences as it would be to use the length of peoples' index fingers or the shape of their knee caps.

Furthermore, physical characteristics like skin colour are continuous variables that are not amenable to simple classifications. It is impossible to classify all of the peoples of the world into discrete categories. It is precisely this problem that has led to the proliferation of classifications of 'races' using combinations of criteria (Miles, 1982: 14). But such efforts are also misplaced because phenotypical features do not co-vary with one another; for instance, not all people with dark skin have curly hair.

A similar set of problems confronts those who attempt to define 'race' in terms of genotypical, or genetic, criteria. Some scientists have suggested that 'races' can be defined as populations that differ in the frequency, or prevalence, of certain genes, and that 'race' differences are therefore relative, and not absolute (Kuper, 1984: 8-11); this argument has been made, for instance, in the context of the frequency distributions of ABO blood groups. Thus 'races' are seen to differ in terms of the frequency distribution of alleles.

But, having suggested that 'races' can be defined in terms of genetic frequencies, these theories also introduce the following qualifications. First, the extent of genetic variation within any population is usually greater than the average difference between populations. Second, although the frequency of occurence of different alleles does vary from one 'race' to another, any particular genetic combination can nevertheless be found in almost any 'race'. Third, because of human migration and inter-breeding, distinctions between 'races' identified in terms of polymorphic frequencies are blurred. Fourth, there is no simple and direct relationship between genetic variation and physical variation: many genotypical variations are not evident phenotypically, while different geographical populations that share certain phenotypical features do not necessarily share the same genotype. And fifth, differences in genotype do not correspond with what we normally think of as 'racial' groups (Miles, 1982: 16).

These qualifications, and the observations noted above concerning 'race' as phenotypical difference, have led some to suggest that the 'race' concept has little or no scientific utility. Indeed, Michael Banton (1970) and Alan Anderson and Jim Frideres (1981: 19) have suggested that the term 'race' should be banished from social-scientific terminology. 'Race' should be seen, then, as a label that has been used to describe and explain patterns of phenotypical and/or genotypical variation: and it is for this reason that the term is used in quotation marks in this paper. It does not refer to objective, biologically based groupings of people.

A similar set of epistemological and methodological problems has also been identified with the notion of ethnicity. Rather than conceiving of ethnicity as a social fact, we must see it too as a label that is used to describe and explain certain forms of difference (see Bolaria and Li, 1988: 17; Cassin and Griffith, 1981; Li, 1988: 27-33). Thus, whereas 'race' should refer to the delineation of group boundaries by reference to phenotypical or genetic criteria, 'ethnicity' should refer to the delineation of group boundaries by reference to cultural criteria (Wilson, 1973: 6-7).

What implications does this argument have for the issue of 'race relations' (and, by extension, ethnic relations)? If 'races' of people do not exist, then we are faced with the problem of whether 'race relations' can refer to a particular category of social relations. In short, how can there be 'race relations' if there are no such things as 'races' of people?

Sceptical 'race-relations' social scientists have responded to this apparent contradiction by agreeing that 'race' is not an objective biological category that refers to biological sub-groups of the human species. What they have argued instead is that the *belief* that 'races' exist is most important (Rex, 1983). Following W.I. Thomas's famous dictum that 'if men define situations as real, they are real in their consequences' (in Coser, 1977: 521), it is argued that because people believe that 'races' exist, and that because these beliefs have certain impacts on the forms that social relations take, then it is possible to speak of 'race-relations' situations. The object of sociological analysis, then, is the study of these beliefs and their consequences for social interaction (Rex, 1983).

For the political economist, however, this is an unsatisfactory justification for 'race-relations' sociology and for the use of the term 'race' as an analytical category. First, these conceptual categories are unscientific. Part of the intellectual task of social science is to question common-sense understandings of the ways in which societies are organized and social relations are structured. In continuing to make use of the notion of 'race', social scientists are simply reproducing inaccurate views of the world. In light of recent history, these beliefs have not been without heinous social consequences for some groups of people. In continuing to use the notion of 'race', social scientists are irresponsibly reproducing, in Ashley Montagu's (1964) terms, 'man's most dangerous myth'.

Second, 'race-relations' sociology reifies the notion of 'race' (the term reification refers to the elevation of an idea, or concept, to the status of an object [Miles, 1982:33]). For the sociology of 'race-relations', 'race' is seen to have determinant, but not necessarily autonomous effects in the real world (Miles, 1982: 219). In this view, 'races' are seen as actors in their own right, and actions are structured by 'race'. The reification of 'race' implies that 'racial' groups constitute a homogeneous social category. People's 'racial' background is said to be the primary determinant of their experience: 'race' shapes the jobs they do, the amount of money they make, where they live, and their relations with the state. In suggesting that 'race' is an active subject, such theories make no mention of the impact of the social relations of production on experience.

Political-economy theorists have, to a certain extent, avoided the problems associated with the reification of 'race', although some continue to make use of the concept as if it referred to real biological groups of people (see for example Centre for Contemporary Cultural Studies, 1982; Sivanandan, 1982; Bolaria and Li, 1988). The conceptual problem that political economists have confronted instead is the process of *racialization*: how and why, within the capitalist mode of production, social significance has been attached to patterns of phenotypical or genotypical variation. Political economy has developed two sets of responses to this question: the first is based on a structuralist approach, and the second on an agency approach, where analysis focuses on the practices and ideologies of classes and other social groups in the course of struggles over scarce resources.

CAPITALISM AND RACIALIZATION

The structuralist approach to racialization has its intellectual roots in the pioneering work *Class, Caste and Race*, by Oliver Cromwell Cox, and more recently in *Immigrant Workers and Class Structure in Western Europe*, by Stephen Castles and Godula Kosack. In Canada it has been most developed by Bolaria and Li in *Racial Oppression in Canada* and in Li's *Ethnic Inequality in a Class Society* (see also Basran, 1983; Daniels, 1987). Structuralist-oriented thinkers link racism and the process of racialization to the demands of economies for quantities of cheap and docile labour. The starting point of this perspective is, in Bolaria and Li's (1988: 7) terms, that 'race problems begin as labour problems'. Initial emphasis is placed on the dynamics of capital accumulation whereby some sectors of capitalist production require the existence of large pools of cheap labour that can be drawn upon when they are needed and displaced when they are not.

In this view, racism emerged as an ideology that justified the allocation of human beings to particular positions in class relations as the reserve army of labour, or as part of a cheap-labour fraction of the working class. Ideas of inferiority and superiority, based on phenotypically defined criteria, justified differential allocation of groups to positions in production relations. Furthermore, once they were so allocated, it also justified differential rewards for the exploitation of their labour power. In other instances, racism was used as a justification for the existence of systems of forced, or unfree, labour. In both cases, superficial biological or physical criteria were used by employers, or sections of the state, to delineate group boundaries, organize the production process, and justify exploitation and unequal treatment.

Thus while particular historical contexts may differ, the essence of the structuralist argument is that racism and the process of racialization were initially developed and propogated by capitalist employers in order to justify the exploitation of labour power and unequal treatment. Racism is seen as an ideology imposed from above, which has additionally divided the working class: it functioned to create class fractions that contributed further to the maintenance of the status quo (Castles and Kosack, 1973: 453-60).

This approach has not gone unchallenged by other political economy theorists; empirical, methodological and theoretical problems have been identified. First, the argument tends to be teleological: it suggests that capitalist societies have certain needs, and that these needs then produce the required response. It implies that capitalists self-consciously developed an ideology of racism that was in accordance with their objective needs. While it cannot be denied that racism may have the effect of dividing the working class, it is illegitimate to argue cause from effect.

Second, racism in certain historical instances can be dysfunctional for capital (Miles, 1982; Bonacich, 1979: 30-1). This is evident, for example, when racist hostility disrupts the workplace, or where property is damaged in situations of conflict. It is also evident in cases where racism results in the exclusion of certain groups of people from a social formation. In the case of Canada, what is particularly significant about racism directed against East Indians during the early years of the twentieth century is not that it made them available as cheap and docile labour (although again this may have been an effect), but rather that it justified their *exclusion* from the country. Exclusion meant that East Indians could not sell their labour power for wages and therefore could not have the opportunity to be exploited by Canadian capitalists. Given that fewer than six thousand East Indians migrated to Canada between 1900 and 1948, it is hard to see why Canadian capitalists either themselves developed, or appropriated from elsewhere, an ideology to justify the exploitation of this comparatively small group of people.

A similar argument can be applied to the analysis of racism directed against the Chinese. For employers, one consequence of racist practices was to make it difficult for them to exploit the labour power of Chinese workers. It was the president of the Canadian Pacific Steamship Company who tried to fight, albeit unsuccessfully, the state's imposition of head taxes on Chinese labour migrants (Avery and Neary, 1977: 26), and it appears to have been an employer who initiated court proceedings to overturn racist laws that restricted Chinese employment within coal mines (Sampat-Mehta, 1973: 43-44).

Third, this approach is silent on the role of the working class in the initiation and reproduction of racism and the process of racialization (Bonacich, 1979). It tends to assume that the working class is an empty vessel that capitalists can fill with any rubbish they like. I will develop this theme more fully in the next section.

The second approach to the issue of racism and racialization, and one that emerged as an alternative to the structuralist position, is based on the agency tradition of political economy. This tradition has its roots in the work of the Italian thinker Antonio Gramsci, and has been popularized more recently in Britain by Stuart Hall, Robert Miles, and Annie Phizacklea. For Hall (1978), racism is not a homogeneous ideology that has been imposed by capitalists 'from above' on groups of people in order to achieve certain predefined ends, but rather is a form of ideological representation that has emerged 'from below' (see also Husband, 1987). Racism is one of the ways in which people attempt to make sense of their lived experiences, to interpret and to explain the world. Thus,

> racism is not a set of false pleas which swim around in the head. They're not a set of mistaken perceptions. They have their basis in real material conditions of existence. They arise because of the concrete problems of different classes and groups in the society. Racism represents the attempt ideologically to construct those conditions, contradictions, and problems in such a way that they can be dealt with and deflected in the same moment (Hall, 1978: 35).

The sociological task, therefore, involves examination of how and why the contradictions of capitalism are experienced and defined by some classes at certain historical conjunctures in terms of 'race' (see also Lecourt, 1980; Centre for Contemporary Cultural Studies, 1982).

Hall's observations regarding the meaning and significance of racism have led to the methodological and theoretical position that what exists is not so much racism, but rather a series and range of *racisms*. The term 'racisms' is more appropriate because the experiences and contradictions that classes and other social groups face differ historically, conjuncturally, and cross-culturally (Satzewich, 1989). The forms of ideological expression that involve evaluations of phenotypical difference and assessments of the superiority and inferiority of groups of people have varied meanings. Thus the meaning of racism is historically specific, and while certain theoretical generalizations may be applicable, detailed historical analysis is required to discern it.

This approach has led to the study of working-class racism in contemporary Britain. For example, Phizacklea and Miles' study of Willesden, part of the London Borough of Brent, suggested that working-class

> racist beliefs are not so much an aberration as a likely response to the current circumstances in which our respondents find themselves: they reflect the perception of disadvantage amongst 'us' who have to take the brunt of inflation, unemployment and the shortage of housing. In this way the 'coloureds' come to be seen as just another problem that has been hoisted upon a beleaguered working class by politicians who 'don't have to mix with them' (Phizacklea and Miles, 1980: 176).

There are few studies of the full meaning of working-class racism in

Canada, and this is an area where further research is required. However, there are studies of the social constitution of ethinicity and gender, and these are discussed in more detail in the next section on the articulation of 'race', ethnicity, and class.

More frequent, in Canada, within the agency tradition are studies of the split labour market. Such research, developed initially by Edna Bonacich in the United States, emerged as a challenge to the structuralist position. Bonacich (1979) suggests that what appear as ethnic and 'racial' antagonisms are rooted in initial differences over the price of labour. These initial differences, which in turn are the result of historically specific conditions, and which in turn come to be associated with various superficial physical or cultural differences, constitute the central point of group conflict. The existence of high- and low-cost labour that in principle can perform the same type of work means that employers, in an effort to maximize profits, attempt to replace expensive labour with cheap labour. Actual or threatened displacement leads to attempts on the part of higher-priced workers to protect themselves. Protection can take the form of blocking access to cheaper labour, or equalizing the price of labour. If the former occurs, working-class action results in the creation of a split labour market whereby some groups of workers are excluded from certain sectors of production. In Bonacich's terms:

> The real division is not between white and non-white, but between high priced and cheap labour. This distinction, because of historical accident, happens to have been frequently correlated with the white/non-white distinction, hence 'race' comes to be the language in which the ensuing conflicts are expressed. When a split labour market . . . falls along other lines, other idioms are used. In other words, the underlying issue is a class issue (price of labour), not biological differences (Bonacich, 1979: 20).

This form of argument has also been applied to Chinese migration to Canada. Creese (1984: 10; see also Li, 1979) demonstrates that Chinese labour in British Columbia was considerably less expensive to purchase than white labour. In general, Chinese workers appear to have earned about 50 per cent of what white workers did for doing the same type of work (Phillips, 1967: 8). The differences in the price of labour were premised on a historically lower subsistence level for Chinese workers, the fact that the reproduction costs of Chinese labour were borne in China rather than Canada, the contract-labour system under which they were brought to Canada, and the political subordination of Chinese workers (Creese, 1984: 10). Differences in the price of labour meant that the higher-cost white workers felt threatened by low-cost labour. They responded by pressuring various levels of government to restrict entry and, failing that, by restricting the occupations they could take up. Thus racialized exclusionary practices were based in large part on working-class practices.

This type of argument has also been applied in the case of black sleeping-car porters employed on Canada's railways. Calliste (1987, 1988), revising somewhat Bonacich's initial formulation, suggests that there was a doubly submerged split labour market, in which there were three levels of stratification. While 'white' trade unions were unable to restrict access to porter positions on the basis of 'race', they were, with the active collaboration of employers, able to impose differential pay scales. Black porters received less than white porters, even when they were doing the same type of work. In this case, the labour market was doubly submerged because black immigrant workers imported from the US received less pay than both black Canadian porters and white porters.

'RACE', ETHNICITY, AND CLASS

A second area of concern within political economy is the articulation, or relationship between, 'race' and class (Solomos, 1987). It is becoming increasingly popular to suggest that 'race' constitutes the major division within capitalist societies, and that the existence of this division is an anomaly that cannot be explained in the context of Marxist theory. This argument has been made by those who work both within and outside the political-economy tradition.

For those otherwise sympathetic to political economy, this argument has been developed primarily in the context of post-war labour migration to western Europe. For example, Castles, Booth, and Wallace (1984), in their interesting account of the patterns of migration to, and settlement in, western Europe, and the political action of immigrants, argue that

> foreign workers . . . experience their class position as the specific result of institutional discrimination and racism, rather than as the result of the relationship between labour and capital (Castles et al., 1984: 217).

In the context of the children of foreign workers, they suggest that the present tendency within political economy to locate them as part of the reserve army of labour is inadequate insofar as the concept

> is not sufficient to describe the growing political consciousness and militance of minority youth. Their struggles are not primarily to secure access to the labour process, but to defend themselves and their communities against racism. Their direct opponent is not the capitalist employer, but the state, represented by school, welfare bureaucracy and police (Castles et al., 1984: 214).

Such findings lead them to question the utility of class theory in understanding the position of migrants in western Europe.

In Canada a non-Marxist version of this argument has been developed by Peter Ward in his analysis of social cleavages in British Columbia (Ward, 1981; but see Warburton, 1981, for a critique). He argues that prior to the Second World War, the fundamental social division in BC was not based on differential relationships to the means of production. The incomplete annihilation of aboriginal people, the migration of 'Asian' races, and the presence of a predominantly white majority created a multiracial community. He suggests that the widespread belief in the perpetual 'racial' inferiority of non-whites, coupled with the denial of the franchise and widespread social and job segregation, meant that major social divisions were based primarily upon 'race': consciousness of 'race' overrode consciousness of class.

In response to these criticisms, it should be noted that attempts to give one set of relations priority over the other are misplaced, making the contradiction between 'race' and class identified in these critiques more apparent than real. The formulations noted above tend to reify the notion of race. They accord equal analytical status to the concepts of 'race' and class, yet the concepts themselves refer to two different dimensions of reality (Cassin and Griffith, 1981: 110-11). As noted above, 'race' is a label that has been used to define group boundaries, and class is an objective relationship to the means of production. The apparent opposition between 'race' and class is therefore a false construction.

In addition, the critique of political economy developed by Castles et al. (1984) is based on a highly economistic and deterministic understanding of class and class consciousness. Their argument implies that if those who occupy particular class positions do not engage in economic struggles over wages and working conditions, then 'class' is somehow inoperative. Marxist historians have argued that class struggles and class actions always occur in particular social and historical contexts, and that there is no necessary correlation between class positions and the content of class struggle. Within the framework of political economy there is no logical reason why those who are part of the reserve army of labour must engage in a struggle for waged employment if they are to really belong to the reserve army of labour. Historically, some of those who have constituted the reserve army of labour have struggled to *resist* proletarianization, and *resist* incorporation as wage labour (Palmer, 1984).

Furthermore, Ward's analysis is based on the abstraction of racialization from its material context and assumes that racism in BC simply had a life of its own that was unconnected to the larger contradictions within the province (Tan, 1987: 76; Warburton, 1981). As noted above, racism took on meaning within the lived experiences and contradictions that classes of people faced in the province.

How, then, have Canadian political economists attempted to understand the articulation of 'race' and class? As noted above, research into the split labour market has been one fruitful line of inquiry into this relationship. A second line of research that unravels the link between 'race', ethnicity and class can be seen in attempts to determine how 'racial' and ethnic categories are used to insert people into the relations of production. 'Race', ethnicity, and gender can be regarded as particular types of mechanisms by which categories of people are incorporated into the labour market and the relations of production. These studies demonstrate that 'race', ethnicity and gender can constitute the substance of class relations.

Ng's (1988) study of an employment agency examines how the category of 'immigrant women' was constructed by employment counsellors, and the way in which these definitions dovetailed with the demands of the labour market and the concerns of state funding agencies. Along with Cassin and Griffith (1981), she criticizes the notion that ethnicity is a 'social fact' that exists independently of peoples' experiences. The agency that Ng studied was formed to facilitate the employment of minority women who were having difficulty finding wage work. She demonstrates that the employment counsellor worked up the information given by the client into certain credentials that could be matched to the demands of employers for unskilled labour:

> The work of the employment counsellors constituted a determinant component in facilitating labour market processes by producing immigrant women as a distinctive kind of labour with certain skills and qualifications—as 'commodities', and in organizing the relation between immigrant women and their potential employers—the buyers of this distinctive kind of labour (Ng, 1988: 50).

The counselling and job-search processes thus drew upon prevailing views of gender, ethnicity, and 'race' to constitute particular categories of women as particular solutions to labour-force recruitment and retention problems.

This argument has also been developed in my own study of the state's recruitment of farmworkers for the Ontario fruit and vegetable harvest since 1945 (Satzewich, 1988). I argue that growers of fruits and vegetables in Ontario faced a two-fold labour problem: that of initially recruiting and then of retaining workers for the duration of the harvest. While the state-organized recruitment of internal reserves of labour and the substitution of capital for labour have partially resolved these problems, farmers have continued to demand amounts of wage labour beyond what is available in Canada.

I demonstrate that farmers turned to various forms of migrant and immigrant labour, which were additionally differentiated as either free or unfree in terms of their ability to circulate in the labour market. Groups of foreign-born workers were differentially incorporated into sites in production relations in part because of particular processes of racialization. For example, black workers from the Caribbean were incorporated as unfree migrant labour because of beliefs that they were beasts of burden, that they were 'racially' incapable of participation as full citizens within political and civil society, and that their presence would cause various social and 'racial' problems. Conversely, people from Holland were incorporated as free immigrant labour because state officials felt that as a 'race' of people, their 'free initiative' could not in good conscience be limited. Thus notions of 'race' had a determinant impact on the manner in which these workers were incorporated into production relations (Satzewich, 1988).

Taken together, these studies suggest that 'race' and class are not opposed to one another, and are not contradictory phenomenon. In Stuart Hall's (1980: 341) terms, 'race is the modality in which class is "lived", the medium through which class relations are experienced'.

A second line of research, which is only now beginning to emerge, and which requires much more careful study, is the examination of the class relations within minority communities, and the manner in which these relations structure community action.

For example, at the turn of the century there were important class divisions within the Chinese population in Canada (see Li, 1979). The two classes of Chinese in the province (working-class labourers and petit bourgeois traders, commodity producers and merchants) were treated differently by the state. The various head taxes that were imposed on the Chinese made a clear distinction between workers and the petit bourgeoisie. Workers and their families were required to pay $50, then $100 and then $500 upon entry into the country, whereas Chinese merchants and their families could enter without paying the tax. Later, one of the few classes of Chinese that could continue to enter Canada after the Passage of the 1923 Chinese Immigration Act were merchants who planned to invest more than $2,500 in the country, while Chinese workers were barred entry. Thus racist immigration controls were not applied to the entire category of Chinese who wanted to migrate to the country (Satzewich, 1989).

More recently, Hari Sharma (1982), in the course of union organizing in British Columbia's fruit and vegetable industry found that the industry employs various groups of minority workers, including

Sikhs, Chinese, and women. In some cases, the employers themselves are of Sikh and Chinese origin, and some of the labour contractors who supply labour to employers and organize the transportation of workers to the work site also appear to be of East Indian and Chinese origin (S. Sharma, 1982). Given the marginal status of the East Indian working class in the rest of the BC labour market, and the difficulty they face in finding well-paid employment under decent working conditions in the 'core' sectors of the market, what needs to be assessed is the extent to which employers and labour contractors are able to manipulate an ideology of 'ethnic solidarity' in order to justify the exploitation of their compatriots' labour power.

Class relations within 'minority' communities also appear to be increasingly important in the context of state funding. Again, research on this issue is only now beginning, but what it seems to suggest is that members of the minority bourgeoisie and petit bourgeoisie have been able to dominate 'community' politics (S. Sharma, 1982: 11; Richmond, 1988: 50; Stasiulis, 1980). It appears that these classes have been able to pursue their own interests within these community associations, and to represent their particular interests as those of the community as a whole. This takes on an increasing level of political significance because the petit bourgeoisie appears to be the more politically conservative element of minority communities, and it is this class that is more likely to attract state funding for its organizations.

The promotion of class divisions, specifically the creation of a petit bourgeoisie, also appears to be a feature of the Canadian state's management of the native population. A common colonization technique throughout the British empire, at present it is used both by the South African government to control the black population, and by Britain's Conservative government to control the population of Caribbean origin resident in economically deprived inner-city areas.

In Canada, the development of a Native middle class appears to have been a state strategy with a relatively long history. It was hoped that members of this middle class would act to exert control over other Native people. In the context of the reserve system, there is evidence to suggest that Indian Agents explicitly promoted the development of class divisions by rewarding with land, machinery, livestock, or political office those 'leading families' who were willing to conform to the Indian Affairs department's assimilationist objectives (Dosman, 1972: 22-6, 47; Silman, 1988).

That this also appears to be a contemporary strategy on the part of the Canadian state is evident in its promotion of the Special Constables Program in which Natives police other Natives, and in its emphasis on economic development through the private enterprise system, whereby Indian-controlled institutions exploit the labour power of the Indian working class (see Driben and Trudeau, 1983). In the future, 'economic development' may mean, in part, that Indians will increasingly discipline other Indians through the wage labour/ capital relationship.

CONCLUSION

While political economy is critical of 'race-relations' sociology for its use of unscientific and reified notions of 'race', there is conceptual space within this theoretical tradition for the analysis of racialization—that is, those social processes whereby social significance is attached to patterns of physical or genetic variation. The structure and agency traditions of political economy approach the problem of racialization from different starting points. The structuralist view examines racism as an ideology imposed from above by those who own the means of production on those who do not; racism acts to mystify social reality, justifies the exploitation of certain groups of peoples' labour power, and contributes to the maintenance of the status quo. Conversely, the agency view examines racism not as a false ideology about the world, but as an ideology that comes from peoples' lived experiences. The delineation and formation of group boundaries around physical differences is one way that people attempt to make sense of their experiences and the day-to-day contradictions they face.

Clearly, there are two major areas where further research within political economy is needed. First, more studies of the meaning and nature of working-class racism are essential. And second, more studies are required on the nature and meaning of class divisions within minority communities, and the manner in which these divisions manifest themselves in community politics, and relations with the state.

REFERENCES

Anderson, Alan and Jim Frideres

1981 *Ethnicity in Canada: Theoretical Perspectives*. Toronto: Butterworths.

Avery, Donald, and Peter Neary

1977 'Laurier, Borden and a White British Columbia'. *Journal of Canadian Studies*. 12: 24-34.

Banton, Michael

1970 'The Concept of Racism'. In S. Zubaida, ed. *Race and Racialism*. London, Tavistock.

Basran, Gurcharn

1983 'Canadian Immigration Policy and Theories of Racism'. In Peter S. Li and B. Singh Bolaria, eds, *Racial Minorities in Multicultural Canada*. Toronto: Garamond.

Beaujot, R., K.G. Basavarajappa, and R.B.P. Verma
1988 *Current Demographic Analysis: Income of Immigrants in Canada*. Ottawa: Statistics Canada.
Bolaria, B. Singh, and Peter Li
1988 *Racial Oppression in Canada*. 2nd ed. Toronto: Garamond.
Bonacich, Edna
1979 'The Past, Present and Future of Split Labour Market Theory'. In C. Marrett and C. Legon, eds, *Research in Race and Ethnic Relations*. Greenwich: JAI Press.
Calliste, Agnes
1987 'Sleeping Car Porters in Canada: An Ethnically Submerged Split Labour Market'. *Canadian Ethnic Studies* 19: 1-20.
1988 'Blacks on Canadian Railways'. *Canadian Ethnic Studies* 20: 36-52.
Cassin, Marguerite, and Alison Griffith
1981 'Class and Ethnicity: Producing the Difference That Counts'. *Canadian Ethnic Studies* 13: 107-29.
Castles, Stephen, Heather Booth, and Tina Wallace
1984 *Here for Good: Western Europe's New Ethnic Minorities*. London: Pluto Press.
Castles, Stephen, and Godula Kosack
1973 *Immigrant Workers and Class Structure in Western Europe*. London: Oxford University Press.
Centre for Contemporary Cultural Studies
1982 *The Empire Strikes Back: Race and Racism in 70s Britain*. London: Hutcheson.
Coser, Lewis
1977 *Masters of Sociological Thought*. New York: Harcourt, Brace Jovanovich.
Cox, Oliver
1948 *Caste, Class and Race*. New York: Monthly Review Press.
Creese, Gillian
1984 'Immigration Policies and the Creation of an Ethnically Segmented Working Class in British Columbia, 1880-1923'. *Alternate Routes* 7: 1-34.
Daniels, Doug
1987 'Canada'. In Jay Sigler, ed., *International Handbook on Race and Race Relations*. New York: Greenwood Press.
Dosman, Edgar
1972 *Indians: The Urban Dilemma*. Toronto: McClelland and Stewart.
Driben, Paul, and Robert Trudeau
1983 *When Freedom is Lost: The Dark Side of the Relationship Between Government and the Fort Hope Band*. Toronto: University of Toronto Press.
Globe and Mail
1989a 'Albania riot broken up in fourth day of unrest'. Toronto, 22 March 1989.
1989b 'Clash in Soviet Georgia leaves 16 dead, 200 hurt'. Toronto, 10 April 1989.

1989c 'Racial issues key to Chicago mayoral vote'. Toronto, 4 April 1989.

Hall, Stuart

1978 'Racism and Reaction'. In Commission for Racial Equality, *Five Views of Multi-Racial Britain*. London: Commission for Racial Equality.

1980 'Race, Articulation and Societies Structured in Dominance'. In UNESCO, *Sociological Theories: Race and Colonialism*. Paris: UNESCO.

Husband, Charles

1987 'British Racisms: the Construction of Racial Ideologies'. In Charles Husband, ed., *'Race' in Britain*. London: Hutchinson.

Kuper, Jessica

1984 *Race and Race Relations*. London: Batsford Academic and Educational Ltd.

Lecourt, Dominique

1980 'On Marxism as a Critique of Sociological Theories'. In UNESCO, *Sociological Theories: Race and Colonialism*. Paris: UNESCO.

Li, Peter

1979 'A Historical Approach to Ethnic Stratification: the Case of the Chinese in Canada'. *Canadian Review of Sociology and Anthropology*. 16: 320-23.

1988 *Ethnic Inequality in a Class Society*. Toronto: Wall and Thompson.

Marx, Karl

1978 *The Communist Manifesto*. In Robert Tucker, ed., *The Marx-Engels Reader*. New York: W.W. Norton.

Miles, Robert

1982 *Racism and Migrant Labour*. London: Routledge and Kegan Paul.

Miles, Robert, and Annie Phizacklea

1985 *White Man's Country*. London: Pluto.

Montagu, Ashley

1964 *Man's Most Dangerous Myth*. Cleveland: World Publishing.

1972 *Statement on Race*. London: Oxford University Press.

Ng, Roxana

1988 *The Politics of Community Services*. Toronto: Garamond.

Palmer, Bryan

1984 'Social Formation and Class Formation in North America, 1800-1900'. In David Levine, ed., *Proletarianization Family History*. New York: Academic Press.

Phillips, Paul

1967 *No Power Greater: A Century of Labour in B.C.* Vancouver: BC Federation of Labour Boag Foundation.

Phizacklea, Annie, and Robert Miles

1980 *Labour and Racism*. London: Routledge and Kegan Paul.

Reitz, Jeffrey

1988 'The Institutional Structure of Immigration as a Determinant of Inter-Racial Competition: A Comparison of Britain and Canada'. *International Migration Review*. 22: 117-46.

Rex, John
1983 *Race Relations in Sociological Theory*. London: Routledge and Kegan Paul.
Richmond, Anthony
1988 *Immigration and Ethnic Conflict*. Toronto: Macmillan.
Sampat-Mehta, R.
1973 *International Barriers*. Ottawa: Harpell's Press.
Satzewich, Vic
1988 *Modes of Incorporation and Racialization: the Canadian Case*. Unpublished Ph.D. thesis, Department of Sociology, University of Glasgow.
1989 'Racisms: The Reactions to Chinese Migrants in Canada at the Turn of the Century'. *International Sociology*. 4: 311-28.
Sharma, Hari
1982 'Asian Indian Struggles in British Columbia: An Interview with Hari Sharma'. *South Asia Bulletin*. 3: 53-69.
Sharma, Shalendra
1982 'East Indians in the Canadian Ethnic Mosaic'. *South Asia Bulletin*. 2: 6-18.
Silman, Janet
1988 *Enough Is Enough: Aboriginal Women Speak Out*. Toronto: Women's Press.
Sivanandan, A.
1982 *A Different Hunger*. London: Pluto Press.
Solomos, John
1987 'Varieties of Marxist Conceptions of "Race", Class and the State'. In John Rex and David Mason, eds, *Theories of Race and Ethnic Relations*. Cambridge: Cambridge University Press.
Star Phoenix
1989 'Native tells story of misery, racism'. Saskatoon, 23 Jan. 1989.
Stasiulis, Daiva
1980 'The Political Structuring of Ethnic Community Action'. *Canadian Ethnic Studies*. 12: 19-44.
Svenson, Ken
1978 *'The Explosive Years': Indian and Metis Issues in Saskatchewan to 2001*. Regina.
Tan, Jin
1987 'Chinese Labour and the Reconstituted Social Order of British Columbia'. *Canadian Ethnic Studies*. 19: 68-88.
Warburton, Rennie
1981 'Race and Class in British Columbia: A Comment'. *BC Studies*. 49: 79-85.
Ward, Peter
1981 'Class and Race in the Social Structure of British Columbia, 1870-1939'. In Peter Ward and Robert McDonald, eds, *British Columbia: Historical Readings*. Vancouver: Douglas and McIntyre.
Wilson, William
1973 *Power Racism and Privilege*. New York: Free Press.

TWELVE

THEORIZING CONNECTIONS: GENDER, RACE, ETHNICITY, AND CLASS

DAIVA K. STASIULIS

This chapter explores the possibilities and problems inherent in analyses that seek to conceptualize the links among relations organized by gender, race, ethnicity, and class.[1] In Canada, as in all multi-racial, multi-ethnic societies, all social relations have class, gendered, racial, and ethnic elements. Within any given context and for any given population, however, one of these social constructions or identities may be perceived to be more salient than the others.

There is a growing body of literature that illustrates the many levels (economic, political, and ideological) and modalities (discourses, practices, institutional mechanisms) through which race, ethnicity, gender, and class are intermeshed. This chapter critically examines selected theoretical debates in the international and Canadian literature[2] that seek to integrate notions of 'class' and 'gender' with 'race' and 'ethnicity'.

In it I will discuss both the strengths and the weaknesses of some of the recent efforts to theorize the connections among class, race, ethnicity, and gender. Given the immense size, richness, and diversity of this literature, I can adequately address only a few major debates. The chapter is organized in three sections. The first considers several approaches to the conceptualization of the relationship between race and class, with reference to the forms of racism experienced in countries such as Britain, the United States, and Canada. A major weakness of socialist feminism in the 1980s has been that, notwithstanding its efforts to incorporate the categories of race and class into its theory and practice, its analysis of racism and its understanding of the relationship between racism and class exploitation are frequently left unspecified or inadequate. Anti-racist feminism would benefit substantially from the some of the analytical directions taken within the race and class debate, which I outline in the first section.

The second section addresses some of the contributions of the debates within feminism that have stemmed chiefly from attempts by Black feminists to confront the racism and Eurocentrism of the white-dominated Western women's movement and analysis of women's oppression.[3] The third section draws out some of the implications of the foregoing analysis for analyses of Aboriginal, immigrant, and racial-minority women in Canada. The chapter concludes with a few remarks about the implications for political practice of multi-dimensional theories of oppression.

THE RACE AND CLASS DEBATES

The protracted and often violent oppression of Black and other people of colour in Britain, the United States, and, above all, South Africa has made racism and racial subordination major and recurrent areas of difficulty for analyses from the left. Debates among Marxists and neo-Marxists focus on the relationship between racism (variously defined as ideologies or subordinating practices involving socially constructed notions of 'race') and the development of capitalism. Given the heterogeneous nature of Marxism and other theories of the left, it is not surprising that the question of what the relationship is between race and class, and between racism and capitalist development, has received many divergent answers.

The most basic disagreement on the 'race-class question' centres on whether racism and racial phenomena can be understood solely in terms of the analytic categories of historical materialism, class, and production relations or, alternatively, whether 'race' must be accorded an analytical status separate and distinct from 'class'. As Solomos (1986) points out, neo-Marxist approaches to race and class vary substantially according to the amount of autonomy from class-based social relations they accord to race, racial divisions, and racism. At both the analytical and the political levels, the central issue is frequently posed in terms of the question 'Which form of power relations—racial oppression or class exploitation—is more determinant in providing the basis of racial inequality, antagonism, and consciousness within social movements for change?' Or, as succinctly put by Harris (1987: 91), 'Which evil—racial oppression or class exploitation—is the more "primary"?'

The seminal work by Cox on *Caste, Class and Race* (1948)—still widely considered to be *the* orthodox Marxist analysis of racism—

represents one extreme position: Cox assumes that racial antagonisms are nothing but the mystified form of the class struggle determined by the clash of economic interests arising out of the development of capitalism. According to Cox, all racist phenomena (ideology, antagonistic attitudes, discriminatory practices) have their roots in the colonial phase of capitalism. The expansion of capitalism via the amassing of vast profits from the enslavement and 'proletarianization' of coloured people necessitated the construction of a commensurate philosophy of justification. Race prejudice is viewed as a social attitude propagated by an exploiting class in order to stigmatize some group as inferior so that exploitation may be justified. The major function of racism is to divide the working class so that the proletariat can be exploited more effectively by the capitalists.

The resulting conflict between racially divided workers is thus epiphenomenal to the conflict between capital and labour. White and Black workers share a political interest in the abolition of capitalism; racial divisions in countries such as South Africa simply reinforce structural divisions, and they emerge as fractions *within* the working class. Racial antagonisms existing between white and Black workers are evidence of 'false consciousness', with the white workers sharing racial attitudes or loyalties with the (white) bourgeoisie that are not in their interests as members of the exploited class.

Although Cox's work has undergone many thorough critiques both by contemporary Marxists (Miles, 1980) and by critics of Marxism (Parkin, 1979), it is representative of one polar tendency within Marxism to view racial and other forms of non-class divisions as mere reflections of production and class-based relations. As elaborated upon below, this reductionist tendency has predominated in contemporary Marxist analyses of immigration and racial oppression in Canada. As Genovese (1971) and Solomos (1986: 87-8) have pointed out, Cox's historical materialism reflected a mechanistic model of determination: racial oppression and antagonism are located in the political and ideological superstructure that is determined by the functional needs of the economic base. Cox did not have the benefit of the sophisticated work on ideology, class, and the state of Antonio Gramsci, the theoretical refinements of cultural and structural Marxists, or the vast body of work within Marxism that has since discredited the base-superstructure model and sought to avoid the obvious forms of class reductionism and economic determinism evident in Cox's work.

In contemporary British debates over race and class, the prodigious work of Miles and Phizacklea (Miles, 1980, 1982, 1984, 1987, 1988; Phizacklea and Miles, 1980) is the clearest instance of application of Marxist political economy to analyses of racism. Beginning with

Marx's fundamental distinction between phenomenal and essential relations, Miles and Phizacklea relegate 'race' and 'race relations' to the realm of phenomenal forms. Although they may appear natural and even inevitable to human agents, 'race relations' constitute merely 'the surface appearance of the way in which the world is organized', and may actually obscure the real underlying (i.e., essential) relations (Miles, 1984: 31; 1988: 430). Thus these authors contend that treating 'race' as an analytical or explanatory concept is fundamentally mistaken. Instead, they argue for the necessity of applying the analytical categories of Marxist political economy—especially class and production relations—to the process of racialization and the reduction of racism.

Central to their analysis of racism against non-white immigrants in Britain during the 1970s and 1980s is the shortage of labour that occurred with the post-war expansion of industrial capitalism. Migrant labour from the countries that had recently exchanged colonial for Commonwealth status in the Caribbean and South Asia provided one important solution to the problem of labour shortage. The position taken up in production relations by Black migrants was both similar to that of white British workers (part of the working class) and different. The difference lay in the disproportionate distribution of Black workers in less desirable semi-skilled and unskilled manufacturing jobs. A second difference was the process of 'racialization' of this 'fraction of the working class' that took place at both the political (state immigration and citizenship policies, practices of the white-led trade union movement) and ideological (e.g., the impact of racist ideology) levels (Miles, 1984: 229).

Miles and Phizacklea deny that even though they reject the idea of 'race' as having any independent analytical value, their argument is economically determinist. Consistent with other neo-Marxists who propose models of complex determination of social class, they argue that in the historical context of Caribbean and South Asian migration to post-1945 Britain, 'the political and the ideological have had determinant effects, simultaneously with the economic, in creating and reproducing a *racialized* fraction of the working class (and other classes)' (Miles, 1984: 229; emphasis in original). The central elements of their formulation are that (a) race is an ideological construction rather than an analytic category, and (b) capitalist relations of production have primary analytic significance and override the effects of 'racialization'. Miles describes racism and racialization as having 'autonomous but limited effects' (1984: 91). This ambiguous statement raises the questions of precisely how much autonomy is conceded, and whether it is necessary to use a conceptual scheme distinct from the concepts of Marxian class analysis in order to account for this autonomous, race-specific ideological and political realm.

Several other theorists in Britain have conceptualized the links between race and class in ways that accord more explicit attention and autonomy to race phenomena. Frequently these theoretical writings navigate a perilous route between the opposite shoals of economic reductionism and the reification of 'race' in isolation from class-based social relations. Solomos (1986) distinguishes between the 'relative autonomy' model of Hall (1980), and the Birmingham Centre for Contemporary Cultural Studies (CCCS, 1982) and the 'autonomy model' of Gabriel and Ben-Tovim (1978).

Hall, a leading proponent of the 'relative autonomy' position, argues that 'although racism cannot be reduced to other social relations, one cannot explain racism in abstraction from them' (Solomos, 1986: 92). He urges that, given that a homogeneous form of racism is not endemic in all human societies, the historical specificity of different forms of racism be made the object of study. All analyses of racism, however, must be anchored in an understanding of the broader framework of economic relations. In other words, while Hall contends that racial antagonisms cannot be accounted for *solely* in terms of economic relations, he insists that racial structures cannot be adequately understood outside the framework of specific sets of economic relations (Hall, 1980). Finally, on the question of primacy, he views race and class as standing in some sort of mutual relationship. As summarized by Solomos (1986: 92), for Hall,

> 'race' has a concrete impact on the class consciousness and organization of all classes and class fractions. But 'class' in turn has a reciprocal relationship with 'race', and it is the articulation between the two which is crucial, not their separateness.

Parmar (1982), one of the members of the Birmingham group (CCCS) who provides a sustained analysis of the articulation of gender with race and class, also rejects the analytical separation of race and class. In a study of South Asian women, she concludes (1982: 296; emphasis added) that the way

> capital, patriarchy and race structure Asian women's oppression and exploitation does not make it possible *or desirable* to separate out the primary cause of oppression; all three factors are intrinsic to the day-to-day experiences of Asian women.

The 'autonomy' approach of Gabriel and Ben-Tovim (1978; Ben-Tovim et al., 1981, 1986) reaches a diametrically opposite conclusion: that race (gender is not mentioned) is irreducible to class and therefore *must* be analytically accounted for in terms of its own autonomous conditions of production. Like Miles and Phizacklea, Gabriel and Ben-Tovim see race and racism as *ideological* concepts. In contrast to the former, however, the latter authors insist that racism cannot be accounted for primarily as the product of economic or class relations, but rather arises out of 'determinant ideological practices, with their own theoretical/ideological conditions of existence and their own irreducible contradictions' (1978: 139). Gabriel and Ben-Tovim are critical of the 'relative autonomy' approach to racism on the grounds that it provides only a more sophisticated form of class reductionism and economic determinism. For them, invoking the nebulous concept of 'relative autonomy' has the effect of replicating the functionalist thrust of Althusser's theory of ideology, whereby 'ideology constitutes the mechanism for the reproduction of production relations' (1978: 140; Solomos, 1986: 95).

The assumption of the autonomous nature of racism leads Gabriel and Ben-Tovim to focus their analyses on the political processes of racist and anti-racist struggles at both the local and national levels of the British state. According to these authors, Marxist and neo-Marxist analyses of racism that take as their starting point the economic laws of capital accumulation are inadequate to the task of analyzing the complex *political* realities of both racist politics and anti-racist struggles (Ben-Tovim et al., 1986: 133-4; emphasis added).

But while Gabriel and Ben-Tovim eschew any formulation that accounts for racism in terms of 'external' economic relations, they deny that their position suggests they are 'entering some kind of autonomous sphere, where action takes over from structural constraints' (Ben-Tovim et al., 1986: 133). Thus economic relations enter into their analysis at the point where they 'can be said to determine in the last instance the *mode of reproduction* of racism' (Gabriel and Ben-Tovim, 1978: 139; emphasis in original). In other words, while racism and reactions to it cannot be explained by reference to capitalism and class antagonisms, such wider structural constraints do play a role in determining the effects of racist ideology, chiefly through limiting the effectiveness of anti-racist struggles (Ben-Tovim et al., 1981, 1986).

There are several problems with the 'autonomy' model of Gabriel and Ben-Tovim, of both a theoretical and a political nature. Theoretically, they deny that economic relations have any influence in the production of racial ideologies. Yet by focusing their analyses on the *political* struggles that structure the effects of racist ideology, they are left with a deficient explanation for the origins, development, and content of this ideology. Politically, their emphasis on anti-racist politics, race-relations legislation, and other 'popular democratic' reforms within the state is premised on the primacy of political struggles over other determining factors. Like other post-Marxists (e.g., Laclau and Mouffe, 1985), Gabriel and Ben-Tovim conceive of the state as devoid of any 'preconceived hierarchy' (Ben-Tovim et al., 1986: 134) and 'unproblematically open to infusions of meaningful democratic, anti-racist practice' (Gilroy, 1982: 279). The neo-conservative agenda of capitalist states vis à vis the massive restructuring of capital currently taking place at both global and national levels is all but completely ignored, as is the extent to which progressive race-relations (and gender-equity and other) reforms are constantly checked by the power and autonomy of capital and central state authorities.

Despite these shortcomings, Gabriel and Ben-Tovim's attempt to give autonomy to the social construction of race represents an important break with the economistic and class-reductionist tendencies of Marxist writings. Other theorists have since become concerned with finding analytic tools with which to comprehend and combat racism. Gabriel and Ben-Tovim's separation of the determination of racial ideology and the reproduction of racism is echoed in the insightful deconstructions of racism by Gilroy (1982, 1987) and Anthias (1988), and in the multi-level approach to racism of West (1982, 1987, 1988).

West's effort to construct a multi-dimensional, non-economistic framework of modern racism consists of three 'methodological moments' that are to serve as guides for detailed historical and social analysis. The three moments (1987: 87-8) consist of:

1. A *genealogical* inquiry into the discursive and extra-discursive conditions for the possibility of racist practices, that is, a radically historical investigation into the emergence, development and sustenance of white supremacist logics operative in various epochs in the modern Occidental (Orient, African, Indian) civilization.
2. A *micro-institutional* (or localized) analysis of the mechanisms that promote and contest these logics in the everyday lives of peoples, including the ways in which self-images and self-identities are shaped and the impact of alien, degrading cultural styles, aesthetic ideals, psychosexual sensibilities and linguistic gestures upon peoples of colour.
3. A *macro-structural* approach which accents modes of over-determined class exploitation, state repression and bureaucratic domination, including resistance against these modes, in the lives of peoples of colour.

It is in the elaboration of the first moment—the inquiry into the rise of white supremacy—that West's unequivocal rejection of economism and reductionism is most evident (1982: 49). He suggests that three white supremacist logics—Judeo-Christian, Cartesian scientific, and psychosexual—operate simultaneously in the West to produce the belief that coloured people are alien and inferior. The justification of 'black ugliness, cultural deficiency, and intellectual inferiority' was made possible by the 'creative fusion' of Cartesian philosophy, the rise of the new disciplines of phrenology and physiognomy (reading of skulls and faces, respectively), and the revival during the Enlightenment of neo-classical aesthetic and cultural norms of human form, proportion, and beauty. The advent of modern science, which routinized empirical observation and measurement, concomitantly incorporated Greco-Roman aesthetic standards and thus played a central role in producing what West calls a 'normative gaze' (1982: 53-4). Through this 'gaze'—namely, a specific ideal from which to order and compare measurements regarding 'what it is to be human, cultured, and intelligent'—all people of colour would be judged and found wanting (West, 1982: 53-4, 64).

West does not purport to explain the rise of modern racism. Rather, he argues that 'the everyday life of black people is shaped not simply by the . . . capitalist system of production but also by cultural attitudes and sensibilities, including alienating ideals of beauty' (1982: 65).

Through the inclusion of macrostructural analysis in the 'third movement', West acknowledges the importance of considering historical structural constraints in constructing an adequate theory of racism (1988: 24-5). Yet he views social formations as complex interactions of economic, political, cultural, and ideological regions where the economic sphere is not the 'ultimate factor in explaining racist practices' (1988: 25; 1987: 89-90).

Before summarizing the race-class debate, I will now briefly examine the treatment of relations between race and class and between ethnicity and class in the context of English Canada.[4] Most Canadian analyses in this area adopt theoretical frameworks developed elsewhere and offer little theoretical refinement on the relationship between race and class.

There are several reasons for this. First, ethnic and racial studies generally tend to form a conservative discipline—a tendency that has been deepened by the state support given to ethnic studies since the early 1970s. Second, Marxist and political-economy theorists have paid in sufficient attention to the role of race and ethnicity, and of both Aboriginal peoples and non-Anglo, non-French minorities, in Canadian capitalist development, state formation, and class relations (Abele and Stasiulis, 1989).

The few Marxist accounts of racism in Canada that exist have tended to be plagued by economic determinism and class reductionism. These analyses incorporate inadequate theorizations of both class (e.g., defined only by economic relations) and the state (e.g., instruments of the ruling class) (Basran, 1983; Bolaria and Li, 1985,

1988; Cappon, 1975). Thus Li and Bolaria have sought to address the silence within Canadian political economy on the role of racial-minority workers by focusing on the functions served by the super-exploited migrants and non-European immigrant workers.

Non-European workers, such as the Chinese, East Indians, and Blacks, have been subordinated through a series of restrictive state policies—most importantly, immigration policy—and racist ideology that is propagated by the state through immigration legislation (Bolaria and Li, 1988: 177). Thus the racist oppression of minorities and the racial antagonisms between white and minority workers are viewed as the direct product of capital's need to divide workers and super-exploit weaker sections, and of an instrumentalist state that automatically does capital's bidding. While these authors are undoubtedly addressing a gap in Canadian research on racism by linking the development of racism to Canadian capitalist development, their formulation exhibits some of the same problems of economism and class reductionism that are found in the work of Cox. No separate level of determination is conceded to ideology, to state interests beyond those of capital accumulation, or to the activities of white and racial-minority workers in reproducing or contesting racial antagonisms and oppression (Abele and Stasiulis, 1989: 263; Creese, 1986: 29-30; Warburton, 1989: 13).

A more nuanced rendition is provided by Creese (1986) in her study of early twentieth-century working-class politics in British Columbia. For Creese, race and gender are constitutive elements in the structuration of classes that, rather than simply functioning to reproduce class domination, generate contradictions and conflicts. She demonstrates this point by showing that in the white labour movement there have been actions that both suppressed and encouraged solidarity with Asian workers. Although she does not offer an analysis of the origins of racist ideology or ethnic consciousness, Creese acknowledges the importance of both in the social identities and structural positions of white and Asian workers respectively (1986: 116, 166). Her approach to the 'race-class question' thus firmly rejects unidimensional and economically determinist notions of class. Instead, her study absorbs an expanded, neo-Marxist definition of class in which classes are shaped simultaneously by economic, political, and ideological relations, with racism conceived as percolating throughout the political and ideological realms.

There is now a growing body of literature by labour and social historians that fruitfully merges Canadian labour and immigration history. The role of ethnicity is rigorously explored in diverse accounts of Hamilton steelworkers, Italian workers in Toronto and Montreal, Finnish and British domestic workers, northern Finnish lumberworkers, Albertan coal miners, and the development of a multicultural patchwork of labour markets within different localities (Barber, 1986; Harney, 1979; Heron and Storey, 1985; Iacovetta, 1986; Lindstrom-Best, 1986; Pentland, 1981; Ramirez, 1986; Seager, 1986). Within these studies, ethnicity is treated not as 'cultural baggage', but rather as the world views, traditions, and practices brought by immigrants to Canada and dynamically reproduced and transformed within the Canadian context.

In addition, a number of studies have examined the relationship between race/ethnicity and class where Native peoples are concerned. Given the distinctive histories—both pre- and post-contact with Europeans—and the often unique relationship to capitalist and non-capitalist (e.g., bush) modes of production of Aboriginal peoples in Canada, this relationship is different, and in many instances more complex, for them than for immigrant groups. Some analysts, such as Bourgeault (1983a, 1983b, 1988), insist that the imposition of class, as well as racist and sexist, divisions occurred with the incorporation of Native (including mixed-blood) people into colonial relations under mercantile capitalism in the days of the fur trade. While not disavowing the importance of the fur trade and early capitalist social relations for the transformation and subordination of Native peoples, other scholars insist that the protracted social interaction and struggle between Europeans and Aborigines involved mutually transformative social relations where 'racial and ethnic lines were far from perfectly correlated with relations of domination' (Abele and Stasiulis, 1989: 248; Ray, 1974; Trigger, 1985; Van Kirk, 1980). While Canadian political economy and labour history have generally banished Native people, some studies—especially of primary industries such as fishing—explore the specifity of Native interests and experience vis à vis class organization and labour radicalism (Clement, 1986; Muszynski, 1986).

Collectively, this research documents a process whereby a number of different Aboriginal and migrant groups—including the nineteenth-century Irish, and East and South Europeans well into the 1950s—who were perceived to depart from white, English norms of physical appearance and culture, have been 'racialized' over the course of Canadian history. Canadian racism has been evoked not only by skin colour, but by 'ethnic' markers as well, based on language, religion, and other components of ethnic culture.

Yet a major contribution of that segment of Canadian labour history which interrogates the role and experiences of Aboriginal, immigrant, and minority workers is its disclosure that race and ethnicity are *prima facie* neither divisive nor facilitative of class mobilization and struggle. Much depends on the larger context of social relations and the institutional practices of capital, labour, and the state.

In addition, ethnic and Native communal and kinship-based organizations frequently have provided crucial resources and social foundations for collective action—both supportive of and at odds with larger class battles. This focus on the often critical role of *ethnic communities* in fashioning social identities and in binding together individuals—with either similar or contradictory class positions—is overlooked in many of the British neo-Marxist and radical debates on race and class (Cole, 1988), where antipathy to both the analytical and the political use of 'ethnicity' is widespread. The choice to dispense with ethnicity as an explanatory concept stems in part from the perceived creation or appropriation by the British state of ethnicity to 'divide and rule' various ethnic communities who share similar experiences of class exploitation and racial oppression (Bourne, 1980: 343-7).

Although it is clear that any given formulation of the class-race problematic is far from conclusive, it is possible to distil some central features and fruitful directions taken in the above debates.

1. Theories conceptualizing the links between race and class are increasingly becoming less economically deterministic and class reductionistic, leading to transformed notions of both 'race' and 'class'.

2. Race and racism are being accorded more autonomy and analytical attention. Rather than being treated as epiphenomenal to class, race and racism are increasingly treated as having their own complex and historically specific modes. As stated by Solomos (1986: 104), ' "racial" and "ethnic" divisions cannot be reduced to or seen as completely determined by the structural contradictions of capitalist societies.'

3. Central to the development of a non-economistic and non-reductionist analysis of the race-class dynamic have been re-worked notions of class. The work of neo-Marxists such as Przeworski (1977) and Wright (1980) has been influential in efforts to conceptualize class formation more broadly to include determinations based upon political and ideological forms of struggle, as well as objective economic relations. Przeworski's broad definition of class struggle encompasses struggles that bring classes into being as well as struggles between organized class forces. This enlarged conception of class struggle can render more intelligible the connections between economic and political structures, on the one hand, and struggles organized around non-class identities such as ethnicity, race, gender, and community, on the other (Gilroy, 1987: 31).

4. The role of structural (economic, political, and ideological) fea-

tures of capitalism on both a global and a national scale has been stressed (Solomos, 1986: 104; West, 1988: 24-5). Several of the emergent formulations on race and class, however, are lax about providing analyses of production relations and the role of the state in the reproduction of the capitalist mode of production, emphasizing instead the state's role in reproducing racial oppression (Miles, 1988). Without an adequate grasp of the long-standing central concern of Marxism with the mechanisms reproducing and transforming capitalism, it is doubtful that all dimensions of racism (such as structural racism) can be adequately grasped and, as importantly, combatted or overcome.

5. Racism, in the sense of exclusionary practices justified on the basis of assumed biological or immutable cultural differences, can be directed against ethnic groups who, on the basis of skin colour or other phenotypical characteristics, may or may not be constituted as separate races from the dominant group. That is, ethnically constituted differences (language, religion, dress, etc.) can become the basis of exclusionary discourses and practices that are obviously racist in their imputation of immutable and repulsive differences and their inequitable outcomes. This remains a highly contested point in theories of race and ethnicity, with those who reject any conflation between ethnicity and race claiming that phenotypical markers of racial boundaries such as skin colour are not *merely* socially constructed, nor are they readily malleable and deconstructed (Mason, 1986: 6). As will be elaborated upon later in this chapter, the issue of racial and ethnic categorization is a matter of considerable debate within feminism as the women's movement attempts to incorporate the antagonistic implications of racial and cultural difference.

6. The race and class debate has thus far not taken gender seriously. For example, classical Marxist analyses of racism frequently treat gender as *parallel* with race, as in the concept of a 'reserve army of labour' comprised of either 'racial minorities' or 'women', without specifying the sex of the former or the race and ethnicity of the latter. The more contemporary Marxist and post-Marxist formulations achieved through the 'modernization' of class concepts in their articulation with race have been silent on gender. This silence should not be read as reflecting sexism on the part of race-class theorists, although the fields of Marxist political economy and race and ethnic studies have been male-dominated. However, the omission of gender in theories addressing the race-class question stems equally from the real difficulties encountered in fashioning a coherent analysis that considers two or more different social divisions—both separately, and in their complex articulation.[5] These difficulties, as well as some of the lessons learned from the race and class debates, will be elaborated

upon in the following section, where I examine feminist theorizing on racial and ethnic divisions.

FEMINIST INCORPORATIONS OF RACE, ETHNICITY, AND CLASS

The necessity of coming to grips with racism and racial/ethnic divisions, both within and outside the women's movement, has posed one of the greatest challenges to contemporary feminist theory and practice in Canada, the United States, and Britain. The task of developing an adequate anti-racist perspective and adopting authentic anti-racist strategies for all segments of the feminist movement is a direct response to the growing collective strength and public voice among Aboriginal, immigrant, and racial-minority women (das Gupta, 1986; Hernandez, 1988; Native Women's Association of Canada, 1988; Silman, 1987; Wallis, Giles, and Hernandez, 1988). It also reflects growing international contact among feminists and growing exposure to analyses by and about women in developing countries (Broom, 1987: 273; Hill, 1987). One effect of this exposure has been to reveal the ethnocentric Western assumptions about women's roles in much North American and European feminist writing.

In Canada and elsewhere, the definition given by socialist feminists in the 1980s to their understanding of the power relations within which women are embedded frequently, if not routinely, includes the category of 'race'. For instance, one recent study of the contemporary women's movement in Canada gives as the framework for analyzing women's oppression 'four intertwining categories: gender, class, race, and sexual orientation' (Adamson, Briskin, and McPhail, 1988; see also Bhavnani and Coulson, 1986; Harriss, 1989).

Within a few short years, socialist-feminist theories have moved from a position providing dismissive or only cursory treatment of racial and ethnic identities and divisions[6] to one claiming to treat 'race' and racism as integral to feminist analysis. The inclusion of race and ethnic identities as lenses through which to understand the diverse experiences of women reflects a serious intent to represent, and free from oppression, *all* women. It is important to inquire, however, whether feminist theories have in the process been transformed, or, alternatively, whether the issue of racism and the categories of race and ethnicity have simply been 'grafted' on to existing analyses of sex and class. In other words, are feminist analyses of connections among gender, race, ethnicity, and class merely a matter of 'bland intersectionism', or are they real theoretical advances that might fruitfully serve to inform not only feminist politics, but those of labour and other social movements? These questions will be pursued through an examination of the critiques of white feminism made by Black feminists, the alternative formulations offered, and some recent efforts to theorize the experiences of native, migrant, and racial-minority women in the Canadian context.

Both the labels 'white feminism' and 'Black feminism' are vast simplications of the diversity—of priorities, epistemologies, politics, levels of abstraction, and incorporation of class analysis and other social categories such as sexual orientation—within feminist scholarship. These admittedly problematic terms will be adopted in this paper in order to show how the omission of analyses of racism in feminist historiography and social science undermines both the analytical strength of these fields and their potential for building political solidarity.

By 'white feminism' I mean the vast majority of Western feminist writing that has been produced by white women and either ignores race and ethnicity or treats these social divisions and identities as accessories to the basic definition of 'woman'. Because it is socialist feminism that most consistently addresses the articulation between gender (or sex) and class, and the relationship between capitalist production and human reproduction,[7] the following discussion will focus on the socialist-feminist writing of white feminists.

By 'Black feminism' I mean the growing body of literature, in the United States, Britain, and, increasingly, Canada, that conveys and conceptualizes the historical and contemporary circumstances of Black women and other women of colour. The vehicles of expression of Black feminist thought and emotions are frequently richly evocative, experiential literature—poetry, short stories, and essays, 'the inter-weaving of protests and laments from women who come from the farm and the ghetto; the factory and the university' (Jones, 1985: 315)—as well as more analytical writings. Although fed by diverse national and group-specific histories and cultures of resistance, Black feminists frequently draw inspiration from the same sources (e.g., the writings of Frantz Fanon and Angela Davis) and from anti-imperialist and Black liberation struggles led and supported by women around the globe. The recent proliferation of analytical Black feminist writings offers a more precise and pointed critique of the Eurocentric bias common to white feminist writings. Black feminist writings also suggest elements for alternative theories sensitive to the differing material circumstances and experiences among women differentiated by race and ethnicity.

The omission of women of colour from white feminist analysis has in itself been regarded as reflective of the racism and ethnic exclusivity of the white women's movement. Minh-ha (1989: 99) has argued that the labels by which feminists refer to racial differences among women—such as 'Western', 'non-Western', or 'Third World'—'take the dominant group as point of reference, and they reflect well the West's ideology of dominance', adding, for dramatic illustration, that 'it is as if we were to use the term "non-Afro-Asian" . . . to designate all white people'.

Equally important, however, is Black feminism's insistence on an adequate incorporation of anti-racism into feminist theory and politics. This task necessitates that white women acknowledge the 'material basis of their power in relation to black people, both women and men' (Bhavnani and Coulson, 1986).

In other words, white feminists must come to terms with the complexities and contradictions of power relations involving the intersection of gender, class, and race, where white women may simultaneously be privileged *and* oppressed. The Janus-faced position that white women have held vis à vis women and men of colour is apparent in the legacy of racism within white feminist politics (Hooks, 1981, 1984). Racist strategies were evident in the first wave of feminism, when American suffragettes broke their alliance with Blacks and co-operated with avowed racists in order to gain the southern vote for female suffrage (King, 1988). More recently, white British feminists involved in anti-rape campaigns have managed to ignore the way their marches through Black areas have reinforced racist stereotypes of the violent sexuality of Black men and legitimized the greater policing of Black communities (Bhavnani and Coulson, 1986).

Black feminists have challenged the hegemony of white feminism and critiqued the tendency of white feminists to generalize from the experiences of Anglo-Celtic women to those of all women, regardless of their respective positions within structures of racial and/or ethnic oppression. In political struggles as well as theoretical debates, Black feminists have expressed their concern over the tendency within white feminism to *a priori* privilege gender divisions and sexism (or, in socialist feminism, gender and class divisions) over race divisions and racism.

Black feminism rejects the claims to universality of the central categories and assumptions of white feminist analyses. The major disagreements centre on the theorized construction of women's oppression in the matrix of social relations formed by the state, the private family household, and the wage-labour system. White feminism's treatment of ideological discourses and symbolic representations (motherhood, sexuality, feminity) that uphold women's dependent and subordinate status as wives, mothers, and workers has also been critiqued for failing to consider the intersection of these ideologies with racist ones.

In addition, Black feminists criticize the treatment of the family by white feminists. Both socialist- and radical-feminist approaches have taken the family to be a significant, if not the primary, source of women's oppression (Barrett, 1980; McIntosh, 1978: 254-90). As Marshall (1988: 211) has observed, 'Whether viewed primarily as the locus of domestic labour, the site of human reproduction and socialization, or as a hegemonic ideology, the family, and women's roles as wives and mothers within it, is central to feminist theory.' The major emphasis given to the family in much feminist theorizing is likely connected to women's role in child-bearing, which cuts across class, time, and space, and the major significance for women (far greater than for men) of domestic and kinship relationships.

Given the salience of the family in white feminist explanations of women's subordination, it has often followed that the predominant role assigned to the state under capitalism is that of upholding a particular form of private family household, characterized by a male breadwinner and a financially dependent housewife (McIntosh, 1978; but see Jenson, 1986, for a critique). The major role of women is then viewed as that of performing domestic labour, especially the bearing and raising of children.

The attention given to the family as a site for women's oppression and its particular conceptualization in white feminism are regarded by Black feminists as highly problematic. They argue that first, in racist societies, the family is commonly experienced by Black women as the *least* oppressive institution; rather, it functions as a site for shelter and resistance, and offers opportunities for egalitarian relations between oppressed minority women and men that are denied in major societal institutions, imbued as they are with racism (Carby, 1982: 214; Davis, 1971, 1983: 15-18; Jones, 1985: 12-13; but for an opposing view, see White, 1984: 7-26).

In defending the Black family, many Black feminists do not deny that domestic violence and struggles over the sexism of Black men are significant issues within the Black community. In order to deal with such painful domestic realities as assaults on women and child sexual abuse, Black women have organized shelters and self-support groups (Bogle, 1988: 132; Mama, 1989). Their reluctance to speak publicly about sexism and domestic violence within the Black community, however, is based on their fear that such disclosure will feed into popular perceptions of the violence of Black males (long represented as dangerous to white women) and the broader criminalization of the Black community (Mama, 1989; Pettman, 1989: 14).

A second and related critique by Black feminists centres on the concept of female financial dependence on male wage-earners, which they regard as racially and culturally bound. In both historical and contemporary contexts, the rates of labour-force participation have generally been higher for Black and minority women than for their white counterparts in Canada, the United States, and Britain. In addition, Black women more often have had the *sole* responsibility for earning an income and supporting dependants than have white women (Brand, 1984; Bruegel, 1989; Davis, 1983; Dill, 1983; Jones, 1985; King, 1988; Wallace, 1980).

Third, the assumption of the 'normal' male-led, female-dependent family household has been absorbed into much social science in a manner that has pathologized both the Black family and Black women's roles in the family-household and labour force. A notorious instance of this occurred in 1965, when Daniel Moynihan, as advisor to the American government, argued that Afro-American oppression could be attributed primarily to the matriarchal structure of the Black family and community (Bhavnani, 1989: 69-70). The 'displacement' of Black men from the position of household head and the relative deprivation of the Black community were attributed to Black women, who were represented as emasculating matriarchs. Among the structural processes Moynihan ignored were the effects of the capitalist labour market and state social welfare policies in marginalizing Black men into the waged economy and propelling Black women into adopting strategies geared towards maintaining the financial survival of Black families.

Somewhat different renditions of the 'Black matriarch' thesis are encapsulated in white social scientists' analyses of Aboriginal societies in both Canada and Australia (for Australia, see Pettman, 1989; Langton, 1981). For instance, on the basis of very little evidence and rather speculative reasoning, LaPrairie argues that the disproportionately heavy involvement of Native women with the Canadian criminal justice system is attributable to a cycle in which the severe role strain and feelings of impotence experienced by Indian men as a result of the failure of traditional economies resulted in aggressive male violence against Indian women and subsequent criminal activity by Indian women (1987: 106-7). Thus, in analysis of female Aboriginal criminality, similar emphasis is placed on the links between female household heads, male impotence, and deviance as in the 'Black matriarch' thesis.

Fourth, the central role accorded by white feminism to the family in enforcing women's oppression ignores the effects on Black families of racially restrictive immigration and citizenship laws. Such laws—in Canada, Britain, Australia, and, above all, South Africa—have historically served to *destroy* rather than to maintain Black families by separating husbands from wives, wives from husbands, and parents from children.[8] Moreover, the critical stance adopted by white feminists towards 'the family' assumes a nuclear family and neglects the range of kinship and household structures in different cultures. The destructive influence of immigration policies that disallow the preservation of family forms other than nuclear families (forms that are important sources for women's strength and solidarity) is similarly ignored within white feminism (Ramazanoglu, 1989: 148).

The failure of white feminists to define immigration and citizenship issues as 'women's issues' is linked to the inadequate theorization of the state within white feminist writings. In specifying the contradictory roles played by the state in mediating relations between gender and class, capitalist production and biological reproduction, socialist feminists neglect the role of the state in organizing the political and ideological conditions under which the nation-state is reproduced (Miles, 1988: 438). Central to this process is the way racism becomes intertwined with issues of nationalism in defining the parameters of the nation-state and what Benedict Anderson (1983) has called 'the imagined community' (see also Anthias, 1988; Gilroy, 1987: 26). It is the combination of patriarchal logic with principles of racial and ethnic exclusivity embedded in immigration and citizenship laws that is particularly devastating for minority women. Immigration policy establishes the parameters for the 'legitimate' entry, settlement, and access to social services and paid work of immigrant women. Citizenship policies (in combination with social welfare policies) severely limit their access and entitlement to the fruits of liberal democratic, feminist, and class struggles (Baptiste, 1988; Boyd, 1989; Pettman, 1989; Sondhi, 1987; Yuval-Davis and Anthias, 1989).

Thus what is at issue in the critiques of white feminism by Black feminists is not merely the conceptualization of women's role in the family, but the role of racism in differentiating the material circumstances of white and Black women in relations of both production and reproduction. This point is elegantly brought forth in a study by Carby (1987) of nineteenth-century literary representations of Black and white women by female Afro-American novelists. Carby begins by delineating the distinct and antagonistic positions held by white mistresses and Black female slaves in the plantations of the southern United States. White women were viewed as the means of consolidating property through the institution of 'marriages of alliance' between plantation families and through their role as bearers of the inheritors of that property. In contrast, 'black women, as slaves, had their reproductive destiny bound to capital accumulation; black women gave birth to property, and directly to capital itself in the form of slaves, and all slaves inherited their status from their mothers' (1987: 24-5).

In addition, renewed attention has been given in feminist writings to the role of symbolic representation in the reproduction of women's subordination (Marshall, 1988: 213). Much Black feminist work has been directed at bringing out the race- and class-specific character of ideologies and images of feminity, domesticity, and female sexuality. Carby's study of the nineteenth-century American discourses and literary conventions of 'true womanhood' sheds light on how ideologies of 'true' (i.e., white) womanhood and Black womanhood in the antebellum South were polarized yet interdependent images of each other: the fragility, modesty, and repressed sexuality of white plantation mistresses existed in sharp contrast to the 'masculine' strength and unbridled sexuality of Black slave women. The cult of true womanhood and the antithetical ideology of Black womanhood were built upon a hierarchical differential in the positions that Black women and white women occupied in the social formation of slavery. Carby's approach is both historical materialist and dialectic. She argues that the discourses of white and Black womanhood were *not* simply reflective of lived sets of material and social relations, but themselves played a role in resolving the contradictions in the sets of social relations in which white women, in particular, were located.

Images of sturdy, asexual, and subservient Black domestics and of exotic, sexually dextrous, and compliant Asian women are pervasive in Western popular culture and mass-media advertising, whereas the images of white women, while sexist, are both different and at least somewhat more diverse (Brand, 1984; Hull, Scott and Smith, 1982; Parmar, 1982). Such racially and culturally specific notions of feminity play an important role in relegating women of different 'races' and ethnicities to specific occupations, in barring them from entry into others, and in conditioning managerial strategies of control (Glenn, 1980). In addition, state practices such as the nature of policing and social services delivered to particular communities frequently capitalize on differential racial/ethnic images of women. Thus Mama accounts for the allocation of far fewer refuges for battered women in Britain to the Black than to Asian communities in terms of the different racial stereotypes of Asian and Afro-Caribbean women: 'If the former are passive, exotic, quiet and inspire paternalism, then the latter are aggressive, promiscuous, violent-like-their-men and more threatening than mysteriously silent' (1989: 43).

Race-specific ideologies of womanhood are also important in directing women's reproductive activities towards meeting race (e.g., eugenic) as well as class ends. For instance, Black women and other women of colour have at various times been encouraged to limit their family size and to aid in the reproduction of *white* children through the provision of domestic service to white families. This contrasts with the periodic drives to encourage Anglo-Celtic women in Britain and 'white settler colonies' such as Canada and Australia to have more babies. Such racially exclusive pro-natalist policies have been legitimated through recourse to nationalist and imperialist objectives (Klug, 1989; de Lepervanche, 1989).[9] The fear of 'miscegenation', or sexual relations between white women and black men, and the birth of 'mixed race' children has also led to legislation restricting the entry, settlement, and many rights of Black men (Carby, 1987: 31; Rich, 1986: 30).

In sum, Black feminism maintains that by ignoring race, the analytical formulations of white feminism are impoverished. Because it treats 'women' as a homogeneous racial category, white feminism is unable to account for the differences and hierarchical structuring in material and discursive conditions that govern Black and white women's lives. Black feminist analyses reveal how, for *both* white women and women of colour, the relationship to the family, state, production, and reproduction has been mediated simultaneously by class interests, gender divisions, and white supremacist logics, in a way that has constructed barriers to sisterhood across racial lines. Finally, Black feminism discloses the important role played by racially specific gender ideologies and images—part of popular 'common sense'—in 'naturalizing' the suitability of Black women and women of colour for jobs in the lowest stratum of a labour market already segmented along gender lines, in aiding (as nannies and domestics) the reproduction of white families, and in justifying differential entitlement and administration of social services.

The challenge posed by Black feminism, then, goes beyond that of merely rendering visible the differential experiences of gender across racial and ethnic lines. It calls for nothing less than the incorporation of systematic analyses of racism into feminism, and a subsequent reconsideration and reformulation of some of the accepted concepts within feminist writings. Central concepts within feminism such as 'reproduction', 'the state', and 'the family' all currently embody white, racist logics. Indeed, the recognition that race and ethnicity, in addition to class, play a central role in defining the nature and extent of relative privilege and oppression of women, renders simplistic and misleading the very notion of 'women's oppression' (Lamoureux, 1987: 64).

BLACK FEMINISM IN THE CANADIAN CONTEXT

Leaving aside for the moment the question of defining 'Black women' or 'women of colour' in the Canadian context, Black feminist arguments appear to strike a deep chord of resonance with the historical and contemporary experiences of several groups of Aboriginal and non-European migrant women. Canadian feminist politics incorporate a history of racial and ethnic exclusion. An instance of this occurred in the early twentieth century, when Anglo-Celtic suffragettes sought the vote for British Canadian women on the grounds that it would enable them to influence immigration policy to ensure the exclusion of undesirable Eastern Europeans (Palmer, 1982).

Aboriginal women have echoed many Black feminist writers in insisting that racism, rather than sexism, is the primary source of their oppression; that solidarity with the men of their community is critical in ameliorating their oppression; and that the concerns of the white, middle-class women's movement are far removed from their own concerns for physical and communal survival (LaChapelle, 1982; Silman, 1987; for a similar position among Aboriginal women in Australia, see Pettman, 1989: 26). Far from acting to preserve the family, the Canadian state has followed coercive paternalistic policies in seizing Native children and placing them in white foster homes or boarding schools. The consequences of these state policies vis à vis Native families and education include a tendency for young people to leave school altogether, destruction of Native culture, and a tragic pattern of Native youth suicides.

The process of migration of Asians and Blacks into Canada has been mediated by two often competing objectives in immigration policy: the desire to populate Canada with white British people and the demands of the capitalist labour market. This has meant that prior to the explicit expunging of racist criteria in Canadian admissions policy in 1967, non-white migrants were accepted into Canada only if they met pressing needs for cheap, exploitable labour. In each case—for instance, the importation of 15,000 Chinese male labourers to construct the transcontinental railway, and the more recent migration of Caribbean women to perform domestic work—state regulations were designed to actively discourage settlement in Canada (Adilman, 1984; Li, 1988: 60). Indeed, a distinctive and subordinate relationship of non-white, non-European women to the state has been encoded in a patchwork of racist immigration policies that actively restricted the entry into Canada of dependants of either male or female non-white migrant workers. This had the effect of severely limiting family size and thus controlling the growth of resident non-white populations.

Thus Black feminism places on the agenda of Canadian feminist historiography a number of important questions. These questions pertain to the race, gender, and class specificity of mechanisms circumscribing the lives of Black women and women of colour in Canada, and the activities of the Canadian women's movement. Black feminism also opens up analyses of the discursive operations that have justified the treat of Black women and other women of colour as 'alien' and undesirable. Yet there are limits to the capacity of Black feminism to comprehend the experiences and incorporation of different 'racial' and ethnic groups of women into Canada's economy, class structure, and political and symbolic orders.

Chief among these limitations is the implicit Black/white dichotomy that is frequently assumed to structure the racist and gendered oppression of women. Indeed, some American and British Black feminist works explicitly state that whatever the degraded conditions of the work and home lives of other women of colour or European immigrant women, Black women 'shouldered unique burdens at home and endured unique forms of discrimination in the workplace' (Jones, 1985: 9; for Britain, see Mama, 1989, and Murphy and Livingstone, 1985).

The arguments most commonly expounded by Black feminism and taken up by Black Canadian feminists such as Brand (1984) have the effect of linking racism to skin colour, rather than to the structural location of particular groups of women in concrete and historically specific social relations and to the accompanying discourses that aid in the processes of denigration, subordination, and exploitation. The insistence on the enduring and unique liability of race or skin colour for Black women (and possibly other women of colour) draws attention to the origins of racism in colonial and imperial relationships, from which white Western women have benefitted. But it would be equally important to point out the distinctive and protracted burdens within Canadian colonialism that have been borne by Aboriginal women (*Fireweed*, 1986; LaChapelle, 1982; Silman, 1987).

The Native Women's Association of Canada has noted the inordinately slow pace at which Bill C-31 (the 1985 amendments to the Indian Act) has been implemented, through which Indian women and their families are having their rights to First Nationhood restored.[10] The organization has attributed the 'tardiness, the inefficiency and the inhuman procedures' of Indian Affairs in administering applications for reinstatement to the fact that 'the applicants are Aboriginal people' (Native Women's Association of Canada, 1988: 128).

The unique histories both of the class, racial, and gender oppression of Native women and of their resistance to that oppression are nurturing grounds for such distinctive political concerns as land claims and self-government. Frequently, however, white feminists, far removed from Native peoples' battles over sovereignty, are quick to recognize the sexist character of the old Indian Act, but are less comprehending of the role of women in Aboriginal self-determination. The unique kinds of oppression experienced by Native women may result in flat stereotypes, useful for categorization of Aboriginal women as a special group. One Native woman related how the organizers of a feminist conference were discomfited by the decision of two Native participants to attend the workshop on 'empowerment' rather than the one on 'poverty' to which they had been assigned (Silman, 1987).

To apply Black feminist arguments in the Canadian context would also require consideration of the impact of French-English divisions and Quebec nationalism. The context for immigration to Canada was not one but two linguistically and culturally defined nations or 'imagined communities'. The elevation of the role of Quebec French women in the home and reproduction (i.e., through the 'revenge of the cradle') was deemed necessary to resist the pressures of external encroachment by the English and other non-French immigrant groups and to maintain the specificity of the Quebec nation (Lamoureux, 1987; Dumont et al., 1987). The extent to which the contradictions involving the role of nationalism in the Quebec women's movement have affected the experiences and well-being of racial-minority and non-French migrant women in Quebec is an important issue.

The fact that a long history of European and non-European immigration has brought to Canada, in different waves, people who have departed from the English model of physical appearance and cultural desirability has led to the development of many different racism*s*. Racisms built upon language, religion, and other cultural markers have historically be directed at white as well as non-white groups who were regarded as threatening to the British and Protestant character of English Canada (Iacovetta, 1986: 209). One effect of structural racism in Canada is that in a multi-racial, multi-ethnic female work force, particular groups of European immigrant women have historically shared disadvantages similar to those of Black working-class women, and continue to do so.

The flowering of ethnic feminist historiography in Canada has made it possible to replace such clumsy and misleading concepts as 'double (or triple) oppression (or jeopardy)' with an increasingly detailed portrait of the social structures, social relations, institutional mechanisms, and discourses that affect the lives of immigrant and minority women (Abele and Stasiulis, 1989: 267-8). Analyses of the multiple disadvantages faced by immigrant women have centred on two related factors: (a) entry statuses within immigration policy that make women dependent on husbands, fathers, and other male relatives, and (b) restricted opportunities to learn the official languages (see Boyd, 1986, 1984; Estable, 1986; Ng and Ramirez, 1981; Stasiulis, 1987). But detailed case studies that take as their setting the workplace (Gannage, 1987; Johnson, 1982), trade unions (Lipsig-Mumme, 1987), the household (Iacovetta, 1986), or the employment agency (Ng, 1986, 1988) reveal many other situations in which immigrant and racial/ethnic-minority women constitute distinct groups facing circumstances that are sometimes unique and sometimes shared with other women. Such histories also document the spirited and creative resistance of these women to male, capitalist, racist, and bureaucratic forms of domination, and thus undercut the image of them as hapless victims of a seamless web of oppression.

The capacity of Black feminism to inform analyses of racial and ethnic minority women in Canada is limited by a second inherent tendency: namely, its treatment of 'Black women' or 'women of colour' as homogeneous, thus avoiding the issue of how class has mediated the effects of race and gender.[11] This is a critical issue in Canada, where significant class differences have emerged within Black, Asian, and other racial categories of women as the result of a selective post-war immigration policy.

Since the early 1960s, Canadian immigration policy has sought to recruit Third World immigrants with high levels of education and professional and technical skills, yet has also brought in many less-skilled and -educated family members of primarily male immigrants. More recently, Canadian immigration has included large numbers of refugees from southeast Asia, whose skills frequently do not match the demands of the Canadian labour market, and who carry a formidable liability in that market: lack of fluency in one of the official languages. The Mulroney government has also aggressively recruited capital via the Immigration Department's Entrepreneur and Investor programs, through which wealthy individuals, including many Hong Kong capitalists seeking solutions to the '1997 jitters',[12] have gained immigration status.

This latter migration of Asians to Canada is guaranteed to foster racism, particularly in British Columbia, which has a long history of anti-Asian hostility, and whose resource-based economy has been rocked by current movements and state policies of capital restructuring (including free trade with the United States) and heightened assaults on the labour movement. But it is important to distinguish between the forms and effects of racism experienced by wealthy female immigrants from Hong Kong and those experienced by Indo-Chinese refugee women who have few income and job options apart from the highly exploitive needle trades. The very different circumstances of these two groups of 'visible minority' women offer but one example where connections among gender, race, and class in the Canadian context defy analyses based on essentialist conceptions of 'women', or indeed 'Black women' or 'women of colour'.

CONCLUSION: POLITICAL IMPLICATIONS

At both the theoretical and political levels, these heated debates about race and class reflect one aspect of the crisis in Marxism. Not only has orthodox Marxism's focus on production and class relations been seen by some academics as incomplete; it has also been widely regarded as inadequate to the task of informing social movements based on other social identities (gay, ecological, anti-militaristic, as well as feminist and anti-racist). Most recently, the task of analyzing the interconnections between these social divisions and identities has been taken up by these movements as well as by many left and socialist parties, particularly in Western Europe.

The era of the 'new social movements' provided the political context for the development of Black feminism and feminisms of other women of colour (American Asian feminism, Chicana feminism, etc.) (Garcia, 1989). By the late 1980s, the assessments of the political efficacy of Black feminism are mixed. For instance, the Black British feminist Mama (1989) emphasizes the continuing need for separate forums for the empowerment of Black women and specialist services for those women who face racism from both state agencies and white feminist organizations. The impact of Black feminism was also felt in the shift in the British feminist politics of reproduction, from emphasis on the single issue of abortion rights to a more inclusive focus on women's reproductive rights in general (Amos and Parmar, 1984: 13).

Reflecting upon the organizational rise and disintegration of the Black women's movement in Britain, Parmar (1989) confirms the historical necessity of such autonomous organization as both empowering and strengthening for the participants. Ultimately, however, the British Black women's movement foundered over a number of conflicts and ended in theoretical and political paralysis. Parmar argues that this immobilization resulted from, on the one hand, 'accumulating a collection of oppressed identities which in turn have given rise to a [destructive] hierarchy of oppression', and on the other, constructing a notion of Blackness that reflected forms of essentialism such as 'cryptic nationalistic sentiments [relying on] biologistic definitions of race' (1989: 58-9).

Other assessments of politics based on a general notion of race/gender/class have critiqued the mechanistic manner in which women are labelled 'as "doubly oppressed" or "triply oppressed" without recognizing that oppressive systems work in highly contextualized ways' (Harriss, 1989: 38). Both Black feminism and the recent debates on race and class have contributed significantly to a clearer understanding of various forms and dimensions of racism. In the rush to embrace a form of politics that incorporates different social divisions and dynamics of power, the women's movement and other progressive movements need to resist the superficial and even rhetorical inclusion of race/class/gender axes of domination. This danger is apparent in the concept of 'classism' adopted by some feminists, which 'served to reduce the whole issue of class exploitation to a set of attitudes or prejudices' (Harriss, 1989: 39).

The need to comprehend the class character of all oppressions is particularly clear when one considers the time-worn strategies of state agencies to use pluralism—the recognition of discrete (and intersecting) social identities such as gender, race, and ethnicity—to divide people into special-interest groups and ignore and obfuscate shared class interests.[13] Versions of feminism whose major preoccupation is incorporating 'difference' risk losing sight of class issues such as the growing power of transnational capital—even in areas, such as China and Eastern Europe, that have long been avowedly anti-capitalist—and the reign of conservative governments in the majority of Western democracies. The post-modernist feminist project of exploring 'gender, race and class as sites of difference' is, as Barrett points out, in danger of failing to recognize that these are also sites of power, exploitation, and oppression (1989: 42). As a guide to politics, organizing around 'difference'—in the sense of taking as a starting point only the personal and experiential modes of being—can lead to a form of closure, a directing of energy inwards, leaving the sources of oppression unchallenged.

Since the 1970s, in Canada and many other Western democracies, the state has developed several specialist programs, advisers, commissions, and bodies to represent women's, Aboriginal, racial-minority, and other sectional interests. During the same decade, conservative governments have been elected whose overall economic and social agendas emphasize principles of 'freeing the market', cost-effectiveness and profitability in the restructuring of the labour market, and delivery of services. As Frigga Haug (1989: 112-13) states, for these conservative governments

> meeting or palliating women's demands were no part of their policy. On the contrary, cutbacks in social spending, shifting the burden to private households and so particularly to women, privatization and the glorification of old feminine virtues are typical of the policies of western conservative governments.

The raising of these stark economic and political realities is not meant to obviate the task of understanding the impact of these larger processes for specific racial- and ethnic-minority women. Nor is it an argument for subordinating all struggles against race/gender/class to a larger class struggle. Totalizing politics are unrealistic and less effective than alliances based upon grass-roots activism, whose social configuration is determined by the specific issue. Rather, what I mean to underscore are the inevitable intrusions of capitalist relations within the construction of intersecting forms of oppression. It is only by keeping in view the larger context of global and national economic and political realities that any movement seeking to understand the complex intersections between gender, race, ethnicity, and class can avoid becoming inward-looking and blandly pluralistic, and develop a politics of social transformation that truly moves beyond the fragments.[14]

NOTES

[1]I have dispensed with the convention, adopted by many social scientists, of placing 'race' within quotation marks to signify that 'race' is a social construction rather than a biological division within humankind, and as a reminder that biologically there exists only the one (i.e., human) race. Marxists also frequently follow this convention in order to differentiate the (epi)phenomenal or ideological character of 'race' from the materialist foundations of class, rooted in the respective relations of individuals and groups to a historically specific mode of production. While I fully support the assumption that within any given society and historical era, the process of racial categorization is social, political, and ideological and profoundly affected by economic relations of exploitation, rather than simply found in nature, it remains that race, like gender, has biological referents and is most commonly associated with physiognomically based difference such as skin colour. Moreover, the emphasis that is rightly placed on the social nature of constitution of races is also applicable to gender, ethnicity, and class, all of which have specific and intermeshed material and ideological modes of reproduction.

[2]The following discussion of race, ethnicity, gender, and class in Canada draws almost entirely on English Canadian literature and treats only tangentially the very important issue of French-English divisions and nationalism among Quebec women.

[3]Notably missing from my discussion of feminist theories are the debates attempting to establish the relationship between gender and class, women's oppression and class exploitation, production and reproduction. A central question underlying these debates concerns the origins of women's oppression, especially as it is related to the development of capitalism (Armstrong and Armstrong, 1986: 208-40; 249-54; Connelly, 1986; Kuhn and Wolpe, 1978; Sargent, 1981). The political question animating Marxist and socialist-feminist analyses is whether women's liberation will be the outcome of the transformation of capitalist into socialist relations, or alternatively whether an end to female oppression requires autonomous feminist or distinctive (combined gender and class) transformative strategies. A significant contribution of socialist-feminist analyses has been to bring to the fore differences in types of oppression and resistance experienced by working-class, middle-class, and bourgeois women. More recently, socialist-feminist writings are revealing the *national divergences* in experiences and sources of female oppression and the national and historical specificity of the role

of the state in constructing and reproducing women's subordination and dependence (see Jenson, 1986; Sassoon, 1987). Similar problems of generalization within feminist theorizing raised by Black feminist critiques have been raised in other areas of feminist historiography and social science that adopt historical comparative frameworks.

[4]For a critical examination of the treatment of Aboriginal peoples, immigrants and ethnic minorities in English Canadian political economy, see Abele and Stasiulis (1989).

[5]Indeed, important contributions to the race and class debate have been made by feminists (e.g., Anthias, Phizacklea). In their efforts to conceptualize the links between race and class, these feminists reveal the same tendencies as non-feminists to leave gender divisions untheorized.

[6]Typical in this regard is Armstrong and Armstrong's (1986) relegation of race, ethnicity, and religion to the sidelines within the socialist-feminist project: 'While the working class may or may not be differentiated by race, ethnicity, religion, occupation, industry or whatever, it is invariably differentiated by sex' (212).

[7]Socialist feminists diverge, however, on the theorized integration of the capitalist mode of production and the sexual or gendered division of labour. While Armstrong and Armstrong (1986) regard the sexual division of labour, premised on the biological role of women in having babies, to be essential to capitalism, forming one integrated system, Barrett (1980) and Connelly (1986) argue that gender divisions are a historically constituted integral part of, but not a necessary condition for, the development of capitalism.

[8]Black feminists in Britain have categorically stated that 'even though the family may be a major site of women's oppression and subordination, it is not for the state to divide families against their wishes. Furthermore, in a racist society, the family can also be a source of support and strength for those under attack by the state' (WING, 1985: 7; see also Amos and Parmar, 1984: 15; Baptiste, 1988; Sondhi, 1987).

[9]Francesca Klug argues that the 1906 social welfare reforms of the Liberal government in Britain were motivated by two concerns: a genuine commitment to boosting the living standards of the poor, and a desire to improve the physical well-being of the British population as defenders of the Empire (1989: 23).

[10]Under the old Indian Act, Indian women who married non-status Indian or non-Indian men were removed from the Indian Register by the Department of Indian and Northern Affairs. Aided by the new Canadian Constitution, and after a protracted process of protest and lobbying (detailed in Silman, 1987), the Canadian government moved to amend the Indian Act. Bill C-31 removed the sexually discriminatory sections of the Indian Act and allowed individuals who had lost their status to be reinstated.

[11]'A middle-class, black American woman who can have a career and employ

a cleaning woman may experience the social impact of racism but she is not in the same structural position as an unemployed Bangladeshi woman worker in Britain who is treated by the state as dependent on her husband even if he is refused entry to Britain. In the west, black women are disadvantaged by racism in relation to white women, but black is not a static or universal category of disadvantage that transcends all other sources of social difference which determine the quality of people's lives' (Ramazanoglu, 1989: 134).

[12]In that year, China formally takes back the British colony into its fold (Malarek, 1987: 215).

[13]This point is persuasively made in Kathryn Harriss's (1989) study of the left-wing municipal socialism of the Greater London Council. The GLC experimented with welding socialist aims with a consciousness of the needs of autonomously organized groups such as Blacks, gays, the disabled, etc. Harriss argues that the identities of race, gender, sexual orientation, etc. provided the GLC with a 'set of convenient pegs upon which to hang [its] policies, insofar as the borough population becomes classified according to what people have in common with their "identity group" rather than with others of the local working-class population' (48). Thus, beset by the pressures of accountability to central government, and finally to capital, the local council, *notwithstanding its socialist philosophy*, attempted to contain the demands of various sectional populations. By focusing on such issues as discrimination, it was able to avoid the fundamental class issues of poverty and decent housing and thus obscure the class-bound character of the local state within capitalism which makes it 'governed by constraints . . . placing it at odds with its working-class population' (51).

[14]*Beyond the Fragments* is the title of a British book that addressed many of the difficulties of developing a form of socialist-feminist organizing that simultaneously avoided the limitations and fracturing consequences of autonomous struggles while respecting the integrity of autonomous organization (Rowbotham, Segal, and Wainwright, 1979).

REFERENCES

Abele, Frances, and Daiva Stasiulis
1989 'Canada as a "White Settler Colony": What about Natives and Immigrants'. Pp. 240-77 in W. Clement and G. Williams, eds, *The New Canadian Political Economy*. Montreal: McGill-Queen's University Press.

Adamson, Nancy, Linda Briskin, and Margaret McPhail
1988 *Feminist Organizing For Change: The Contemporary Women's Movement in Canada*. Toronto: Oxford University Press.

Adilman, T.
1984 'A Preliminary Sketch of Chinese Women and Work in British Columbia 1858-1950'. In B.K. Latham and R.J. Padro, eds, *Not Just*

Pin Money: Selected Essays on the History of Women's Work In British Columbia. Victoria, BC: Camosun College.

Amos, Valerie, and Pratibha Parmar
1984 'Challenging Imperial Feminism'. *Feminist Review* 17 (July): 3-19.

Anderson, Benedict
1983 *Imagined Communities*. London: Verso.

Anthias, Floya
1988 'Race and Class Revisited: Conceptualizing Race and Racism'. Paper presented at the International Sociological Association's Research Committee for Race Ethnic and Minority Studies, Amsterdam, December.

Anthias, Floya, and Nira Yuval-Davis
1983 'Contextualizing Feminism—Gender, Ethnic and Class Divisions'. *Feminist Review* 15: 62-75.

Armstrong, Pat, and Hugh Armstrong
1986 'Beyond Sexless Class and Classless Sex: Towards Feminist Marxism', and 'More on Marxism and Feminism: A Response to Patricia Connelly'. Pp. 208-40, 249-54 in R. Hamilton and M. Barrett, eds, *The Politics of Diversity: Feminism, Marxism and Nationalism*. Montreal: Book Center.

Baptiste, Mary John
1988 'The Implications of the New Immigration Bill'. *Critical Social Policy* 23: 62-9.

Barber, Marilyn
1986 'Sunny Ontario for British Girls, 1900-30'. Pp. 55-74 in Jean Burnet, ed., *Looking into My Sister's Eyes: An Exploration in Women's History*. Toronto: Multicultural History Society of Ontario.

Barrett, Michele
1980 *Women's Oppression Today*. London: Verso.
1989 'Some Different Meanings of the Concept of "Difference": Feminist Theory and the Concept of Ideology'. Pp. 37-48 in E. Meese and A. Parker, eds, *The Difference Within: Feminism and Critical Theory*. Amsterdam: John Benjamins.

Basran, G.S.
1983 'Canadian Immigration Policy and Theories of Racism'. Pp. 3-14 in P.S. Li and B.S. Bolaria, eds, *Racial Minorities in Multicultural Canada*. Toronto: Garamond.

Ben-Tovim, Gideon, et al.
1981 'Race, Left Strategies and the State'. In *Politics and Power 3*. London: Routledge and Kegan Paul.

Ben-Tovim, Gideon, John Gabriel, Ian Law, and Kathleen Stredder
1986 'A political analysis of local struggles for racial equality'. Pp. 131-52 in J. Rex and D. Mason, eds, *Theories of Race and Ethnic Relations*. Cambridge: Cambridge University Press.

Bhavnani, Kum-Kum
1989 'Complexity, Activism, Optimism: An Interview with Angela Davis'. *Feminist Review* 31 (Spring): 66-83.

Bhavnani, Kum-Kum, and Margaret Coulson

1986 'Transforming Socialist-Feminist: The Challenge of Racism'. *Feminist Review* 23 (June).

Bogle, Marlene T.

1988 'Brixton Black Women's Centre: Organizing on Child Sexual Abuse'. *Feminist Review* 28 (January): 132-5.

Bolaria, B. Singh, and Peter S. Li

1985 *Racial Oppression in Canada*. Toronto: Garamond.

1988 *Racial Oppression in Canada*. 2nd ed. Toronto: Garamond.

Bourgeault, Ron

1983a 'The Development of Capitalism and the Subjugation of Native Women in Northern Canada'. *Alternate Routes* 6: 110-40.

1983b 'The Indian, the Metis and the Fur Trade: Class, Sexism and Racism in the Transition from "Communism" to Capitalism'. *Studies in Political Economy* 2: 45-80.

1988 'Race and Class Under Mercantilism: Indigenous People in Nineteenth-Century Canada'. Pp. 41-70 in Bolaria and Li (1988).

Bourne, Jenny

1980 'Towards an Anti-racist Feminism'. *Race and Class* 25 (1): 1-22.

Boyd, Monica

1984 'At a Disadvantage: The Occupational Attainments of Foreign Born Women in Canada'. *International Migration Review* 18 (Winter).

1986 'Immigrant Women in Canada'. Pp. 47-75 in Rita J. Simon and Caroline Bretell, eds, *International Migration*. Towota, NJ: Rowman and Allenheld.

1989 'Immigration and Income Security Policies in Canada: Implications for Elderly Immigrant Women'. *Population and Policy Review* 8: 5-24.

Brand, Dionne

1984 'A Working Paper on Black Women in Toronto: Gender, Race and Class'. *Fireweed* 19 (Summer/Fall): 26-43.

Broom, Dorothy

1987 'Gender and Inequality: An Overview: Another Tribe'. Pp. 264-81 in C. Jennet and R.G. Stewart, eds, *Three Worlds of Inequality: Race, Class and Gender*. Melbourne: Macmillan.

Bruegel, Irene

1989 'Sex and Race in the Labour Market'. *Feminist Review* 32 (Summer): 49-68.

Cappon, Paul

1975 'The Green Paper: Immigration as a Tool of Profit'. *Canadian Ethnic Studies* 7: 50-4.

Carby, Hazel

1982 'White Women Listen! Black Feminism and the Boundaries of Sisterhood'. Pp. 212-35 in Centre for Contemporary Cultural Studies (1982).

1987 *Reconstructing Womanhood: The Emergence of the Afro-American Woman Novelist*. New York: Oxford University Press.

Centre for Contemporary Cultural Studies
1982 *The Empire Strikes Back*. London: Hutchinson.
Clement, Wallace
1986 *The Struggle to Organize: Resistance in Canada's Fisheries*. Toronto: McClelland and Stewart.
Cole, Mike
1988 '"Race" and Class or "Race", Class Gender and Community?: A Critical Appraisal of the Radicalised Fraction of the Working-class Thesis'. *British Journal of Sociology* 40 (1): 118-29.
Connelly, Patricia
1986 'On Marxism and Feminism'. Pp. 241-8 in R. Hamilton and M. Barrett, eds, *The Politics of Diversity*. Montreal: Book Center.
Cox, Oliver
1948 *Caste, Class and Race*. New York: Monthly Review Press.
Creese, Gillian
1986 'Working Class Politics, Racism and Sexism: The Making of a Politically Divided Working Class in Vancouver, 1900-1939'. PhD dissertation, Department of Sociology and Anthropology, Carleton University.
das Gupta, Tania
1986 *Learning from Our History: Community Development with Immigrant Women, 1958-86, a Tool for Action*. Toronto: University of Toronto Press.
Davis, Angela
1971 'Reflections on the Black Women's Role in the Community of Slaves.' *Black Scholar* 3 (4): 2-15.
1983 *Women, Race and Class*. New York: Women's Press.
de Lepervanche, Marie
1989 'Women, Nation and the State in Australia'. Pp. 36-57 in Yuval-Davis and Anthias (1989).
Dill, Bonnie Thornton
1983 'Race, Class and Gender: Prospects for an All-Inclusive Sisterhood'. *Feminist Studies* 9 (1): 131-50.
Dumont, Micheline, Michele Jean, Marie Lavigne, and Jennifer Stoddart
1987 *Quebec Women: A History*. Toronto: Women's Press.
Estable, Alma
1986 'Immigration Women in Canada—Current Issues'. A Background Paper for the Canadian Advisory Council on the Status of Women.
Fireweed
1986 Special Issue by Native Women (Winter).
Gabriel, J., and G. Ben-Tovim
1978 'Marxism and the Concept of Racism'. *Economy and Society* 7 (2): 118-54.
Gannage, Charlene
1986 *Double Day, Double Bind*. Toronto: Women's Press.
1987 'A World of Difference: The Case of Women Workers in a Canadian Garment Factory'. Pp. 213-28 in H.J. Maroney and M. Luxton, eds, *Feminism and Political Economy*. Toronto: Methuen.

Garcia, Alma M.
1989 'The Development of Chicana Feminist Discourse, 1970-1980'. *Gender and Society* 3 (2) (June): 217-38.
Genovese, E.
1971 *In Red and Black*. New York: Vintage.
Gilroy, Paul
1982 'Stepping out of Babylon—Race, Class and Autonomy'. Pp. 276-314 in Centre for Contemporary Cultural Studies (1982).
1987 *'There Ain't No Black in the Union Jack': The Cultural Politics of Race and Nation*. London: Hutchinson.
Glenn, Evelyn Nakano
1980 'The Dialectics of Wage Work: Japanese-American Women and Domestic Service, 1905-1940'. *Feminist Studies* 3 (Fall): 432-71.
Hall, Stuart
1980 'Race, Articulation and Societies Structured in Dominance'. In UNESCO, ed., *Sociological Theories: Race and Colonialism*. Paris: UNESCO.
Harney, Robert
1979 'Montreal's King of Italian Labour: A Case Study of Padronism'. *Labour/Le Travailleur* 4.
Harris, Leonard
1987 'Historical Subjects and Interests: Race, Class and Conflict'. Pp. 90-105 in Mike Davis et al., eds, *The Year Left 2*. London: Verso.
Harriss, Kathryn
1989 'New Alliances: Socialist-Feminism in the Eighties'. *Feminist Review* 31 (Spring): 34-53.
Haug, Frigga
1989 'Lessons from the Women's Movement in Europe.' *Feminist Review* 31 (Spring): 107-18.
Hernandez, Carmencita R.
1988 'The Coalition of Visible Minority Women'. In Frank Cunningham, Sue Findlay, Marlene Kadar, Alan Lennon, and Ed Silva, eds, *Social Movements/Social Change*. Toronto: Between the Lines.
Heron, Craig, and Robert Storey, eds
1985 *On the Job*. Montreal: McGill-Queen's University Press.
Hill, Helen
1987 'The Gender Variable in Development Policies: Was Nairobi a Turning Point?'. Pp. 340-60 in C. Jennett and R.G. Stewart, eds, *Three Worlds of Inequality: Race, Class and Gender*. Melbourne: Macmillan.
Hooks, Bell
1981 *Ain't I A Woman? Black Women and Feminism*. Boston: South End Press.
1984 *Feminist Theory: From Margins to Centre*. Boston: South End Press.
Hull, Gloria, Patricia Bell Scott, and Barbara Smith, eds
1982 *All the Women Are White, All the Blacks Are Men, but Some of Us Are Brave*. New York: Basic Books.

Iacovetta, Franca
1986 'From Contadina to Worker: Southern Italian Immigrant Working Women in Toronto, 1947-62'. Pp. 195-222 in Jean Burnet, ed., *Looking Into My Sister's Eyes*. Toronto: Multicultural History Society of Ontario.

Jenson, Jane
1986 'Gender and Reproduction, or Babies and the State'. *Studies in Political Economy* 20: 9-46.

Johnson, Laura
1982 *The Seam Allowance: Industrial Home Sewing in Canada*. Toronto: Women's Press.

Jones, Jacqueline
1985 *Labor of Love, Labor of Sorrow*. New York: Basic Books.

King, Deborah
1988 'Multiple Jeopardy, Multiple Consciousness: The Context of a Black Feminist Ideology'. *Signs* 14 (1).

Klug, Francesca
1989 '"Oh to be in England": The British Case Study'. Pp. 16-35 in Yuval-Davis and Anthias (1989).

Kuhn, A., and A. Wolpe, eds
1978 *Feminism and Materialism*. London: Routledge and Kegan Paul.

Laclau, Ernesto, and Chantal Mouffe
1985 *Hegemony and Socialist Strategy: Towards a Radical Democratic Politics*. London: Verso.

LaChapelle, Caroline
1982 'Beyond Barriers: Native Women and the Women's Movement'. Pp. 257-64 in M. Fitzgerald, C. Guberman, and M. Wolfe, eds, *Still Ain't Satisfied!* Toronto: Women's Press.

Lamoureux, Diane
1987 'Nationalism and Feminism in Quebec: An Impossible Attraction'. Pp. 51-68 in Heather Jon Maroney and Meg Luxton, eds, *Feminism and Political Economy*. Toronto: Methuen.

Langton, Marcia
1981 'Urbanizing Aborigines: The Social Scientists' Great Deception'. *Social Alterantives* 2 (2): 16-22.

LaPrairie, Carol
1987 'Native Women and Crime in Canada: A Theoretical Model'. Pp. 103-12 in Ellen Adelberg and Claudia Currie, eds, *Too Few to Count: Canadian Women in Conflict with the Law*. Vancouver: press gang.

Li, Peter
1988 *The Chinese in Canada*. Toronto: Oxford University Press.

Lindstrom-Best, Varpu
1986 'We Won't be Slaves!' In J. Burnet, ed., *Looking Into My Sister's Eyes*. Toronto: Multicultural History Society of Ontario.

Lipsig-Mumme, C.
1987 'Organizing Women in the Sewing Trades: Homework and the 1983 Garment Strike in Canada'. *Studies in Political Economy* 22 (Spring): 41-72.

McIntosh, Mary
1978 'The State and the Oppression of Women'. Pp. 254-90 in Kuhn and Wolpe (1978).
Malarek, Victor
1987 *Haven's Gate: Canada's Immigration Fiasco*. Toronto: Macmillan.
Mama, Amina
1989 'Violence Against Black Women: Gender, Race and State Responses'. *Feminist Review* 32 (Summer): 30-47.
Marshall, Barbara
1988 'Feminist Theory and Critical Theory'. *Canadian Review of Sociology and Anthropology* 25 (2).
Mason, David
1986 'Introduction. Controversies and Continuities in Race and Ethnic Relations Theory'. Pp. 1-19 in John Rex and David Mason, eds, *Theories of Race and Ethnic Relations*. Cambridge: Cambridge University Press.
Miles, Robert
1980 'Class, Race and Ethnicity: A Critique of Cox's Theory'. *Ethnic and Racial Studies* 3 (2): 169-87.
1982 *Racism and Migrant Labour*. London: Routledge and Kegan Paul.
1984 'Marxism Versus the Sociology of "Race Relations"?'. *Ethnic and Racial Studies* 7 (2): 217-37.
1987 *Capitalism and Unfree Labour*. London: Tavistock.
1988 'Racism, Marxism and British Politics'. *Economy and Society* 17 (3): 428-60.
Minh-ha, Trinh T.
1989 *Women, Native, Other*. Bloomington: Indiana University Press.
Murphy, Lindsay, and Jonathon Livingstone
1985 'Racism and the Limits of Radical Feminism'. *Race and Class* 36 (4): 61-70.
Muszynski, Alicja
1986 'Class Formation and Class Consciousness: The Making of Shoreworkers in the BC Fishing Industry'. *Studies in Political Economy* 20 (Summer).
Native Women's Association of Canada
1988 'The Implementation of Bill C-31 (Amendments of the Indian Act)'. *Resources for Feminist Research* 17 (3): 125-8.
Ng, Roxana
1986 'The Social Construction of Immigrant Women in Canada.' In R. Hamilton and M. Barrett, eds, *The Politics of Diversity*. Montreal: Book Center.
1988 *The Politics of Community Services: Immigrant Women, Class and the State*. Toronto: Garamond.
Ng, Roxana, and Judith Ramirez
1981 *Immigrant Housewives in Canada*. Toronto: Immigrant Women's Centre.

Palmer, Howard
1982 *Patterns of Prejudice: A History of Nativism in Alberta*. Toronto: McClelland and Stewart.

Parkin, Frank
1979 *Marxism and Class Theory: A Bourgeois Critique*. London: Tavistock.

Parmar, Pratibha
1982 'Gender, Race and Class: Asian Women in Resistance'. Pp. 236-75 in Centre for Contemporary Cultural Studies (1982).
1989 'Other Kinds of Dreams'. *Feminist Review* 31 (Spring): 55-65.

Pentland, Clare
1981 *Labour and Capital in Canada, 1650-1860*. Toronto: James Lorimer.

Pettman, Jan
1989 '"All the Women are White, All the Blacks are Men" . . . Racism, Sexism and the Re-presentation of Black Women'. Peach Research Centre, Australian National University, Canberra, mimeo.

Phizacklea, Annie, and Robert Miles.
1980 *Labour and Racism*. London: Routledge and Kegan Paul.

Przeworski, A.
1977 'Proletariat into Class: The Process of Class Formation from Kaul Kautsky's *The Class Struggle* to Recent Controversies'. *Politics and Society* 7 (4): 343-401.

Ramazanoglu, Caroline
1989 *Feminism and the Contradictions of Oppression*. London: Routledge and Kegan Paul.

Ramirez, Bruno
1986 'Brief Encounters: Italian Immigrant Workers and the CPR, 1900-30'. *Labour/Le Travailleur* 17 (Spring): 9-27.

Ray, A.
1974 *Indians in the Fur Trade*. Toronto: University of Toronto Press.

Rich, Paul B.
1986 *Race and Empire in British Politics*. Cambridge: Cambridge University Press.

Rowbotham, S., L. Segal, and H. Wainwright
1979 *Beyond the Fragments: Feminism and the Making of Socialism*. London: Merlin.

Sargent, L., ed.
1981 *Women and Revolution: A Discussion of the Unhappy Marriage of Marxism and Feminism*. London: Pluto Press.

Sassoon, A.S., ed.
1987 *Women and the State*. London: Hutchinson.

Seager, A.
1986 'Class, Ethnicity and Politics in the Alberta Coalfields, 1905-1946'. In D. Hoerder, ed., *Struggle a Hard Battle: Essays on Working Class Immigrants*. Dekalb, Ill.: Northern Illinois Press.

Silman, Janet
1987 *Enough is Enough: Aboriginal Women Speak Out*. Toronto: Women's Press.

Solomos, John
1986 'Varieties of Marxist Conceptions of "Race", Class and the State: A Critical Analysis'. Pp. 84-109 in J. Rex and D. Mason, eds, *Theories of Race and Ethnic Relations.* Cambridge: Cambridge University Press.

Sondhi, Ranjit
1987 *Dividied Families: British Immigration Control in the Indian Subcontinent.* London: Runnymede.

Stasiulis, Daiva
1987 'Rainbow Feminism: Perspectives on Minority Women in Canada'. *Resources for Feminist Research* 16 (1): 5-9.

Trigger, Bruce
1985 *Natives and Newcomers.* Montreal: McGill-Queen's University Press.

Van Kirk, Sylvia
1980 *'Many Tender Ties': Women in Fur Trade Society 1670-1870.* Winnipeg: Watson and Dwyer.

Wallace, Phyllis A.
1980 *Black Women in the Labor Force.* Cambridge, Mass.: MIT Press.

Wallis, Maria, Wenona Giles, and Carmencita Hernandez
1988 'Defining the Issues on Our Terms: Gender, Race and the State'. *Resources for Feminist Research* 17: 3 (September): 43-8.

Warburton, Rennie
1989 'Towards a Synthesis of Theory on Ethnic Relations in Canada'. Paper presented at the annual meetings of the Canadian Sociology and Anthropology Association, Laval University, Quebec, June.

West, Cornel
1982 'A Genealogy of Modern Racism'. *Prophesy Deliverance! An Afro-American Revolutionary Christianity.* Philadelphia: Westminister Press.
1987 'Race and Social Theory: Towards a Genealogical Materialist Analysis'. Pp. 73-89 in Mike Davis et al., eds, *The Year Left 2: An American Socialist Yearbook.* Stony Brook, NY: Verso.
1988 'Marxist Theory and the Specificity of Afro-American Oppression'. Pp. 17-29 in Cary Nelson and Lawrence Grossberg, eds, *Marxism and the Interpretation of Culture.* Urbana: University of Illinois Press.

White, E. Frances
1984 'Listening to the Voices of Black Feminism'. *Radical America* 18 (2-3): 7-26.

Women, Immigration and Nationality Group (WING)
1985 *Worlds Apart: Women Under Immigration and Nationality Law.* London: Pluto Press.

Wright, Erik Olin
1980 'Varieties of Marxist Conceptions of Class Structure'. *Politics and Society* 9 (3): 323-70.

Yuval-Davis, Nira, and Floya Anthias
1989 *Woman-Nation-State.* London: Macmillan.

SUBJECT INDEX

AUTHOR INDEX